A LEVEL
BRITISH
HISTORY

D1352783

David Weigall
Head of History, Anglia Polytechnic University
and Michael Murphy

EDUCATIONAL

ST JULIAN'S
SCHOOL LIBRARY
HEATHER ROAD
NEWPORT NP19 7JZ

Letts Educational
Aldine Place
London W12 8AW
Tel: 0181 740 2266
Fax: 0181 743 8451
e-mail: mail@lettsed.co.uk

Every effort has been made to trace copyright holders and to obtain their permission for the use of copyright material. The author and publishers will gladly receive information enabling them to rectify any reference or credit in subsequent editions.

First published 1982
Reprinted 1983 (twice), 1985, 1986
Revised 1984, 1986, 1991
Reissued 1993
Reprinted 1994, 1996
Revised 1997

Text © David Weigall, 1982, 1984, 1986, 1991, 1997

Typeset by Jordan Publishing Design

Design Watermark Communications Ltd (cover), Jonathan Barnard (text)

Illustrations: Illustra Design

Design and illustrations © BPP (Letts Educational) Ltd

All our rights reserved. No part of this publication may be reproduced, stored in a retrieval system, or transmitted, in any form or by any means, electronic, mechanical, photocopying, recording or otherwise, without the prior permission of BPP (Letts Educational) Ltd.

British Library Cataloguing in Publication Data
A CIP record for this book is available from the British Library

ISBN 1 85758 600 X

Printed and bound in Great Britain by
Progressive Printing Limited, Leigh-on-Sea, Essex

Letts Educational is the trading name of BPP (Letts Educational) Ltd

PREFACE

This book is designed to meet the needs of students covering the popular late modern period of British history for A-level, AS and Scottish Higher examinations. It is intended to be used as an aid throughout the course, as a book for constant reference and as something which will be particularly helpful for revision.

This book is a companion guide to *A-level European History*, which covers the modern period in Europe. In preparing this book we have received indispensable help and advice from A-level History examiners and specialist historians in schools, colleges and universities. This means that we have been able to benefit from the practical experience of teachers and examiners and the insights of professional historians.

Our particular thanks are due to Mr Harry Browne and to Dr Boyd Hilton for their invaluable contributions and advice throughout, to Mr Ritchie Greig for his advice and help over the Scottish syllabuses, and, for their special contributions to particular topics, to the following: Professor Norman McCord, Dr Stephen Beller, Mr Christopher Catherwood, Mr Alan Griffiths, Dr Eunan O'Halpin, Dr Martin Moriarty, Dr John Pollard, Dr David Stevenson and Dr Don Watts.

We are grateful, too, to the staffs of all the examination boards for their prompt helpfulness and advice.

We are, further, very indebted to all the staff of Letts Educational Ltd who have helped with this publication, and to their advisers, for their encouragement, expertise and forbearance. Rachel Grant deserves special mention for all her work with the new edition in two companion volumes.

Use of past questions

We are grateful to the examination boards for allowing us to use past A-level and Scottish Higher questions in this publication and to their subject officers for details and History syllabuses.

Acknowledgement is due to the Longman Group Ltd for permission to use the diagram on page 209.

David Weigall
Michael J Murphy

CONTENTS

SECTION 1: STARTING POINTS

How to use this book 2

    The structure of this book 2

Syllabus checklists and paper analysis 3

    Examination boards and addresses 5

Studying and revising History 6

    The difference between GCSE and A/AS level 6

    Study strategies and techniques 7

    Revision techniques 11

The examination 12

    Examination techniques and question styles 12

SECTION 2: A-LEVEL BRITISH HISTORY 1815–1951

Introduction 16

Chapter 1   Lord Liverpool's Administration, 1815–27 17

Chapter 2   The Whig reforms, 1830–41 30

Chapter 3   Chartism and the Anti-Corn Law League 44

Chapter 4   Peel and the Conservative Party 58

Chapter 5   British foreign policy, 1815–65 70

Chapter 6   Disraeli and Conservatism 85

Chapter 7   Gladstone and Liberalism 98

Chapter 8   Joseph Chamberlain 111

Chapter 9   Gladstone and Ireland 124

Chapter 10 The Liberal Governments, 1906–14   138

Chapter 11 Britain's interwar economy   152

Chapter 12 British politics in the 1920s   166

Chapter 13 The National Governments, 1931–9   180

Chapter 14 British foreign policy in the 1930s   194

Chapter 15 Labour in power, 1945–51   206

SECTION 3: TEST RUN

Test your knowledge quiz   220

Test your knowledge quiz answers   221

Mock exam   229

Mock exam suggested answer plans   232

INDEX   235

STARTING POINTS

In this section:

How to use this book

   The structure of this book

Syllabus checklists and paper analysis

   Examination boards and addresses

Studying and revising History

   The difference between GCSE and A/AS Level

   Study strategies and techniques

   Revision techniques

The examination

   Examination techniques and question styles

HOW TO USE THIS BOOK

THE STRUCTURE OF THIS BOOK

The 15 chapters in this book do not pretend to be an introduction to all aspects of British History for the period since 1815. They concentrate, however, on topics which are essential to a proper understanding of the nineteenth and twentieth centuries and which, year after year, are recognised as such in the questions set by the examiners.

The period from the end of the Napoleonic Wars is an extremely popular and widely studied one. It is also a very complex one, for which there is a greater abundance of historical material than for any previous period. The chapters are intended to guide you to greater comprehension of the period and help you acquire and practice historical skills.

The years after 1815 were years of unprecedented and dramatic transformations, rapidity of social and economic development and of major political change. In many respects this period forms a natural unit of historical development for study. When one considers such topics as the growth of Nationalism, parliamentary democracy and Communism, it can also be seen to offer the basic background of knowledge for an understanding of present-day developments, institutions and ideas.

The chapter objectives provide a comprehensive synopsis for the chapter. It indicates what you should be looking out for in your reading and the considerations which your examiners, at the end of your course, will require you to bear in mind. It encourages you to approach your reading analytically, as explained in the following section. It also challenges you to relate various aspects to one another.

Before you embark on your reading for a given topic, you should read through the relevant list of study objectives very carefully to assess the full scope of the topic. When you have completed your reading and note-taking, check through the objectives and ask yourself if you have mastered enough knowledge and acquired enough understanding of what you have read to be able to give an account of each of them. When you have mastered all these points you should be confident that you will be prepared to answer questions on that topic at A level, from whatever angle they may come.

The main text should be read as a supplement to your textbook and other reading. It is important to remember that the text is *not* an alternative to other reading but is a guide to what is of significance to your needs for A-level History. It is condensed and written with an emphasis on analysis of the topics, covering such considerations as the causes, effects and wider historical significance of events and developments. It includes definitions of key concepts and, organised under clear headings, will help you with the process of historical selection, comprehension, comparison and interpretation. Remember, though, that they are an aid for you to master A-level History and do not do all the work for you!

The chronologies include a list of events, enactments, etc., arranged by topic. Those in capitals are of special significance. These can help you make sure, with the help of your textbooks and other sources of information, that you make notes on these key facts.

As you work through your reading, it may be helpful to clarify the order of events by referring to the chronologies. The chronologies are also excellent memory aids during your pre-examination revision.

QUESTION PRACTICE

Each chapter contains a question section with worked answers divided under the following headings:

Tutorial note: an analysis of what the question is really getting at. This examines the wording of the question and any confusions that arise from it, points out any implications you should be aware of and also gives you general advice on how to answer the question.

You need to know about: a summary of those areas of the topic which you should have mastered in order to be able to answer the question proficiently.

Suggested essay plan: an essay plan showing you how to construct a comprehensive and relevant answer to the question. This shows you how to use evidence to present a historical argument – on the use of what you have read and learned to present a well-reasoned response to the question *as set*.

These are *not* full model answers. Examiners will be looking for knowledgeable, convincing, well-planned answers, but in history essay writing at this level there is no such thing as an *exclusively 'right' answer*, in contrast to, say, the solution of mathematical problems. The suggested essay plans are presented, therefore, as exercises for you to consider, discuss and work through – and emphatically *not* as the only right answer. They should be studied when you have done your reading and note-taking and thought out the topic. Again, they are not intended as substitutes for your own efforts.

Remember that the construction, presentation and ordering of historical material are most important. Practice in constructing and appropriately supporting a historical argument is essential. Very often A-level History candidates fail to do justice to what they know because of weak presentation and incompleteness in their essays.

The illustrative questions are followed by question banks, consisting of document questions and further essay questions. Use the question banks at the end of each chapter to draw up your own essay plans. There is no more effective way of building up your confidence in your ability to use what you know to answer specific questions and to produce essays that are wholly relevant.

The document questions can be used either with your textbooks to hand as an exercise to find out more about the topic, or, after you have finished your reading for the topic, to test your grasp of it. Note how marks are weighted for these questions. They give you some indication of the amount of space you should be prepared to allocate to each. While the straightforward factual questions on the document, for which two marks are awarded, probably only require a few lines, you may well need to spend half a page or more on the demanding analytical question which offers eight marks.

The reading list at the end of each chapter refers you to a number of the most commonly used textbooks for nineteenth and twentieth-century British History outlines, as well as to titles recommended for *further* reading on the topic concerned. Wide reading is essential for a good, rounded grasp of history. In-depth study of History leads you beyond your textbooks to other sources. One of its major purposes is to encourage the spirit of enquiry.

Maps and diagrams are included where necessary and you should study them carefully when you are reading the text.

SYLLABUS CHECKLISTS AND PAPER ANALYSIS

The following details indicate relevant units for study for papers offered by the examining boards. For full information on the nature of the syllabus, papers on offer, objectives of courses and weighting of marks you should consult your teachers or lecturers, or the examining board concerned. What follows is based on the most recent information available to the authors. But syllabus and paper contents are liable to change and examination regulations or rubrics to be altered.

This list is therefore indicative rather than comprehensive or necessarily completely up-to-date in all particulars. Booklets containing all details are available from the individual boards.

Note, also, that this book will be useful for a number of courses other than A level, for example access and return-to-study courses for the older student.

A-level Examinations

Associated Examining Board

Syllabus 0630	Paper 02 Period Study	British and European History c.1760–1980	Chapters 1–15
Alternative Syllabus 0673	Paper 02 Period Study	British and European History c.1760–1980	Chapters 1–15
Syllabus 0630	Paper 07 Depth Study	British Politics, Economy and Society 1830–1850	Chapters 2–5

Edexcel, London Examinations (formerly ULEAC)

Syllabus A 9266	Paper 5	Early Industrial Britain 1783–1850	Chapters 1–4
Syllabus A 9266	Paper 6	Politics and Reform in Britain 1830–1886	Chapters 2–7
Syllabus A 9266	Paper 8	British Politics and Government 1886–1939	Chapers 8–14
Syllabus A 9266	Paper 9	British Society and Politics 1939–1979	Chapters 11, 12, 13, 15
Syllabus B 9267	Paper 13	English History 1688–1974	Chapters 1–15
Syllabus D 9269	Paper 1	International Problems since 1931	Chapters 11–15

Northern Examinations and Assessment Board

Syllabus A	Paper 2 M	Britain 1783–1906	Chapters 1–9
Syllabus A	Paper 2 N	Britain 1851–1951	Chapters 5–15

Oxford and Cambridge Examinations and Assessment Council

Syllabus 9020	Paper 4	English History 1783–1974	Chapters 1–15
Syllabus 9020	Paper 5	English History 1450–1974	Chapters 1–15
Syllabus 9020	Paper 18	British Society 1815–50	Chapters 1–15
Syllabus 9930	Option C Unit 2 (Core)	English History 1740–1980	Chapters 1–15
Syllabus 9625	Paper 3	English History 1689–1980	Chapters 1–15
Syllabus 9625	Paper 27	English History/The Age of Peers 1830–1850	Chapters 2–5

Welsh Joint Education Committee

Syllabus A	Paper A1 (D)	Outline History of Wales and England 1815–1914	Chapters 1–10
Syllabus A	Paper A1 (E)	Outline History of Wales and England 1900–1974	Chapters 10–15
Syllabus B	Paper A4 (3)	Popular Movements in Wales and England, 1815–1850	Chapters 1–4
Syllabus B	Paper A4 (5)	Britain between the Wars, 1919–1939	Chapters 11–14

Scottish Qualifications Authority (formerly SEB)

Scottish Certificate of Education Higher Grade

Option C: Later Modern History Section (a)	Britain 1850s–1979	Chapters 5–15
Option C: Later Modern History Special Topic 11	Appeasement and the Road to War	Chapter 14

Certificate of Sixth-Year Studies			
Option (f)		Economic Development of Britain 1820–1880: its Social and Political Impact	Chapters 1–7
Option (k)		Britain at War and Peace 1939–1956	Chapter 15

Northern Ireland Council for the Curriculum Examinations and Assessment			
	Paper 1	British and Irish History c.1815–c.1900	Chapters 1–9
	Paper 1	British and Irish History c.1900–c.1964	Chapters 10–15

AS-level Examinations

Associated Examining Board			
Syllabus 0991		British and/or European History c.1760–1980	Chapters 1–15

Edexcel, London Examinations (formerly ULEAC)			
Syllabus 8265		British and European History	Chapters 1–15

Northern Examinations and Assessment Board			
Syllabus A	M	Britain 1783–1906	Chapters 1–9
Syllabus A	N	Britain 1783–1906	Chapters 5–15

Oxford and Cambridge Examinations and Assessment Council			
Syllabus 8470/8392		British History	Chapters 1–15
Syllabus 9930	Option C Unit 2 (Core)	English History 1740–1980	Chapters 1–15

EXAMINATION BOARDS AND ADDRESSES

AEB	The Associated Examining Board Stag Hill House, Guildford, Surrey GU2 5XJ
EDEXCEL	Edexcel, London Examinations Stewart House, 32 Russell Square, London WC1 5DN
NEAB	Northern Examinations and Assessment Board Orbit House, Albert Street, Eccles, Manchester M30 0WL
NICCEA	Northern Ireland Council for the Curriculum Examinations and Assessment 29 Clarendon Road, Belfast BT1 3BG
OCEAC	Oxford and Cambridge Examinations and Assessment Council Syndicate Buildings, 1 Hills Road, Cambridge CB1 2EU Ewert House, Ewert Place, Summertown, Oxford OX2 7BZ
SQA	Scottish Qualifications Authority Ironmills Road, Dalkeith, Midlothian EH22 1LE
WJEC	Welsh Joint Education Committee 245 Western Avenue, Cardiff CF5 2YX

STUDYING AND REVISING HISTORY

THE DIFFERENCE BETWEEN GCSE AND A/AS LEVEL

Before you start your A-level History course it is essential that you are clear about the sort of skills that are required. What qualities will the examiners will be looking for? What is being tested? How do the demands of A-level differ from those of any history you may have done before?

Anything you write, either in course essay work or for your exams, should display a sound factual grasp, a clear sense of the order of events and of their relationship to one another: you should be able to *describe* and to *narrate* accurately. But it is a great mistake to imagine that these skills alone will satisfy A-level History requirements. While a sound factual and chronological grasp is essential, it is only the beginning.

Historical analysis

As examiners' reports show, the most frequent failing among History candidates is an unwillingness, or inability, to *apply* what they know and to *analyse* it in the context and within the bounds of a specific question. It is not so much a lack of knowledge but an apparent absence of thought about that knowledge, and of practice in using it, which lose marks. These skills can only be mastered with practice and experience, not least in sorting out what is relevant in your reading. Answers to A-level History questions come from the process of selection and analysis.

The style and demands of these questions involve you in discussing, comparing, judging and justifying. A grasp of the narrative of historical events and the ability to prescribe are presupposed in the good A-level candidate. At GCSE the basic skills of memorising, understanding historical sequence and presenting it in an orderly fashion may be adequate accomplishments for examination success. This is not to say that the good GCSE candidate may not attempt more than this, either in course work or in exams. The A-level student, however, *must* attempt more and must always resist the temptation to drift into a *simply narrative* response to a question where *analysis* is required.

This is not to disparage narrative, nor to say that narrative and analysis cannot be very satisfactorily combined. They can; and in history – which is the study of individuals, institutions and developments in time – narrative sequence is an essential component. However, A-level History is not simply a matter of offering historical details but of using what you know in interpretation and explanation – not just of knowing but of giving the clearest indications that you understand the implications both of what you know and of the further questions to which that knowledge may give rise.

As the ULEAC examiners have stated, they are 'not looking for the mere regurgitation of received truths.... The highest marks are reserved for answers which clearly provide a cogent and coherent response to the question as set out on the examination paper, and which are supported by substantial illustrative material intelligently selected'. They warn that 'other work may display accurate and relevant knowledge but fails to use this knowledge as an effective contribution to an answer to the question set. Such work will be considered for Grade E equivalent but seldom more. On the other hand, any answer which shows real endeavour to focus relevantly on the question set, and achieves some success in this, will always be treated sympathetically'. NEAB is even more specific, saying that 45% of the marks awarded for an A-level History answer will be given for knowledge and 55% for the ability to assess evidence and to select and organise material. A-level History papers, it insists, demand more than narrative answers and a wholly narrative answer would only secure a maximum of 10 out of 25.

Historical assessment

A-level History requires the assessment of problems in their context. The demands of an A-level essay, in terms both of depth and of sophistication, mark a considerable advance on what you were prepared for in GCSE History. While a typical GCSE question may ask you to describe, for instance, how the Great Reform Act came about, an A-level examiner will want you to discuss its significance and implications, e.g: for subsequent reforms in the nineteenth century.

In addition to analysis and a capacity for well-supported and soundly constructed historical argument, you should be able to show an appropriate sense of historical period and a clear understanding of the framework of ideas and attitudes of the age about which you are writing. The good historian is able to intuit and to convey (1) a feeling of the way that people's minds reacted in a particular period, and (2) an understanding of their situation. He is able, in short, to display historical imagination.

The less able student all too often shows himself confined in his judgment by contemporary perspectives. This shows particularly in those essays where students deliver harsh (and often unsubstantiated) verdicts on past figures, institutions or developments. To criticise the past out of hand for not living by what you consider to be the values of the present demonstrates a failure of historical imagination. It will be more important for you to show the examiner that you understand how the unreformed pre-1832 British parliamentary system worked than to tell him how 'undemocratic' you consider it was!

STUDY STRATEGIES AND TECHNIQUES

A-level History, particularly with all the '-isms' of the late modern period, requires you to be able to understand and handle concepts. Questions often demand a mastery of technical historical vocabulary, and the instructions of examiners to 'discuss', 'consider' and 'examine' make essential a high level of discrimination in the meaning of words and in their use in historical writing. An extremely common failing among history students is the misuse of staple words in the history textbook vocabulary – words such as *absolutist*, *totalitarian*, *radical*, *reactionary* and *protectionist*. An imprecise grasp of such concepts leads to confused and inadequate answers in course or examination work. You have only to consider the following A-level questions to appreciate that any proper answers to them are inconceivable without a clear definition in one's mind of what the concepts mean and imply in their context:

> Explain and illustrate what you understand by the term 'Radical' in the period 1815–1906.

> 'Ireland destroyed Gladstonian Liberalism.' Did it?

It is not just misunderstanding and misuse of concepts which lead to poor and waffly answers and essays. Another frequent weakness is the attempt to explain historical events by the sweeping use of broad concepts, such as *Nationalism* and *technological change*, without using specific examples or sufficient discrimination between different sorts of nationalism or kinds of technological change. It is essential for you to master sufficient detail to be able to illustrate and clarify such general concepts.

Note that a good number of concepts are what have been called 'essentially contested'. For instance, the description 'democratic' has been frequently appropriated by authoritarian or totalitarian regimes (e.g. as in 'democratic centralism'), as well as Western-style pluralistic societies. Again, what an Athenian meant by 'democracy' two and a half thousand years ago is very different from contemporary representative democracy. It is very easy to misuse concepts, applying them anachronistically to a period in which they were not known, or undiscriminatingly, without pointing out that they denoted something quite distinct in the period you are writing about.

Historical debate and interpretation

The topics which you cover in your History course, and on which you will be questioned in the examination, may have produced considerable controversy and a wide variety of interpretations among historians. There are few entirely simple problems in modern history and you should be aware of the major debates, at least in outline. At A-level, one of the purposes of studying history is to introduce you to historical interpretation and to particular approaches to the study. The skill of constructing and sustaining a historical argument depends, in the first instance, on analysis and the sifting of available evidence. You will rapidly gain confidence in coming to terms with history through practice in evaluating the arguments for and against particular interpretations. You will also discover that it is ill-advised to opt unhesitatingly for one interpretation against all others unless you can sustain this view with a compelling display of evidence supporting it. At all events, one should avoid giving the impression of one-sidedness.

The wider context of 'factors'

Though the analytical approach to history will lead you to identify separate factors as in the causes of a war or revolution, you should be prepared to discover the wider context, i.e. the interrelatedness and linkage between them, as well as identifying their individuality. Though they help to clarify and define, such categories as *economic*, *political*, *social*, *constitutional* and *ideological* overlap and, in explaining any event or development, are often found to be interrelated.

A rote learning approach to your studies tends, quite simply, to make for pedestrian and unimaginative answers when you come to write a course essay or take your examination. The uninspired reeling-off of factors will suggest that you have not thought either sufficiently deeply or thoroughly about what you have been studying.

The importance of relevance

The most frequent loser of marks at A-level is the sort of answer which is either plainly irrelevant to the question, or only of marginal relevance. Many students who may well have written comprehensive essays on a topic during their course are disconcerted to find that the questions in the examination cover aspects for which they were not prepared or are posed from an unexpected angle. All examiners are well aware that some candidates may have prepared a number of major topics and virtually memorised answers on them – quite frequently with stock quotations. In such papers a question on Peel becomes *the* answer on Peel. This fundamental failing goes back to the question of historical analysis.

You should remember that, in preparing course work and examinations, your historical material should always be shaped to provide a relevant answer, supported by apposite allusion and factual illustration. The narrative and descriptive parts of your essays should be at the service of your analysis of the question. In good historical writing, the writer is seen to be in control of the evidence in presenting a historical argument. It is obvious to the examiner which answers sort out the relevant considerations, make analytical use of reading and display the skills of identifying the significant points and of relating them.

Note-taking and essay-writing skills

Every History student should have clear, comprehensive and well-ordered notes. These are essential both for course work and in preparing for examinations. In addition, practice in note-taking is of more general value, encouraging clear-headedness and mental discipline.

The key skills here are: selectivity, precision and neat presentation. Before you take notes from a chapter, pamphlet or article, read it through first to establish a general idea of its information and argument. Then carefully re-read and draft notes from this second reading. Finally, check through and see if you have missed anything of significance. If you have, amend your work accordingly. Keep your notes brief, to the point and, as far as possible, prepare them in your own words. Make sure you note down your source. Ensure above all that they are legible and comprehensible. For instance, if you use abbreviations, make sure you will be able to understand them when you come to write your essay or revise for the exam. Anything you note down should be instantly comprehensible afterwards.

Break your notes into clearly differentiated sections. The judicious use of underlining also helps. Underline the key points, but ensure you have significant factual illustration to support these points. Good notes convey some idea of the variety of motivations and their interrelationship; and they give you plenty of hard facts to back up analysis. You will find effective notes absolutely invaluable when you come to revise. Re-reading your old essays before your exams is no alternative to having a file of lucid and pithy notes to hand! Finally, when you are note-taking, remember to leave space in the margin or at the bottom of the page or section so that you can add any useful additional material from further reading. This is particularly helpful when you are refreshing your memory of a topic during revision.

A good essay needs reasoned judgement and a comprehensive range of evidence. Good note-taking is the first step. Before you put pen to paper for your essay make sure you have a clear idea of your answer to the question as set. Draft an essay plan when you have asked yourself what points you are going to make, how you are going to relate them in a coherent and relevant argument and what facts/evidence you have to support your argument. Before you do this you should make sure that you have explored all the implications of the question before you and that you are ready to do them justice. When you write the essay out, express yourself as clearly and accurately as you can. It is essential for you to read it through when you have finished, checking for inaccuracies and vagueness of expression. You will find it useful also to list those books, articles or other sources of information you have used at the end of the essay, noting author, title, edition, place and date of publication, publisher and (where relevant) the pages consulted.

The questioning approach

The good student develops, from his reading and thought about the subject, a questioning habit of mind. He goes on from a question to ask further questions. He requires the clarification of any ambiguous term. To give an example: when faced with a question on the causes or results of of any particular event or development he will take care to distinguish between the immediate and the longer-term causes or results. If he is asked to explain the outbreak of the First World War, he has an awareness of the far-reaching considerations – of all those things which produced the international climate in which the Powers were quite likely to go to war – as well as the immediate occasion, being the course of events following the assassination of Archduke Francis Ferdinand in 1914. The good answer illuminates the relations between the longer-term and the immediate causes.

Documents

You will be required to answer questions on source material/documents. This requires sharp critical assessment. As Marc Bloch the French historian noted, source material like this is a witness, 'and like most witnesses it rarely speaks until one begins to question it'. Faced with a document, one should ask the following questions: a) What kind of statement is it? b) What do we know about its author and the circumstances in which it was produced? c) Is it a primary or secondary source? d) Did it have an intended audience or readership? For instance, was it intended as a public statement, or purely as private comment, as in a diary which the author regarded as entirely personal and never intended to be published? e) Was it an immediate reaction to an historical event, or a later reflection, as with memoirs?

You must be able to evaluate the extract(s) and to interpret them. This is a two-way process. On the one hand, your knowledge about a particular historical event or development will help you to understand the source material before you. On the other, this material should add to and illuminate what you already know about it. You should ask yourself, then: how does this contribute to my understanding? How does my knowledge of the historical context enable me to interpret what is before me? You may have one or a variety of documents. The questions may simply test your factual grasp. They may probe your understanding of concepts. They may ask you to evaluate their reliability or perspective; or you may be asked to compare and contrast various accounts and/or assess to what extent they provide a full understanding and explanation. In your examination, the marks awarded for each of the questions on documents or statistical material will be specified after the question. The higher the marks, the more testing the question. The quality of your overall answer to a document question will be indicated by the way in which you are able to combine knowledge extracted from the documents themselves with wider appreciation of the historical context and other sources.

Projects

Several of the Examining Boards offer history candidates the opportunity of writing an individual assignment or personal study. This is a special test of your capacity for independent investigation and enquiry and many students find that this is one of the most fulfilling parts of their course and a real opportunity to display particular enthusiasm and investigative and evaluative skills on a topic which particularly interests them.

Ensure that you read carefully any instructions and advice from the Board on the kind of topic envisaged, the required length, scope, procedures for approval and rules for presentation. It is essential that you choose an appropriate topic, that you have a clear idea of the time you will have to allocate to it and that you have adequate and accessible sources for your research. You must discuss it thoroughly with your teacher or lecturer who will normally have to submit the topic for approval to the Examining Board.

Preparation of a good project requires considerable self-discipline, precision and close attention to detail and presentation. You will need to establish the answer to a variety of questions. Some are procedural, relating to approval of the idea, deadline for submission, whether or not you will have an interview on your project and are expected to bring your notes with you, whether you are to provide a log of your research. Others relate to the research and writing-up of your project, its parameters and the expectations of your examiners. What do they emphasize in their instructions?

One Board, for instance, specifies that you should place the problem investigated in its historical background and relate it to its context, meaning here both background and historical continuum. Another Board advises that you are likely to gain most from studies which ask a definitive question or attempt to solve a problem and that if you choose a local topic you should be prepared to relate it to the wider historical frame. Some topics may present themselves because you are aware of an interesting cache of documents or source material. Others offer themselves first in the form of a question which you would like to try and resolve.

Be absolutely clear about presentation. For instance, how will you be expected to present your footnotes and bibliography? Tidy professionalism is most important. However original your contribution, if it is submitted in an unclear and disorganized form it may well confuse and will certainly detract. A good project should be something standing in its own right, a product of considerable thought and academic self-criticism and of a willingness to re-write, the result of what Dr Samuel Johnson called 'slow diligence'. If you decide to take history either as a Single or Joint-Honour subject at university or college you will very likely have to prepare a dissertation in the course of your studies, usually in your last year. Previous practice in researching a topic thoroughly and presenting your conclusions in a cogent form will serve you in good stead.

Conclusion

A sound piece of work for A-level History shows an intelligent understanding of the past, a clear analysis based on a sound grasp of fact and a capacity for lucid expression. The criteria by which you are judged in the examinations are: relevance, accuracy and quantity of factual knowledge; effectiveness of presentation and the ability to communicate knowledge in a clear and orderly fashion with maximum relevance. You should show that you can present and justify a historical argument, that you are capable of exercising historical judgment and are aware of period and context. These skills can only be acquired over a period of time, with wide reading and much practice.

Two journals, *History Review* and *Modern History Review* are strongly to be recommended for the A-level History student. Not only do they include authoritative articles on historical topics; they also provide useful advice on historical skills and methods. Recent useful books include Mary Abbott (ed.) *History Skills* (London, Routledge, 1996); Derek Rowntree's *Learn How To Study* (3rd edition, London, Macdonald, 1988); R Brown and C Daniels *Learning History: A Guide to Advanced Study* (London, Macmillan, 1986); M Stanford *The Nature of Historical Knowledge* (Oxford, Blackwell, 1986); J A Clarke, V Crinnion and S M Harrison *The Modern History Manual* (Lancaster, The Framework Press, 1987) and A Marwick *The Nature of History* (3rd edition, London, Macmillan Education, 1989). Note, too, that examining boards publish and make available reports on how candidates collectively handle the questions they set. These are very instructive, both as to what the examiners expect and how candidates fall short.

REVISION TECHNIQUES

Effective revision for A-level History is not simply passive absorption, but a very active process. It is an opportunity for you to reassess what you have written in your notes and essay assignments, not just an exercise in re-reading.

You should remember, as explained in the previous section, that you are being examined not simply on your memory, but on your capacities for thought, analysis and judgment. After revising each topic, you should be able to feel confident that you will be capable of answering questions on it from whatever perspective they may come.

In order to encourage this confidence and flexibility of approach, you should practise drafting skeleton essay plans for past questions. List the main points you want to make in the order in which you will present them (remember that a clear structure is most important in essay-writing), and jot down key information to use in supporting them.

In drafting either full or outline answers in your revision, remember that your material should provide a fully specific and relevant answer. Any narrative and descriptive parts of your essays should be used to serve your analysis of the question. At the same time, though, you should never allow the weight of factual information to obscure the argument of your answer, neither should you assume that the examiner will be aware you know the facts if you have not stated them, or that he will find your assertions and generalisations self-evidently correct.

Further, you should allow yourself practice in fully answering questions under mock examination conditions, timing yourself for this exercise. Section 3 of this book contains a full mock British History examination for this purpose.

A planned programme

Revision should be clearly and systematically planned. If you are taking the summer A-level examinations, you should have covered the great majority of the syllabus topics by the end of the spring term (if you are taking the winter examinations, by the beginning of the autumn term). Draw up a schedule for your revision, starting, in the case of the summer examinations, at the beginning of April.

Try to give at least an hour to your History revision each day. Use your mock examination to highlight those topics which need more attention in your revision.

A clearly thought-out programme of revision is one which you can complete without panic and which you can combine with additional reading for the subject. Leave a period of, say, a week to a fortnight at the end for comprehensive re-revision, during which you can refine key points from your notes and clarify any final difficulties. A thorough schedule along these lines will give you the confidence which is such an important element in achieving success.

THE EXAMINATION

EXAM TECHNIQUES AND QUESTION STYLES

Some of the following points may appear very obvious to you. They are, nevertheless, frequently disregarded by candidates and neglect of them is again and again noted in examiners' reports as leading to poor or indifferent answers and to failure in the examination.

You should try and ensure that you observe the following rules:

❶ Read the rubric for each paper and section of paper very carefully and answer the full number of questions required of you. Pay particular attention to subdivisions, i.e. where you are asked to answer questions from more than one section.

❷ Be sure that you have an absolutely clear idea of what any question you choose to answer means and answer it *as set*. Pay particular attention to the precise requirements of the examiners, i.e. are you being asked to 'explain', 'comment upon', 'illustrate', etc.? If the wording of a question is genuinely ambiguous or confusing, be prepared to point this out in your answer.

❸ Choose the questions you are confident you can answer rather than those, however interesting, which you *think* you might be able to answer. Your answers should be pointed and precise. If you use quotes, make sure that they are pertinent to your argument. Do not quote in a random way simply to impress, because you will not. Avoid the vague, weak and general introduction to a question which does not go straight to the point.

❹ Attempt as far as possible to apportion your time equally between the questions, unless there are indications in the rubric or marks (as in some document questions) to the contrary. An overlong first answer only forces you to scramble to finish the last question. Far too many candidates every year submit scripts which show they have not properly familiarized themselves with exam conditions. Give yourself plenty of practice in writing against the clock.

❺ Answer all parts of the question. For instance, in the following question:

> Why, how, and with what consequences did Britain abandon a policy of 'splendid isolation'?

You should note *why*, *how* and *consequences*. The examiner will be looking for answers which deal with all three.

❻ This is equally true of questions which require you to 'compare' or 'contrast'. Candidates often fall down badly by simply concentrating on one side of the question and making only a passing reference to the other(s), e.g:

> Compare the circumstances in which the Irish Home Rule Bills were introduced in 1886, in 1893 and in 1912.

Any treatment of this question which concentrates almost exclusively on one of the Home Rule Bills – however detailed and thorough – will not be even a partial answer: it will not really be an answer at all, since the purpose of the question is to elicit a comparison.

❼ Remember to use what you know to provide an answer which is strictly relevant to the question. It is useful to draft an essay outline and to check its relevance to the question, as set, before you answer it.

❽ Avoid essay conclusions which are simply repetitions of what you have already written.

❾ Provide a clear structure and sequence in your answer. The art of presenting a historical argument is extremely important.

❿ Always write clearly, avoiding vagueness either of expression or in factual allusions, e.g: 'There were several social reforms.' Which reforms? When did they come about?

⓫ In answering document questions, read the extract(s), not just the questions, very carefully. If asked to explain them, do so in your own words. Make sure the examiner sees that you understand what the document means and its relevance. Look out particularly for differences of emphasis or tone if there is more than one extract on a topic.

On no account leave your compulsory document question till last. The extracts will require careful reading and reflection. Examiners frequently comment how easily marks are lost in rushed answers to the document questions.

⓬ Give yourself time at the end to re-read what you have written, to correct any errors, or to make any necessary additions.

A-LEVEL BRITISH HISTORY 1815–1951

In this section:

Chapter 1: Lord Liverpool's Administration, 1815–27

Chapter 2: The Whig reforms, 1830–41

Chapter 3: Chartism and the Anti-Corn Law League

Chapter 4: Peel and the Conservative Party

Chapter 5: British foreign policy, 1815–65

Chapter 6: Disraeli and Conservatism

Chapter 7: Gladstone and Liberalism

Chapter 8: Joseph Chamberlain

Chapter 9: Gladstone and Ireland

Chapter 10: The Liberal Governments, 1906–14

Chapter 11: Britain's interwar economy

Chapter 12: British politics in the 1920s

Chapter 13: The National Governments, 1931–9

Chapter 14: British foreign policy in the 1930s

Chapter 15: Labour in power, 1945–51

Each chapter features:

■ *Units in this chapter:* a list of the main topic heads to follow.

■ *Chapter objectives:* a synopsis of the topics which will be covered in the chapter.

■ *Commentary and chronology:* a concise text, analysing key concepts and incidents, followed by a list of significant events arranged in chronological order.

■ *Worked questions and answers:* typical examination questions, with tutorial notes, an indication of the knowledge required and a suggested answer plan.

■ *Question bank:* further examination questions for you to attempt.

INTRODUCTION

During the Napoleonic War, a new Britain had come into being. Few nations have experienced so rapid and disturbing a process of change as occurred in Britain in the two decades before 1815. During the eighteenth century the population almost doubled, open fields were enclosed, farming was rationalised and many yeomen were driven from the land.

Industrial changes after 1780 meant the advent of the machine and steam power, great new industrial cities, the rise of coal, iron and cotton and the decline of the old woollen and cottage industries. Changes of such magnitude meant anxiety and misery for many but they also meant great opportunities and profits for others.

The impact of war

War had intensified this process and had accelerated the pace of change. In agriculture it had hastened the enclosure movement and encouraged much investment in land that would not normally be profitable. The coal, iron and textile industries received enormous stimulation from the demands for war goods and uniforms. European trade was severely disrupted for over 20 years and new markets, for example, in South America, had to be found for British trade. The financial burden of the war was enormous (the National Debt grew from £240 million to £860 million) and the introduction of income tax and higher indirect taxes meant that all classes suffered.

The war on the whole was profitable for producers, i.e. farmers and industrialists, but oppressive for the lower orders who were forced to work long and hard in the new mills and factories, live in squalid, overcrowded conditions in the new industrial towns, bear the brunt of higher indirect taxes and be severely repressed in the name of 'Church and King' if they objected.

Perspectives

During the war, conflicts of interest were hidden as all energies were devoted to defeating France, but what would happen when the pressures and the artificial demands of war were removed? Would the lower orders continue to accept unquestioningly their new way of life? Would the new industrial middle class be satisfied to be ruled by an old-fashioned aristocracy that looked back to the agricultural world of the eighteenth century rather than forward to the industrial and manufacturing world of the nineteenth? How would the old ruling order respond if challenged on such key issues as 'cash, corn and Catholics'? Would they resist, adapt or reform?

By 1815, therefore, the world of the eighteenth century had been shattered. The agricultural and industrial revolutions had destroyed the balance of society and new classes had appeared for whom there was no place in the established order. Dissatisfaction was aggravated and intensified by the French Revolution, with its radical ideals of civil and religious liberty. It was exacerbated also by the repressive policy of the Younger Pitt's government in the 1790s, and by the disruptive demands of a war that dragged on intermittently for over 20 years.

LORD LIVERPOOL'S ADMINISTRATION, 1815-27

Units in this chapter

1.1 *The return to peace*
1.2 *Distress and discontent, 1815–20*
1.3 *The policies of transition, 1820–22*
1.4 *Government policy, 1815–20*
1.5 *Reconstruction and reform, 1822–27*
1.6 *Tory Party disintegration, 1828–30*
1.7 *Chronology*

Chapter objectives

❶ Lord Liverpool, his political talents and philosophy: how could the man whom Disraeli called the 'arch-mediocrity' retain power for longer than any Prime Minister since? Liverpool managed to display consummate political skill, despite his irritable temper; Asa Briggs's assessment was that Liverpool was 'a mediator of men and ideas'.

❷ The composition of the ministry and the changes of 1822. Was there a reactionary period 1815–22 (associated with Castlereagh) followed by a liberal awakening 1822–7 (associated with Canning)? What was the effect on policy-making of Peel's and Robinson's displacement of Sidmouth and Vansittart, Canning's succession to Castlereagh, Huskisson's promotion to the Board of Trade, and the adhesion of the Grenville party?

❸ The division of the ministers into 'liberal' Tories (e.g. Canning and Peel) and 'high' Tories (e.g. Eldon and Wellington); the difficulties in the way of such a neat classification – for instance, the 'high' Tory Castlereagh took the 'liberal' side on Catholic emancipation, while Peel championed the Protestants. Did the 'liberals' and the 'highs' appeal to different classes in the country? Did the distinction correspond to the chronological break in 1822 or not?

❹ Support for the ministry in parliament was very strong among the independently-minded country gentlemen who, though willing to defeat the government on specifics (e.g. the 1816 Property Tax), could not forgive the Whigs for Fox's support of the French Revolution, and so always supported the government on issues of confidence. The Whigs were further weakened by internal divisions, poor leadership and the implacable hostility of George IV. A general mood of reaction in the nation, dating from the 1790s, also helped the Tories.

❺ Castlereagh's diplomacy at Vienna and the subsequent rejection of the Holy Alliance (1820 State Paper): Canning pursued a similar policy but in a more flamboyant and publicity-seeking style – e.g. the French invasion of Spain, the Greek Revolt and the Latin-American revolts. The bitter cabinet divisions (1825–6) as Wellington led the Tory rebels against Canning's more independent line in foreign policy.

❻ The switch from a protectionist economic policy (e.g. 1815 Corn Law) to Huskisson's and Robinson's freer trade policies – tariff reductions, the relaxation of the Navigation Code and of the Combination Laws; the new policies associated with 'dear money' economics (deflation), following the resumption of cash payments in 1819, and with retrenchment; the 1828 Corn Law began the slow process towards the repeal of 1846.

❼ The move towards the more efficient control of law and order, following the fiasco at Peterloo; Peel's penal reforms and the development of the Metropolitan Police; law-and-order considerations forced the grant of Catholic emancipation (1829).

❽ Political and personal motives combined to persuade the 'high' Tories not to serve under Canning (1827); the reasons for the fall of Goderich's ministry; the reasons for the fall of Wellington (1830) and of the 50-year-old Tory regime itself; the revolt of the Ultra-Tories (e.g. Knatchbull) against the economic (and especially the currency) policy and Catholic emancipation.

The main problem facing Lord Liverpool's government was the widespread distress and discontent of the postwar world. Protests were treated as unsympathetically as in the 1790s. Informers and *agents provocateurs* were employed by a government which feared that 'English Jacobins' would imitate the French Revolution and attempt violently to overturn the existing political order. Consequently, the military was used to break up peaceful meetings and laws were introduced to deter working-class expression through speech, meeting or writing. Only after the return of prosperity in 1822 did the government relax its vigilance and introduce some limited, but welcome, reforms.

1.1 THE RETURN TO PEACE

The coming of peace in 1815 did not bring the stability and prosperity that the nation desperately hoped for. To the landed classes peace brought falling prices, lower profits and the inability to pay the large investment mortgages taken out during the war. The result was often bankruptcy and widespread distress on the land. As foreign corn became available once more, English corn prices collapsed. The response of a parliament dominated by the landed classes was to bring in the Corn Law of 1815, which immediately antagonised the two other emerging groups in the state – the middle and lower orders.

The wartime demand for coal, iron, armaments and profitable government contracts ceased. Trade with Europe stagnated as many European nations had brought in protective tariffs. As a result, industrial production had to be scaled down, priorities rearranged and new markets discovered. Unemployment in agriculture, industry and trade rose alarmingly. Demobilisation aggravated the problem.

You must ask yourself to what extent were these economic, trading and financial problems due to the effects of war – or were the changes wrought by the industrial and agricultural revolutions bound to have serious and disruptive consequences in any event?

The radical protest

Each class in society, therefore, was damaged by the return to peace but in the general ruin and confusion the lower orders suffered most. As their economic plight deepened, they became willing listeners to the growing band of radicals such as William Cobbett, Major Cartwright and 'Orator' Hunt, who demanded fundamental reforms in Church and State. Find out what you can about the ideas of the Radicals and the changing nature of working-class protest during the period 1790–1830. Note that the government particularly resented the radical tendency to link social distress to politics.

1.2 DISTRESS AND DISCONTENT, 1815–20

Whatever the nature of the protest, the discontent that burst forth from 1815 was so menacing that law and order could be maintained only by the use of the armed forces. At Ely and Littleport, county agricultural labourers, faced with unemployment and high bread prices, marched under banners inscribed 'Bread or Blood' and rioted throughout the area. In the industrial towns of the Midlands and the North unemployed workers smashed machinery. London did not escape disorder and, after the Spa Fields meeting in 1816, *Habeas Corpus* was suspended. In 1817 fresh disturbances occurred in the provinces. There was an attempt at armed insurrection at Pentrich in Derbyshire.

Fig. 1 Social unrest in Britain 1815–21

19

The Tories won the general election of 1818 – mainly because the disaffected had no vote. More importantly, however, it was due to the weakness of the Whigs in opposition. Dispirited, divided and leaderless, they failed to offer an alternative to the Tory policy of rigorously maintaining law and order.

The revival of *Habeas Corpus* set the Radicals free. More disorder followed, culminating in the 'Peterloo Massacre' at St. Peter's Fields, Manchester, in 1819. The Regent congratulated the magistrates and Yeomanry for their prompt and decisive action, but the nation was outraged. Early disorders seemed to paralyse the Whigs but Peterloo encouraged them to challenge Tory policy and put themselves at the head of the constitutional movement for parliamentary reform.

Undaunted, the government passed the Six Acts in the autumn of 1819. This further suppression of English liberties was followed by the Cato Street conspiracy in 1820. This attempt to murder the Cabinet proved to be the final act of lawlessness of these disturbed and unhappy years.

1.3 THE POLICIES OF TRANSITION 1820–22

Problems in the economy and trade brought about by the abrupt change from war to peace had by now largely been solved. Despite the continued efforts of the radical journalists and the attacks of the unstamped press on Tory policy, their cause declined as employment picked up – apparently confirming Cobbett's dictum: 'I defy you to agitate a fellow with a full stomach.'

You must know the chronology of distress during these years and the details of major events like Peterloo and Pentrich. Why did the Whigs provide such ineffective opposition?

The cabinet had, nevertheless, one final popular agitation to survive when, on the death of George III in 1820, Caroline, the estranged wife of the Prince Regent, returned from six years' exile to claim her position as Queen. George's attempt to divorce her precipitated a crisis.

The importance of the event is not in the unsavoury revelations that emerged about the Queen's conduct, but in its political effects. The stock of the monarchy was further reduced; a humiliated government was forced to bow to the pressure of public opinion. On the other hand, note how Whigs and Radicals, who had supported the Queen, gained in popularity and how thus an understanding was forged between Whigs, Radicals and the people which was to bear fruit in the reform crises of 1830. For the moment, however, it was clear that political radicalism had burnt itself out.

1.4 GOVERNMENT POLICY, 1815–20

The Lord Liverpool government may have weathered the immediate postwar storm but the Radicals attacked its policy as cruel, repressive and uncaring. Shelley, in his sonnet *England in 1819*, called the Prime Minister and his colleagues 'Rulers who neither see, nor feel, nor know.' This predominantly aristocratic administration appeared to equate reform with revolution and blindly crushed the symptoms of economic distress without considering the underlying causes.

Furthermore, the Radicals argued that the government actually added to the general distress by introducing the Corn Laws, abolishing income tax and returning Britain to the gold standard. In general they reacted to general unrest not by reconsidering their policies but by political repression. Is the radical case too one-sided in its approach?

In defence of the policy of the Lord Liverpool administration, one could argue that the first duty of any government is to maintain law and order. Also, it was well known that the means at the disposal of the government were unequal to the task. With party discipline in its infancy, they had to show a determination to govern or the result might have been catastrophic. Having seen the effects of the revolution in France, the ruling classes, as their every letter to the Home Office appeared to confirm, feared violence and imminent revolution in England.

Firmness, then, they thought was essential. As to the economic distress, the government believed that – in an age of laissez-faire – intervention in economic affairs was undesirable and that, because of the absence of information, the lack of a trained government bureaucracy and the limited administrative and financial resources available, it would in any case be ineffective. They introduced the Corn Law because agriculture was the main factor of production and still the major employer in the country. It offered the best chance of helping the whole nation out of depression.

According to conservative apologists, the government was not unduly repressive in its handling of the situation, nor was it greatly obsessed with disorder and treason. Ministers were alarmed but generally pragmatic in their response. Both centrally and locally they did what they could to alleviate distress and subscribed generously to soup kitchens and relief funds.

On the whole, it is claimed that government reaction was largely what might reasonably be expected of a cabinet who had seen the French Revolution and were determined to prevent a British one. According to Professor Gash, 'they were often urged to do more; they could hardly have done less.' This explanation may appear to you to excuse too much. You must, however, be able to argue effectively both the 'repressive' and 'pragmatic' explanations of government policy.

How near to revolution?

What is remarkable about the years 1815–20 is that a people so oppressed by economic exploitation, unemployment, hunger and political repression, and so used to violence in their everyday lives, did not act more violently than they did. Make a list of points explaining why a revolution did not occur. Halévy maintained that Methodism prevented the middle-class leaders of postwar disaffection from going too far. E P Thompson agrees that there was a real possibility of revolution during the period but suggests that there were not enough Methodists to influence events more than marginally, although, paradoxically, some radical leaders did benefit from Methodist instruction in reading, writing and public speaking. More important than the influence of religion may be the government's unwavering determination to maintain law and order. Would you agree that the potential leaders of a revolution, such as Cobbett, Cartwright and Hunt, had neither the will nor the means to bring one about?

1.5 RECONSTRUCTION AND REFORM, 1822–27

The suicide of Castlereagh gave Lord Liverpool the opportunity to reconstitute the ministry in 1822. Younger men in the Party were given key posts. Peel became Home Secretary; Huskisson, the President of the Board of Trade; Robinson, the Chancellor of the Exchequer, and Canning, Leader of the House of Commons and Foreign Secretary. These men were all capable administrators and, as they all had middle-class origins, were much more likely to be in tune with the needs of a developing industrial society. More importantly, they strengthened the performance of the Ministry in the House of Commons, where it had previously been weak.

They also realised that, after the alarms of the period 1815–20, a wider basis for popular support had to be found. Basically, it was the return of prosperity, rather than any preconceived policy by Liverpool, that gave them the opportunity to introduce some modest reforms. Note that the reforms of the Liberal Tories were mainly economic and legal. Their political outlook did not change; it was simply not challenged in the 'twenties.

You must know the details of the work of Peel and Huskisson. The most important contribution of 'Prosperity' Robinson was that he consistently balanced the budgets and cut taxation. Until his death in 1827, Canning gave the military an aura of liberalism by his open rejection of the Holy Alliance and his confident vindication of nationalism abroad. Note that some very important reforms were carried out by the Tories after 1827. The Corn Laws were modified and a sliding scale was introduced to give some flexibility. Dissenters were given civil and religious liberty by the Repeal of the Test and Corporation Acts in 1828, but O'Connell had to wrest Catholic emancipation from a reluctant government in 1829.

These concessions on cash, corn and Catholics, however, merely sowed dissent in the rain of the Tories. The challenge to their most fundamental beliefs, especially in the granting of Catholic emancipation, prompted charges of betrayal against Peel and Wellington. These post-1827 reforms under Wellington were basically concessions. Pressured from outside parliament, and, after Canning's death, divided within, these constitutional changes finally brought about the destruction of 'Liverpool Toryism.'

1.6 TORY PARTY DISINTEGRATION 1828–30

During this period the importance of Liverpool's leadership qualities suddenly became apparent as Canning, Goderich and Wellington all failed to hold the party together. Some of the divisiveness was due to personal ambitions and antagonisms, but much more was due to religion as the party divided into pro-Catholic (Canning) and anti-Catholic (Wellington and Peel) sections. Note that it was religion rather than pressure for parliamentary reform that brought about the collapse of Wellington's government in 1830. As Professor Eric Evans says, 'the religious changes of 1828 and 1829 should be considered an integral part of the history of reform in 1832 – not as a prelude to it'.

An enlightened administration?

Armed with the details of the major reforms of the ministry and your knowledge of the policies of governments immediately before and after 1822, you should now be able to tackle the central question of this section: how 'liberal' were the Liberal Tories? They were, indeed, responsible for some important reforms.

Huskisson's free-trade measures, which upset the protectionists, were liberal in outlook. He dismantled the Navigation Acts and put the Corn Laws on a sliding scale. His policies were strongly supported by Canning's foreign policy, in which the promotion of trade was always a basic principle. Peel's improvement of prison conditions, his reduction of the number of capital offences, his reform of the Criminal Code, and his establishment of the Metropolitan Police Force in 1829 – these were reforms that would not have been contemplated by Sidmouth and Eldon. Certainly these reforms appeared liberal compared to what had gone before but less so when compared to the Whig reforms of the 1830s.

There remain, however, certain important factors to be borne in mind. Lord Liverpool did not consciously encourage reform in the 'twenties: all the new appointments had served during the repressive period. In most cases the process of reform had already begun or was being investigated. The 'Liberal Tories' were not innovatory. Before and after 1822 they had sought to foster commerce and trade, to protect property and to strengthen law and order. Apart from the Corn Laws – which they believed to be vital for the national interest – their economic measures were progressive.

There was, however, no bold commitment to improvement: the reforms that occurred did not attempt to alter the fundamental constitutional structure. Parliamentary reform was never seriously considered and pressing problems of a new urban industrial society, such as public health, poverty, education and factory reform, were ignored. The 'Liberal Tories' *could* have attempted reforms similar to those of the Whigs in the 1830s, but did not.

Finally, consider the argument that there is a real continuity in government policy from 1815–27 and that 'the essence of the Liverpool system was opposition to constitutional changes combined with innovation in administrative and social policy.'

1.7 CHRONOLOGY

1815	January	CORN LAW: prohibited the import of foreign corn until the price of English corn reached 80s. a quarter.
1816	March	REPEAL OF THE PROPERTY (i.e. INCOME) TAX: necessitated the introduction of more indirect taxes which, proportionally, fell heaviest on the poor. LUDDISM: machine-breaking in the East Midlands, Yorkshire and Lancashire.
	May	ELY AND LITTLEPORT RIOTS: the seizure of Littleport by agricultural labourers; dispersed by military force.
	December	SPA FIELDS RIOT, London: organised by the Spenceans and led by Thistlewood with the object of seizing the Tower: they were dispersed at the Royal Exchange.
1817	January	A London crowd attacked the Prince Regent's coach.
	February	HABEAS CORPUS SUSPENDED.
	March	Act against Blasphemous and Seditious Libels. MARCH OF THE BLANKETEERS from Manchester to petition the Regent for relief.
	June	PENTRICH REVOLT: organised by J Brandreth, partly owing to the influence of a government spy 'Oliver'; easily suppressed by a small military force near Nottingham.
1819	May	BULLION COMMITTEE, chaired by Peel, recommended a return to the gold standard.
	16 August	PETERLOO MASSACRE: meeting in St Peter's Field, Manchester for parliamentary reform; magistrates sent a body of Yeomanry into the 80,000 crowd to arrest 'Orator' Hunt; they panicked; the Hussars charged the crowd; 11 were killed and 400 injured. The government introduced THE SIX ACTS: these aimed to prevent delay in the administration of justice, seditious libels and training in the use of arms; they gave power to seize arms, imposed a 'newspaper stamp' tax and proscribed seditious meetings. They were not strictly enforced. Factory Act: forbade the employment of children under nine in cotton mills.
1820	January	Death of George III, accession of George IV.
	February	CATO STREET CONSPIRACY: a plot formed by Thistlewood to assassinate the cabinet. Conspirators were seized in Cato St. in north-west London. Thistlewood and four others were executed.
	August	THE QUEEN'S TRIAL. George IV attempted to divorce Caroline, his estranged wife; public sympathy for the Queen (as George was unpopular) led to widespread disturbances in London.
1821	May	RETURN TO THE GOLD STANDARD, whereby the Bank of England gave gold for notes. This was a deflationary measure, causing some distress.
1822	August	Castlereagh committed suicide. RECONSTRUCTION OF THE MINISTRY: Liverpool gave Canning, Peel, Huskisson and Robinson key posts in the government.

1823	June	HUSKISSON'S RECIPROCITY OF DUTIES ACT substantially increased British trade. Revision of the Navigation Acts: lifted restrictions on foreign trading vessels. PEEL'S REVISION OF THE CRIMINAL CODE: modified the severity of the criminal code and improved prison administration.
1824	June	REPEAL OF THE COMBINATION ACTS of 1799 and 1800 which had prevented liberty of association among working men. Organised by F Place and carried by J Hume in Parliament.
1825	December	NEW COMBINATION ACT limiting freedom passed in 1824, after a wave of strikes. Financial crisis: wild speculation led to the collapse of 60 banks in seven weeks.
1826	July	General election, followed by trade recession.
1827	April	CANNING BECAME PRIME MINISTER on the disablement, by illness, of Lord Liverpool. Unity of the Tory Party broken.
	August	Death of Canning. GODERICH BECAME PRIME MINISTER. FAILED TO FORM A CABINET.
1828	January	WELLINGTON BECAME PRIME MINISTER.
	May	TEST AND CORPORATION ACTS against the nonconformists were repealed.
	June	REVISION OF CORN LAWS: sliding scale – imports prohibited when corn was below 54s. a quarter; progressive tariff from 54s. to 73s. – when corn entered free.
1829	April	CATHOLIC EMANCIPATION ACT: Daniel O'Connell's Catholic Association, plus his election as MP for County Clare, forced the government to grant emancipation. Catholics were no longer excluded from major public offices (such as MP). A further Act, however, raised the qualification for the franchise in Ireland from 40s. to £10 in order to mitigate the consequences of emancipation.
	September	ESTABLISHMENT OF THE METROPOLITAN POLICE FORCE by Peel.
1830	November	Fall of Wellington's Government.

Illustrative questions and answers

1 Compare and examine the attitude of Lord Liverpool's government to social and economic problems before and after 1822.

Tutorial note

The most difficult problem of interpretation concerning Liverpool's government is the extent to which the ministerial changes of 1822 affected the content of policy-making. This question requires you to adjudicate on this matter with respect to economic and social policy.

You need to know about

The social and economic condition of England 1815–30. The economic and social policies of Liverpool, Vansittart, Huskisson and Robinson.

Suggested answer plan

1 Superficially, the social and economic policies (especially the reduction of tariffs in the 1820s) seem to fit the picture of a reactionary government turning 'liberal' after 1822. Robinson replaced Vansittart as Chancellor, and Huskisson became President of the Board of Trade. On the other hand, Robinson and Wallace had previously been at the Board of Trade, and Vansittart was not intrinsically hostile to free trade.

2 The causes of postwar distress 1815–21; loss of wartime demands on the economy, and the disruption to major industries (e.g. iron); unemployment was exacerbated by the return of ex-soldiers from the continent; prices were still high from wartime inflation.

3   The causes of agricultural distress 1819–22; good harvests reduced the price of corn; much of the wartime cultivation had to be abandoned because it was on land not inherently suitable for wheat crops; many farmers with mortgages were also damaged after 1819 by the government's deflationary policy.

4   Social and political consequences of the economic situation 1815–22; severe industrial unrest culminated in Peterloo; a back-bench agricultural revolt threatened the government's position in parliament (1819–22). All government policies before 1822 were determined by the need to maintain social calm, i.e. to minimise urban distress and agrarian political discontent.

5   The main threat to law and order was thought to be the possibility of inadequate food supplies; until c 1821 ministers thought that home production must always be the basis of food supply; this belief led to the 1815 Corn Law to protect agriculture.

6   In 1821 ministers perceived that, given the exhaustion of suitable arable land, Britain could not always be self-sufficient in food; it would therefore be necessary to import food more regularly in order to keep foreign farmers in production; moreover, irregular imports were disrupting the gold standard; so, despite the political dangers, ministers began the cautious move towards free trade in corn, which resulted in the 1828 Corn Law, and finally in the 1846 repeal.

7   Until c.1822 ministerial freedom of action was limited by the lack of any financial surplus; the 1816 loss of property tax meant that Vansittart had to live from 'hand to mouth'. An upswing in the business cycle (1821–6) increased government revenue, which enabled Robinson and Huskisson to reduce indirect taxation. Such 'freer trade' made them appear very liberal but Vansittart would probably have done the same if he had still been in office.

8   Anyway, Huskisson's 'free trade' policies were cautious and based more on bilateral and reciprocal agreements with other countries than on unilateral action; but he did significantly relax the Navigation Laws and also amended the Combination Laws.

9   A determination to preserve law and order prevailed throughout the period. The return to prosperity after 1821, not a change in government attitude, explains the absence of social unrest from 1822 to 1830.

10 The real division in policy concerned attitudes not to social or trading problems but to the currency; here the turning-point came in 1819, with the triumph of the bullionists; 1822 made no significant difference to this, most crucial, issue.

2   Would you agree that Lord Liverpool's government 1822–7 was a 'Liberal Tory' administration?

Tutorial note

Do not waste too much time defining 'Liberal Toryism'. You are mainly required to examine the ideology of the Liverpool administration in its post-1822 phase, and also the nature of its political appeal.

You need to know about

The policies and philosophy of the Liberal Tories. The political support for them in the country at large. An assessment of the 'liberality' of the reforms.

Suggested answer plan

1   The implications of the word 'liberal' in the 1820s; usually used by enemies as a term of abuse; 'Liberal Toryism' was not a half-way house between Tory and Whig but rather a set of political attitudes and instincts (especially free trade and laissez-faire) which were growing within both the Tory and Whig parties, and which would eventually develop, through 'Peelism', into Gladstonian Liberalism. Quote Peel, 1820, as saying that 'the tone of England is more *liberal* than that of the government'.

2 Obviously, Liverpool's government remained 'Tory' in the sense of wishing to maintain the unreformed constitution and to suppress radical discontent by strengthening the forces of law and order (e.g. Canning's support for the Manchester magistrates after Peterloo); they all wished to maintain the established Church but differed as to whether this could best be done by resisting or conceding Catholic claims. The prominence of Liberal Tories like Canning after 1822 did not help the 'Catholic' cause, as Liverpool kept this an 'open' question in cabinet.

3 Nevertheless, in 1822–7 Liverpool's government undoubtedly divided into 'liberal' and 'high' Tory camps; by 1825–6 the cabinet was fundamentally split, with some ministers barely on speaking terms. Liverpool's personal support ensured the dominance of such 'liberals' as Canning, Huskisson and Peel, while Wellington, Vansittart (Bexley) and Eldon attempted to undermine policy from within the government. The main sources of dispute were commercial and monetary policy, the recognition of the South American colonies and attitudes to the Greek revolt.

4 Some important 'liberal' (but non-controversial) reforms were carried out by Peel at the Home Office and Huskisson at the Board of Trade. Canning, by his flamboyant statements on foreign affairs, gave the ministry a 'liberal' aura. Compared to the period 1815–20, these reforms did appear enlightened but they were limited. The government refused to tackle the big constitutional, political and social questions of the day – e.g. the Poor Law, factory and parliamentary reform, etc. Compared to the Whig reforms which follow, they appear restrained.

5 It is sometimes thought (see W R Brock and Asa Briggs) that 'liberal' Tories appealed to mercantile and manufacturing interests (Canning and Huskisson were both MPs for Liverpool) as against the agricultural bias of the 'high' Tories. In fact, Liberal Tories were as much attached to the landed establishment as anyone, and the fact is that – except in the case of corn – free trade was not then popular with commercial interests. If Liverpool's government after 1822 had any class-based appeal, it was rather to the 'rentier' interests who benefited from their 'sound money' policies.

6 And yet Canning was willing to compromise on policy (as over Greece), and Huskisson partially retreated on the Combination Acts. It is probable, therefore, that the divisions over Liberal Toryism can largely be explained in simple personality terms, especially the 'high' Tory distrust of Canning. Their policy of conservatism, however 'liberal', was still fundamentally a policy of preserving the essential basis of aristocratic power and the constitution inherited from the eighteenth century.

3 How near did England come to revolution between 1815 and 1832?

Tutorial note

This question requires, not only your assessment of the strength, unity and potential for violence of the radical movements during the years 1815–32 but also of the readiness and efficiency of the forces of law and order.

You need to know about

The social and political history of the years 1815–32. The structure of government and the organisation of repression.

Suggested answer plan

1 Professor Gash has called the years 1815–48 the most prolonged period of social discontent in English history; certainly, it came nearer to revolution during these years of industrial transformation and dislocation than at any other time – but 'how near' remains open to question.

2 Economic and social factors making for discontent: the growth of population

and pressure on food supplies, led to high prices and resentment against the 1815 Corn Law ('the most naked piece of class legislation in English history', according to Lord Blake); economic fluctuations caused cyclical unemployment and the permanent *under*-employment of skilled workers (hand-loom weavers, stockingers, frame-work knitters) displaced by technological advances; cholera, overcrowding and insanitary conditions in the new industrial cities.

3   The course of political defiance, 1815–21; Spa Fields, the Blanketeers, Luddism, Peterloo, the Queen Caroline riots, the Cato Street Conspiracy; the recurrence of violence 1830–32; 'Captain Swing' riots in Nottingham, Bristol, etc. The chronology of violence suggests that it was closely connected to the economic depression – a fact which perhaps suggests that it was a response to short-term difficulties, not an endemic aspect of society.

4   As Lenin (an expert on the subject) argued: deterioration plus activity does not equal revolution. Three preconditions are required for revolution: (a) an active revolutionary group ready to seize power; (b) a weakness, or inability to enforce law and order; (c) a loss of nerve, or a crisis in the affairs of the ruling order. These preconditions did not exist.

5   There is more reason for believing that the radical leadership of working-class protest (Cobbett, Hunt, Place, etc.) was fundamentally cautious, believing in 'moral' rather than 'physical' force and in courteous appeals to parliament rather than direct action.

6   The Establishment was more vulnerable in 1829–32 than in 1815–21 because it was bitterly divided over the Reform Bill crisis, and because working-class malcontents found allies in the middle class who were demanding political representation (Attwood, Prentice, Baines and the Political Unions). On the other hand, the forces of law and order had been strengthened during Peel's period at the Home Office; London even had its Metropolitan Police – a much more effective peace-keeping force than the yeomanry – and the government's nerve never failed.

7   Conclusion: protest during the years 1815–32 was less truly revolutionary than Chartism later, if only because it was *not* directed against the State as such; resentment was directed against landlords, fundholders, master-manufacturers, or at particular laws and inventions (e.g. threshing-machines), and against corruption in the state (what Cobbett called 'the Thing') but not against the State itself; once the latter was cleansed, it was thought that it would once again protect the common people. It was the 1832 Reform Act which – defining for the first time ever full citizenship (i.e. the possession of the vote) in material, socio-economic terms (the £10 householder, the 40s. freeholder) – directed working-class anger against the State itself and thereby turned it into a genuinely revolutionary movement.

Question bank

1   Document question (Lord Liverpool's government, 1815–27): Study the extract below and then answer question (a) to (g) which follow:

line

1   'As I lay asleep in Italy
    There came a voice from over the Sea,
    And with great power it forth led me
    To walk in the visions of Poesy.

5   'I met Murder on the way –
    He had a mask like Castlereagh –
    Very smooth he looked, yet grim;
    Seven blood-hounds followed him;

'All were fat; and well they might
10 Be in admirable plight,
For one by one, and two by two,
He tossed them human hearts to chew
Which from his wide cloak he drew.

'Next came Fraud, and he had on,
15 Like Eldon, an ermined gown;
His big tears, for he wept well,
Turned to mill-stones as they fell.

'And the little children, who
Round his feet played to and fro,
20 Thinking every tear a gem,
Had their brains knocked out by them.

'Clothed with the Bible, as with light,
And the shadows of the night,
Like Sidmouth, next, Hypocrisy
25 On a crocodile rode by.

'And many more destructions played
In this ghastly masquerade,
All disguised, even to the eyes,
Like Bishops, lawyers, peers, or spies.

30 'Last came Anarchy: he rode
On a white horse, splashed with blood;
He was pale even to the lips,
Like Death in the Apocalypse... .

'Let the charged artillery drive
35 Till the dead air seems alive
With the clash of clanging wheels,
And the tramp of horses' heels.

'Let the fixed bayonet
Gleam with sharp desire to wet
40 Its bright point in English blood
Looking keen as one for food.

'And let Panic, who outspeeds
The career of armed steeds
Pass, a disregarded shade
45 Through your phalanx undismayed... .

'Men of England, heirs of Glory,
Heroes of unwritten story,
Nurslings of one mighty Mother,
Hopes of her, and one another;

50 'Rise like Lions after slumber
In unvanquishable number,
Shake your chains to earth like dew
Which in sleep had fallen on you –
Ye are many – they are few.'

(Stanzas from Shelley's *The Mask of Anarchy*, written
on the occasion of the Massacre at Manchester, 1819)

(a) What office did Castlereagh hold in Lord Liverpool's government? For what reasons and with what justification could lines 5–6 ('I met Murder on the way – He had a mask like Castlereagh') be applied to the way he carried out the duties of that particular office? (4)

(b) For what other reason did Shelley associate Castlereagh personally with 'Murder'? (2)

(c) What posts in Liverpool's government were held by Eldon and Sidmouth respectively and why did Shelley attack them so bitterly in lines 15–25? (6)

(d) Explain the reference to 'spies' in line 29. (3)

(e) Describe and account for the importance attached to the incident referred to in lines 34–41. (6)

(f) What were the reasons for the 'Panic' referred to by Shelley in line 42? (4)

(g) Name the man who might be said to have attempted, a year after this was written, to act in the spirit of lines 50–54, and why did Englishmen in general *not* 'Rise like Lions after slumber' in the 1820s? (6)

2 How do you explain the ability of the Tories to remain in office until 1830?

(NISEAC, June 1990)

3 Had Liverpool's government any valid and practicable alternative to its repressive public order policies in the period 1812–1820?

(London, June 1990)

4 How liberal were the 'Liberal Tories' of the years 1822–30?

(Cambridge, June 1990)

5 Was there any serious threat of revolution during Lord Liverpool's Ministry?

(Oxford and Cambridge, June 1990)

READING LIST

Standard textbook reading

A. Briggs, *Age of Improvement* (Longman, 1959), chapter 4.

E. J. Evans, *The Forging of the Modern State* (Longman, 1983), chapters 6, 7, 11, 19, 20.

R. K. Webb, *Modern England* (Allen and Unwin, 1980 edn.), chapter 4.

A. Wood, *Nineteenth-Century Britain* (Longman, 1960), chapters 3, 5.

Further suggested reading

M. Bentley, *Politics Without Democracy 1815–1914* (Fontana, 1984).

J. E. Cookson, *Lord Liverpool's Administration: the Crucial Years* (Scottish Academic Press, 1975).

J. R. Dinwiddy, *From Luddism to the Reform Bill* (Blackwell, 1986).

E. J. Evans, *Britain Before the Reform Act* (Longman, 1989).

N. Gash, *Lord Liverpool* (Weidenfeld and Nicholson, 1984).

A. Mitchell, *The Whigs in Opposition 1815–30* (OUP, 1967).

W. Reitzel ed., *The Autobiography of William Cobbett* (Faber and Faber, 1967).

E. Royle and J. Walvin, *English Radicals and Reformers 1760–1848* (Harvester, 1982).

M. I. Thomis and P. Holt, *Threats of Revolution in Britain 1789–1840* (Macmillan, 1977).

E. P. Thompson, *The Making of the English Working Class* (Gollancz, 1963).

THE WHIG REFORMS, 1830–41

Units in this chapter

2.1 *The need for reform*
2.2 *The reform crisis*
2.3 *Effects of reform*
2.4 *Further reforms, 1833–41*
2.5 *Whig achievements*
2.6 *Chronology*

Chapter objectives

❶ Background to the Reform Act: the Tories won the 1830 election but Wellington failed to appease the ultra-Tories or Canningites; the government was defeated on the Civil List issue and resigned. Lord Grey became Prime Minister against a background of political, social and economic unrest. The Whigs were strengthened by the adhesion of the Canningites and Radicals. The ministry was predominantly aristocratic but was determined to solve the problem of reform.

❷ Note the content of the Reform Bill, the struggle to pass the Bill, the influence of economic distress, the publicity of the radicals, the pressure of the Political Unions (mark especially Attwood and the BPU), and the NUWC. The riots and disorder at Nottingham, Bristol, etc. (1831) and 'the days of May' (1832) – 'to stop the Duke', etc. The object of the Whigs was to appease the middle classes – 'the wealth and intelligence of the country'. The Tories resisted fiercely; Peel was 'unwilling to open a door'.

❸ The terms of the Reform Act – were they conservative and modest? Or a revolutionary enactment? There was little change in the composition of the House of Commons, few concessions to Radicals, and corruption continued. The Crown, the Church, the House of Lords, the aristocracy – all survived the trauma. However, a first breach had been made – the Act had complemented the religious changes begun in late 1820s. The Reform Act was 'great' because of the struggle for its passing rather than the significance of its contents.

❹ The Radicals demanded further reforms; the Whigs were reluctant but continued – at least up to 1836. The cause of reform was helped by utilitarian doctrine and Benthamite procedures – i.e., the Royal Commission, legislation and central (supervised) control. The importance of Chadwick in this 'revolution in government'.

❺ Whig legislation: the abolition of slavery was finally forced through by the pressure of the Dissenters and the evangelicals; £20 million was allocated to assuage the West Indian lobby – which was less vociferous now that profits of the sugar trade were in decline. The Benthamites, however, were unable to get state control of education: Benthamite intrusion was fiercely resisted by the Anglicans and the Dissenters. The Benthamites had to be content, therefore, with an annual education grant of £20,000. The campaign for a Factory Act – by Tory landowners (i.e., Oastler), the Radicals, evangelicals and factory operatives – was successful but disappointingly utilitarian in character. The creation of a Factory Inspectorate prepared the way for later, more effective, legislation.

⑥ The 1834 Poor Law Amendment Act; the deficiencies of the old system; the middle-class attack on Speenhamland. The Act, which was Benthamite utilitarian in conception and execution, finished independent, parochial administration by amalgamating parishes into Unions, managed by elected Boards of Guardians; the results of the Act, the attitudes of the working class and of the Radicals; the Anti-Poor Law movement.

⑦ The 1835 Municipal Corporations Act: this was a corollary of the 1832 Reform Act. It swept away corrupt municipalities and gave 'shopocracy' the vote. The Act was largely permissive and so postponed municipal reforms until the 1870s. The Act was 'poison for the Tories' as it made the boroughs Whig strongholds.

⑧ Reactions: the Radicals were disappointed as there was no Church disestablishment. However, the civil registration of births, marriages and deaths was introduced, tithes were commuted, and the non-denominational University of London was founded. Working-class leaders, however, were irritated at the suppression of the trade unions and the lack of further constitutional reforms. The middle classes were irritated by the continuance of the Corn Laws. The failure of the Whigs to tackle these questions led to the rise of Chartism and of the Anti-Corn Law League in the later 1830s when Whig reforms had dried up.

⑨ The Whigs were divided and weakened after 1834 by the rifts with the Radicals and the O'Connellites, the weakness of Melbourne's leadership, the inability to solve financial problems and the constancy of the Irish difficulties. Note the re-emergence of the Tories under Peel; the Tamworth Manifesto offered a new Conservative creed for the nineteenth century. Peel's qualities of leadership contrasted with those of Melbourne; the 'Bedchamber Question'. The Whigs continued in office but not in effective power; the 1841 election ended Whig rule.

⑩ The Whig reforms were creditable: they laid the foundation of a modern administrative state but the governments had their failures. They failed in Ireland despite their reforms (viz. Education, Poor Law, Municipal Corporations, tithes); they failed in finance (this was less excusable); and they failed to satisfy working-class aspirations. However, they had appeased the middle classes, they had tackled fundamental problems and had made sure that England's progress to democracy would be an orderly one.

This is a period of active reform and political reorganisation. The most important change was the Reform Act of 1832, effected largely through the mobilisation of public opinion by assorted radicals. The campaign which developed was a very different one from that which led up to Peterloo. By this stage the middle classes in the new towns had come to regard the heavily aristocratic and Anglican established ruling order as no longer acceptable. With their allies, the radicals in the new areas, they organised themselves into political pressure groups, such as the Birmingham Political Union, to campaign for reform.

The Whigs, elected in 1830 on a reform platform, saw their task as remedying the main grievances of the people. Although the reform measure they passed in 1832 was essentially conservative in nature, their action probably saved England from revolution.

Encouraged by their own belief in progress, and helped by the Benthamite doctrine of utilitarianism, they proceeded to introduce several major reforms before their reforming zeal petered out in 1836.

2.1 THE NEED FOR REFORM

Lord Grey's government faced a difficult situation in 1830. His Cabinet contained men of both parties but was predominantly made up of the great landed Whig aristocrats, most of whom would be unenthusiastic about fundamental reform of the political system. (It was said that his Cabinet surpassed in acreage any previous Cabinet.) It dealt severely with the 'Captain Swing' riots before, ironically, turning its attention to reform. In fact, Wellington's government had reluctantly begun the reform of the constitution in 1828. The question now, unlike then, was not whether reform should be allowed, but how much should be granted.

The unreformed system

Prior to 1832 the unreformed electoral system was a confusing and antiquated mixture of local customs, practices and abuses. The industrial revolution and population growth of the late eighteenth century had rendered the system obsolete and unrepresentative. The most obvious defects were: the existence of nomination (or 'rotten') boroughs; the widely mixed urban franchises; the unrepresented industrial cities; regional under- or over-representation; the limited numbers who had the vote (only 160,000 out of 16 million); the few elections that were contested and the almost complete domination of the system by the landed élite. You must be able to give examples of each of the above defects.

The Tories had the major, though not exclusive, share of the unreformed system and they (with the Church and the Army) were its fiercest defenders. They argued in its defence that (a) it had stood the test of time, (b) it allowed all classes and interests representation and (c) that it was a deliberative assembly, not a congress of delegates. Even the much-attacked 'rotten' boroughs, it was alleged, had given men of ability (like Pitt, Burke, Fox, Canning and Peel) a means of entry into the Commons. Finally, the Tories maintained that reform would undermine the habits of obedience, deference and respect for property.

In short, they favoured a system based on the ruling aristocracy, the landed gentry, the primacy of the countryside and the Anglican Church. You must now find out what those who wished to change the system wanted.

2.2 THE REFORM CRISIS

The actual pace of change, however, was to be dictated as much by events within parliament as outside it. Hence the crucial importance of the break-up of the Tory Party after Liverpool, and the first adjustments to the constitution that followed. The religious bastion of Anglicanism had now been breached.

The radical campaign which had begun in the 1760s with Wilkes, and had continued under Wyvill, Cartwright, Cobbett and Burdett, at last appeared to be achieving success. You should consider the question of why reform was delayed until 1832 and what combination of circumstances made it possible then. (Note that the reform

- ● Rotten Boroughs
- ● Large Towns with no MPs

Representation in the Commons 1830 – 32

	County Seats		Borough Seats		University Seats		Totals	
	1830	1832	1830	1832	1830	1832	1830	1832
England	82	144	403	323	4	4	489	.471
Wales	12	15	12	14	–	–	24	29
Scotland	30	30	15	23	–	–	45	53
Ireland	64	64	35	39	1	2	100	105
Totals	188	253	465	399	5	6	658	658

Fig. 9 Representation in the unreformed Parliament, 1830

movement was made up of ultra-Tory discontent after Catholic emancipation, the economic distress of 1830, the outpourings of the press on reform and the activities of the Political Unions – especially Attwood's BPU.)

Wellington's determination to oppose reform forced the Whigs' hand. Lord Grey, realising that the price of power and general law and order was a Reform Bill, and knowing that he could rely on support across party lines, determined to act boldly.

He entrusted the drafting of the Bill to a committee of four – which included the two most prominent reformers in the party, Lord John Russell and Lord Durham.

The passing of the Bill

The political complexion of Grey's cabinet assured the propertied classes that reform would not mean revolution: the object of the first Bill introduced by Russell was primarily to rally middle-class support around the prevailing aristocratic system. With the Tories incredulous at the proposed changes – 163 seats were to disappear – the struggle to pass the Reform Bill began.

Some historians argue that over the next year England was in a near-revolutionary state. The public, roused by the Political Unions, demanded 'the Bill, the whole Bill and nothing but the Bill.' When it was jeopardised they rioted, threatened a run on the Bank of England, and burned the castle at Nottingham, the Bishop's Palace at Bristol and the gaol at Derby. There were threats of a refusal to pay taxes and fears of mutiny in the Army. The ingredients for a revolution seemed present as the Radicals and Political Unions tried to impress on the government that a failure to grant reform might precipitate a revolution. How did Lord Grey respond and why was he able to avert this threat? Make sure that you master the sequence of the main events from March 1831 to June 1832 (see Chapter objectives and Unit 2.6 Chronology).

The Whig case

The Reform Act attacked the most obvious defects of the unreformed system: the 'rotten' boroughs, unequal franchises, unrepresented cities, regional under- and over-representation. Could it be argued that some of the changes reinforced the landed hold on power? (Check on this aspect and pay particular attention to the Chandos and secret ballot clauses.)

The Whigs, of course, maintained that the Bill was a moderate, conservative, final measure. They could not afford to lose the support of too many aristocrats or Tory partisans. Lord Brougham stressed that only half a million of the propertied and educated class – 'the wealth and intelligence of the country, the glory of the British name' – would get the vote. Macaulay neatly summed up their fundamental objective: 'that we may exclude those whom it is necessary to exclude, we must admit those whom it is safe to admit.' According to W R Brock, 'the poachers were to be turned into gamekeepers.'

The strength of the Whigs' case was that they were offering a practical remedy for a felt grievance, the most that parliament would tolerate and the least that the country at large would accept. The fear of violence and revolution persuaded many MPs to support them – though more out of fear than conviction. The Whigs also maintained that it would preserve aristocratic rule, and the events of the decades that followed showed that their political judgement was sound.

The Tory case

The Tories rejected all these arguments and insisted that the Reform Act would destroy the balance of the constitution. According to Peel, their chief spokesman, royal power and patronage would be undermined and the Church and House of Lords threatened. The Act, he insisted, could not be final. Once the principle of change was accepted, more reforms would inevitably follow. Hence he demurred, 'I am unwilling to open a door I see no prospect of being able to close'. Wellington foresaw the decline of the landed interest and a fresh onslaught on the Corn Laws. Alexander Baring, MP for Thetford, prophesied that 'the field of coal would beat the field of barley.' In general the Tories rejected Whig arguments about 'finality' and 'moderation' and viewed with alarm the prospect of a House of Commons filled with merchants, tradesmen and radicals.

2.3 EFFECTS OF REFORM

About effects of the Act, there are two schools of thought. One tries to minimise the importance of the Act because, for example, the worst fears of the Tories were not realised. It is argued that the Act lessened but did not eliminate bribery, that most of the basic radical demands were ignored and the working classes were denied the vote. Furthermore, the middle classes, who gained the franchise, failed to make use of it to vote into parliament the financiers, manufacturers and bankers who might have represented them.

In fact, the new House of Commons looked very like the unreformed chamber – 150 MPs still related to members of the Lords; 400 had no profession; 71 were lawyers; 75 had Church patronage; 64 were Army or Navy officers. Only 49 merchants were elected. According to Greville, 'the reformed parliament was very much like every other parliament.' You can discover further arguments for minimising the effects of the Act if you study its impact on the powers of the Crown, Church and House of Lords. Would you agree that each seemed to survive this testing ordeal in the 'thirties and emerged with its powers largely unimpaired?

On the other hand, the Act did effect certain important changes. It got rid of the most notorious 'rotten' boroughs, made the system more representative and gave a substantial number of the middle classes the vote. The manner of its passing was also significant; the Commons had asserted its power over the monarchy and the House of Lords. The force of public opinion and public pressure had been acknowledged. The Act stimulated more interest in both local and national politics and, as more elections were contested, both parties had to reconsider their political outlook and their attitude to the new voters.

Do these changes, however, amount to a revolution? Perhaps the fundamental significance of the Reform Act was that it sanctioned change in the constitution when the time was ripe, showed how this change could be achieved and peaceably opened the door to democracy.

2.4 FURTHER REFORMS, 1833–41

Many political leaders hoped that after 1832 the country would settle down to a period of relative calm. In the event the 1830s proved to be one of the more turbulent decades in British history, with emerging middle- and working-class movements challenging and, in some cases, seeking to overturn, violently, the prevailing political system. Initially the governments of Grey and Melbourne proceeded to tackle the problems posed by the new industrial society. Unlike the high and liberal Tories, the Whigs believed in doing things.

The governments of Grey and Melbourne proceeded to tackle the problems posed by the new industrial society. The predominantly landed parliament accepted the passing of a series of acts which in the event only appeared to sharpen class divisions and emphasise class consciousness. Consequently, reforms dried up after 1836 as the Whigs tired of attempting to satisfy the parliamentary Radicals and their working-class allies.

Nevertheless, by then they had many important reforms to their credit. Slavery in the colonies was abolished in 1833 and the first government subsidy was given to education in the same year. A Factory Act remedied the worst abuses in most textile mills in 1833 and, more important in the long run, appointed four inspectors to supervise the working of the Act. The old Poor Law was amended in 1834. Local government was reformed by the Municipal Corporations Act of 1835 and finally some minor concessions were made to Dissenters in 1836.

Study the details of these measures and note how the influence of Benthamite utilitarianism runs through most of the reforms. Benthamism provided a procedure for reform: investigate, legislate, centralise and, using 'feedback' information (mainly supplied by the new government inspectors), amend where necessary. This procedure was a tremendous asset to reformers and more especially to Edwin Chadwick, who was the driving force behind the most important of the Whig reforms.

The Benthamites did not have it all their own way, however, for they were continually challenged by Tory humanitarians and Evangelicals such as Lord Shaftesbury. Historians now often stress that Victorian reform politics are impossible to comprehend if the religious impulse is not given full weight. Also note that some progressive manufacturers (such as Robert Owen and his followers) offered alternatives to the individualist, capitalist laissez-faire system, e.g. the more communally-inspired Co-op and trade union movements. There was a clear conflict of outlook, then, between these groups in the 1830s and 1840s. You must examine their distinctive ideas and see where they differed, clashed and overlapped in their attitude to the above reforms.

The new Poor Law

The most important of the Whig reforms was the Poor Law Amendment Act of 1834. This clearly revealed the utilitarian spirit of the age; Chadwick played a major part in its formulation and application. The new Act rested firmly on Benthamite convictions – the greatest happiness of the greatest number – and recommendations – the workhouse test and the principle of 'less eligibility.'

Find out what you can about the arguments used to justify this reform, e.g. the spectre of overpopulation raised by Malthus in his *Essay*, escalating poor rates, the motives of Chadwick, the terms of the Act and its effects in the decade that followed. Evaluate the arguments of those who opposed the Act. You should also have some knowledge of the activities of the anti-Poor Law movement. Was the Act a brave, rational approach to a problem which, by the introduction of the Speenhamland system in 1796, had undermined the will of the labourer to work and, as a result, encouraged idleness and pauperism? Or was it, as many humanitarians maintained, 'a vast engine of social degradation' which punished people for being poor and unemployed through no fault of their own? The choice for the poor now seemed to be work, workhouse or starve.

2.5 WHIG ACHIEVEMENTS

Although the Whigs were by 1835 clearly in decline, they had many achievements to their credit. True, they failed in Ireland and in finance but they had seen the need to make a place in the constitution for the middle classes and they had, at least, sought to grapple with the conditions of life and work in the new industrial society. Because of the conflict of interests involved, many of the reforms were compromises, as in factory reform, or permissive, as in municipal reform. They did, however, try to solve the problems posed by the old and muddled local arrangements by promoting a system of administration that was national, standardised and efficient.

Reform before 1830 in many ways was a matter of expediency; now, under the pressure of utilitarianism and social needs, it was becoming more a matter of policy. The pattern of government had been changed in a decade and the foundations of an administrative revolution laid.

Whig failures

But perhaps the significance of the work of the ministry lay less in what it achieved than what it failed to achieve. Many people came to recognise that they were not the beneficiaries of reform. Why were the radicals and their working-class followers so bitterly disappointed? Why did Oastler call the Whigs 'bloody, base and brutal'?

It would appear at first sight that the middle classes should have been happy with these reforms which, on the whole, favoured their utilitarian and entrepreneurial outlook. Yet they were also disappointed. Find out why. What were the immediate results of this widespread dissatisfaction with the Whig reforms?

Decline of the Whig party

By 1840 the Whigs were in disarray. Death and retirement had deprived the Party of its ablest leaders. They failed to balance the budget, to agree on a policy for Ireland, or to deal with the intransigence of the House of Lords. Under the disinterested Melbourne, the Party withered away, allowed Peel to emerge as the most positive politician in the Commons and, thereby, win decisively the general election of 1841.

2.6 CHRONOLOGY

1830	September	'SWING' RIOTS: agricultural labourers burned hayricks and smashed threshing machines in southern agricultural counties.
	June	Accession of William IV. JULY REVOLUTION in Paris: ultra-conservative government of Charles X overthrown; the liberal Louis-Philippe was made King.
	November	Lord Grey became Prime Minister. Union of Canningites and Whigs.
1831	March	FIRST REFORM BILL passed by the House of Commons. Defeated in Committee.
	April	General Election. Reform fever; demand for 'the Bill, the whole Bill and nothing but the Bill'.
	June	SECOND REFORM BILL introduced. Passed by the House of Commons.
	October	Rejected by the House of Lords. REFORM RIOTS in Nottingham and Bristol.
	December	THIRD REFORM BILL introduced.
1832	May	Amended by Lords. Grey resigned. KING PROMISED TO CREATE ENOUGH WHIG PEERS to get the Bill through the Lords.
	June	GREAT REFORM ACT passed. It redistributed 143 seats and extended the franchise to the £10-householder in the towns.
1833	August	ABOLITION OF SLAVERY: ended slavery in the British colonies. £20 million given in compensation. FACTORY ACT prohibited the employment of children under nine, granted an eight-hour day to young persons under 13, and appointed inspectors. EDUCATION ACT: first government grant of £20,000 to the two religious societies (Anglican and Non-conformist) which controlled education. The grant was increased and inspection introduced in 1833.
	September	OXFORD MOVEMENT founded: publication of TRACTS FOR THE TIMES.
	October	G.N.C.T.U. founded by Robert Owen.
1834	March	Trial and transportation of the Tolpuddle Labourers.
	July	Lord Melbourne became Prime Minister.
	August	POOR LAW AMENDMENT ACT abolished the Speenhamland system and instituted a new system of poor relief based on the workhouse. Collapse of G.N.C.T.U.
	November	Robert Peel became Prime Minister.

	December	Tamworth Manifesto: Peel's electoral address to his constituents at Tamworth. Clear assertion of Conservative principles.
1835	March	ECCLESIASTICAL COMMISSION established to investigate the question of Church reform.
	April	Lord Melbourne became Prime Minister.
	September	MUNICIPAL CORPORATIONS ACT instituted a more uniform system of local government in the towns. It diminished corruption and abolished municipal privileges.
1836	August	REGISTRATION ACT: births, marriages and deaths to be recorded. DISSENTING MARRIAGES ACT: marriage in Church, chapel or before a registrar allowed. Removed a major Nonconformist grievance. Tithe Commutation Act. Stamp duty on newspapers reduced from 4d to 1d.
1837	June	Death of William IV. Accession of Queen Victoria.
1838	May	PUBLICATION OF 'THE PEOPLE'S CHARTER'.
	September	FORMATION OF THE ANTI-CORN LAW LEAGUE.
1839	May	Lord Melbourne resigned on the Jamaica Bill. 'Bedchamber Crisis': Peel refused to take office unless the Whig ladies of the Royal Household were dismissed. The Queen refused his request and Melbourne was restored as PM.
1840	January	PENNY POST established.
	10 February	Marriage of Queen Victoria to Prince Albert of Saxe-Coburg-Gotha.
1841	May	Government defeated in the Commons.
	June	General election. Conservative victory.
	September	Robert Peel became Prime Minister

Illustrative questions and answers

1   How far is it true to say that the Whig governments of the 1830s began the 'Age of Reform'?

Tutorial note

This calls for a discussion of whether or not the governments of Grey and Melbourne embarked upon a major programme in ways which marked their achievements as different from those of previous ministries, and began a new era in British politics.

You need to know about

The major legislative enactments of the Whig governments concerned. Some knowledge of the work of the governments of the 1820s and their attitude towards reform. Some knowledge of the progress of reform later in the nineteenth century.

Suggested answer plan

1   It would be an obvious mistake to say that there were no reforms before the Whig return to office in 1830. For example, the first Factory Act in 1802, and further modest measures of factory regulation in 1820, 1825 and 1830. Peel created the new Metropolitan Police in 1829; the Combination Acts (which restricted trade unions) were partially repealed in 1824–5. Small beginnings were made in parliamentary reform – two members from the corrupt borough of Grampound were transferred to Yorkshire. In 1828–9 the repeal of the Test and Corporation Acts and Catholic emancipation brought significant extensions of religious equality.

2   The first five years of the Whig ministries saw an unmistakable quickening of the pace of reform: the Great Reform Act brought the first large instalment of parliamentary reform and removed many of the more discreditable features of the old electoral system. This measure seemed to be much more sweeping and thorough in the Britain of 1832 than it may do to later observers. In 1833 slavery was abolished throughout the British Empire, there was the appointment of the first factory inspectors and, in 1834, the Poor Law was reformed. In 1835 the Municipal Corporation Act provided a new basis for local government by reforming the government of existing boroughs and setting up municipal institutions in urban areas previously without them.

3   An important distinction may be made between the reforms enacted before and after 1830. In the 1820s the Tory governments were willing to make some improvements to the existing system but shied away from major fundamental reforms; the repeal of the Combination Acts was the work of Place and Hume; even the creation of the Metropolitan Police was given the appearance of a government response to a study on policing by a House of Commons Select Committee, though in fact the committee was guided by Peel. In general the Tories were willing to consider 'judicious improvements' but no sweeping measures of reform.

4   Where important constitutional reforms did take place in the 1820s they were forced on the government rather than welcomed by it; the repeal of the Test and Corporation Acts in 1828 was proposed by an opposition member, Lord John Russell; the granting of Catholic emancipation in 1829, though opposed by Peel, was conceded because of the Clare by-election in Ireland and the threat of serious trouble there.

5   On the other hand, the Whig reforms of the 1830s saw a different spirit. The reforms which the government itself devised and enacted were much more sweeping. Instead of the disfranchisement of individual boroughs, a broad plan of parliamentary reform was implemented; the abolition of slavery covered *all* British possessions; the Poor Law system throughout England and Wales was investigated and altered, and town governments were adjusted on a national basis. The government embraced major reforms as an absolutely essential part of its work.

6   Some measures provided an important foundation for future reforms – e.g. inspectors appointed under the 1833 Factory Act provided a model for later inspectorates of schools, mines and lunatic asylums; reformed town councils provided a basis for future growth in the work of local government; the registration of births, deaths and marriages provided new statistical resources for future governments, and this was only part of the increased information made available. The Poor Law Commission and the factory inspectors, for instance, had the duty to lay regular reports before parliament, and the orderly accumulation of evidence about social problems was an important prerequisite for further reforms in future years.

7   In conclusion, though the Tory governments of the 1820s enacted some reforms, this was done so gingerly and sometimes so reluctantly that the much more thoroughgoing work of the Whigs entitles them to be regarded as the real pioneers of the 'Age of Reform'.

2   How far did the 1832 Reform Act fulfil the aims of its creators?

Tutorial note

This question cannot be answered properly by a narrative account of the reform crisis of 1831–2. It requires first of all an examination of the objectives which the framers of the measure had in mind, and then a consideration as to how far the nature and effects of the 1832 Act matched those objectives.

You need to know about

The nature of the leadership in Grey's government. The pre-1832 electoral system. The main features of the 1832 Reform Act. The post-1832 electoral system.

Suggested answer plan

1   The Grey Cabinet was composed mainly of aristocrats – including a number of important ministers, e.g. Melbourne and Palmerston, who had recently served in Tory governments. They did not believe in democracy and there is no reason to expect that they might have done in the Britain of 1832. The cabinet committee which drafted the Bill included Lord Durham, Lord John Russell, Sir James Graham, Bart. and Lord Duncannon.

2   The reform of Parliament was one of the ministry's main aims. Grey and Russell were advocates of reform for many years before 1830; they wished to preserve the predominance of the aristocracy, to broaden the basis of support for the constitution, and to eliminate, or greatly reduce, aspects of the electoral system which brought the representative system into disrepute. In particular, they wished to conciliate the 'middle classes', though this term was not used with any great precision. They aimed for 'a better representation of the property and intelligence of the country'. In this context the word 'intelligence' was used in the older sense of 'information' (surviving in the modern term of 'intelligence corps'). This meant improving the electoral influence of the propertied and educated sectors of society. To do this they sought a modest extension of the franchise, together with provisions which would:
    *   make the franchise more uniform throughout the country;
    *   make elections simpler and cheaper;
    *   reduce corruption.

3   Before 1832 both the franchise and distribution of MPs had changed little for very many years; the counties returned only about a quarter of MPs, though a minority of the population and the wealth of the country was in the towns; the borough franchise was very varied, usually depending on the provisions of the charters governing individual boroughs. In some – Preston, for example – the franchise was quite wide; in others – like Portsmouth – only members of the corporation had the vote. There were also many other varieties of borough electorate; some ancient boroughs – such as Old Sarum – had decayed but still returned MPs; in other boroughs bribery was an established part of the electoral scene; newer urban areas – e.g. Manchester and Leeds – were without representation.

4   The government's reform proposals included: the removal of MPs from boroughs too small or decayed to justify their retention, giving MPs to new towns, increasing the number of county MPs and introducing standard electoral qualifications. In the counties, 40s. freeholders kept the vote, but the Act also enfranchised certain groups of copyholders, leaseholders and tenants. In the boroughs, the main category of voters was to be those who owned or occupied property of a rateable value of £10 or more – the £10-householders.

5   The results of the 1832 Act in practice represented partial fulfilment of its creators' aims; the redistribution of seats went some way to correct the earlier imbalance between county and borough members; the important newer towns received their own MPs. Many smaller boroughs lost their MPs or now returned one instead of two. Over 300,000 new voters were added to the half million existing before 1832.

6   Corruption did not disappear, but the number of very corrupt constituencies diminished with the disappearance of many of the smaller ones. Some of the new post-1832 voters proved as willing to accept bribes as their predecessors; more than 50 seats were still under the control of individual patrons, most of them aristocrats.

7   The Whigs largely succeeded, in the immediately following years at least, in broadening the support for the electoral system. When the Chartist movement

developed a few years later, many of the most strenuous reformers of 1831–2 had been conciliated by the reform of 1832, and were now strong defenders of the reformed system against the Chartists. The electoral changes of 1832 greatly strengthened the existing order, and the aristocracy continued after 1832 to enjoy a predominance very similar to that in pre-1832 years.

3   Why did the Whig hold on power decline in the years after their great victory in 1832?

Tutorial note

After the triumphant passing of the Great Reform Act in 1832, the Grey government scored a sweeping electoral victory in the first reformed general election in December, 1832 but, by 1841, they were defeated and out of office. The question requires an explanation of this transition.

You need to know about

The results of the general elections of 1832,1835,1837 and 1841. An appreciation of the difficulties encountered by the Whigs in holding their followers together and maintaining their popularity. The strong recovery of the Conservatives during the 1830s and the reasons for it.

Suggested answer plan

1   By the end of 1832 the old Tory Party had been crushingly defeated in the battle over the Reform Act and reduced to a small minority in the new House of Commons. The victorious government went on to enact important reform measures (1833–5), including the abolition of slavery, and factory, poor law and municipal reform.

2   However, Whig parliamentary supporters were not a coherent body: they ranged from an important bloc of aristocratic Whigs to Radicals and Irish nationalists under Daniel O'Connell. Even the Radicals were not united and included different groups unable to work together even on agreed policies. It was very difficult for the government to hold together these varied segments, and impossible to prevent a great deal of bickering and public disunity.

3   The general election of 1835 saw Conservatives under Peel gain about 100 seats – though not enough to keep Peel's minority government of 1834–5 in office. In this, and in the following election in 1837, losses among Whig supporters were particularly marked within the radical wing of the 'coalition'. When, after 1835, Whig reform measures ceased, Radicals blamed their losses on their link with the supine Whigs, while Whigs attributed their increasing weakness in parliament to public hostility against the militant pronouncements of some radical groups.

4   Some of the reforms enacted by the Whigs also aroused opposition. The new Poor Law brought much popular hostility and opposition to the elements of centralisation and interference in local affairs included in the 1834 changes. Also, the Whig government reform of the Church of England, especially the control of its property and income was disliked by many Anglicans at a time when the Church was a very influential body. Attempts to impose unwelcome reforms on the established Church of Ireland, especially to divert that Church's revenues to social purposes, lost the government important supporters – two senior cabinet ministers, Stanley and Graham. Grey himself resigned in 1834, mainly for the same reason.

5   Meanwhile, under Peel's skilful leadership, the opposition, now taking the name of the Conservative Party, experienced a distinct recovery. For the general election of 1835 Peel issued the celebrated Tamworth Manifesto, offering the electorate the concept of an attractive Party which, while determined to conserve the vital foundations of British society, was not a reactionary body but a Party itself willing to contribute useful reforms. Peel was careful to

present a public image of conspicuous moderation, while Conservative propaganda stressed the need to defend the reformed establishment against the excesses of radicalism and the nationalist Irish. A closer alliance between the Whigs and the Irish, under the Lichfield House compact (1835), did nothing to prevent this impression gaining ground.

6   Other elements in Whig policy also contributed to the growing support for the Conservatives: the moderation of Whig Home Secretaries towards the early activities of the Chartist Movement; this may have been wise, but the restraint in dealing with democratic agitation was unpopular with the reformed electorate, which showed no desire to extend its privileges. The deepening economic depression from 1837, plus the widespread distress it entailed, exposed the Whigs to heavy criticism. They seemed incapable of devising a financial policy to solve these problems, and their last budgets saw a series of deficits in the national accounts.

7   The Whig government, therefore, declined in strength for a variety of reasons: the basic disunity of their wide range of followers was a serious weakness, while some of their policies brought opposition in their train. They lost important adherents, and successive general elections cut away the great majority they had won in 1832. The 'Bedchamber Crisis' of 1839 showed how precarious their hold on power had become. On the other hand, thanks largely to the dexterous leadership of Peel, the opposition was better able to appeal to influential public opinion, and by 1841 was well placed to eject the Whigs and win a sweeping electoral victory.

Question bank

1   Document question (The Problem of the Poor Rate in the Early Nineteenth Century): study the extract below and then answer questions (a) to (g) which follow:

'We, the undersigned magistrates of Suffolk, beg leave respectfully to submit to the Committee for the Revision of the Poor Laws, the following observations.

'In the present alarming state of the poor rates it must be obvious that there must have been some very unexpected and extraordinary alterations when these rates are swelling to an amount not only unprecedented but beyond what any actual change in the situation of the agricultural population might appear to warrant. We trust it will appear that one cause among many others has added very materially to the burden of the assessment; and that it is indefensible as being <u>unjust, impolitic and cruel</u>.

'The circumstances to which we allude is a practice which has prevailed of giving reduced and insufficient wages to labourers in husbandry and sending them to the poor rate for the remainder of the sum necessary for their support. A practice like this becomes an assessment, not so much for the relief of the poor as of their employers. If the poor rates were levied solely on those who employed labourers, the evil, though great, would be less oppressive. But when it is recollected that the small occupier who cultivates his little farm by his own labour and that of his family; that the tradesman, the mechanic and (where cottages are rated, or where a little land is attached to them) even the labourer is compelled to pay to this assessment, the hardship and partiality of the practice is most evident. Further, the professional man, the shopkeeper, the artisan all are taxed for the payment of labour from which they derive no immediate benefit and in the profits of which they have no participation.

'The practice tends to debase the industrial labourer to the class of the pauper: it habituates him to the reception of poor relief; it teaches him <u>to look to the rates for his usual maintenance instead of apply it reluctantly in sickness or old age</u>.

'For the evils thus detailed, the existing laws furnish no relief. If the labourer whose earnings are insufficient for his support, applies to the magistrate, the magistrate, having no power to fix the rate of wages, MUST, however reluctantly, ORDER relief from the poor rate; and, as this order is <u>final and conclusive</u>, the several classes aforementioned as aggrieved by this unequal assessment, are precluded from the benefit of appeal against <u>the overseers</u> account and left without remedy against this glaring act of injustice and oppression.'

(From a *Memorial of the Magistrates of the County of Suffolk to a Select Committee of the House of Commons on the Poor Laws*, 1817)

(a) What system of poor relief is described in the extract? Where and when is it supposed to have originated? (4)

(b) What other systems of poor relief were also in use in rural areas? (4)

(c) Under what legislation had a magistrate 'final and conclusive' power to order relief from the poor rate? (2)

(d) Explain the term 'the overseers'. (2)

(e) Comment on the nature and validity of the grievances detailed and on their description as 'unjust, impolitic and cruel'. (6)

(f) What measures were eventually taken to teach the labourer not 'to look to the rates for his usual maintenance instead of applying to it reluctantly in sickness or old age'? (6)

(g) Examine the public response to the measures eventually taken in removing the grievances complained of by the Suffolk magistrates in this memorial. (7)

2 'Reform of Parliament in 1832 was much more a matter of political opportunism than of constitutional principle.' Do you agree? (Cambridge, June 1991)

3 Why was the passage of the 1832 Reform Act so contested when its impact on the size of the electorate was so small?

(Oxford and Cambridge, June 1992)

4 'Though the Whigs had no consistent plans of reform, they still deserve credit for major improvements in the machinery of governing Church and State'. Discuss this comment on the period 1833–41. (JMB, Summer 1988)

5 Compare and contrast the impact of the Reform Acts of 1832 and 1867.

(AEB, June 1988)

READING LIST

Standard textbook reading
A. Briggs, *Age of Improvement* (Longman, 1959), chapter 5.
E. J. Evans, *The Forging of the Modern State* (Longman, 1983), chapters 22, 23, 24, 25, 26.
R. K. Webb, *Modern England* (Allen and Unwin, 1980 edn.), chapter 6.
A. Wood, *Nineteenth-Century Britain* (Longman, 1960), chapter 5.

Further suggested reading
M. Brock, *The Great Reform Act* (Hutchinson, 1973).
A. Brundage, *The Making of the New Poor Law* (Hutchinson, 1978).
E. J. Evans, *The Great Reform Act* (Methuen, 1983).

G. B. A. M. Finlayson, *England in the Eighteen-thirties* (Arnold, 1969).
N. Gash, *Reaction and Reconstruction in English Politics 1832–52* (OUP, 1968).
I. Newbold, *Whiggery and Reform, 1830–41* (Macmillan, 1990).
J. D. Marshall, *The Old Poor Law 1795–1834* (Macmillan, 1974).
M. E. Rose, *The Relief of Poverty 1834–1914* (Macmillan, 1972).
E. A. Smith, *Lord Grey*, (Oxford, 1990).
D. Southgate, *The Passing of the Whigs 1832–36* (Macmillan, 1962).
J. T. Ward (ed.), *Popular Movements c. 1830–1850* (Macmillan, 1970).

CHARTISM AND THE ANTI-CORN LAW LEAGUE

Units in this chapter

3.1 *A divided society*
3.2 *Chartism: the causes*
3.3 *The Anti-Corn Law League*
3.4 *Chronology*

Chapter objectives

❶ Chartism was the product of industrialisation but was also a part of the radical tradition dating back to Major Cartwright's *Take Your Choice* (1776); it represented the fundamental belief that economic exploitation and political subservience could be righted by parliamentary means.

❷ Background to Chartism: the emergence of the provinces; the desperation of the hungry 1840s; born out of working-class hunger and anger – 'a knife and fork question' (Harney); Chartism as a phase in the 'social tension' chart. There was also anger at exclusion from 1832, the crushing of the trade unions and the introduction of the New Poor Law. The unstamped press publicised these discontents and provided an organisational network.

❸ Institutional background: the LWMA and articulate, artisan, London radicalism; later joined by Attwood and BPU (idea of petition). Reinforced by popular, local, radical activity – especially that of O'Connor (and his newspaper *The Northern Star*) in Leeds and the West Riding.

❹ The local nature of the Chartist movement: it was strongest in centres of old decaying industries – e.g. textiles, wool, stockings, in Nottingham, Leeds, etc. Also London, Birmingham, Tyneside, South Wales, Glasgow. The handloom weavers were the backbone of the movement, which was weak in the South-East and in agricultural areas. The movement was class-conscious – 'fustian jackets, blistered hands and unshorn chins'; it was singularly working-class (it rejected the overtures of the ACLL and of the Complete Suffrage Union). Note the Irish contribution – especially that of O'Connor and *The Northern Star*. It was a disparate movement held together by its leaders and by rallies, by its organisation and its press.

❺ Strategy: the debate in the London Convention, 1839; 'moral or physical force', petition or rebellion? The rejection of the petition, the Newport

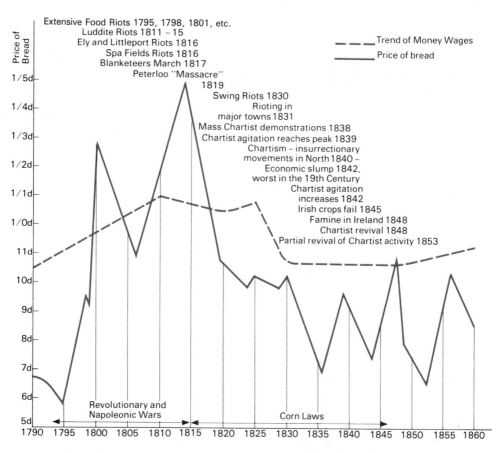

Fig. 10 This diagram represents an index of social tension in Britain between 1790–1860 in relation to the trend of money wages and the price of bread

Rising, the Chartist arrests, the collapse (1840). This was mainly due to a lack of organisation and by government determination to stand firm. The excellent use by the government of the Army (General Napier), of the railways and the electric telegraph to maintain control. The Chartists reorganised and founded the National Charter Association (1840). The rejection of the second petition (1842), the Plug Plot fiasco, the disintegration of the leadership as each leader pursued his own objective. O'Connor offered his land scheme; Lovett offered his on education; others Owenism, religion, etc.

❻ The decline of the Chartist movement as economic conditions improved; Kennington Common (1848), the rejection of the third petition, the loss of mass appeal. Was failure due to the defects in the movement's leadership? To defective strategy? To localism? To dependence on hunger? Or was it that the government and the middle class were determined to resist and that Chartism was doomed from the outset – i.e., that failure was due more to middle-class strength than to working-class weakness? The significance of the movement.

❼ Background to the Anti-Corn Law League: the trade depression post-1836; middle-class dissatisfaction with the results of the 1832 Reform Act; their irritation with their continued social and political inequality. The failure of the Whigs to repeal the Corn Laws. The ACLL was eminently a Manchester and middle-class movement, comprising industrialists, manufacturers, etc., together with humanitarians and some radicals. They believed that the landed classes were idle, feudal and immoral (John Bright); for them the battle was not simply about a customs duty but was a challenge to the social and political order.

⑧ Motives: free trade and enlightened self-interest. Argued that, apart from economic benefits, free trade would bring international interdependence and peace. (The Chartists were sceptical and refused overtures to join.) The ACLL's strategy was for peaceful persuasion by the use of the press, by propaganda, by pamphlet; there was also the annual motion in parliament, the buying of freeholds, etc. The contribution of Cobden and Bright, the excellence of the central, well-funded organisation in Manchester – but the movement was struggling after 1842.

⑨ The impact of the Irish famine: yet, many ACLL members saw repeal as *their* triumph; they felt that they had convinced Peel and the nation of the justice of their case. These claims were exaggerated, as were their predictions (and the protectionists' fears) about the results. Agriculture was not ruined, corn prices did not collapse, the aristocracy did not relinquish power; neither incidentally did mid-Victorian prosperity rest solely on Corn Law repeal and the alleged benefits of free trade.

During the late 'thirties England was plunged into depression. The condition of the lower classes was miserable. The manufacturing middle classes were also affected by the slump and condemned the Corn Laws as an interference with free competition and free trade.

Both classes founded movements to express their discontent and to challenge the prevailing political structure. The Victorian age opened, therefore, with the threat of revolution in the air – a threat the ruling orders could not afford to ignore.

3.1 A DIVIDED SOCIETY

By the mid-forties England had attained industrial maturity, symbolised by the advent of the railways and proudly celebrated in the Great Exhibition of 1851. She had become the workshop of the world. Most Englishmen welcomed the age of improvement and gloried in the rapid and startling changes that occurred. Others feared the consequences of the changes and the class, material and social divisions resulting from them.

In his novel *Sybil or the Two Nations*, published in 1845, Disraeli captured brilliantly the mood and contrasts of this new England, and the gulf that had emerged between the rich and poor. It is important that you understand why England had become such a divided society in the 1830s. Consider also in what ways the economic crisis of the late 'thirties quickened the pace of politics and encouraged the working and middle classes to express their discontent by forming two of the most important political pressure groups of the nineteenth century.

3.2 CHARTISM: THE CAUSES

Chartism, said Carlyle, was 'bitter discontent grown fierce and mad'. It was an attempt to remedy the social and economic evils of the 1830s by political methods and thereby bring about the regeneration of English society. It also expressed the desire of the working classes for social justice. The major demand of the Chartists was for parliamentary reform.

The six points of the People's Charter – adult manhood suffrage, vote by ballot, annual parliaments, equal electoral districts, payment for MPs and the abolition of property qualifications for MPs – already had a chequered radical history which

Fig. 3 Centres of Chartist activity

stretched back to the 1760s. In this respect Chartism did not create, but gave expression to, a working-class movement that had been growing for many years. From its inception therefore, although it may have had economic and social undercurrents, recent research emphasises that it was a political movement, with political objectives to be achieved by political means.

According to Professor Briggs, however, Chartism was born out of 'hunger and anger'. It was a gut reaction to the economic depression of the late 'thirties and an angry response to the Reform Act of 1832, to the collapse of Owenite Unionism and to the introduction of the New Poor Law. It encouraged every person or group with a grievance, mission or political demand to enrol. Its strength derived from its ability to encompass all the dissatisfactions of a discontented Britain.

Make a list of the different groups that belonged to the Chartist movement and be able to discuss the aims and objectives of each of the leaders.

Nature

The institutional origins of the People's Charter are to be found in the London Working Men's Association – which many prominent Radicals of the day were invited to join. The document itself was drawn up in May 1838, by William Lovett (with the advice of Francis Place) and, with Attwood's help, was launched nationally in 1839. Originally, therefore, Chartism was a movement dominated by the educated and politically experienced sector of the working class.

Gradually, however, as the depression deepened and the unemployed joined in greater numbers, the rights of labour were added to their original demands for the rights of man. Feargus O'Connor did most to emphasise this new development as he stressed the proletarian origins of the mass of the Chartists, their 'fustian jackets, blistered hands and unshorn chins'. To him Chartism was fundamentally an expression of the struggle between the 'the haves and have nots'.

Local diversity

It is very difficult to understand Chartism without a full understanding of its regional and local diversity. According to Professor Briggs, Chartism was strongest where economic hardship was greatest, i.e. in the decaying centres of the older industries or in new single-industry towns like Stockport. It was predominantly an urban and industrial phenomenon. The impact in agricultural areas was feeble.

The movement included superior craftsmen such as carpenters and printers, as well as factory operatives, handloom weavers, miners and nailmakers. There was, then, widespread, if locally concentrated, support.

It is important to note that each area had its own grievances, its own leaders and its own priorities. In Manchester it was an expression of class conflict between cotton masters and men. Across the Pennines in Leeds it was galvanised by O'Connor into an aggressive physical-force movement for all those handloom weavers displaced by machinery. In Birmingham, a centre of small workshops, it was, according to Engels, more radical than Chartist. In Tyneside it had strong support from the aristocracy of labour – the better-off artisans.

National unity, then, was more apparent than real. Some modern historians argue that it is more accurate to talk about 'Chartists' than 'Chartism.'

Find out what you can about the conflicting aims and personal rivalries of the Chartist leaders, and the local nature and differing demands of their supporters.

Events

It was Feargus O'Connor who gave the movement whatever appearance of national unity it possessed. His fiery oratory, perfected in the anti-Poor Law movement, backed by his radical newspaper *The Northern Star*, won him the support of the handloom weavers of the West Riding. In 1838 he made his bid for leadership. His appeal to physical force thrilled his discontented followers but alienated the more moderate moral-force leaders such as Lovett and Attwood.

At the People's Convention (an ominous title to those who remembered the French Revolution), held in London in 1839, a compromise solution to this difference of approach was agreed in the slogan 'peaceably if we may, forcibly if we must'. All the plans of the first phase failed – the petition, the 'national holiday', Frost's Newport rising. The Convention eventually broke up late in 1839 in disarray; most of the leaders were soon imprisoned.

A new organisation – the National Charter Association – was formed in 1841 but more disappointments followed in 1842 with the rejection of the second petition and the failure of the 'Plug-Plot' strikes in Lancashire and Staffordshire. Chartism was visibly weakening. Undaunted, O'Connor founded a Chartist Co-operative Land Society in 1843 but by 1848 this was also in difficulty and was wound up in 1851.

You should make notes on the major events (listed above) and be able to explain their importance in the history of the movement.

1848

Inspired by the recent revolutions in Europe, the Chartists decided, in April, 1848, to make a final effort. It was agreed to hold a monster meeting in London at Kennington Common. The proposed march to Parliament was banned. In the Commons a third petition was derisively rejected. This was not, however, the 'fiasco' as asserted by many text books. What that day entailed was not folly and cowardice by Chartists but an enormous propaganda victory for a government which did much to conjure up the danger of a revolution in the first place. In fact Chartism continued to cause problems in June, July and August – all repressed by the government though now with less flamboyance.

In any case, this marked the end of the movement, which was dispersed rather than destroyed. It struggled on into the 1850s. Some aberrations, like Christian Chartism and Teetotal Chartism, continued to be popular but the great days of Chartism and the 'mass platform' had effectively ended by the mid 'forties. In this respect the meeting at Kennington Common was but a disappointing postscript.

Failure

Clearly then, Chartism failed. This is not surprising as the Chartists set themselves an almost impossible task. Their main problem was how to attain a revolutionary goal by constitutional means. Essentially, the movement failed to obtain middle-class (or parliamentary) support for the Six Points.

Satisfied by the extension of the franchise in 1832, or active in the Anti-Corn League, the middle classes ignored, shunned or condemned Chartism. The leadership itself was divided and often confused in its aims. Most projects, including the petitions, were poorly organised. O'Connor may have given Chartism what unity it possessed but his egocentric attitude, his bitter denunciations of alternative approaches (such as Temperance Chartism and the Complete Suffrage Union) and his physical-force speeches alienated many sections of the movement. His calculated revolutionary bluff (the trump card of the masses) failed to move a government that was determined to stand firm.

The government used troops, the railways and the new telegraph system to contain early Chartist meetings and marches; and in General Napier they had made a masterly choice to control events in the North. Secure in the knowledge of the undivided support of English property-owners, the government handled the movement intelligently and effectively.

Moreover, because Chartism was heavily dependent on economic slump for its vital driving force, the return to prosperity under Peel fatally weakened it. The irrelevance of some sources of Chartism (such as the Land Plan), and the elimination of others, all contributed to its decline. In this respect the Kennington Park rally and the rejection of the petition in 1848 were an anticlimax after the early years of marching, drilling, demonstrating and talking about physical force.

Chartism, then, had major weaknesses but these were not – as Kitson Clark maintains – the fundamental causes of its failure. Against a strong government and the middle classes – both totally determined to preserve law and order and thereby save England from revolution – Chartism, well or badly led, was bound to fail.

Significance

The movement was not, however, without significance. It gave a severe shock to the established order and made clear to the government and to the middle class the extent of the 'condition of England' question.

It encouraged Peel's efforts 'to make England a cheap country for living' and his success in putting the country back to work constituted a kind of Chartist success and lends weight to J S Mill's later verdict that 'Chartism was the victory of the vanquished'. It improved the morale of the working class, and provided excitement and a sense of community. It showed the more intelligent leaders how, and how not, to agitate and indicated the importance of middle-class support.

Epilogue

The conclusions of historians a decade ago which presented Chartism as a social protest of impoverished male handloom weavers, poorly led and ultimately betrayed by the unstable Irish demagogue O'Connor, may now have to be reassessed. Recent research stresses the occupational diversity of the movement, the role of women, its predominantly political nature, the importance of the 'mass platform' and the underestimated qualities of its most famous leader. Consequently, essays may now need to show an awareness of all these factors, stress the political rather than the economic context of the movement and display an awareness of O'Connor's skill rather than his folly!

3.3 THE ANTI-CORN LAW LEAGUE

The problem

Most of the newly enfranchised middle classes were satisfied with the Reform Act of 1832 – though some were still unhappy at their social inferiority and the continued domination of parliament by the landed aristocracy. The Corn Laws still rankled but while England was prosperous, up to 1836, resentment by the middle classes was held in check and their energies were concentrated on schemes such as currency and education reform.

When trade collapsed in 1836 and their manufacturing profits were threatened, they turned their attention once more to the campaign for free trade. If they could get rid of the Corn Laws and the remaining tariffs, the prospect was an endlessly expanding market for their goods. Cobden argued persuasively that Corn Law repeal and free trade would give manufacturers more outlets for their production, tackle the 'condition of England' question by expanding employment and lowering the price of bread, make British agriculture more efficient and productive by exposing it to foreign competition and, perhaps most important of all, promote international peace through contact and trade. Bright, meanwhile, broadened the basis of support by introducing the moral element. He stigmatised the landlords as parasites collecting unearned rents and oppressing the agricultural labourers with Game Laws and other remnants of feudal power. Supporters of the League were largely, but not exclusively, the manufacturing and trading classes. They were joined by Dissenters and humanitarians and all those who believed that cheap bread was a fundamental need. The Chartists remained suspicious.

Economic or political?

The most significant aspect of this efficiently led campaign, however, was psychological. The Corn Laws were the symbol of the privileged position of the old aristocratic order. Destroy the Corn Laws and the landed order would also collapse. For this reason, Morley said, 'it was not a battle about a customs duty but a struggle for political influence and social equality'. 'Repeal,' Croker said, 'would bring the overthrow of the existing social and political system.'

Find out what you can about the ways and means adopted by the League in its efforts to gain the repeal. You should also discover some biographical facts about Cobden and Bright and be able to assess their contribution to the movement.

Repeal

Masterly as their campaign was, it did not effect repeal and had, in fact, begun to falter after 1842 as harvests improved and bread prices fell. Encouraged by these events and stung by ACLL abuse, the Protectionists also began to fight back. Despite some ACLL support in parliament (including Charles Villiers' annual motion for reform), the ruling order stood fast under Peel. Unlike the Chartists, spokesmen of the ACLL made it clear that their constitutional agitation had to succeed by persuasion or not at all. Yet by 1845 it was clear that they also had failed to win over the Commons.

However, as N McCord says, although 'the legend of the success of the ACLL dies hard' it was 'Peel in Parliament' that repealed the Corn Laws. He did it in direct response to the Irish famine and furthermore insisted that he did it in the national, as opposed to middle-class, interest.

The propaganda of the League, however, provided sound arguments and had prepared society for the acceptance of repeal. Russell declared the Whigs in favour in 1845 (the Edinburgh letter) and by that date Peel had already been convinced by Cobden's arguments. All that was needed was an occasion and that was provided by the Irish famine. Cobden generously acknowledged Peel's role, while an elated Bright declared that 'the middle class have effectively vindicated their right to rule.'

Price of Wheat per quarter 1811–1864 (yearly average)

	s.	d.		s.	d.		s.	d.
1811	95	3	1829	66	3	1847	69	5
1812	126	6	1830	64	3	1848	50	6
1813	109	9	1831	66	4	1849	44	6
1814	74	4	1832	58	8	1850	40	4
1815	65	7	1833	52	11	1851	38	7
1816	78	6	1834	46	2	1852	41	0
1817	96	11	1835	39	4	1853	53	3
1818	86	3	1836	48	9	1854	72	7
1819	74	6	1837	55	10	1855	74	9
1820	67	10	1838	64	4	1856	69	2
1821	56	1	1839	70	6	1857	56	5
1822	44	7	1840	66	4	1858	44	3
1823	53	4	1841	64	5	1859	43	10
1824	63	11	1842	57	5	1860	53	4
1825	68	6	1843	50	2	1861	55	5
1826	58	8	1844	51	3	1862	55	6
1827	58	6	1845	50	9	1863	44	9
1828	60	5	1846	54	9	1864	40	5

Fig. 4 Table showing the average price of wheat per quarter between 1811–64

Effects

The possible effects of repeal had been exaggerated by both Protectionists and Free Traders. For a start, repeal seemed to help the starving Irish very little and the famine continued remorselessly until 1849. Neither did English farming collapse. Rationalised under the threat of foreign competition, it made use of new technology and entered a golden era of 'high farming' and prosperity. Prices were stable in the 1850s (wheat averaging 52s. a qr).

The real effects came in the 1870s after the revolution in sea transport and the opening of the vast American prairies, which completely undermined British ability to compete in corn growing. The Protectionists had abandoned their opposition to Free trade long before – Disraeli himself declared in 1852: 'Protection is not only dead but damned'.

3.4   CHRONOLOGY

1836	June	LONDON WORKING MEN'S ASSOCIATION founded by William Lovett.
1837	May	Birmingham Political Union reorganised; now publicising an ultra-radical political programme initiated by Thomas Attwood.

	November	*NORTHERN STAR* published, with Feargus O'Connor as its owner, soon selling 50,000 copies per week.
1838	May	THE PEOPLE'S CHARTER PUBLISHED.
	September	MANCHESTER ANTI-CORN LAW ASSOCIATION FOUNDED.
1839	February	CHARTIST CONVENTION in London.
	March	ANTI-CORN LAW LEAGUE FOUNDED: led by Richard Cobden and John Bright. ANTI-CORN LAW CIRCULAR published: 15,000 circulation.
	May	FIRST CHARTIST PETITION: 1.28 million signatures rejected by 235 votes to 46.
	November	FROST'S NEWPORT RISING: Chartists from the valley marched on Newport; they were scattered, with casualties, by troops. The leaders were transported to Australia.
1840	July	NATIONAL CHARTER ASSOCIATION founded.
1841	September	Richard Cobden was elected MP for Stockport.
1842	January	COMPLETE SUFFRAGE UNION founded in Birmingham by Joseph Sturge.
	May	SECOND CHARTIST PETITION: contained 3.3 million signatures rejected by the House of Commons – 287 votes to 49.
	August	PLUG-PLOT STRIKES in Lancashire and Staffordshire. Five hundred Anti-Corn Law League delegates marched to Westminster to lobby MPs.
1843		THE LEAGUE: ACLL newspaper published.
1844	August	Cobden and O'Connor debate the Corn Laws at Northampton.
1845	April	CHARTIST LAND PLAN: a cooperative venture. Units of four acres distributed; three estates established before the Company crashed in 1848.
	October	Partial failure of the Irish potato crop.
	November	'Edinburgh Letter': Russell accepted the need to repeal the Corn Laws.
1846	June	CORN LAW REPEAL. Repeal was to be effected over three years. Farmers were to receive some government aid as a palliative.
1847	July	Feargus O'Connor elected MP for Nottingham.
1848	March	Riots in London, Glasgow and Manchester prompted by rising unemployment and the European revolutions.
	April	Chartist Convention in London.
	10 April	CHARTIST MEETING AT KENNINGTON COMMON. O'Connor was persuaded to abandon the march; the government enrolled 150,000 special constables. The Third Chartist Petition (2 million signatures, many forgeries) rejected.
	May	Chartist National Assembly. Chartist riots in Northern England.
1851	May	The Great Exhibition (Crystal Palace) opened in Hyde Park.
	August	Chartist Land Company wound up.
1855	August	Death of Feargus O'Connor; he was buried at Kensal Green Cemetery, London. An estimated 50,000 people attended his funeral.
1858	February	Chartist Conference agreed to cooperate with moderate Radicals.

Illustrative questions and answers

1 How far was the Anti-Corn Law League responsible for the repeal of the Corn Laws?

Tutorial note

It is very important that a question like this, which demands analysis and discussion, should *not* be answered by a simple narrative account of the League. Much to be preferred is a response carefully confined to an assessment of the League's responsibility.

You need to know about

The working of the political system in early Victorian Britain. The nature and activities of the Anti-Corn Law League. An appreciation of other forces which contributed to the repeal of the Corn Laws.

Suggested answer plan

1   The Anti-Corn Law League was one of the most famous political pressure groups in British history. The contribution of Cobden and Bright is well known; the contrast between the failure of the Chartist movement and the success of the League is often noted.

2   It is natural to assume a clear connection between the work of the League and repeal; the organisation and expenditure involved in the League's campaigns was scarcely to be seen in any earlier political pressure group. After a shaky start (1838–41), it quickly established itself on a footing of continuous activity with a headquarters organisation, regionally distributed agents, a propaganda machine and formidable public speakers; all contributed to an impression of power. Moreover, after 1846 the Leaguers were keen to emphasise their role in bringing about repeal. Note Peel's remarkable tribute to Cobden in 1846, attaching to him the principal responsibility for the coming of free trade in corn.

3   It is, however, possible to suggest that these evaluations of the League's achievements are exaggerated. Consideration of the post-1832 system will suggest difficulty for radical agitation to grasp real power. The Corn Laws could only be repealed by an Act of Parliament, and it is not clear that the League was ever in a position to control the legislature. In practice the electoral system was still dominated by aristocratic Whigs and Conservatives. It is difficult, perhaps impossible, to measure the effects of the League's propaganda campaign: property and influence remained of crucial importance in determining political power, and political agitation never succeeded in shifting that balance of power to any great extent. The House of Commons only had a small minority of MPs closely connected with the League and, in comparison, the serried ranks of landed Whigs and Conservatives, were formidable.

4   Moreover, other factors unconnected with the work of the League were moving in the direction of repeal; economists advocated free trade, and the political establishment had already begun the process before the League was founded. The tariff system had already been considerably reduced, including modifications of the Corn Laws in 1823. Although the Conservative victory in 1841 owed something to the defence of those laws, Peel revised the Corn Law in 1842, reducing the level of protection; his budgets contained many tariff reductions. By 1846 the Corn Laws stood out as a survival of the policy of protection which in other areas had been substantially discarded. The success of Peel's policy of free trade (1842–5) in restoring prosperity provided a cogent argument for going further. Peel himself had privately decided against the Corn Laws long before the League's final agitation. The Irish famine provided him with an opportunity to take a step he had been contemplating for several years.

5   Of course, the League's work certainly had some success: its greatest achievement was to hasten the conversion of the Whig opposition, which meant that by late 1845 the only possible alternative government was committed to repeal. Whig votes were an important component in the Commons majority which voted for repeal in 1845, enabling Peel to overcome dissentients in his own Party on the issue. The threat of continued, even heightened, agitation by

the League may have persuaded the House of Lords to accept repeal. The League, however, played no part in drafting the term of the repeal measure – it played a supporting rather than a leading role in 1846.

6 Conclusion: the primary responsibility for the repeal of the Corn Laws lay with Sir Robert Peel and his government. The League played a part in preparing public opinion and in converting the Whigs but, despite all this, they were never in a position to exert decisive political influence.

2 'Social and economic distress gave rise to Chartism, the advent of prosperity killed it'. Discuss.

Tutorial note

This calls for a discussion of how far Chartism can be seen simply as a response to social conditions, with hard times producing popular pressure for radical reform while easier conditions led to political apathy or acceptance of the existing order.

You need to know about

The nature and history of the Chartist Movement. The shifts in economic conditions during and after the main period of Chartist activity.

Suggested answer plan

1 The coincidence in the timing of economic depression and the peaks of Chartist activity is sufficiently obvious to demonstrate the existence of an important connection between the two. Many areas suffered during the depression which became obvious in 1837 and deepened. These years saw the growth of Chartism into a widespread movement – the first Chartist convention, the first petition and the extremism involved in the Newport Rising of 1839 and other smaller outbreaks. The 'Plug Plot', sparked off by wage reductions resulting from the depression, led to Chartist involvement in widespread strikes; hope of transforming them into a national strike for a People's Charter. The last great flare-up of Chartism, culminating in the Kennington Common fiasco, also owed much to economic troubles in that year. In contrast, more prosperous years, the mid-40s, did not see such strenuous mass support for the Charter. It was not surprising, then, that Chartism was often seen as a 'knife-and-fork' question, or that subsequently historians saw the movement as a barometer of early Victorian economic and social troubles.

2 Although there was a close connection between Chartism and distress, things were not as simple as the link might suggest; it is important to remember that Chartism was an episode in the lives of many people, rather than the full story of those lives. Many Chartists were active reformers long before the Charter was drafted and many remained active reformers long after 1848. The connection with immediate economic and social conditions does much to explain the extent and fluctuations of mass support for Chartism but cannot provide a complete picture of the nature of the movement.

3 None of the six points was a *new* radical demand: most of them were advocated in the later eighteenth century, and indeed earlier. The concept of universal manhood suffrage had a long history; the secret ballot was also not a new idea, having been advocated in the earlier 1830s by Radicals like MP George Grote, who had introduced in parliament several motions in its support. Also, the committee which drafted the 1832 Reform Bill gave the ballot serious consideration. The Charter, therefore, brought together an important group of long-standing radical proposals and welded them into a single programme. This was hardly a response to immediate social conditions.

4 Similarly, many of those who rallied to the Chartist cause had already been active in earlier political campaigning – including the struggle over parliamentary reform in 1831–2, the campaign for factory reform and the protests against the new Poor Law. For many, Chartism was only one phase in a long record

of radical political activity. It was not, then, the case that all Chartists were motivated by the immediate pressures of the economic depression.

5 This concept of Chartism cannot do justice to the considerable intellectual and ideological elements within the movement. The original members of the LMWA who played a key role in the drafting and launching of the Charter were not men suffering distress but men convinced of the need for fundamental change on rational grounds. Other prominent Chartists, e.g. George Julian Harney, were democrats on intellectual rather than immediate 'bread-and-butter' considerations.

6 Although Chartism as a mass movement disappeared as economic prosperity grew, it is too much to say that prosperity killed it, for not all Chartists abandoned their cause. In many parts of the country small groups of dedicated Chartists held together for many years after the failure of 1848; some played a part in the parliamentary reform campaigns of the 1860s. What prosperity did was to eliminate *mass* popular support, which in the late 1830s and 1840s had intermittently enlisted under the Chartist banner. A hard core of dedicated radicals remained faithful after 1848 but were never able to recruit such an extensive following as distress and suffering had brought to the Chartist cause during the worst depressions of the early Victorian years.

7 Conclusion: the quotation in the question contains a good deal of truth but is less satisfactory as a *total* explanation of the rise and decline of Chartism.

3   Did the Chartist Movement have any chances of achieving its aims?

Tutorial note

It is sufficiently obvious that the Chartists did not succeed in placing their six points on the statute book. The question requires discussion of whether the movement ever could have been victorious, given the context in which it had to operate.

You need to know about

An appreciation of early Victorian society and the distribution of power within it. The nature and the resources of the Chartist movement and the difficulties facing it.

Suggested answer plan

1 At first sight it may seem obvious that a movement which could enlist such mass support must have had some chance of success. At the peaks of its activity Chartism could claim millions of supporters, and the dedication of many cannot be questioned.

2 However, an examination of the nature of the society in which Chartism operated casts doubt upon this first impression. In the early Victorian years most people lived in small scattered rural communities, which presented any radical crusade with serious problems of organisation and communication. Not until 1851 did the census show a bare majority living in towns, many of these places being quite small; though industrial and urban society was growing fast, Britain was still very far from being a predominantly industrialised and urban society. In 1851 the biggest single occupational groups were still agricultural labourers and domestic servants, both being groups which were very difficult to enlist in radical political activities.

3 The majority of Chartists were poor, some desperately so; many had little or no education. While this could provide material for mass demonstrations in hard times, it did not provide a promising foundation for sustained organisation. Mass support fluctuated according to social conditions, eager to protest in bad years but likely to drift away when better times came.

4 Democracy was now an accepted doctrine; it is important to realise how drastic the demands of the Charter were in the Britain of 1840. Society was profoundly unequal at that time, and always had been. The seemingly modest provisions of the 1832 Reform Act appeared startlingly sweeping at the time. How much

more radical, then, was the People's Charter, which demanded a fundamental change in the organisation of British society and its ruling elite.

5 Sometimes revolutionary change can be introduced because of the weakness or lack of nerve of those in power at the time, but there was never any chance of this in early Victorian Britain, where the aristocratic ruling élite possessed a serene confidence in its right to rule. Britain's rulers occupied strong positions in the economic, political and social life of the country and Chartism was never able to shake this predominance. The armed forces remained loyal and could be used to restrain or repulse Chartist pressures. The Whig government during the years 1838–40 was confident enough to adopt a moderate and restrained line of resistance to Chartism, avoiding executions and, thereby, martyrs. When alarmed by Chartist activities, they were provoked into displays of strength rather than thoughts of surrender. The House of Commons was confident enough to reject repeated Chartist petitions, with many MPs not even bothering to attend the debates.

6 Moreover, the Whig reforms of the earlier 1830s – the Reform Act of 1832, the Poor Law and the Municipal Corporation Act – reinforced support for the existing order by conciliating many men of influence previously opposed to the unreformed system. The leaders in the reform agitation were by 1839 councillors, aldermen, mayors or Poor Law guardians, possessing the vote and unwilling to see their privileges diluted by the coming of democracy under Chartist auspices. Instead of joining the Chartists these men were now inclined to join or lead the special constables, or issue anti-Chartist proclamations from the reformed town councils.

7 When to these factors we add the disunity always present in Chartist ranks – e.g. the various sub-divisions such as 'moral-force' or 'physical-force' Chartism, Christian Chartists and Temperance Chartists – we see it to be an umbrella movement covering a wide variety of differing local groups of reformers. So we may well conclude that Chartism had little real chance of success. And yet, it is well to remember that some successful revolutions have been the work of small groups of dedicated men. Such successes, however, do not occur against resistance so strongly entrenched as that of the aristocratic rulers of early Victorian Britain.

Question bank

1 Document question (Thomas Attwood introduces the Charter): study the extract below and answer the questions (a) to (g) which follow:

'MR. ATTWOOD was thankful for the indulgence extended to him, and would only trespass a few minutes longer upon the attention of the House. But he wished to say a few words in explanation of his own peculiar situation. Although he most cordially supported the <u>petition</u>, was ready to support every word contained in it, and was determined to use every means in his power in order to carry it out into a law, he must say that many reports had gone abroad, in regard to arguments said to have been used in support of the petition on different occasions, which he distinctly disavowed. He never, in the whole course of his life, recommended any means, or inculcated any doctrine except peace, law, order, loyalty, and union, and always in good faith, not holding one face out of doors, and another in that House; but always in the same manner, and in the same feeling, fairly and openly doing all that he could as a man, a patriot, and a Christian, to work out the principles which he maintained; and to support the views of the petitioners. <u>He washed his hands of any idea, of any appeal to physical force.</u> He deprecated all such notions – he repudiated all talk of arms – he wished for no arms but the will of the people, legally, fairly, and constitutionally expressed – and if the people would only adopt his views, and respond to his voice – if they would send up similar petitions from every parish in England, and go on using every argument which justice, reason, and wisdom dictate, they would create such an action in the public mind, which would again act upon Members of that House – that giving due allowance for the prevalence of generous feeling among English gentlemen and the English people, if the people would act in that manner – <u>if they proceeded wisely and discreetly</u>, washing their hands of all insolence and violence – he was confident they would <u>ultimately secure the attentive consideration of that House</u>. Having said so much, he should now read <u>the prayer of the petition…</u> '

(Hansard 3/ XVLIII, 222)

(a) Where was Attwood's political base and what cause first brought him into politics? (2)

(b) In what year was the speech made? (2)

(c) Comment on the background and nature of the petition. (4)

(d) Attwood rejected physical force. Who was the leader of physical-force Chartism? Outline (briefly) his contribution to the movement. (5)

(e) Did the Chartists subsequently proceed 'wisely and discreetly'? (5)

(f) What, in essence, was 'the prayer of the petition'? (3)

(g) Why did Chartism fail to 'ultimately secure the attentive consideration of that House'? (6)

2 Should Chartism be seen chiefly as the product of a decaying society, or a society in a state of growth? (NISEAC, June 1990)

3 Why, despite social change and popular protest, was there no political revolution in Britain between c 1820 and c 1850? (AEB, June 1991)

4 Why did many working people become Chartists? (JMB, June 1989)

5 Discuss the political and economic consequences of the Repeal of the Corn Laws (Oxford and Cambridge, June 1990)

READING LIST

Standard textbook reading

A. Briggs, *Age of Improvement* (Longman, 1959), chapter 6.

E. J. Evans, *The Forging of the Modern State* (Longman, 1983), chapters 16, 18, 28, 29.

R. K. Webb, *Modern England* (Allen and Unwin, 1980 edn.), chapters 5, 6.

A. Wood, *Nineteenth-Century Britain* (Longman, 1960), chapter 8.

Further suggested reading

A. Briggs (ed.) *Chartist Studies* (Macmillan, 1959).

G. D. H. Cole, *Chartist Portraits* (Macmillan, 1941).

J. Epstein, *The Lion of Freedom: Feargus O'Connor* (Croom Helm, 1982).

J. Epstein and D. Thompson (eds.) *The Chartist Experience* (Macmillan, 1982).

P. Hollis (ed.), *Pressure from Without in Early Victorian England* (Arnold, 1974).

D. Jones, *Chartism and the Chartists* (Lane, 1975).

N. McCord, *The Anti-Corn Law League* (Allen and Unwin, 1958).

D. Read, *Cobden and Bright* (Arnold, 1967).

E. Royle, *Chartism* (Longman, 1980).

J. Rule, *The Labouring Classes in Industrial England* (Longman, 1986).

D. Thompson, *The Chartists* (Temple Smith, 1984).

PEEL AND THE CONSERVATIVE PARTY

Units in this chapter

4.1 *Peel's background*
4.2 *Peel's Second Ministry, 1841–46*
4.3 *Ireland*
4.4 *Corn Law repeal*
4.5 *Assessment of Peel*
4.6 *Chronology*

Chapter objectives

❶ Peel's family background, personality, and upbringing; a shy, withdrawn boy who got his own back on the world by coming top in examinations (double First at Oxford).

❷ Peel's success as Irish Secretary; his businesslike approach to politics and methods of dealing with Irish discontent (Ribbonism, etc).

❸ His role as chief 'protestant' politician and the development of a 'Peelite' group within the Liverpool party.

❹ Peel's role in the resumption of cash payments (and his later determination, culminating in the 1844 Bank Act) to safeguard that settlement. His absorption of political economy and cautious move towards an income tax (finally realised in 1842) and freer trade.

❺ Peel's penal reforms as Home Secretary (not original, note the influence of Bentham, Romilly and Macintosh) and the Metropolitan Police; more 'liberal' than Sidmouth and Eldon, but less so than Russell and Brougham.

❻ Wellington's government of 1828–30 and events leading to Catholic emancipation; Ultra-Tory revolt against Peel, and his basic disgust with the Tory Party thereafter; quit Oxford seat.

❼ Peel's opposition to the 1832 Reform Act (he was unwilling to open a door which would not easily be closed) but refusal to form an anti-reform ministry made the passage of reform inevitable.

❽ Peel's 1834–5 administration and the Tamworth Manifesto led to a resurgence of the Tory Party (or the new Conservative Party). Its principle was attachment to the Crown, Church and Aristocracy, coupled with cautious, non-organic, reforms.

⑨ As the leader of the opposition – he was moderate, often sustaining the Whig government against its own radical supporters – Peel built up a reputation for supreme honesty and statesmanship, see e.g. the setting up of the Ecclesiastical Commission in 1836.

⑩ Extra-parliamentary speeches (mainly to respectable artisans and manufacturers) and a surge of Tory support in the counties and the boroughs led to a national swing and victory in the 1841 election. Peel's remarks on corn were ambiguous, trying to distance himself from supporting protection – but protection, nevertheless, was instrumental in bringing the Tories to success.

⑪ Though he recognised his debt to the Party, Peel was unwilling to allow it to dictate policy. He regarded himself as a minister of the Crown whose duty it was to govern in the national interest. The main problem was finance; he quickly demonstrated his administrative superiority in the field by the brilliance of his budgets.

⑫ Peel's radical financial policies and decision to reimpose income tax meant a review of the tariff structure, which in turn brought up consideration of the Corn Laws. These were modified in 1842; protectionist MPs made their displeasure felt. Farmers founded the Anti-League and Central Agricultural Protection Society in 1844. The split between Peel and the Party widened in 1845 over the Maynooth grant.

⑬ The social condition of England in the 1840s (e.g. the suffering in Paisley and Stockport horrified Peel); his policies to relieve distress (direct for indirect taxation) aimed to do this through increased prosperity; this culminated in the Corn Law repeal, for which the Irish Famine was probably used as a mere pretext. He rejected the back-to-the-land paternalism of the Young England and Ten Hours movements because of the effects it would have on productivity.

⑭ The political condition of England in the 1840s (Chartism and the Anti-corn Law League spearheading working- and middle-class attacks – albeit separate – on the aristocracy). The Corn Law repeal was partly to appease the League, which might otherwise have swept the board at the next election; and partly to persuade the Chartists that not all statesmen were indifferent to their discontents (i.e. it was a symbolic gesture); but the repeal was primarily to save the aristocracy from its mistaken – and, to Peel, suicidal – attachment to a Corn Law which was ineffectual and, in the long run, untenable. For him repeal was essentially a preserving measure.

⑮ Out of office, Peel was still regarded as the greatest statesman of the day; he was the darling of the mercantile, manufacturing and professional classes of the North, and was popular with the workers because of cheap bread and national economic recovery. The failure of Chartism vindicated the work of his ministry.

⑯ Peel's posthumous political influence; the slow peregrination of his closest disciples (Oxford High-Church 'Peelites') into the Liberal Party, together with his ideals of little England, free trade, and self-help individualism. An alternative view is that Peelism went into the development of Conservatism.

Peel was a great, if not the greatest, Prime Minister of the nineteenth century. He was also one of the most capable Victorian statesmen. He dominated early Victorian England more completely than Gladstone or Disraeli dominated the later years. He reconstructed the Tory Party after the Reform Act of 1832 but was always inclined to put nation before party in matters of policy.

He demonstrated his leadership by helping to modernise Britain during his 1841–46 administration but then split the party he had built by repealing the Corn Laws in 1846. Ironically, this enabled his opponent, Disraeli, to become leader of the Tories and left his ablest lieutenant, Gladstone, without a party.

4.1 PEEL'S BACKGROUND

By the time of the Great Exhibition in 1851 the world of Peterloo and the Six Acts seemed only an uncomfortable memory. This was largely due to the successful policies of Robert Peel. *The Times*, in Peel's obituary in 1850, remarked: 'Peel has been our chief guide from the confusions and darkness that hung around the beginning of the century to the comparatively quiet haven in which we are now embayed'.

Though he started his career as a Tory, he ended as a Liberal Conservative and became a good guide primarily because of his ability to adapt to changing circumstances and changing needs. He was the son of a successful and enlightened cotton manufacturer who left him a wealthy inheritance and an understanding of the outlook and standards of the business class. By education (Harrow and Oxford: he was the first undergraduate to receive a double First in Classics and Mathematics), and temperament he became associated with the ruling class. It was to prove an uneasy relationship.

Cash and reform, 1819–27

Entering Parliament in 1809, Peel was, from 1812 to 1818, the Chief Secretary for Ireland where he established a reputation for firm but honest and impartial administration. He became MP for Oxford University in 1817 and, in 1819, was chairman of the 'Bullion Committee', which advocated a return to the gold standard – a move to check inflation and put the currency back on a sound footing.

This deflationary measure, however, was bound to upset the landed classes who, on the strength of high prices, had during the war years invested large sums at high mortgage repayment rates in agricultural improvements. Attwood, in 1820, argued that 'Peel's Act' and the ending of cheap money was at the root of the economic difficulties of farmers in the 1820s. From 1822 Peel, as Home Secretary, was busy with a series of legal and criminal reforms. In 1829 he crowned this work by founding the London Metropolitan Police Force.

Catholic emancipation

The problem which concerned Peel in the 1820s, however, was Catholic emancipation, which he firmly resisted until 1829. Events in Ireland, organised by O'Connell and the Catholic Association, left Peel with the choice of two evils in 1828 – emancipation or rebellion. Peel wished to resign, but Wellington persuaded him to stay on to carry the Bill.

As the MP for Oxford, a bastion of the High Church, he was immediately branded a traitor and apostate by angry, resentful Anglicans and Protestants. In the circumstances it is not surprising that he opposed the Reform Bill, and his strong defence of the established Church after 1832 was partly an attempt to reinstate himself with the Party. His break with Wellington during the reform crisis gave him more political independence. Hence it was no surprise when, after Melbourne's dismissal, Peel was called back from Italy by the King to form his first government in December 1834. Look carefully at Peel's decisions on 'cash and Catholics' and try to discover why these issues were so important to the Tories. Do you consider that Peel betrayed the Party on these issues?

The Tamworth Manifesto, 1834

Although Peel lost the election, he gave the Tory Party what it desperately needed in the 1830s – leadership and direction. In the Tamworth Manifesto (which N Gash says 'caused a prodigious sensation') he outlined his plans and policy 'for the Party which from now on will be called Conservative.'

In seven pages of print he stated his policy – a policy designed to appeal to all moderate men interested in maintaining order and good (i.e. non-partisan) government. He accepted the 1832 Reform Act and the possibility of future moderate reform of proven abuses. Peel was trying to turn the Tory Party of one particular class into the Conservative Party of the nation. He gradually built up Party strength in the 'thirties.

In the interests of good government, he refrained from factious opposition. He supported the Whigs when he believed their measures were just and for the national good.

When Peel became Prime Minister for the second time, in 1841, his control of the Party was absolute. During the 'thirties he had proved his ability and potential for leadership; yet he remained unpopular with at least half the Party. Many Tories did not like his middle-class background, his commercial ideas, his liberal outlook and his occasional attempts to put policy before the Party. His relationships, both Party and private, were often strained and uneasy (note the details of the 'Bedchamber Question' in 1839.) Many regarded him as cold and aloof – 'an iceberg with a slight thaw on the surface.'

4.2 PEEL'S SECOND MINISTRY, 1841–46

By 1841 the Whigs were in total disarray. Facing a deficit of £2 500 000, they seemed utterly bereft of political enthusiasm or ideas. Peel won a clear majority of 80 seats at the general election and gathered a strong team around him – Wellington, Aberdeen, Stanley and, later, Gladstone. In an England in the depths of depression those suffering, and those concerned, proposed many different remedies such as Chartism, Corn Law repeal and cooperation.

Note that Peel made the surprising – and radical – decision that a bold policy of fiscal and financial reform was needed to resolve England's economic problems. 'We must,' he wrote to Croker, 'make this country a cheap country for living.'

Free trade budgets

Peel first turned his attention to the Corn Laws and revised the sliding scale of 1828. For prohibition, he now wanted to substitute 'fair protection'. Corn imports were allowed below 73s. a quarter but, to the Tories, this was unpalatable medicine and precipitated a ripple of apprehension among Protectionist back-benchers. Cobden, on the other hand, saw it as a tinkering measure – 'a bitter insult to a suffering nation.'

It was to tariff revision, however, that Peel looked for rapid improvement in the country's economic position. By lowering tariffs (currently paid on over 1200 articles) he hoped to stimulate trade and manufacturing in Britain.

It is essential that you know the details of what came to be known as Peel's great 'free-trade' budgets of 1842 and 1845. Basically, a sliding scale of tariff duties and selective remissions was introduced during the ministry and, by 1847, over £8 000 000 in government customs and excise revenue had been remitted. In 1841 Peel reintroduced income tax to make good the current deficit left by the Whigs and then continued it to balance his future tariff concessions.

Despite the remission of £8 000 000 in tariffs, Peel's government was in surplus by 1846. This was a magnificent achievement, fully vindicating Peel's bold fiscal approach. Admittedly, he was aided by a run of good harvests and a railway-building boom which encouraged investment, industry and employment. But it was an ambitious programme which deserved success.

To support these free-trade measures he introduced a Bank Charter Act in 1844. This completed the work he had begun in 1819, prepared the way for the supremacy of the Bank of England and restored confidence in the pound. Opinion is divided on the success of this Act, but all agree that the Companies Act followed (which enacted that all companies must now register and display an annual balance sheet), encouraged business and public confidence, and stimulated investment.

An alternative view of the work of his ministry, however, might be that Peel's interest in the economy was not his only preoccupation. As PM he was concerned with national defence and, indeed, increased expenditure on the army and navy from 1841–6. Secondly, he was concerned with problems of law and order and dealt firmly with Chartism in England and O'Connell's attack on the Union in Ireland. Peel was also concerned about national unity and pursued policies such as taxation and tariffs which would benefit all citizens and not just special interest groups. Nor was he inflexibly opposed to social reform.

Social reforms

Peel, once characterised as 'a businessman who brought business methods to government', is justly famous for his financial and administrative measures. He was a brilliant administrator and financier, rather than a social reformer. As was shown by his monetarist approach to the 'condition of England' question when he took office in 1841, he did not believe that the state could solve problems by intervention. Yet his ministry was not devoid of social reform achieved by state intervention: a Mines Act was passed in 1842, a Factory Act in 1844, and – after Chadwick's investigations into the sanitary condition of the labouring poor had prompted the setting up of a Royal Commission – a Public Health Act under Russell.

The complicated and detailed administrative work of Peel's ministry was helped enormously by the 'administrative revolution in government' which occurred in the 1830s and 1840s. During these years the foundation of the Civil Service was laid, more efficient procedures were devised to speed up parliamentary legislation and more dedicated administrators appointed to supervise all aspects of government work.

4.3 IRELAND

Peel cleverly withstood O'Connell's attempts to repeal the Act of Union but his later Irish policy created apprehension in the Conservative Party. He aimed to persuade reasonable, middle-class Catholics to forsake O'Connell's repeal agitation and support the Union. In an attempt to bridge the sectarian gap between Protestants and Catholics, he founded three secular national colleges in Belfast, Cork and Galway, only to have them attacked by both denominations as 'godless'.

The greatest stir in England, however, was caused by his decision in 1845 to increase the annual grant to the Catholic Training Seminary at Maynooth from £9 000 to £26 000. Emancipation may have been granted but not, it appears, toleration. The Commons was inundated with hundreds of hostile petitions. Gladstone resigned, but Peel stubbornly forced through the Commons what he regarded as a just and beneficial measure – a statesmanlike but not very popular action.

The Irish famine

It was Ireland, in fact, that brought about Peel's downfall. As soon as the news of the Irish famine came through in 1845, Peel thought about repealing the Corn Laws. It was an idea that had been maturing in his mind for some time and derived from the inescapable logic of his financial and fiscal measures.

Although Wellington argued that 'it was potatoes that put Peel in his damned fright', it was not Ireland – according to Professor Gash – but the condition of England that provided the underlying motive for repeal, i.e. the success of his free trade budgets; the belief that agricultural prosperity depended on efficient techniques (not protection) and that continued middle-class antagonism was undermining the position of the landed aristocracy and undermining, therefore, the political stability of the nation.

Peel, then, was prepared to repeal the Corn Laws for what he believed to be the best interests of the whole nation. He seems to have underrated the strength of opposition among Tory backbenchers. Although a successful leader, he was not a popular one; many Tories had come to resent his liberal brand of Conservatism. It is important that you understand the apprehensions of Tories during this period. Why did they consider the Corn Laws to be so important?

4.4 CORN LAW REPEAL

Peel's Cabinet was divided. Russell's 'Edinburgh Letter', in which he declared for free trade, encouraged Peel to resign. Russell, however, was unable to form a government and 'passed the poisoned chalice back to Sir Robert'. Peel generously refused to leave the Queen in extremity and agreed to come back. The Party was irretrievably split. The rebels in the Commons, led by George Bentinck, who was ably supported by the young Disraeli, attacked Peel with bitter and personally wounding invective.

With the aid of the Whigs and a third of the Conservatives, Peel forced the Bill through, only to be defeated the same night on a Coercion Bill for Ireland. Bentinck and Disraeli maintained that Peel had betrayed his Party on the three great issues of the day – cash, Catholics and corn.

Find out what you can about the motives of the Protectionists and pay particular attention to the underrated contribution of Bentinck. Would you agree that Peel could perhaps, be accused of desertion but not betrayal?

Kitson Clark maintains that Peel had simply put nation before Party in an effort to solve one of England's bitterest social issues. Furthermore, it could be argued that the terms of repeal demonstrated that he wished to be the surgeon, not the executioner, of the landed interests.

Repeal was to be spread over three years, accompanied by a £2 000 000 drainage loan, a revision of Poor Law rates and a cut in import duties on seeds and fertilisers. Peel wanted to encourage 'high farming' rather than attempt to guarantee 'high prices' by maintaining the Corn Laws. Above all, by repeal he felt that he was defusing the bitter, anti-aristocratic feeling that permeated the middle classes. Finally, you should consider the argument that Peel, unlike the Protectionist Tories, believed that retaining the Corn Laws was more dangerous than repealing them.

4.5 ASSESSMENT OF PEEL

According to Professor Gash, Peel's lifework was to fashion a compromise between the system he inherited and the necessities of a new industrialising society. It is most important that you understand that this system did not posit two rival parties advocating alternative policies: it was designed primarily to enable the king's government to carry out national policy. Peel's primary aim, then, was to be a loyal minister of the Crown and to secure efficient, stable government. He was prepared to do whatever was necessary to achieve this.

The growth of the party system and its prejudices after 1832 was a dilemma for Peel because, as an old-fashioned royal minister, he favoured government by a centre group in the Commons – an alliance of moderates which would exclude the extremists of both parties. Note that it was a combination of Whigs and moderate Tories together that ensured that Catholic emancipation and Corn Law repeal were carried; Peel for his part supported moderate Whig reforms in the 1830s.

His conservatism, therefore, was not a party label, for eventually he was prepared to break the Party in the national interest. As he said in 1846: 'If I fall I shall have the satisfaction of reflecting that I do not fall because I have shown subservience to a party (and) preferred the interests of a party to the general interests of the community.' Peel put policy before Party and, by insisting on flexibility in the face of national problems, he helped to preserve the prevailing system (and aristocratic power) in a period of economic distress and political challenge.

One can, however, praise Peel too much. Recent historians have been more critical. They deny that he was a 'flexible' statesman on economic matters, and much more a prisoner of the ideology of laissez-faire than was earlier claimed. Neither did he rebuild the party during the 1830s – the Conservative Party elected in 1841 remained very narrow in its support. It is possible to be severely critical of Peel's handling of his party. He hid his real free-trade sentiments in 1841, took backbenchers' support for granted and despised their lack of political knowledge and understanding. He failed to consider seriously their legitimate fears and rode roughshod over their political and religious sensitivities. Peel's belief that as an expert only he had the truth did not endear him to everyone in the House.

Peel's relations with his Party were, therefore, perpetually strained. As its leader it was his task to convince the Party of his brand of Conservatism and the value of 'centrist' politics. He failed. It was his merit as a statesman that he was prepared to adapt his policies to the need for change. It was his defect as a party leader that he did so in a manner which seemed high-handed and autocratic.

It would be wrong, however, to think that his political career ended in failure. He split the Party but retained the loyalty of its ablest members – Gladstone, Graham, Cardwell, Aberdeen. His repeal of the Corn Laws gave him immense national popularity, his fiscal reforms solved the depression of the 'hungry 'forties' and the combination of the two probably saved England from revolution in 1848. The 'forties were, indeed, 'Peel's decade.' More than any other, he had shown himself to be 'the statesman of the industrial revolution.'

4.6 CHRONOLOGY

1788	February	Born; son of Sir Robert Peel, a Lancashire cotton spinner.
1812	August	Chief Secretary for Ireland until 1818; established the Royal Irish Constabulary.
1817	June	Became MP for Oxford University.
1819	May	Became CHAIRMAN OF THE 'BULLION COMMITTEE'; he recommended a return to the gold standard.
1822	November	Became HOME SECRETARY; modified the severity of the criminal code.
1827	April	Peel refused office under Canning (because he opposed Canning's policy of Catholic emancipation).
1828	January	As Home Secretary under Wellington, Peel founded the Metropolitan Police Force.
1829	March	Peel INTRODUCED CATHOLIC EMANCIPATION; the break-up of the old Tory Party.
1831	March	Peel opposed the Great Reform Bill during its two-year passage through parliament.
1834	December	Peel's First Ministry; lasted until April 1835. TAMWORTH MANIFESTO; Peel's address to his constituents at Tamworth; an electioneering document on a grand scale, it advocated 'a careful review of institutions, civil and ecclesiastical...the correction of proved abuses and the redress of real grievances'.

1835	April	Peel was defeated by an alliance of O'Connell and the Whigs – the 'Lichfield House Compact'.
1836		ECCLESIASTICAL COMMISSION created with power to redistribute Bishops' incomes.
1839	May	THE BEDCHAMBER QUESTION; Peel refused to take office on Melbourne's resignation unless Whig ladies of the Royal Household, in attendance on the Queen, resigned.
1841	September	Prime Minister; as PM he was 'masterful and autocratic'.
1842	March	FIRST FREE TRADE BUDGET; reduced the import duty on 700 articles. Income Tax of 7d in the pound was introduced to offset the fall in income.
	April	MODIFICATION OF THE CORN LAW further eased the restrictions on the entry of grain during periods of dearth. MINES ACT; women, and children under ten years of age, forbidden to work underground.
	July	BANK CHARTER ACT: this was the logical development of Peel's work on the 'Bullion Committee' of 1819. COMPANY ACT: companies now had to register with the Board of Trade and produce an annual balance sheet. This gave some public accountability and encouraged investment.
	August	RAILWAY ACT: instituted 'parliamentary train' – third-class passengers to be carried at 1d per mile. This Act was basically a victory for laissez-faire. The railway lobby resisted attempts at further government control. FACTORY ACT: children aged eight to 13 to work a six-and-a-half-hour day. Maximum 12–hour working day for women. Dangerous machinery to be fenced.
1845	February	MAYNOOTH GRANT: despite strong opposition, Peel increased the annual grant to this College, which trained Irish Catholic priests. Gladstone resigned. Queen's Colleges founded: Belfast, Cork and Galway added to the existing Anglican college – Trinity, Dublin; this was opposed by Anglicans and condemned as 'godless' because of the absence of religious teaching.
	October	IRISH FAMINE: outbreak of potato blight in autumn.
	November	'EDINBURGH LETTER' Lord John Russell's letter to his constituents in London accepting the necessity for repeal of the Corn Laws.
	December	THE TIMES stated the government's intention to repeal the Corn Laws. Peel resigned; Russell failed to form a government.
1846	June	CORN LAW REPEAL. Conservative Party split. Government defeated on Coercion Bill for Ireland by a combination of Whigs, Irish MPs and Protectionists. Peel resigned.
1850	2 July	Peel died (from injuries sustained after a fall from his horse).

Illustrative questions and answers

1 Examine the role of Peel in contemporary British politics.

Tutorial note

This is a searching question. In considering his political role you should understand the way Peel functioned as a politician, what he stood for in contemporary estimation, and what effect he had on the development of politics in his lifetime.

You need to know about

All aspects of British political history in the first half of the nineteenth century.

Suggested answer plan

1   Peel is often credited with founding the Conservative Party (Gash, Blake), in the sense of a nationalist, pragmatic, unideological, executive Party, above sectional interest. More plausibly, he can be seen as the founder of the Liberal Party, into which most of his supporters (Gladstone, Cardwell, etc.) drifted,

taking with them his 'little England' internationalism (see Aberdeen's foreign policy and hostility to Palmerston), free trade, self-help and individualist ethos. Whichever version is correct, Peel's was a formative and creative role in politics.

2 Until 1828, Peel's role was to defend the protestant establishment, which made him the darling of the Ultra-Tories. The latter badly needed a political leader with talent.

3 After 1828 Peel never filled this sort of role, being not quite trusted. Many saw him in the role of weather vane, judging the correct moment to implement reversals of policy (see Bagehot, 'he was converted at the conversion of the average man'); others simply saw him in the role of traitor.

4 As Home Secretary Peel grew into the role of the supreme executive politician. He could boast that 'he never proposed any measure that he did not carry.' This was most obvious during 1841–6, when he dominated all departments and even introduced some of Goulburn's budgets. A tireless administrator, he commanded all aspects of government business.

5 After a brief negative role from 1830–3, Peel bounced back with the Tamworth Manifesto; this was vacuous enough – defending the virtues of the status quo and opposing extremism – but it inaugurated his image (emphasised in several extra-parliamentary speeches, mainly to master manufacturers and respectable working-men's organisations) as a champion of Crown, Church, and Aristocracy.

6 His 'responsible' behaviour as leader of the opposition in the late 1830s, sometimes even supporting the Whig ministers against their own supporters, contributed to his perhaps rather spurious image as a supremely honest politician.

7 His role in office was to solve the 'condition of England' question through radical finance; confirm England as a progressive industrial nation by promoting economic recovery; remove the dissension between the social classes by Corn Law repeal, thereby saving the landed aristocracy from being overthrown and England from revolution.

8 Despite Peel's aspiration to be an executive politician, Disraeli's judgement is correct: that Peel was the 'greatest parliamentarian that ever lived'. Though no orator, he was a superb debater, deploying arguments and statistics with aplomb, and always gave an impression of solid reasonableness which belied a really rather doctrinaire and stubborn personality.

9 The role he played with most conviction, however, was that of political martyr (1846–50). His opponents found this insufferable, but disciples were inspired.

2 What were the motives of those who brought about Peel's downfall?

Tutorial note

This question calls for an analysis of the political crisis of 1845–6. You must consider the motives of those individuals and groups that opposed Peel's actions in those years.

You need to know about

Details of the events of 1845–6. The structure and beliefs of the Tory Party in parliament and the country.

Suggested answer plan

1 A narrative of the events of 1844–6; backbench revolts against Peel on the sugar duties and the ten-hour day (1844); agitation over agricultural relief and Maynooth (1845); the Irish famine and the Corn Law repeal (1846); a vote on Irish coercion toppled the government.

2 The role of Russell and of the Whig opposition; did he deliberately hand 'a poisoned chalice' back to Peel in December 1845? Outline the reasons for supposing that Russell's attempts to form a ministry (frustrated by a quarrel between Grey and Palmerston) were genuine.

3   The motives of the Tory malcontents: their long-standing dislike of Peel's dear-money and deflationary policies; and their suspicion that he might betray them on corn, as he had on the Catholics. The Corn Laws were to them a guarantee of high rents and a vital symbol of status and power; both threatened by the Manchester manufacturer. Also landlords urged on by Richmond's Anti-League of mainly tenant farmers.

4   Peel would probably have survived, albeit with difficulty, but for the personal venom and persistence of Disraeli and Bentinck. Bentinck's motives easy to fathom: an honest, unpolitical man, he felt that he had been 'sold'. He also blamed Peel for having augmented the cares which led to the death of Canning in 1827; this added a personal bitterness to his criticism.

5   Disraeli's motives more ambiguous: what will clearly not do is to say that he was paying Peel back for not being given office in 1841. It was the convention for MPs to offer their services, as Disraeli had done then; moreover, Peel's government had no more consistent or loyal back-bench supporter than Disraeli throughout 1842–3. It was 1844 that marked the turning-point.

6   Probably Disraeli sincerely believed what he alleged – that Peel had been intellectually seduced by the utilitarians, economists, sophists and calculators. Disraeli's 'Young England' (Smythe, Manners, etc.), which called for a return to organic, agrarian, paternalist protectionism, struck a widespread response in Tory hearts ('the finest brute vote in creation') during 1844–6 – as the Ten Hours and Anti-Poor Law movements showed.

7   But it is obvious too that Disraeli deeply disliked Peel personally, and also that he felt snubbed by him, not in 1841, but subsequently. Peel openly despised the Party that 'spent their days in hunting and shooting and eating and drinking', and never took it into his confidence. Disraeli was a Party man before all things, and longed to participate in the great game of politics. Peel, with his executive mentality, quite starved Disraeli's political appetite, and reaped the consequences.

3   'The paradox is that on the issues of corn, cash and Catholics, Peel was at odds with his Party.' Discuss.

Tutorial note

Unquestionably Peel thwarted his supporters' wishes on these issues. You must decide whether he was 'at odds with' them all along, or whether he acted reluctantly and under the pressure of circumstances.

You need to know about

Peel's policies with regard to the gold standard and the Corn Laws. Their economic implications for different sections of the community. The nature of the Catholic question and reasons for its political importance. Attitudes of the Tory backbenchers.

Suggested answer plan

1   The nature and background of the Catholic question: anti-Catholicism was the most heartfelt instinct of the English squirearchy since the seventeenth-century; even 'the immortal Mr Pitt' had offended on this issue, so it was Peel's staunch protestantism that mainly accounted for his swift rise to prominence in the Tory party – a rise otherwise inexplicable as he was a manufacturer's son who rarely courted support.

2   Peel's refusal to serve under the 'Catholic' Canning in 1827 reassured the Party. But Peel had also been Irish Secretary and Home Secretary, and so had a pragmatic approach to law and order. Returning to office in 1828, he quickly perceived that the Catholic Association threatened the civil peace, and his reaction to O'Connell's victory in the Clare by-election was swift and decisive. So on this issue, Peel was probably not 'at odds with' the Party, but saw the need to 'about-turn' in a crisis.

3   The currency issue: the decision to return to gold in 1819 ('Peel's Bill') led to an increase in the value of money and a decline in the price of primary and secondary produce. This benefited investors ('fundholders') and exporters, but damaged debtors and producers for the home market. Many agricultural Tories were heavily mortgaged (having expanded cultivation in wartime) and suffered on both counts. By 1822 a hostile agricultural lobby had formed; monetary discontent (Knatchbull, Chandos) contributed to Wellington's and Peel's fall in 1830.

4   Peel, being devoted to sound money, was always at odds with most of the Party (see the March 1833 division on Attwood's distress motion); the 1844 Bank Act, intended to 'safeguard' the gold standard, was even more deflationary.

5   Peel's intentions on corn were more uncertain. Theoretically he favoured free trade; politically he wished to leave it alone. The requirements of government forced him gradually towards repeal. Especially he feared that protection was jeopardising food supplies, disrupting the currency, increasing manufacturing unemployment, and creating public strife (spearheaded by the Anti-Corn Law League).

6   Anyway, he thought agriculturists could survive repeal by capitalising, and so did many back-benchers. The *real* pressure for protection came from farmers, who often forced their landlords' hands. When they lined up behind Bentinck and Disraeli the protectionists made it clear that what they were against was Benthamism, Whiggery, Peelism and consensus politics. Hence Disraeli's peroration: 'Let men stand by the principle by which they rise; right or wrong... . Above all maintain the line of demarcation between the parties...' The real charge against Peel was not free trade but 'betrayal'.

Question bank

1   Document question (Peel and Conservatism): study Extracts I, II and III below and then answer questions (a) to (h) which follow:

Extract I

'To the electors of the Borough of Tamworth.

Gentlemen,

On the 26th of November last...I received from His Majesty a summons <u>wholly unforeseen and unexpected</u> by me...(to assist) His Majesty in the formation of a new Government... .

'I <u>never</u> will admit that I have been, either before or after the Reform Bill, the <u>defender of abuses or the enemy of judicious reforms</u>. I appeal with confidence, in denial of the charge, to the <u>active part</u> I took in <u>the great questions of the currency</u>...(and)...in <u>the consolidation and amendment of the Criminal Law</u>... . With respect to the Reform Bill itself...I consider the Reform Bill <u>a final and irrevocable settlement</u> of a great constitutional question... .

'Then as to the spirit of the Reform Bill and the willingness to adopt and enforce it as a rule of government. If by adopting the spirit of the Reform Bill it be meant that we are to live in a perpetual vortex of agitation...I will not undertake to adopt it. But if the spirit of the Reform Bill implies merely a careful review of institutions...combining with the firm maintenance of established rights <u>the correction of proven abuses and the redress of real grievances</u>; in that case, I can, for myself and colleagues, undertake to act in such a spirit and with such intentions... .'

Our object will be – the maintenance of peace – the honourable fulfilment of...all existing agreements with Foreign Powers...(and) the <u>just and impartial consideration of what is due to all interests – agricultural, manufacturing and commercial</u>.'

(From Peel's election address, 1834)

Extract II

'Hush!' said Mr Tadpole. 'The time has gone by for Tory governments; what the country requires is a sound Conservative government.'

'A sound Conservative government,' said Taper, musingly, 'I understand: Tory men and Whig measures.'

(From Disraeli's novel *Coningsby* published 1844)

Extract III

'A Conservative government is an organised hypocrisy.'

(From Disraeli's speech in the House of Commons, 10th March 1845)

(a) Explain the circumstances in which Peel received the 'wholly unforeseen and unexpected' summons. (3)
(b) What part did Peel play in 'the great questions of the currency'? (2)
(c) Explain Peel's reference to 'the active part' he took in 'the consolidation and amendment of the Criminal Law'. (3)
(d) What comment might a hostile critic make on Peel's claim that he had 'never', before 1834, been a 'defender of abuses or the enemy of judicious reforms'? (4)
(e) Why did Peel feel it necessary in 1834 to declare that he considered the Reform Bill 'a final and irrevocable settlement'? (2)
(f) What 'proven abuses' did Peel 'correct' and what 'real grievances' did he 'redress' in the years 1841–46? (6)
(g) Explain what 'Tadpole' and 'Taper' understood as the differences between 'Tory', 'Conservative' and 'Whig' in Extract II. (5)
(h) What connection can you trace between Peel's promise to give 'just and impartial consideration of what is due to all interests – agricultural, manufacturing and commercial' and Disraeli's reference to 'organised hypocrisy' in Extract III? (6)

2 Would you agree that throughout Peel's 1841–46 administration the basic principles of Toryism were consistently betrayed? (WJEC, June 1991)

3 Why, and with what consequences, did the Conservative Party split in 1846? (Cambridge, June 1991)

4 Discuss the view that 'the weakness of the Tory Party in the twenty-five years following the repeal of the Corn Laws was due entirely to the events of 1846?' (AEB, June 1988)

5 'Peel's Character as a liberal Tory did not become apparent until the minority of 1841–46'. How far do you agree? (London, June 1990)

READING LIST

Standard textbook reading
A. Briggs, *Age of Improvement* (Longman, 1959), chapter 6.
E. J. Evans, *The Forging of the Modern State* (Longman, 1983), chapter 27.
R. K. Webb, *Modern England* (Allen and Unwin, 1980 edn.), chapter 6.
A. Wood, *Nineteenth-Century Britain* (Longman, 1960), chapter 9.

Further suggested reading
P. Adelman, *Peel and the Conservative Party 1830–50* (Longman, 1989).
R. Blake, *The Conservative Party from Peel to Thatcher* (Fontana, 1985).

T. L. Crosby, *English Farmers and the Politics of Protection* (Hassocks, 1977).
E. J. Evans, *Sir Robert Peel* (Routledge, 1991).
N. Gash, *Sir Robert Peel* (Longman, 1986).
N. Gash, *Politics in the Age of Peel* (Harvester, 1977).
G. I. T. Machin, *Politics and The Churches in Great Britain 1832–68* (OUP, 1978).
D. Read, *Peel and the Victorians* (Blackwell, 1987).
R. M. Stewart, *The Foundations of the Conservative Party 1830–67* (Longman, 1978).
R. M. Stewart, *The Politics of Protection: Lord Derby and the Protectionist Party 1841–52* (CUP, 1971).

BRITISH FOREIGN POLICY, 1815–65

Units in this chapter

5.1 *The principles of foreign policy*
5.2 *Viscount Castlereagh, 1812–22*
5.3 *George Canning, 1822–27*
5.4 *Lord Palmerston, 1830–65*
5.5 *Chronology*

Chapter objectives

❶ The changed patterns of European international relations after 1815. Allied reasons for fighting France differed; their attitudes to the Vienna settlement also differed but all were determined that France would not threaten Europe again. Castlereagh favoured the Quadruple Alliance for this purpose, the Tsar a Holy Alliance. The importance of Nationalism and Liberalism as factors in post-1815 European affairs; Britain's attitude to these new developments.

❷ The basic principles of British foreign policy – maritime and commercial; politically and territorially satisfied but economically insatiable; aggressively free trading; 'nation of shopkeepers'. Worked for a European balance dividing France and Russia (England's two most likely enemies). Castlereagh tried to maintain a balance by the Congress system, Canning by independent action and Palmerston by a mixture of the two. In the Near East, British policy was to check Russian expansion and defend our trade. Britain appeared to favour Liberalism, especially when it coincided with strategic or commercial considerations – e.g. Belgium or the Spanish-American colonies.

❸ Castlereagh (1812–22): his contribution to European diplomacy at Vienna; the Quadruple Alliance, and his attitude to the Holy Alliance – a 'sublime piece of mysticism and nonsense', the Congresses; his attitude to collective intervention; his European outlook, belief in discussion, mediatorial role. His rejection of principles of Nationalism, Liberalism and public opinion. He failed to explain his aims, was accused of associating with European despots, and was, therefore, unpopular at home. Yet he laid down the basic principles of British foreign policy in his State Paper (May 1820). His approach basically pragmatic – refusing to act on questions of 'abstract and speculative principles'.

❹ Canning (1822–27): considered an opportunist, Nationalist in approach, and less European-minded, he rejected diplomacy by conference – believed in the principle 'each nation for itself'. Was he a supporter of Liberalism? Or only when the Navy could be used to maximum effect?

He was unable to intervene when France invaded Spain but warned her against attempts to regain the Spanish-American colonies. More positive aid to the Portuguese constitutionalists. Canning's surprising intrusion into the Eastern Question – usually he worked with Russia to effect a solution; Navarino (1827). After his death, Wellington and Aberdeen returned to traditional ways – the 'Greek affair no substitute for Turkish power'. In domestic issues, Canning was conservative. Perhaps his liberal reputation is exaggerated. Did he digress from basic principles as laid down by Castlereagh?

⑤ Palmerston (1830–65): an alleged disciple of Canning, also a shrewd mixer of diplomatic and nationalist bluster: popular at home and disliked abroad. Followed the basic principles but was sometimes inconsistent. Was he a champion of nationalism, of liberalism, of public opinion or was he more narrowly insular? His statement, 'We have no eternal allies and no perpetual enemies' suggests that he was basically an opportunist. He supported Belgium (fear of French expansion), Spanish and Portuguese constitutionalists, and Italian unification (but he refused to intervene in 1848).

⑥ The Aberdeen interlude under Peel 1841–46. Negotiation and diplomacy averts potential war with France and the United States. Aberdeen later unsuccessful over the Crimean War in 1853.

⑦ Palmerston's attitude to Mehemet Ali and the Eastern Question: his pursuit of Britain's commercial interests – even to forcibly opening China to western merchants (e.g. the two Chinese Wars). His use of the Navy, and his brinkmanship (e.g. Don Pacifico): his relations with Queen Victoria and Albert. Palmerston's failure to see that times had changed after the Crimean War; his error in encouraging the Poles in 1863 and the Danes (over Schleswig-Holstein) in 1864.

⑧ How closely did British Foreign Secretaries of this period follow the basic principles? To what extent did they stand for intervention or non-intervention? Did their differences lie less in ideology than in temperament, less in Party than in whether they were activists or passivists? Were they pragmatic opportunists who always had a clear idea of Britain's needs – and tailored their policies and actions to suit?

The year 1815 marked the end of the long struggle with Revolutionary and Napoleonic France. At Vienna a new, more stable world had to be fashioned from a Europe ravaged and changed by almost 23 years of war. Britain favoured a balance of power that would contain French expansionist policies in Europe and restrain Russian imperialism in the Near and Far East. Initially Castlereagh was prepared to work with Metternich to achieve these ends but, under Canning, British foreign policy gradually became more independent and isolationist as European reaction became more pronounced.

Lord Aberdeen presents something of a contrast to Canning. He was Wellington's Foreign Secretary 1828–30, Peel's 1841–46 and later presided over the outbreak of the Crimean War. He was in the Castlereagh tradition of foreign policy, favouring quiet diplomacy in preference to the more vocal nationalism of Canning and Palmerston.

Palmerston typified British power and confidence in mid-century and consequently he followed a jingoistic policy favoured by the mass of the British electorate. Many did not like his diplomatic approach or political style but his colourful assertion of British power made him 'the most English minister' – loved at home and hated abroad. Though he remained the archetypal 'John Bull', nevertheless his actions demonstrated his awareness of the complexity of European problems and his determination to follow the interests of Britain in them all.

Fig. 5 Europe after 1815

5.1 THE PRINCIPLES OF FOREIGN POLICY

There was a noticeable continuity and consistency underlying the principles of British foreign policy from 1815 to 1865. All British Foreign Secretaries saw their main task as the upholding of what they believed to be British interests. Though there were some constraints on their actions, e.g. royal and parliamentary, in cabinet they were generally unchallenged.

Commerce and trade

Britain's most vital interests arose out of her position as a great maritime and commercial power. Politically and territorially she was satisfied; commercially her appetite was rapacious. Her pursuit of markets – as in China – was vigorous and, on occasions, aggressive. Generally, merchants could rely on the support of the government which, incidentally, did not ask other nations for preferential treatment; all that was needed to guarantee British success was free trade and open competition.

The Navy

To protect and extend this worldwide trading network a powerful Navy was vital. A strong Navy, furthermore – by facilitating the acquisition of bases from Latin-America to China, from which, without occupation, Britain could control trade incursions by foreign rivals – enabled her to adopt a policy of 'informal empire'.

Despite Admiralty conservatism and policies of economic retrenchment, the government accepted responsibility for keeping the sea lanes open and, to a lesser extent, for keeping rivals out of British spheres of influence. This, then, was the period of the 'Pax Britannica' when, virtually unchallenged, the British Navy ruled the seas.

The balance of power

To British Foreign Secretaries, foreign policy signified Europe; Britain was quite capable of dealing with minor imperial problems on her own. British foreign policy was forged in the fires of the Revolutionary and Napoleonic Wars. What they all sought, therefore, was peace and stability in Europe. They were pragmatists with no doctrinaire attachment to either Legitimacy or Constitutionalism.

In Europe, Britain was suspicious of France and Russia – both aggressively expansionist powers – the former in Europe, the latter in the Near and Far East. Believing in a balance of power, Britain decided that a strong central bloc, comprising Austro-Hungary, Prussia and Italy, was essential to keep her two most likely enemies apart. Secure as an offshore island, and believing in a policy of non-intervention, Britain could not, however, afford to be isolated. What she wanted was a system of limited liability – preferring to add her weight to European affairs only in times of crisis. For Britain, therefore, the balance of power meant the independence of each nation and the predominance of none.

Other areas

Britain also desired neutral or friendly relations with the Netherlands, Portugal and the United States – all-important for strategic or commercial reasons. Her main interest in the Near East was to check Russian expansion and defend her own Mediterranean trade – a policy that imposed the unpopular task of supporting the declining autocratic power of the Ottoman Empire – and in the Far East the British aim was to secure the northern borders of India (our major piece of 'formal Empire') against Russian encroachments. Britain was also determined to gain an economic foothold in China before Russia could do so.

Insofar as there is any general statement of the principles of British foreign policy, it is to be found in Castlereagh's State Paper of May, 1820. Note that although the methods and style of each Foreign Secretary (even the lesser ones) might have changed, the principles, from 1815 to 1865, remained unaltered.

5.2 VISCOUNT CASTLEREAGH, 1812–22

As victor, Britain made no European territorial claims at the Congress of Vienna, but Castlereagh cleverly acquired a string of islands and ports to add to her 'informal empire'. His main object at Vienna was to curb the power of France and restore Europe once more to peaceful normalcy.

Though aware of Britain's interests, Castlereagh had a European outlook. He believed that European problems could be solved in congress by discussion and negotiation. He had little time for the new forces of Nationalism, Liberalism or public opinion and was more concerned with implementing policies which he regarded as possible and immediately relevant. Thus, he dismissed the Czar's scheme for a Holy Alliance as 'a piece of sublime mysticism and nonsense' and instead persuaded the Allies to continue with the Quadruple Alliance.

Many contemporaries could not distinguish between the two alliances; and

Castlereagh, because of his association with European despots, was branded a reactionary. But Castlereagh was no hardened reactionary: he perceived that Britain could secure her interests by working with the other Powers. His mistake was that he neglected to explain this policy to cabinet, parliament or people. Note, however, that the congress system, though it perverted Castlereagh's aims, contained the germ of a most important concept in European diplomacy – the Concert of Europe – an idea later favoured by Gladstone.

The congresses

At Aix-la-Chapelle in 1818 it was agreed that the Allied army of occupation should be withdrawn from France and that she should rejoin the European community of Powers. But among those powers the publication of Metternich's Carlsbad Decrees and the subsequent revolutions in Spain and Naples quickly exposed divergencies. The Holy Alliance favoured collective intervention, which Castlereagh firmly opposed. As a result, Britain sent an observer instead of a delegate to Troppau in 1820 and to Laibach in 1821. Another congress, to consider the Greek revolt, was planned for Verona in 1822, but Castlereagh committed suicide before it was convened.

Assessment of Castlereagh's policy

Castlereagh's policy after 1815, built on the personal contacts he established during the Napoleonic War, was one of the most personal ever pursued by a British Foreign Secretary. He had no obvious successor. While in office he intelligently exploited Britain's position of strength and worked well with Austria to restrain Russia and France. His fault was that he tended to see political affairs too much in terms of the status quo and refused to acknowledge that fundamental new forces were affecting events in Europe.

In his obituary, the *Scotsman* stated: 'The name of Castlereagh will long be connected with tyranny abroad and all that is slavish and oppressive at home.' On the other hand, M E Chamberlain reminds us that Castlereagh worked unfailingly to abolish the slave trade and supported Catholic emancipation. She maintains, therefore, that Castlereagh, who has never been accused of neglecting British interests, was not a reactionary and that there was much in his foreign policy that was 'distinctive and original'. Where do you think the truth lies?

5.3 GEORGE CANNING, 1822–27

The change from Castlereagh to Canning produced no break in the continuity of foreign policy. But 'where Castlereagh made discreet signals, Canning waved a flag in conversations, despatches and speeches'. Canning openly rejected the congress system and was much more nationalist in outlook: 'each nation for itself and God for us all.'

As he was not on intimate terms with the rulers of Europe, few of whom knew or trusted him – his more independent approach was to be expected. More brilliant than Castlereagh, he saw the weakness of a system which did not encourage the support of parliament and people. On the whole, Canning followed and developed the principles outlined by Castlereagh in his State Paper of 1820.

Spain, Portugal and the New World

During his period in office, Canning was confronted with four major problems. In his handling of these he smashed the already frail structure of the Holy Alliance. Powerless to do anything when France invaded Spain in 1823, he was, through Britain's control of the seas, the master in the dispute about the Spanish American colonies. In 1825, he recognised the independence of a number of these with the now famous justification: 'I resolved that, if France had Spain, it should not be Spain with the Indies. I called the New World into existence to redress the balance of the Old.' In the old world of Portugal, where constitutionalists and reactionaries struggled for control, Canning also showed his sympathy for the constitutionalists by sending the Navy to help them in 1824 and 1826.

The Greek Revolt

When the Greeks rebelled in 1821, Canning was mindful of Castlereagh's advice: 'Barbarous as it is, Turkey forms in the system of Europe a necessary evil.' He had a choice: to support Turkey and oppose Russia (traditional) or work with Russia to ensure a peaceful solution. Because of widespread support for the Greek cause in England (Philhellenism) he chose the latter: the Petersburg Protocol advocating that Greece become an autonomous state under Turkish suzerainty. An Allied fleet was sent to enforce a blockade on the unwilling Turks in 1827 and the battle of Navarino followed. The news of the destruction of the Egypto-Turkish fleet caused a sensation when it became known. Despite Navarino, however, his policy eventually proved successful: the Greeks got their independence at the London Conference of 1830.

Assessment of Canning's policy

When making an assessment of foreign affairs under Castlereagh and Canning, the most important fact to bear in mind is that there was no fundamental change of policy when Canning took over in 1822. Canning merely accelerated existing trends. His policy differed from Castlereagh's in method rather than principle.

According to P J Rolo, Canning also fostered a legend – the legend of his own liberalism. Indeed, a close examination of the motives behind his policies demonstrates that liberalism to Canning was something to exploit rather than to follow. Much of his domestic policy was reactionary: until his dying day he remained an opponent of parliamentary reform.

Nevertheless, his style and his use of the press to publicise his policies made him popular. If the interests of Britain are taken as a criterion he must be judged a most successful Foreign Secretary.

Comparing Canning with Castlereagh

When comparing the two, one should remember that both their reputations are exaggerated – Canning being less, and Castlereagh more liberal than is usually stated. Both were Tories, both served under Lord Liverpool, both were primarily concerned with British interests and both were moving away from the congress system.

Canning, however, was more in tune with nineteenth-century developments and, unlike Castlereagh, cleverly turned everything into a publicity campaign. The public enjoyed his 'liberal' victories but Canning was, in fact, well aware of the limits of both British power and British interests when it came to encouraging liberalism or nationalism. 'Let us not', he once said, 'in the foolish spirit of romance, suppose that we alone can regenerate Europe. However, his independent approach led Metternich to complain that the ministry of Canning 'marked the end of an era in the history of England and Europe'.

5.4 LORD PALMERSTON, 1830–65

Castlereagh had been a great European figure; Canning had been much more nationalist. So also was Palmerston, who added a lively sense of Britain's honour and prestige to Canning's policy of liberal-nationalism. Like Castlereagh, Palmerston was also prepared to use negotiation and conferences to solve European problems. A master of improvisation, he chose his allies (and his policies) according to the situation – now absolutist, now liberal: 'We have no eternal allies and no perpetual enemies. Our interests are eternal and perpetual and those interests it is our duty to follow.'

The cornerstone of his policy was national interest. He was careful to avoid any firm European commitments. A J P Taylor maintains that, in general, he tried to use Britain's strength to preserve the European balance of power. In the ideological struggle between absolutism and Liberalism, Palmerston carefully adhered to a policy of neutralism. Palmerston, then, did not deviate from the basic principle laid down by his predecessors. Firmly believing that Britain should be 'the arbiter of Europe', he wanted to have a free hand in dealing with problems as they arose. He also hoped that British opinions would be listened to and respected.

Remember that behind Palmerston's bluff 'John Bull' exterior there was an experienced and confident diplomat (who could speak several languages), a skilled drafter of despatches and a shrewd assessor of international relations.

1830–41

Palmerston's career can best be understood if divided into three sections. His period of greatest success was from 1830 to 1841, when he triumphantly resolved major international problems in Belgium, the Iberian Peninsula, the Ottoman Empire and China. You must be familiar with the details of these important events but, more important, be able to explain the reasons for the policies that Palmerston adopted in all of them and why he was successful.

1841–46

Aberdeen's period at the Foreign Office presented a real contrast. By remaining calm in the face of mounting public excitement, it could be argued that the more subtle diplomacy prevented two potentially disastrous wars. Though accused by Palmerson of being both weak and a pacifist, in fact he understood the European dimension of British foreign policy more clearly than his two predecessors.

1846–51

Palmerston's middle period in office revealed mixed fortunes but no obvious failures. After an uncertain beginning, with the affair of the Spanish marriages in 1846, he resisted the attempt to partition Switzerland in 1847 and, for all his talk of liberalism, he maintained a rigorous neutrality during the 1848 revolutions. His use of the Navy over Kossuth and Don Pacifico eventually induced the Queen to send him a memorandum deploring his unconstitutional methods. When he recognised the coup d'état of Louis Napoleon the following year, Russell took the opportunity to dismiss him.

1855–65

Palmerston returned as Prime Minister in 1855 to a changed international scene. After the Crimean War (see A. Wood, *Nineteenth-Century Britain*, Chapter XI), the European balance constructed at Vienna was finally destroyed. Industry and science had made new and powerful European armies controlled by dedicated and unscrupulous nationalists such as Cavour and Bismarck. Palmerston and Russell were out of place in this new diplomatic environment and, predictably, made mistakes. Where the Navy was supreme, however, they were still able to take a strong and successful line – as in China and Italy. Finally they misjudged two European crises – the Polish revolt in 1863 and the Schleswig-Holstein affair in 1864 – events, at that time, well outside the range of British power.

Assessment of Palmerston's policy

Palmerston undoubtedly strengthened the influence of Britain in Europe but his dictatorial and aggressive methods made him unpopular with her wartime allies. Conversely, he enjoyed great popularity at home where, according to Jasper Ridley, the people had become 'more Palmerstonian than Palmerston himself'. Much of this was due to his careful use of the newspaper press to bolster his reputation. He did this brilliantly, but on occasion (e.g. the Orsini Bomb Plot and Schleswig-Holstein) he unwisely let public opinion dictate policy. Abroad, his bullying methods upset some. But generally he possessed a shrewd understanding of European diplomats and events and fashioned his policies accordingly.

Perhaps one should conclude with his own vindication of 'bluster' (used against Russia during the Mehemet Ali crisis): 'I am all for making a clatter against Russia – depend upon it, that is the best way to save you from the necessity of making war against her.'

5.5 CHRONOLOGY

1814	March	THE TREATY OF CHAUMONT arranged by Castlereagh.
1815	June	CONGRESS OF VIENNA. Napoleon defeated at Waterloo.
	September	HOLY ALLIANCE signed. Rulers of Russia, Austria and Prussia agreed to prevent war and work for European unity on a Christian basis. Castlereagh refused to join.
	November	QUADRUPLE ALLIANCE made between Britain, Russia, Austria and Prussia. These nations agreed to work together in a concert to keep the peace. This treaty was largely the work of Castlereagh.
1818	September	CONGRESS OF AIX-LA-CHAPELLE. Allied armies of occupation withdrawn from France.
1820		Revolts in Spain, Naples and the Spanish-American colonies.
	May	CASTLEREAGH'S STATE PAPER: outlined the principles of British foreign policy.
	October	CONGRESS OF TROPPAU. Castlereagh for non-intervention in European revolts but the other Powers issued a protocol sanctioning the use of force to maintain the status quo.
1821	January	CONGRESS OF LAIBACH to discuss the revolt in Naples. Britain sent an observer.
	February	Greek revolt against the Ottoman Empire: English sympathies pro-Greek.
1822	August	Death of Castlereagh. Canning became Foreign Secretary.
	October	CONGRESS OF VERONA to consider the Greek revolt. Britain sent an observer.
1823	April	FRENCH TROOPS INVADE SPAIN. Ferdinand VII restored.
	December	Monroe Doctrine of 'America for the Americans' enunciated by President Monroe. Any interference by European Powers in the American hemisphere would be deemed an unfriendly act by the US.
1824	December	Independence of Mexico, Columbia and Buenos Aires recognised by Canning.
1825		Independence of Chile, Bolivia and Peru recognised by Canning.

1826	April	PROTOCOL OF ST PETERSBURG with the new Tsar Nicholas. Agreement to mediate in Greek-Turkish War.
	December	Combined naval and army force to support Portugal against Spain, despatched by Canning.
1827	July	TREATY OF LONDON ratified the Protocol. France and Prussia became signatories.
	August	Canning died.
	October	BATTLE OF NAVARINO. Turkish-Egyptian fleet sunk by an Allied fleet under Admiral Codrington. Greeks now assured of independence.
1828	April	Russo-Turkish War. Aberdeen became Foreign Secretary.
1830	July	Revolution in France: Charles X replaced by Louis Philippe.
	August	STRUGGLE FOR BELGIAN INDEPENDENCE which Britain favoured, but feared that French help might become French ownership. Palmerston's diplomatic skill and Louis Philippe's good sense saw it to a successful conclusion in 1839.
	November	Palmerston became Foreign Secretary.
1831	November	WAR BETWEEN OTTOMAN SULTAN AND MEHEMET ALI. Turkey defeated but Russian intervention saved her.
1833	July	TREATY OF UNKIAR SKELESSI between Turkey and Russia; they agreed to give each other mutual help. Palmerston feared a Russian protectorate over Turkey.
1834	April	NEW QUADRUPLE ALLIANCE – Britain, France, Spain and Portugal. Palmerston strongly supported the constitutionalist girl queens in Spain and Portugal. Helped to expel their reactionary uncles.
1839	June	WAR BETWEEN OTTOMAN SULTAN AND MEHEMET ALI renewed. Mehemet Ali was victorious and the major Powers, alarmed at the possible destruction of the Ottoman Empire, intervened.
	November	CHINESE OPIUM WAR. Chinese authorities tried to stamp out the illicit opium trade with British India. Disputes led to violence, demands for compensation and, eventually, war.
1841	July	TREATY OF LONDON. Unkiar Skelessi revoked. The great Powers agreed to maintain the integrity of Turkey.
	September	Peel and the Conservative Party in office. Aberdeen appointed Foreign Secretary.
1842	August	Aberdeen and Guizot agree compromise over French annexation of Tahiti. Dispute with the United States over the frontiers of Maine and Oregon with Canada settled peacefully. Treaty of Nanking, in which Britain received Hong Kong, ended Chinese War.
1846	July	Palmerston became Foreign Secretary. THE SWISS SONDERBUND. Attempted secession by seven Catholic Cantons from the Swiss Federation. Palmerston prevented European intervention on their behalf. Protestant Cantons suppressed the Sonderbund (November 1847).
	August	Affair of the Spanish Marriages: this broke friendly relations between France and Britain.
1848		Year of revolutions. French monarchy overthrown (February). Metternich overthrown (March). Palmerston remained neutral but supported the Sultan when he refused to hand over the Hungarian leader, Kossuth to Austria.
1850	June	DON PACIFICO. Palmerston's 'Civis Romanus sum' speech.
1851	August	QUEEN'S MEMORANDUM: commented unfavourably on Palmerston's individualistic methods.
	December	LOUIS NAPOLEON'S COUP D'ETAT recognised by Palmerston without Cabinet approval. Palmerston forced to resign; succeeded by Earl Granville.
1854	March	CRIMEAN WAR BEGAN. Britain and France declared war on Russia.
1855	February	Palmerston became PM; Clarendon became Foreign Secretary.
1856	March	CRIMEAN WAR ENDED. Paris Peace Conference.
	October	Chinese wars (second and third) ended in October 1860 by the TREATY OF PEKIN.
1857	May	Indian Mutiny; ended April 1859.

1858	January	ORSINI 'BOMB PLOT': attempt to assassinate Louis Napoleon. Palmerston's 'Conspiracy to Murder' Bill rejected and he resigned.
1859	June	Palmerston became PM; Russell became Foreign Secretary.
1860	May	Garibaldi's campaign for Italian unification in Sicily and Naples. Palmerston and Russell gave moral support by maintaining a benevolent neutrality.
1861	February	American Civil War began. Britain remained neutral despite difficulties over the TRENT in November, 1861, and the ALABAMA in June, 1863.
1863	February	POLISH REVOLT. Russell led the Poles to expect British help against Russia but sent them none.
1864	February	WAR OVER SCHLESWIG–HOLSTEIN: Prussia and Austria invaded Denmark. Russell sympathised with the Danes and led them to expect British help; encouraged them to resist. No help was sent.

Illustrative questions and answers

1 'National interest was always his overriding objective.' Is this an accurate assessment of Castlereagh's foreign policy after 1815?

Tutorial note

The question demands an analysis of the principles underlying Castlereagh's foreign policy. Remember that his contemporaries accused him of allowing general European concerns to override British interests. You may choose to assess the accuracy of the above statement in the light of this popular criticism.

You need to know about

A thorough understanding of the principles of British foreign policy. A detailed knowledge of Castlereagh's foreign policy from 1815–22.

Suggested answer plan

1 Introduction: Castlereagh became Foreign Secretary in 1812. His outlook was coloured by his experiences as Chief Secretary for Ireland in the 1790s. His ability was respected but he was not revered. A combination of the Irish experience of rebellion and the European experience of the French Revolution made him a determined advocate of peace and maintenance of the status quo. As leader of the House of Commons he was acknowledged as the main driving force of Liverpool's administration; consequently he was blamed for its repressive policy at home and its association with foreign despots abroad.

2 The continuity of ideas underlying British foreign policy during this period. Peace, non-intervention, the balance of power, economic expansion. The way in which the objectives were approached may have differed, but the principles were permanent. The basis of these principles was that of Britain's national interests, and this was clearly expounded by Castlereagh in his State Paper of May 1820.

3 At Vienna, Castlereagh accepted that the aim of the Congress was European peace and a new balance of power after the upheavals of the Napoleonic War. Castlereagh was generous to France; he was also agreeable to national sentiment being ignored for the sake of shaping the new Europe. Territorially satisfied, he added to Britain's 'informal empire' by acquiring a string of islands across the globe. When faced with the Tsar's apparently interventionist Holy Alliance, he refused to join and offered instead the continuation of the more practical Quadruple Alliance. To maintain the ideals of European peace, stability and the balance of power he was willing to try the Congress system –

but to him the system was always one of limited liability. Britain still favoured the policy of a free hand, not wishing to become too entangled in European affairs – an involvement which, above all, could have detrimental economic effects.

4   Increasingly, Castlereagh was out of step with the reactionary interpretation of the Vienna Settlement, which encouraged intervention, and wished to stifle Liberalism and emergent Nationalism. Revolts in Spain and Naples were a setback to Castlereagh's attempts to curtail collective action. To Castlereagh the Congress 'system' was not a system for the government of other states. He began to withdraw – only sending an observer to Troppau and Laibach. This concern prompted him to produce his State Paper of May 1820, in which he reaffirmed the fundamental principles of British foreign policy.

5   Did Castlereagh follow national interests in these events, or was he the dupe of foreign reactionaries, the pawn of Metternich? An examination of these policies demonstrates clearly Castlereagh's proper regard for the interests of his country – a stable France, the control of the seas, economic expansion (note his opposition to possible Franco-Spanish intervention in the South American colonies), the balance of power, etc. His withdrawal from the congress system indicated his increasing dissatisfaction with its activities. European-minded he may have been, but his actions indicated clear limitations to the primacy of European considerations in his policies.

6   Castlereagh's support for the international method of maintaining peace was not popular in an era of nascent nationalism. Yet he believed that Britain's interests could best be secured by working in concert with the European Powers. His failure was in neglecting to explain this to the cabinet, parliament or people. What Castlereagh sought to achieve by cooperation and personal contact with the European Powers, Canning tried to accomplish by more independent methods – but even he failed to prevent France from intervening in Spain. Castlereagh may have favoured a system of international cooperation, but he rightly believed that European peace and security were as much British interests as European ones.

2   To what extent can we describe Canning's foreign policy as liberal?

Tutorial note

Canning's foreign policy has always been regarded as liberal – the key question is *how* liberal? The question implies that his reputation for liberalism may have been exaggerated, that there may be more continuity in the aims of British foreign policy than is sometimes suggested.

You need to know about

An understanding of the aims and objectives of Castlereagh's foreign policy from 1815–21. A detailed knowledge of Canning's foreign policy and actions in Spain, Portugal, the New World and the Near East.

Suggested answer plan

1   Castlereagh is often said to have represented the more repressive side of the Younger Pitt's character; equally Canning may have inherited the more progressive ideals of his master. It is useful to remember that Canning began life as a Whig but soon settled comfortably into the role of a Pittite Tory. Like Pitt, he favoured Catholic emancipation but displayed few liberal tendencies in other domestic affairs. He was an enemy of Jacobinism, of parliamentary reform and of Corn Law repeal. He also supported the repressive policy of Liverpool's administration from 1815–22.

2   It was in foreign policy that Canning gained his reputation as a liberal. This was primarily based on his rejection of the Holy Alliance, together with Metternich's attempt to rule Europe by the congress system – which Canning openly

denounced. Metternich's consequent dislike of Canning simply added to the latter's reputation as a progressive.

3   How liberal was Canning? He condemned the French invasion of Spain in 1823 and expressed the hope that the Spanish constitutionalists would eventually triumph. He warned about French intervention in Portugal or the rebellious Spanish American colonies. These sentiments may have been liberal, but they also admirably expressed British foreign policy objectives – particularly with regard to protecting our burgeoning trade with South America. His 'New World' speech (a piece of retrospective bravado giving political recognition to the 'New World') was made as much to support and protect a rapidly expanding market for British goods, as to uphold the cause of Liberalism. What he wanted was the preservation of Portuguese independence and the denial of the Spanish colonies to France.

4   Unable to act over the French invasion of Spain, Canning was determined to maintain Britain's interest in the Iberian Peninsula by supporting Portugal – note the strategic importance to Britain of its Atlantic coastline and harbours. He sent a naval squadron to the Tagus in 1824, followed in 1826 by a detachment of British troops to Lisbon to help the constitutionalists and to prevent further instability or foreign interference. In the years up to 1826, therefore, he had successfully defended British interests abroad, increased his own reputation and won the admiration of many liberals in Europe.

5   The Greek revolt presented Canning with his greatest problem. British foreign policy demanded that she support Turkey as a barrier against Russian expansion. However, British public opinion was very pro-Greek (e.g. Byron, Philhellenism). The main danger was a Russo-Turkish war which Canning worked hard to avert – the Petersburg Protocol. Canning rejected the congress approach by reaching an understanding with Russia that Greece be allowed autonomy under Turkish suzerainty. An allied fleet was sent to force this solution on a reluctant Sultan. Navarino was the result but Canning was dead before the news reached London and the Russo-Turkish war, which he had striven to avoid, followed. Nevertheless, the Greeks got their independence in 1830 but Canning had left the congress system in ruins.

6   The liberals claimed that Canning's innovative policy was in the Near East. They claimed that his attempt to work with Russia to effect a solution to the Eastern Question was bold and imaginative. It is unlikely, though, that Canning was doing this solely to further the cause of Greek nationalism. There was British trade in the Mediterranean to consider and the strength of the Ottoman Empire as a barrier to Russia. Others maintained that his Near Eastern policy was a return to working with the other Powers (the concert system), excluding Metternich, whom he personally disliked, from the negotiations.

7   Canning's policies over Spain, Portugal, the New World and Greece certainly appeared progressive. His main motives were, however, not the furtherance of European Liberalism but the implementation of the basic principles of British foreign policy (and the flashy pursuit of personal power and admiration). He was not an unqualified supporter of Liberalism but his political style seemed to mark him as the symbol of resistance to European despotism. While acknowledging the more overtly progressive nature of his policies (compared, say, to Castlereagh) and his dedication to ending the slave trade, his reputation for liberalism in foreign affairs is probably exaggerated. As Professor Gash says: 'under his flamboyant liberal guise, Canning was an acute, cautious and conservative foreign minister.'

3   To what extent could Palmerston be described as a disciple of Canning?

Tutorial note

You should begin with a consideration of the aims and style of Canning's foreign policy. To what extent did Palmerston continue Canning's approach in style and method? Is there enough similarity to justify the title 'disciple'? Did Palmerston consciously model his foreign policy on Canning's? Or was he sufficiently independent in thought and action for one to reject this description?

You need to know about

An understanding of the basic principles of British foreign policy. A detailed knowledge of foreign policies and diplomatic methods of Canning and Palmerston.

Suggested answer plan

1   Palmerston had been a supporter of Catholic emancipation and a Canningite before he left the Tory Party in 1830. He had attacked Wellington's government in 1829 for not following Canning's foreign policy over Portugal and his political style, nationalistic fervour and 'liberal' pronouncements indicate him as a 'disciple' of Canning's. His speeches – 'We have no eternal allies...' for instance – have about them the ring of Canning's 'Each nation for itself...' and mark Palmerston as vigorous a nationalist as his predecessor. His despatches condemn European autocrats and, like Canning, he displayed a lively contempt for foreigners. Similarly, he voiced his support for liberal and constitutional states claiming that they were the 'natural allies' of Great Britain. Decisive in action, eager to protect and extend Britain's foreign trade, capable of appealing directly to the public – often over the heads of cabinet colleagues (he also wrote for a daily newspaper), tenaciously pursuing the slave traders or castigating Metternich, he did appear to be more a disciple of Canning than Castlereagh.

2   Yet this may be a superficial judgement. An examination of his methods shows a willingness to negotiate and collaborate with the other Powers in a way more reminiscent of Castlereagh than of Canning. In the Belgian question he realised that a satisfactory solution was only possible in concert with the other Powers. He worked with Russia and Austria – both of which he personally disliked – to solve the Mehemet Ali crisis in the Near East in the 1830s. In both he was not afraid to 'throw down the gauntlet' to bring France to her senses, but the ultimate objective was to preserve peace and the balance of power.

3   In the 1848 struggle in Europe between Liberalism and autocracy, Palmerston remained neutral. Despite the popularity in England of the Hungarian cause, he maintained an astute diplomatic silence. He retained his popularity, however, by privately commending Kossuth's bravery and, to the annoy-ance of the Queen, by condemning Austrian brutality in suppressing the revolt. In other areas Palmerston showed that he was prepared to be more of an interventionist than Canning – e.g. in Belgium, the Near East, China, Poland and Schleswig-Holstein. Palmerston also went beyond Canning in his support for the extension of British trade (two China wars) and in giving protection to British merchants legitimately following their business interests abroad. The same can be said for his wide-ranging and effective use of the Navy.

4   On balance it is difficult to argue convincingly that Palmerston was a 'disciple' of Canning, displaying as he did such an opportunistic approach to foreign affairs. Like Canning, he cultivated through his speeches and the press the image of a powerful, independent, liberal Britain. Some of this (as with Canning) was to encourage popular support for himself and his policies. Furthermore, behind the image and the bombast, Palmerston displayed a shrewd understanding of the realities and complexities of European diplomacy. What made him successful, popular and uniquely individual was his opportun-ism – be it in conference, negotiation, bluff or independent action – which best guaranteed the paramountcy of British interests, the balance of power and European stability.

Question bank

1 Document question (Canning in the 1820s): Study each of these 10 short quotations from the speeches of Canning and then answer questions (a) to (h) which follow:

1 'I do not believe that I shall learn what England thinks from the King, from great lords and ladies or from great families.'
2 'The middle way means the middle class, which interposes between two extremes... . The middle class is the most valuable part of the community, in which its stable interest and sterling good sense reside.'
3 'We are on the brink of a great struggle between property and the populace which can only be averted by the mildest and most liberal legislation.'
4 'Those who reject improvement because it is innovation will have to accept innovation when it is no longer improvement.'
5 'Our business is to preserve peace and the independence of nations.'
6 'Our influence abroad must be secured in our strength at home in sympathy between people and government, in the union of public sentiment in public councils and in the cooperation of House of Commons and the Crown.'
7 'After being the saviours we have become the model of Europe. Let us hope the model will be generally followed.'
8 'England cannot avoid seeing ranked under her banner all the restless and discontented of every nation.'
9 'We cannot treat as pirates a population of a million and we must try to bring within the bounds of civilisation a contest most barbarously conducted on both sides.'
10 'The issue at Verona has split the one and indivisible alliance into three parts as distinct as the constitutions of England, France and Muscovy. So things are getting back to a wholesome state, each nation for itself and God for us all.'

(a) In view of their content, as well as of the fact that he was a leading figure in a cabinet headed by Lord Liverpool, what do you consider the most significant single word used by Canning in Nos. 1, 2, 3 and 4? Explain briefly your reasons for this choice. (3)
(b) What could the Canningites claim to have done in the 1820s to demonstrate Canning's belief that 'The middle class is the most valuable part of the community' (No. 2)? (4)
(c) What examples can be found, from the years when Canning was in office, of measures by Liverpool's government designed to avert 'a great struggle between property and the populace' (No. 3)? (4)
(d) What 'innovation' that was not, in his opinion, an 'improvement' (No. 4) did Canning wish to avoid in England? (2)
(e) Suggest how far Nos. 5, 6, 7 and 8 indicate that Canning's aims in foreign affairs resembled, and how far they differed from, those of Castlereagh? (5)
(f) What 'contest' is referred to in No. 9; who were the 'population of a million'; and with whom did Canning cooperate in order to bring the contest 'within the bounds of civilisation'? (5)
(g) What was 'The issue at Verona' (No. 10) which 'split the one and indivisible alliance' and which of the other nine quoted sayings of Canning did his action on the issue most clearly illustrate? (5)
(h) Apart from any difference of aim and policy, what personal asset that Castlereagh lacked do these sayings suggest that Canning obviously possessed? (3)

2 'His conduct of foreign policy was one long crime.' Discuss this view of Palmerston's foreign policy. (Oxford and Cambridge, June 1992)

3 To what extent was British foreign policy from 1815 to 1865 motivated by consistent principles?   (AEB, June 1988)

4 To what extent did the foreign policy of Canning follow the lines laid down by his predecessor Castlereagh?   (Cambridge, November 1990)

5 How far do you agree that 'Anglo-French cooperation was the key to British policy towards Europe from about 1830 to the mid-1860s'?   (NISEAC, June 1990)

READING LIST

Standard textbook reading

A. Briggs, *Age of Improvement* (Longman, 1959), chapter 7.

E. J. Evans, *The Forging of the Modern State* (Longman, 1983), chapters 21, 33.

R. K. Webb, *Modern England* (Allen and Unwin, 1980 edn.), chapters 4, 7.

A. Wood, *Nineteenth-Century Britain* (Longman, 1960), chapters 10, 11, 13.

Further suggested reading

K. Bourne, *The Foreign Policy of Victorian England* (OUP, 1970).

M. E. Chamberlain, *Foreign Policy in the Age of Palmerston* (Longman, 1984).

M. E. Chamberlain, *Pax Britannica: British Foreign Policy 1789–1914* (Longman, 1988).

M. E. Chamberlain, *Lord Aberdeen* (Longman, 1983).

P. Dixon, *Canning, Politician and Statesman* (Weidenfeld and Nicolson, 1976).

W. Hinde, *Castlereagh* (Collins, 1981).

J. Joll (ed.), *Britain and Europe 1793–1940* (OUP, 1967).

J. Ridley, *Lord Palmerston* (Constable, 1970).

D. Weigall, *Britain and the World 1815–1986* (Batsford, 1987).

D. Southgate, *The Most English Minister... the Policies and Politics of Palmerston* (Macmillan, 1966).

C. K. Webster, *The Foreign Policy of Castlereagh 1815–22* (Bell, 1925, 1963).

DISRAELI AND CONSERVATISM

Units in this chapter

6.1   *The Corn Laws and after*
6.2   *The Second Reform Act*
6.3   *Disraeli in power 1874–80*
6.4   *Chronology*

Chapter objectives

❶ Disraeli's background and personality; his novelistic and journalistic approach to politics – a combination of extreme egotism and unscrupulousness with political nonchalance.

❷ Background of the Conservative Party to 1846; the reasons for regarding Peel as the 'founder' of Conservatism (his pragmatic, parochial, bureaucratic approach to government); better reasons for regarding Peel as the 'founder' of the Liberal Party and as the antithesis of Conservatism (his moralistic, individualistic, laissez-faire European approach). The 1846 split and Disraeli's part in it. Point out that Disraeli was the government's warmest backbench supporter during the years 1841–3, so he cannot have attacked Peel merely out of pique at not being given office in 1841. Note that Disraeli did not defend protection in 1846, merely the duty of Party leaders not to betray their supporters.

❸ Disraeli's position in the Conservative Party, 1846–74 – he was indispensable but never quite trusted; there were attempts to oust him (in favour of Stanley, Cranborne, etc.).

❹ Disraeli's political philosophy: he adapts his 'Young England' paternalism from an agrarian, pastoral, nostalgic idyll, as depicted in his novel, *Sybil*, into an urban phenomenon. He was one of the first politicians to see politics as a *medium* for satisfying public opinion, full of symbol and gesture (e.g. the purchase of Suez Canal shares, the Empress of India, etc.).

❺ The Second Reform Act: the reasons for regarding this as merely a tactical coup ('stealing the Whigs' clothes', gerrymandering re-distribution of seats) or a pragmatic response to disorder (e.g. the Hyde Park riots). But there were also serious political motives, such as to tap working-class resentments against the aspiring, lower-middle-class, moralistic, Lord's-Day observing, and temperance fanatics of the new Gladstonian Liberalism.

❻ Disraeli's Crystal Palace and Manchester speeches promoted the Empire and social reform; his conquest of the Queen; his 1874–80 government fulfils this type of Conservatism, with its paternalist legislation (artisans dwellings, trade unions, etc.) and Palmerston-style nationalism.

❼ But the actual development of Conservatism after 1870 owed little to Disraeli's romantic, paternalist, vaguely populist philosophy. The main factor was the movement of the middle classes from Liberalism to Conservatism: the business classes were offended by Gladstone's and, later, Chamberlain's radicalism (especially the Workmen's Compensation Act), and looked to the Tories for tariff reform and a strong foreign policy; the lower-middle classes turned Conservative as they grew in respectability (what Salisbury called 'villa Toryism').

❽ The 1885 election gave the Conservatives a majority in the English boroughs for the first time ever – and a minority in the counties. This transformation had little to do with Conservatism as Disraeli had idealised it. Yet Disraeli has to be credited with having kept Conservatism going through its years in the wilderness, when it seemed likely to disappear without trace, or become merely the agrarian wing of a Liberal-capitalist party, as politics reoriented themselves horizontally on a 'capital' versus 'labour' basis. That this did not happen owes as much to Disraeli as to anyone.

❾ Consider Disraeli's abiding influence in the Conservative Party and on Conservative 'one nation' thinking.

Benjamin Disraeli is one of the most contentious political leaders of the nineteenth century. Contemporaries and historians have never ceased to argue over his contribution to the Tory Party, and over the merits and demerits of his personality and his political beliefs. Did he have political principles, or was he merely a political opportunist whose one settled aim was to reach the top?

Whatever the answer to these questions there is no doubt that his success as a politician is amazing. Even Gladstone, his main rival and enemy, said after his death: 'The career of Lord Beaconsfield is in many respects the most remarkable in our parliamentary history... .'

Disraeli's background

Benjamin Disraeli was born in 1804 in Gray's Inn, London. His background was Jewish; his father was a well-known writer. He attended no famous school or university but was self-taught in his father's immense library. His was not the best background for a career in politics. In the 1830s he unsuccessfully fought three elections as an Independent before finally entering parliament, at the fourth attempt, as a Conservative.

Throughout his life, politics and literature were his major interests (his first novel, *Vivian Grey*, was published in 1826) and he enjoyed success in both. He eventually decided to make his career in politics and, armed with a burning ambition, superb courage and a brilliant intellect, he was determined to reach the top.

Within 12 years of entering parliament this eccentric MP, who dressed so outrageously and opposed so determinedly, had become leader of the Tory Party in the House of Commons.

6.1 THE CORN LAWS AND AFTER

Unhappy with the direction of Peel's Liberal Conservatism, and feeling that Peel and Derby underrated him, Disraeli grew restive and hostile and finally challenged Peel, first on the Maynooth Grant and then on the issue of the Corn Laws. He followed Bentinck in alleging that Peel had betrayed the Conservative Party and rallied the Tory backbenchers to his side. Peel's ideal of nonparty government was condemned by Disraeli, who insisted that the Conservatives should 'above all maintain the line of demarcation between the parties.'

His success in overthrowing Peel (whom he called 'a great parliamentary middleman') propelled him into the Party hierarchy – much to the discomfiture of many of the Ultra-Tories, who were not a little suspicious of this Jewish novelist-dandy. What the Party needed at that time, however, was a leader who shared its apprehensions about Peel's particular kind of Conservatism. Disraeli clearly fulfilled this role. This was not mere opportunism on his part. He had shown sympathy with the aristocratic 'Young England' party of the 'forties and with its idealistic notion about the alliance between the old aristocracy and the new industrial classes in the towns. In his novels *Coningsby* (1844) and *Sybil* (1845) he, too, professed belief in the historic factors that had made England great: the Crown, the Church, the constitution and the aristocracy.

The years 1846–66 were critical in Disraeli's career. He dropped his 'Young England' ideals of agrarianism in the late 'forties, abandoned protection in 1852 and introduced a Reform Bill in 1859. In 1866 he accepted a more radical extension of the franchise than Gladstone ('the People's William') would tolerate.

Questions you must research are: was Disraeli re-educating his Party, reverting to 'Peelism' or merely trying to get the Conservatives into power in order to secure his position as leader?

6.2 THE SECOND REFORM ACT

Disraeli's success in passing a Reform Bill in 1867 was a personal triumph achieved with political skill, superb improvisation and not a little deviousness. Neither he nor Lord Derby had any set ideas on reform, nor did they believe in advancing the cause of democracy. After their initial announcement that some measure of reform was necessary, they allowed the Commons and public disorder (though not Gladstone), to dictate the nature of the Bill. The passage was, as Blake perceptively states, 'a moonlight steeplechase'.

It would appear then that their aim was merely to 'dish the Whigs' and thus stay in power as an effective government with a secure majority. In 1867 (and later in 1877 over the Eastern Question) Disraeli showed real genius in reducing the Liberals to their constituent parts in the House of Commons, and this at a time when the Liberal impetus seemed unstoppable. His performance was dazzling enough for the Party to accept him as leader on Derby's resignation in 1868. He had survived every attempt to oust him from the leadership of the Party and his remark on becoming Prime Minister was characteristic: 'Yes, I have climbed to the top of the greasy pole.' Thus, Disraeli's first major ambition was fulfilled. His initial calculation that the Conservative Party offered the better prospects for political advancement than the more 'pedigree-conscious' Whigs had proved correct.

The passing of the Second Reform Act was the greatest parliamentary success of Disraeli's career. It was also a major milestone in England's advance to democracy. You must know the most important events that led up to, and influenced the passing of the Act, the general details of the struggle to get it through parliament – particularly the rivalry between Gladstone and Disraeli – and the results of the Act. And you should also now make a careful comparison of the effects of the First and Second Reform Acts.

Disraeli's political philosophy

When the electorate failed to give him a mandate to govern in 1868, Disraeli was forced to think about developing a political programme. In the main, however, he reacted to Gladstone's Liberalism, as exemplified in the ministry of 1868–74, rather than innovated. He attacked Liberalism as a peculiarly European, un-English doctrine typified by Gladstone's concern for the rights of every nation but his own. It was also, he alleged, a middle-class, nonconformist, sectarian ideology which excluded too many social groups and concerned itself with narrow, Benthamite administrative reforms rather than with the general condition of the people.

Encouraged by a real Tory democrat, J E Gorst, Disraeli set forth his alternative paternalist philosophy in two speeches at Manchester and at the Crystal Palace in 1872. The Tory Party, he maintained, was the national party of England, uniting all groups, all outlooks, all creeds. He stressed the attachment of majority of English people to the Crown, the Church, the constitution and the Empire: these institutions had made England great, had stood the test of time and should be preserved.

Gorst impressed on Disraeli, however, that the extension of the franchise in 1867 meant that the Tories had to broaden the basis of their electoral support – the traditional county vote was no longer enough. The problem was how to implement a social reform programme without alienating the country gentry – who were largely unsympathetic to the new democracy.

6.3 DISRAELI IN POWER, 1874–80

At Berlin in 1878, Disraeli lamented that power had come too late to please him but it could be argued that he was interested in attaining power, not in using it. As Prime Minister he appeared to pursue without a qualm the policy of Liberal Conservatism for which he had denounced Peel. He formed a strong cabinet and, thanks to the efforts of R A Cross at the Home Office, he redeemed his Crystal Palace election pledge to improve the condition of the people. More important, his new Conservatism, a combination of *sanitas et imperium*, gave to the Party a sense of identity and purpose that it had not enjoyed since the days of the Younger Pitt and gave to the new electorate an attractive alternative to Gladstonian Liberalism.

You must now study the government's domestic and social legislation. You should know the main provisions of the Public Health Act, the Artisans' Dwelling Act, Employers' and Workmen's Act, and the Conspiracy and Protection of Property Act – all passed in 1875 – and the Education Act, the Merchant Shipping Act and the Enclosure of Commons Act – passed in 1876. Do not overlook Disraeli's attitude to the Anglican Church (e.g. the Public Worship Act), or the agricultural interests, who formed the backbone of the Party and who were now facing a severe economic depression.

Note that many people still felt that state intervention on the scale of the these Acts endangered the individual liberty of the subject. Most of this paternalistic legislation was aimed at the new urban workers and helped to make Disraeli popular in the country. It led Alexander MacDonald, of the Amalgamated Society of Engineers, to declare 'The Conservative Party has done more for the working class in five years than the Liberals have done in fifty.'

Tory democracy?

Were these reforms 'Tory democracy' in action? This is a question which must be carefully considered. First of all, remember that this was a phrase used some years later by Randolph Churchill when describing the work of the ministry. Disraeli himself never used the term. Nor was radical-Toryism a new phenomenon; individual Tory humanitarianism and concern for social reform already had a notable nineteenth-century history. Furthermore, one can easily exaggerate the importance of the social reforms of the ministry and Disraeli's personal contribution. In fact, he displayed little capacity for administration or executive leadership.

It was Gorst's idea that the Party should organise the Conservative working man and develop a programme of social reforms aimed at attracting him. Furthermore, the detailed reform work of the ministry was carried out by the Home Secretary, Richard Cross. Disraeli failed to mention the Conservatives' social reform contribution in the election of 1880 or make it policy thereafter.

In some ways Disraelian Conservatism was a practical response to the needs of the community left untouched by Gladstone's more administrative reforms. Most of the reforms were, however, moderate, limited or permissive. Very little of it involved the spending of Exchequer funds. They expressed, as Paul Smith emphasises, a policy of 'empiricism tempered by prejudice'.

The onset of economic depression, plus difficulties in Ireland (which Disraeli was prepared to ignore) and abroad, also meant that reforms quickly dried up after 1876. Disraeli's social reform proposals were, therefore, primarily electioneering gestures but they did achieve their major objective; they got the Tory Party into power and showed that it was capable of governing.

Despite the usefulness of the Conservatives' reforms it would be wrong to regard their reform outlook as in principle different from that of the Liberals or to see it as an attempt to implement a reform programme based on a belief in 'Tory democracy'. Disraeli knew that such an outlook did not command wide support in the Party but recognised its usefulness in maximising the tide of Conservative sentiment now flowing away from Gladstone in the English boroughs.

Foreign imperial policy

Foreign policy was a field where Disraeli appeared, paradoxically, to do both very well and very little. In 1874 he caught the mood of the nation when he said of Gladstone: 'It would have been better for us all if more energy had been expended in foreign affairs and less in our domestic legislation'. He insisted that the Conservative Party was the true representative of Britain's national interests abroad and his own actively interventionist outlook meant that he took over the mantle of Palmerston rather than of Castlereagh.

From the moment he took office his gaze turned to the East. At Crystal Palace in 1872 he had reminded the English people that they were at the centre of a great maritime Empire 'whose flag floated over many oceans.' He wished to encourage (at least verbally) an active policy of imperial growth. Suez canal shares were purchased; slavery was abolished in the Gold Coast in 1874, Fiji was annexed, the Queen was made Empress of India, and a 'forward policy' was pursued in Afghanistan and the Transvaal.

You must know the general details of these events, be able to assess the importance of each and decide whether you think they added up to a policy of 'new imperialism.' You should also consider Gladstone reactions to this active imperial policy (e.g. in the first Midlothian campaign) and why he opposed it. Remember also that he had to deal with the legacy of these events in his second ministry.

Next, you must study Disraeli's handling of the Bulgarian crisis and the Eastern Question. Why did Disraeli get involved in the crisis and why did he support the Ottoman Empire rather than the other European powers? Why did he reject the Treaty of San Stefano (1878) and what did he gain at the Congress of Berlin?

The 1880 election

Gladstone had come out of retirement to attack Disraeli's 'inhuman' Eastern policy and denounced his imperialism in a second Midlothian campaign as aggressive, immoral and expensive. Disraeli failed to refute Gladstone's accusations and clearly outraged Christian and humanitarian sentiment in Britain. Disraeli was also under attack from within his Party because, as the economic depression deepened, this earlier (apparent) champion of protection now resisted every demand for aid. Consequently the more militant agricultural interests eventually abandoned the government for the Liberals.

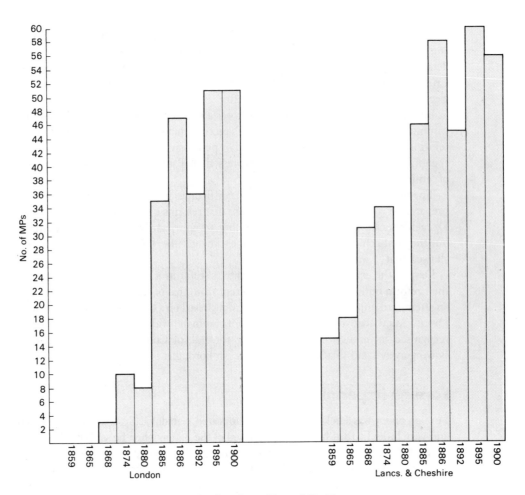

Fig. 6 The 'New Conservative Party' in London, Lancashire and Cheshire

The impact of the depression was more severe in Ireland, where the collapse in production and rents led to the formation of the Land League and a more aggressively obstructionist Irish Party in the Commons. Tired and in ill-health, Disraeli failed to campaign effectively; an elated Gladstone won the election with an overall Liberal majority of 46. Disraeli did not long survive the defeat and died in April, 1881.

Comparative analysis

Once you have studied the different personalities and political philosophies of these two great rivals – Gladstone and Disraeli, or as Bismarck called them, 'the Professor' and 'the old Jew', you must be able to compare their policies in domestic reform, foreign affairs and imperialism (see Chapter 7).

There were fundamental differences. Yet, although the Liberals favoured individualism and the Conservatives paternalism in their approach to domestic affairs, there remained some common ground. After all, did not Gladstone, as well as Disraeli, firmly believe in the Crown, Church, constitution, aristocracy and reform? Besides, most of his radical outbursts against imperialism occurred while he was in opposition – when in government he was forced to invade Egypt in 1882.

Both have many excellent acts to their credit but neither came near to founding a welfare state and, though both were concerned for democracy, they both kept the people at arm's length. Disraeli certainly had a successful rapport with the Queen, which Gladstone could never match, but perhaps Gladstone's more formal approach was the more prophetic for the future role of a constitutional monarch?

Disraeli's Conservatism was the product of a literary and imaginative mind – a mind that seemed to lack the ability to cope with the detailed legislative and administrative work needed for a reforming ministry. He liked to deal in romantic generalities, but as an intuitive politician he saw the weaknesses of moralistic Liberalism.

Gladstone was a born administrator who possessed the ability to master detail in a manner that astonished contemporaries, but his moral crusades often blinded him to practical realities. Morally and intellectually Gladstone was Disraeli's superior. Disraeli's greatness was as a politician, but overall, his character inspired more distrust than respect. Recent research has shown that most of the worst things said about Disraeli appear to be true, while most of the things said in his favour seem to have little foundation. There is a real sense in which it is possible to argue (as Professor John Vincent did) that in terms of accomplishments – financial, legislative, social, foreign and even party – the years before 1867 were a failure and the years after that 'renewed failure'. His one settled aim appeared to be to reach the top and this success alone in the Victorian era was indeed remarkable.

Most historians, however, are not as critical as Vincent. They argue that Disraeli had taken a Party which was antiquated and unpopular, held it together in opposition for 20 years, and gave it a modern outlook and popular philosophy which in the end saw it decisively outlast Liberalism. It is not surprising, therefore, that modern Conservatism regards him, and not Peel, as its principal architect.

6.4 CHRONOLOGY

1804	December	Disraeli was born, the son of Isaac D'Israeli, a well-known author.
1826	April	His book, *Vivian Grey*, was published; this largely autobiographical work brought him into London society, where his ringlets and extravagant dress made him notorious.
1837	July	Disraeli became MP for Maidstone.
1842		JOINED THE 'YOUNG ENGLAND' PARTY, an aristocratic, cavalier movement founded by George Smythe (eldest son of Lord Strangford) and Lord John Manners (second son of the Duke of Rutland). It was against the liberal-utilitarian spirit of the day and offered an alliance of the old aristocracy and the working classes against the new middle-class manufacturers and radicals; it betrayed a nostalgic wish for the pre-industrial age.
1844	May	Disraeli published his book *Coningsby*, which was an acid analysis of Peel's Conservatism.
1845	May	*Sybil* published. In both novels he attacked the Whigs and advocated monarchy, social democracy and Anglicanism; showed awareness of, and sympathy with, the plight of the poor.
1846	June	CORN LAW REPEAL: Disraeli cooperated with Lord George Bentinck and the Protectionists in the attack on Peel; this was the turning point in Disraeli's career.
1849	February	DISRAELI APPOINTED LEADER OF THE PARTY after the death of Lord George Bentinck in September, 1848.
1852	February	Lord Derby's first administration: Disraeli, Chancellor of the Exchequer, abandoned protection as a policy; his first budget was demolished by Gladstone.
1858	February	Lord Derby's second administration.
1859	March	DISRAELI'S REFORM BILL, with 'fancy franchises', rejected.
1866	July	Lord Derby's third administration.

1867	August	SECOND REFORM ACT, which established household suffrage, was passed by Disraeli; this was referred to by Lord Derby as 'a leap in the dark'. REDISTRIBUTION ACT passed to exclude urban and suburban voters from the counties.
1868	February	DISRAELI'S FIRST ADMINISTRATION.
	December	Gladstone's first administration.
1870	May	Disraeli published his book *Lothair*, which portrayed the aristocracy as attractive and dignified but unpractical and aimless.
1872	June	CRYSTAL PALACE SPEECH: Disraeli advocated 'imperialism and social reform'; those policies received strong support from Joseph Chamberlain (and later Lord Rosebery) and proved a popular alternative to Liberalism and Home Rule.
1874	February	DISRAELI'S SECOND ADMINISTRATION.
	August	PUBLIC WORSHIP ACT: suppressed ritualistic practices in the Church of England.
1875	June	PUBLIC HEALTH ACT: consolidated previous statues.
	August	ARTISANS' DWELLING ACT: encouraged slum clearance and rebuilding in towns of more than 25 000 inhabitants. CONSPIRACY AND PROTECTION OF PROPERTY ACT: allowed peaceful picketing. EMPLOYERS AND WORKMEN ACT: made breaches of contract civil and not criminal offences. SALE OF FOOD AND DRUGS ACT: prevented food adulteration. MERCHANT SHIPPING ACT: introduced 'Plimsoll line'.
	November	PURCHASE OF SUEZ CANAL SHARES; this secured control of the route to India.
1876	April	QUEEN MADE EMPRESS OF INDIA.
	August	SANDON'S EDUCATION ACT: a step towards compulsory education. Disraeli made Earl of Beaconsfield.
1877	April	ANNEXATION OF TRANSVAAL. Russo-Turkish War.
1878	March	Treaty of San Stefano.
	June	CONGRESS OF BERLIN: a triumph for Disraeli; he returned from Berlin bringing 'peace with honour'.
	November	Afghan War.
1879	January	Zulu War. British defeated at Isandhlwana.
1881	April	Death of Disraeli in London.

Illustrative questions and answers

1 Would you agree that Disraeli 'educated his Party' or had a coherent policy of Tory democracy?

Tutorial note

This question asks you to assess Disraeli's contribution to the Conservative Party before and after 1868. Did he take over an antiquated Party and modernise it in preparation for government in 1874? While in office did the Party follow a coherent, i.e. consistent, (Disraeli-inspired) programme of Tory democracy? Be able to define and analyse the term 'Tory democracy'.

You need to know about

The development of Disraeli's political philosophy. His main contribution to Party thinking and action prior to 1868. The major legislative enactments of his ministry. The practical or philosophical reasons for introducing this legislation.

Suggested answer plan

1   Criticism of Disraeli's political philosophy is both easy and justified. He was not a serious politician and, despite occasional enthusiasms, he rarely followed up his ideas. Often he seemed to latch on to slogans ('empire', 'social reform') for their vote-catching potential only. His behaviour was certainly incoherent; he seemed prepared to say anything or adopt any policy to secure parliamentary allies, even such unlikely allies as the Irish or radical parties.

2   But it does not follow that his ideas were necessarily incoherent. In fact, they were probably more consistent (unlike his behaviour) than that of most politicians, if only because they were more romantic, less pragmatic. They were worked out at leisure in his books *Sybil* and *Coningsby* and in the rhetoric of 'Young England'. And despite certain adjustments – during the later 1840s Disraeli came to realise that his 'back-to-the-land' agrarianism was impossible – these early theories were held (albeit cynically and sporadically) throughout his career.

3   The word 'democratic' is misleading, however; although Disraeli introduced household suffrage in the boroughs, this was only because he thought the working classes would be more socially conservative, and more easy to manipulate, than the largely dissenting middle and artisan classes supporting Gladstone. He opposed individualism and the ballot, and believed that popular participation should be limited to receiving 'charity' (better housing, protection against adulterated food, etc.) from upper-class paternalists and paternal local cooperations.

4   In fact, Disraeli's 'democracy' consisted in his direct appeal (that is, when he could be bothered) to popular sentiment; he did this occasionally by outdoor speeches, but more by slogans and gestures (his nationalistic foreign policy, the Suez Canal purchase, the Empress of India). Gladstone did the same, but spoke to a different – more moralistic, self-righteous, often dissenting – audience.

5   Of course, he didn't educate his Party. He was deeply mistrusted until the election victory of 1874. The country squires shared his dislikes (i.e. Gladstone, political economists, bureaucrats and centralisers) but had no time for his romantic, paternalist idealism.

6   Moreover, the Party was being transformed under Disraeli after 1865, but in quite the opposite direction to aristocratic paternalism. It was becoming a middle-class Party, whose goals included individualism and orthodox political economy. Only on the question of nationalism was Disraeli in line with Conservative thought.

7   And yet, posthumously, Disraeli has proved a potent force in Conservative thinking; the Party has consistently oscillated between 'one-nation' paternalism (as with, in more recent times, Edward Heath) and laissez-faire, middle-class competition (as with, even more recently, Margaret Thatcher). The former always appeals to Disraeli's example, although it has abandoned his localism (government by landlords, churches, corporations, trade unions) for government by bureaucracy and the corporate state. But at least Disraeli's influence survives, notwithstanding its lack of widespread appeal in his own lifetime.

2   Compare and contrast the domestic legislation (excluding Irish) of Gladstone and Disraeli's ministries between 1868 and 1880.

Tutorial note

This calls for a detailed knowledge of the main legislative work of Gladstone's ministry of 1868–74 and of Disraeli's ministry of 1874–80. It asks you to emphasise similarities and differences in the legislative programme enacted by the two governments. Note that Irish legislation is excluded.

You need to know about

The major legislative enactments of Gladstone's first and Disraeli's second administrations. The practical reasons each government had for introducing this legislation. An understanding of the political philosophy which motivated each government and the wishes and demands of its supporters.

Suggested answer plan

1   Because of the personal hatreds of Disraeli and Gladstone, and the highly developed two-party political system, the first example perhaps of 'adversary politics' in Britain, it is easy to imagine that the policies of the Liberal and Tory governments must have been vastly different, but there was much common ground.

2   Both parties accepted the essential features of Victorian society. Few Liberals wished to move society in a more socialist or interventionist direction; few Conservatives still thought of trying to reverse the industrial progress of the previous 70 years. Thus it was Disraeli who refused to protect agriculture against cheap American corn.

3   Moreover, by 1870 there was (thanks to Palmerston's negative influence) a backlog of administrative and legislative reform waiting to be enacted. Much of this was promulgated behind the scenes by civil servants and other public officials. The main thrust of reform was departmental rather than political (for example, Simon at the Board of Health, Sclater-Booth at the Poor Law and Local Government Boards). The main inspiration behind the Conservative reforms was the Home Secretary (Cross), who worked well with official advisers but had few party-political instincts. Disraeli, who had many such instincts, did not even try to claim credit for his domestic reforms in the 1880 election.

4   When Parliament did become involved in reform legislation, it usually operated on a cross-bench rather than a party line – e.g. Pakington and Forster cooperated on educational reform, Mundella and Cross on trade union legislation. Both parties were against centralisation and believed that legislation should be permissive rather than mandatory. The fact that the Liberal Education Act of 1870 was passed with a majority of Conservative votes and against a majority of Liberal votes illustrates the cross-bench nature of the proposal.

5   However, there were differences. Liberals, concerned mainly with individual freedom, concentrated on political, institutional, and legal reform (e.g. the ballot, university tests, and the legal rights of trade unions) which would create equality of opportunity, so that the clever, ambitious, and hard-working might thrive. Conservatives had a more paternalist approach and were prepared to see practical improvements imposed on the working classes, even on the less respectable and ambitious of them (e.g., the Artisans' Dwellings Act and the Sale of Food and Drugs Act).

   In theory, Sandon's Conservative Education Act was prepared to force parents to send their children to school, which the Liberal Act refrained from doing. More important still, Disraeli was prepared to allow peaceful picketing, whereas Gladstone believed that blacklegs and strikers had equal rights.

6   In conclusion, while there was much common ground between Liberal and Conservative domestic legislation – they were, after all, fighting for the support of the same new electorate – the main contrast lay in the greater attachment of the Liberals to individualism and of the Conservatives to paternalism.

3   What did the Disraelian Conservative party stand for?

Tutorial note

This is a straightforward question which calls for an understanding of the political beliefs – in domestic, imperial and foreign policy – of Conservatives under Disraeli's leadership. The question is, did the beliefs of Disraeli and the Party coincide? Did he educate the Party or simply respond to changing political and electoral circumstances?

You need to know about

An understanding of what policies the main body of Conservatives believed in after 1846. The development of Disraeli's own political beliefs. Disraeli's position in the Party. To what extent the work of the 1874–80 ministry reflected Disraelian and Conservative ideals at home and abroad.

Suggested answer plan

1 Start by pointing out that the Conservative Party only just managed to stand Disraeli. Despite the posthumous adoration, he was never really trusted and only tolerated because he had Lord Derby's support. As late as 1871 there were moves to oust him in favour of Derby's son. So Disraeli and Conservatism should not be regarded as synonymous.

2 Therefore the Party did not *necessarily* stand for what he stood for. Some historians believe it stood for Peelite pragmatism – sound administration, a 'governmental ethic', cautious, un-ideological, essentially middle-class reform. They believe that Disraeli destroyed the Party in 1846, spent 20 years in the wilderness as a punishment, and laboriously put together a Peel-type Party after 1867.

3 In fact, the Tory Party was never Peelite – it was a collection of squires who disliked the pretensions of central government (which is why they ejected Peel) and had no burning desire for office; they were perfectly content with government by the 'conservative' Palmerston; Derby was not particularly ambitious for office, being too fond of his horses, and Disraeli – despite his ambition – was too much a political playboy for single-minded place-hunting.

4 Palmerston's death (1865) and Gladstone's accession (1868) changed all this. Thenceforward Conservatives had to seek office for fear that the 'mad' Gladstone would dismantle all that was dear in society. Office for its own sake, but backed up with a claim that they were the Party of sound government and national security, became the Conservatives' main raison d'être.

5 So Conservatism was essentially a negative reaction to Liberalism. Disraeli himself had a political philosophy, though he was hardly serious or consistent in applying it. It appears in his books *Sybil* and *Coningsby* and in the slogans of 'Young England'. It, too, was stronger on negatives than positives; it reacted against the utilitarian, centralising, bureaucratic and individualistic tendencies of the age, and also against its widespread evangelical morality (as expressed in temperance reform and Lord's Day observance); to begin with it was also anti-industrial and agrarian, but Disraeli surrendered these features as they became impractical (declaring the Corn Laws 'dead and damned' in 1852).

   The positive ideas were vague, but centred round an ideal of organic communities, in which aristocratic paternalists would protect the poor against the exploiting viciousness of middle-class entrepreneurs. Hence his interest in permissive social reform legislation, like artisans' dwellings and public health. Above all, he preferred group action, even peaceful picketing by organised workers, to individualistic action, such as the rights of blacklegs, which Gladstone defended.

6 Prior to 1868 Disraeli had described the colonies as 'millstones round our necks' but after Palmerston's death he intuitively played on the nation's innate jingoism. His Crystal Palace speech advocated imperialism (at least verbally) and he liked to behave as though Britain was still Europe's strongest power. He had no coherent strategy, and his Palmerstonian-style nationalism was never completely popular in the Party (for example, on the Eastern Question).

7 To conclude, Disraeli was not the Conservative Party and it is unlikely that many in it shared his vague ideals. All it stood for was power, and its main aim was to limit the damage done by the dreadful 'old man in a hurry'.

Question bank

1 Document question (Disraeli and the Suez Canal shares): study extracts I and II below and then answer questions (a) to (g) which follow:

Extract I

'As you complain sometimes…that I tell you nothing, I will now tell you a great State secret, though it may not be one in 4 and 20 hours…a State secret, certainly the <u>most important of this year, and not one of the least events of our generation</u>. After a fortnight of the most unceasing labour and anxiety, I…have purchased for England <u>the Khedive of Egypt's interest in the Suez Canal</u>.

'…The day before yesterday, Lesseps…backed by the French government… <u>made a great offer</u>. Had it succeeded, the whole of the Suez Canal would have belonged to France, and they might have shut it up !

'We have given the Khedive 4 millions sterling for his interest, and <u>run the chance of Parliament supporting us</u>… .

'<u>The Faery</u> is in ecstasies about 'this great and important event' (and) wants 'to know all about it when, Mr D. comes down to–day'.

'I have rarely been through a week like the last – and am today in a state of prostration…sorry I have to go down to Windsor… .'

(From a letter by Disraeli to Lady Bradford, dated 25 November 1875)

Extract II

'Lord Derby…the Foreign Secretary is a responsible statesman…with that straightforwardness and common sense for which he is eminent, he told us at Edinburgh that the affair which had created so much sensation at home and abroad was not at all the sort of thing it had been represented to be… . <u>He repudiated with scorn the idea that England aspired to an Egyptian protectorate… . What had really been accomplished was a very ordinary affair</u>… . The Khedive had certain shares…the English government…have acquired them, not to give England any <u>special…influence</u>, nor to secure any <u>exclusive advantage</u>, but to keep open a communication for the benefit of all, which to England is of supreme importance…I gladly take Lord Derby at his word. But now this grand affair is reduced to…moderate dimensions…we may criticise it… . Upon the main ground by which this purchase is justified – namely, the determination to secure a <u>free passage between the Mediterranean and the Indian Ocean</u>, there will be no conflict of opinion. That is a policy in which England is <u>profoundly interested</u>… . But that which has not hitherto been explained, and what remains to be shown, is in what manner and to what extent <u>this investment really does conduce to that desirable object</u>.'

(From a speech by Sir William Harcourt at Oxford, 30 December 1875)

(a) What was 'the Khedive of Egypt's interest in the Suez Canal', why was that 'interest' for sale at this time, and why had the French 'made a great offer'? (5)

(b) Explain the circumstances of Disraeli's government having to 'run the chance of Parliament supporting us'. (5)

(c) Comment on Disraeli's reference to 'the Faery'. (3)

(d) Why did Disraeli claim that the affair was the 'most important of this year, and not one of the least events of our generation' whereas Lord Derby was at pains to say that 'He repudiated with scorn the idea that England aspired to an Egyptian protectorate' and that 'What had really been accomplished was a very ordinary affair'? (5)

(e) Why was England 'profoundly interested' in securing 'a free passage' between the Mediterranean and the Indian Ocean'? (3)

(f)   What were the grounds for Harcourt questioning whether 'this investment really does conduce to that desirable object'?   (4)

(g)   Why and how did England come, during the next ten years, to have the 'special influence' and to secure the 'exclusive advantage' which Lord Derby had repudiated?   (7)

2   What were Disraeli's political motives for pursuing 'Tory democracy' during the Conservative administrations 1866–8 and 1874–80?

(WJEC, June 1991)

3   Did the domestic policies of Disraeli's Second Ministry (1874–80) make a truly important contribution to social reform?   (JMB, June 1988)

4   How far did the policies of Disraeli's ministry (1874–80) mark a new departure for the Conservative Party?   (Oxford, June 1990)

5   Was the political rivalry of Gladstone and Disraeli based more on differences in personality than on differences in political principle?

(Oxford and Cambridge, June 1992)

READING LIST

Standard textbook reading

E. J. Evans, *The Forging of the Modern State* (Longman, 1983), chapters 30, 36, 38, 39.

R. Shannon, *The Crisis of Imperialism* (Paladin, 1976), chapters 3, 5, 6.

R. K. Webb, *Modern England* (Allen and Unwin, 1980 edn.), chapter 8.

A. Wood, *Nineteenth-Century Britain* (Longman, 1960), chapters 14, 15.

Further suggested reading

P. Adelman, *Gladstone, Disraeli and Later Victorian Politics* (Longman, 1970).

M. Bentley, *Politics Without Democracy* (Fontana, 1984).

R. Blake, *Disraeli* (Methuen, 1966).

R. Blake *The Conservative Party from Peel to Thatcher* (Fontana, 1985).

B. Coleman, *Conservativsm and the Conservative Party* (Arnold, 1988).

C. C. Eldridge, *Victorian Imperialism* (Hodder, 1978).

E. J. Feutchwanger, *Disraeli, Democracy and the Tory Party* (OUP, 1988).

R. R. James, *Lord Randolph Churchill* (Weidenfeld and Nicolson, 1959).

F. B. Smith, *The Making of the Second Reform Bill* (CUP, 1966).

P. Smith, *Disraelian Conservatism and Social Reform* (Routledge, 1967).

J. Vincent, *Disraeli* (OUP, 1990).

J. K. Walton, *Disraeli* (Routledge, 1990).

J. K. Walton, *The Second Reform Act* (Methuen, 1987).

GLADSTONE AND LIBERALISM

Units in this chapter

7.1 *The rivalry*
7.2 *Gladstone's First Ministry, 1868–74*
7.3 *Gladstone's Second Ministry, 1880–85*
7.4 *Gladstonian Liberalism*
7.5 *Chronology*

Chapter objectives

❶ Gladstone's background and early political beliefs; *The State and its Relations with the Church*, makes him the rising hope of 'stern and unbending Tories'. His abandonment of high Tory principles while at the Board of Trade under Peel; the effect of Maynooth, Corn Law repeal, and the collapse of the Oxford Movement on his ideas; his work as Chancellor under Aberdeen, followed by his resignation in 1855 and four-and-half years in the political wilderness.

❷ The background to English liberalism; provincial, middle-class, predominantly nonconformist culture; the contributions of the *Edinburgh Review*, philosophic radicalism, and the Whig Party; the contribution of the Peelites; free trade, meritocracy, equal opportunity, 'respectability', self-help, 'peace, retrenchment, and reform' the main Liberal tenets.

❸ Political aspirations of middle-class liberals in the 1850s and 1860s; the rise of the *Daily Telegraph* and the provincial press; the impact of the Crimean War in galvanising such elements against the old aristrocracy; Manchester liberalism (Cobden and free-trade pacifism) against Birmingham liberalism (mainly radical and dissenting); the Education League, Liberation Society, and the United Kingdom Alliance all focus extra-parliamentary liberal enthusiasms; grassroots party organisation and the formation of the National Liberal Federation.

❹ Formation of the Liberal party in parliament after the Willis's Tea Rooms meeting; the impact of the American Civil War, Italy, Schleswig-Holstein, and Governor Eyre; Gladstone's budgets and the battle against Palmerston on defence spending; his demagogic extra-parliamentary appeals make him the 'People's William'; his alliance with Bright.

❺ The death of Palmerston; Gladstone's defeat at Oxford and 'unmuzzling'; put himself at the head of the Radical section of the Party; parliamentary reform, church rates, and Irish disestablishment consolidated this position – but placed him in a false position since he did not wish to travel much further than this; the landslide electoral victory of 1868 and the formation of a balanced 'Whig-Radical' ministry.

⑥ The First Ministry led to the collapse of the alliance between parliamentary and popular liberalism; Irish land, the Education Act, and the Irish Universities were the main areas of controversy; the positive achievements of the ministry (Army purchase, the ballot, Civil Service, and judicature reforms, licensing) could not prevent the defeat of 1874.

⑦ Gladstone's retirement; his return on the back of the Bulgarian agitation; the Midlothian campaign and Second Ministry; the Union of Hearts with the Irish Party, and land legislation; problems with Chamberlain and the Radicals; the occupation of Egypt and other colonial entanglements; the third Reform Act and its effects.

⑧ The 1885 election caused the first-ever Liberal defeat in the English boroughs; Gladstone's adoption of Home Rule; moral conviction, political manoeuvre (especially the wish to subordinate Chamberlain), and administrative convenience (the direct rule of Ireland was too costly for a cheese-paring government) all contributed to Gladstone's decision; the secession of the Liberal Unionists and fall of the third government.

⑨ Gladstone's final years and brief fourth government; the Newcastle Programme and the possibility that Gladstone became more interventionist in his political philosophy at this time; his powerful posthumous legacy on the Liberal Party was not altogether beneficial.

William Ewart Gladstone, one of England's greatest statesmen, was the archetype of Victorian Liberalism. He regarded politics as a Christian duty in the pursuit of which, according to his biographer Philip Magnus, he 'incurred martyrdom for himself as well as for the Liberal Party, which became his instrument, and which, before it broke in his strong grip, owed its unity and enthusiasm almost entirely to him'.

Yet he began his political career as a most reactionary Tory and High Churchman, displaying little sympathy with either Liberalism or democracy. He ended his days as the People's William, the prophet of Liberalism, and supporter of all nations 'rightly struggling to be free'.

7.1 THE RIVALRY

British politics from 1868 to 1881 were dominated by the rivalry between two of England's most gifted political personalities – William Ewart Gladstone (1809–98) and Benjamin Disraeli (1804–81). This rivalry – arising from differences in race, birth, education and temperament – was both personal and political.

Gladstone was the incarnation of Victorian Liberalism; serious, determined, progressive; powerful in oratory and intellectual energy. Disraeli also had great gifts. His superb courage, driving ambition, exceptional political intelligence and a mastery of clever speech and witty repartee made him a disconcerting political opponent.

The early years

Gladstone, the fourth son of a wealthy Liverpool merchant, had a brilliant career at Eton and Oxford. A deeply religious man (he was originally destined to enter the Church), he became increasingly interested in politics, which he came to regard as a moral crusade based on the best instincts of the people. To Gladstone, every important political question was in part a moral one: whatever was morally right could never be politically wrong.

In Lord Macaulay's words, Gladstone, who had begun his political career as 'the rising hope of those stern and unbending Tories', and had denounced the Reform Act of 1832 as 'anti-Christ', yet ended his days as the prophet of enlightened, Victorian Liberalism. He translated into fact the ideas of Smith, Bentham and Mill. More than any other man he was responsible for laying the foundations of modern government and making possible the transfer of power from the aristocracy to the new democracy.

During the 1830s he came under the influence of Peel and, though he abandoned his high-Tory principles, he remained a conservative for the remainder of his life – wanting to preserve a hierarchical society, ruled by an efficient, benevolent and landed élite. As Michael Barker says, Gladstone was 'a curious combination of conservative instincts and radical opinions.' From Peel he learned that politics was not about the pursuit of power but the use of power to achieve noble objectives that were national or, in his own case, Christian. An appreciation of the influence of Peel and Gladstone's conception of religious freedom is crucial to an understanding of the evolution of his political thinking.

As Chancellor of the Exchequer under Palmerston in the 'fifties and 'sixties, Gladstone demonstrated his belief in economic freedom. In Colin Matthew's words, he became 'the codifier, legislator and guardian' of the canons of Peelite finance. Like Peel, he sought to improve the condition of the people through fiscal and financial measures.

You must know the details of his famous budgets that made England a completely free-trade nation. Note that, although the economic achievement was admirable, there was a social cost to Gladstone's attempts to build a 'minimalist' state, for his policy of retrenchment meant a halt to government expenditure on much-needed social reforms. His clashes with Palmerston over the latter's expensive foreign policy also drove him along the road of political radicalism.

Because of Disraeli's attack on Peel in 1846 he emphatically refused to rejoin the Conservative Party. Instead, after some typical Gladstonian soul-searching, he joined the Whig-Peelite-Radical alliance which formed around a key issue of national freedom in 1859 – Italian unification.

Emergent Liberalism

Liberalism was also emerging in the constituencies tutored by liberal editorials in the new, daily provincial press. These consistently advocated civil and religious liberty

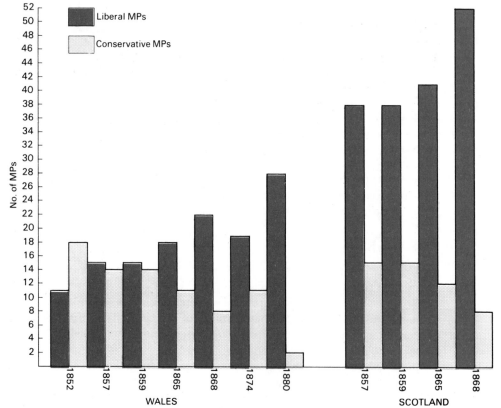

Fig. 7 The growth of 'Celtic fringe' Liberalism

and the belief in the idea of progress. Nonconformists also hoped that the new Liberal Party would adopt their progressive policies in education, politics and religion. From their militant religious outlook came their adoption of 'good causes' that gave them their dynamic quality in politics. The new 'labour aristocracy' were also potential supporters. They wanted more legal freedom for trade unions and recognition from the government of their new-found respectability and independence.

The men who noticed the emergence of these groups and the need to bind them to the newly-founded Liberal Party in the Commons were Gladstone and Bright. After Gladstone's 1864 speech ('every man... is morally entitled to come within the pale of the constitution') he was hailed as the 'People's William.' Bright cultivated this image during the Reform Bill crisis of 1866 – and indicated Gladstone as the natural leader of the next Liberal government.

Gladstone's part in the reform struggle was a confused one. In truth, he advocated only a modest extension of the suffrage but managed to sound more democratic than he was. The people, however, did not forget his 1864 speech and, despite Disraeli's success in passing a Second Reform Act in 1867, voted Gladstone into power in the election that followed in the autumn of 1868.

Gladstone succeeded, therefore, in building up in the 1850s and 1860s a national party of many diverse groups and interests. The problem was how to maintain unity within a party which included workers and employers, Whigs and radicals, Nonconformists and Anglicans. Though Gladstone had affinities with most sections of his party, he wholly belonged to none.

7.2 GLADSTONE'S FIRST MINISTRY, 1868–74

When Gladstone was informed of the Liberal victory at the polls he said: 'Praise be to God. My mission is to pacify Ireland.' Accordingly, his early efforts were devoted to Irish land and religious problems. After these, his carefully balanced Whig-Radical ministry embarked on a programme of constructive legislation. As Michael Bentley has reminded us, Gladstone's mission was also to pacify the competing interests in the Liberal Party. The new Party stood for progress and improvement.

Uninterested in social reform, Gladstone lacked Disraeli's understanding of the material needs of the working class. To Gladstone this would be taking into the hands of the state the business of the individual man. Like the Whigs of the 'thirties, the Liberals were much better at institutional than social reforms. Nevertheless, the new Cabinet initiated a series of fundamental administrative reforms – attacking entrenched privileges, encouraging individualism and merit and thereby laying the foundations of the modern state.

The Liberal reforms

You must now turn to the reforms of Gladstone's first ministry and familiarise yourself with the main details of Forster's Education Act, Cardwell's Army reforms; and the Civil Service, Trade Union, Law, Secret Ballot and Licensing Acts. Try to find out why each Act was introduced – especially the Party pressures or supposed needs that prompted this major programme of legislative activity. Ask yourself also which social groups benefited most from the reforms and in what ways they were especially 'liberal' in nature.

Ireland

Note Gladstone's attempts to pacify Ireland by disestablishing the Anglican Church of Ireland (1869), introducing the first Irish Land Act (1870) and his proposed Irish

University Reform Bill (1873) which helped to bring about the government's downfall the following year. (See Chapter 9).

Foreign policy, 1868–74

Gladstone's main preoccupation was with domestic and administrative matters. He had little interest in foreign affairs, which he approached with some caution. Having, like Castlereagh, a European outlook, he was willing to work in concert with the great Powers to maintain peace.

Rejecting Palmerston's jingoism, in matters of Empire he tended to favour nonintervention. His moral instincts, however, were inclined to make him interventionist – for example, in the Bulgarian massacres. Unlike Disraeli, he believed in the right of small nations to govern themselves. Italian unification made him a Liberal – a commitment emphasised by his attitude to Ireland and the Bulgarian Christians.

He had to deal with three major problems during his first ministry: the Franco-Prussian war (1870), the Black Sea clauses and the Alabama affair. After reading about Gladstone's handling of these issues, you may feel that his responses were wise and statesmanlike in the circumstances but that the electorate felt that he had failed. Try to discover why this was so. Finally, you must investigate the reasons for the fall of the government in 1874.

Assessment of the first ministry

By 1873 the Government had clearly run out of steam. More importantly, Gladstone was now finding it extraordinarily difficult to maintain the units of this diverse, loosely organised Party. The great Liberal problems had been tackled and solved, and the question now was – what next? The radical and Nonconformist members of the party in the newly formed Liberal Associations were especially disappointed with the reforms of the ministry and broke the alliance between the parliamentary and the more militant grass-roots Liberals in the constituencies.

In general, however, the record of the administration was still impressive. The traditional perks of a caste society had been thrown open to merit. Having, by his policy of free trade, prepared the way for the emergence of the middle classes economically, Gladstone had now opened the doors of administrative opportunity to the most ambitious.

It is not surprising that the landed classes believed that he was undermining the old order but it was precisely this attack on prejudice and privilege in England and Ireland which was the essence of Gladstonian liberalism. His government had satisfied many middle-class demands and was a triumph of utilitarianism and efficiency – the victory of the Manchester school of values. Little wonder, then, that the parliamentary Front Bench in 1874 looked, in Disraeli's words, like 'a range of exhausted volcanoes'.

7.3 GLADSTONE'S SECOND MINISTRY, 1880–85

By 1880 the political situation had changed. Gladstone felt that the essential tasks of liberalism had been performed; but he had been inspired to return to politics by the Bulgarian massacres in 1876.

In general, his second ministry proved to be a somewhat barren session in domestic affairs, made bitter by the Bradlaugh incident and the Dilke divorce scandal. The Liberals were clearly a fragmented party in search of a unifying set of policies. Gladstone was overwhelmed by difficulties in Ireland and abroad and proceeded cautiously. He relied almost entirely on the old Whigs – much to the annoyance of emerging young radicals like Chamberlain.

Gladstone disliked Chamberlain's brand of 'social liberalism', with its emphasis on state interference. Such ideas, he believed, might put Party unity at risk. Nevertheless, note that three important democratic reforms were passed – the Corrupt Practices Act (1883), which set a limit on electioneering expenses; the Third Reform Act (1884), which gave the vote to every adult male and thereby enfranchised two million agricultural voters; and the Redistribution Act (1885), which set up single-member constituencies. Salisbury got his reward for insisting on the latter at the 1885 election, when the Conservatives, for the first time ever, won a majority of the English urban seats.

Foreign policy, 1880–85

While in opposition, Gladstone had vigorously opposed Disraeli's jingoistic imperialism and, in 1880, he saw his task as one of returning England's foreign policy to normalcy. However, the legacy of 'Beaconsfieldism' proved intractable; Gladstone's idealistic attempts to create a new, liberal, European foreign policy failed. Gordon's death at Khartoum even managed to dissipate popularity earned by domestic reforms.

Find out why Gladstone's foreign policy in Egypt, the Sudan, Afghanistan and the Transvaal was unconvincing and unpopular.

Ireland

Gladstone's second Irish Land Act 1881 failed to solve the Irish problem and by 1886 his total commitment to Home Rule had split the Party and had dominated the work of his last two ministries 1886 and 1892–94. (See Chapter 9.)

7.4 GLADSTONIAN LIBERALISM

What, then, were the main planks of Gladstonian Liberalism? In general, Victorian Liberalism was a mixture of ideology, morality and self-interest. It was a doctrine as much as a political party. Its meaning has to be sought in its practice. Liberalism should be seen as what Liberals did.

It advocated civil and religious liberty. This religious element often led to the adoption of good causes and occasionally to political militancy. It favoured peace and free trade, a non-aggressive foreign policy, equality of opportunity and material progress at home. It believed in political democracy but not social equality. It accepted selective state intervention but only to organise conditions in which individualism might flourish. Every movement away from laissez-faire was thought to be a movement away from the ideal.

The parliamentary Liberal Party, on the other hand, remained Peelite in outlook and adopted the more practical objectives of sound administration, limited reform, efficiency and careful, but not generous government expenditure. It was still dominated by the great Whig landed magnates. While these were prepared to accept measures to encourage efficiency and improvement, they found many of the Radical demands unpalatable and some of Gladstone's schemes unacceptable.

Gladstone approved these basic tenets of peace, retrenchment and reform but added his own fundamental belief in morality and dedication to Christian purpose. Although his moral outbursts gained him popular support, he was not a democrat. Even in the 1870s he still believed that the landed classes were the only class trained for government: 'I am a firm believer in the aristocratic principle – the rule of the best.'

Many of his progressive reforms – his attacks on privilege – were made in order to make aristocratic government more acceptable in the eyes of the people. Hence his lack of interest in, or sympathy with, Chamberlain's collectivist policies and his failure to foresee the coming age of mass, class-based politics. In later years he became disenchanted with the selfishness of the ruling classes and, after the success of his crusade against the 'Bulgarian horrors', he directed his appeal more and more to the moral and religious instincts of the masses.

Gladstone's true interests were outside politics – to him, politics was simply a means to an end, a method of striving for great and noble achievements such as Home Rule for Ireland or aid for oppressed Bulgarian Christians. By the 'eighties he came to appreciate that in these policies he could usually rely on the support of the masses – rarely the classes. It seemed that it was always the politicians at Westminster who let him down and so he grew more and more disenchanted with the narrowness and selfishness exhibited by most of his parliamentary colleagues.

Not surprisingly, Gladstone became increasingly out of place in an era of cabinet committees and disciplined party politics. His sense of mission hindered him as Prime Minister. Once he convinced himself of the justice of a cause, he found it impossible to compromise and often fought a lone battle in the cabinet in an effort to preserve a favourite political policy.

Consequently, although four times in office, as Prime Minister he was not a success. On such issues as Home Rule he could not compromise or be expedient, nor deal with Radicals like Chamberlain, nor capitulate to the baser needs of party. Gladstone wanted to conceive and execute policy on a grand scale and refused to be tied down by the more mundane matters of party political business.

In John Vincent's words, 'Gladstone ruled the country, not the party'. He understood man but not men. Gladstone's serious view of life, his passionate devotion to progress, his insistence on justice and right – this made him a leader who was idolised or hated. In the final analysis, Gladstone, the embodiment of Victorian Liberalism, was more important for what he was than for what he did.

7.5 CHRONOLOGY

1809	December	Gladstone born, son of John Gladstone, a Liverpool merchant.
1832	December	Gladstone elected as a (protectionist) Tory MP for Newark.
1838	December	Gladstone's first book published, *THE STATE IN ITS RELATIONS WITH THE CHURCH*. In this he showed his support for the Oxford Movement and identified himself with the attitudes of the Tractarians on important public issues. Lord Macaulay, in his review of the book, referred to Gladstone as 'the rising hope of those stern and unbending Tories'.
1841	September	Became Vice-President (1843, President) of the Board of Trade. Introduced Railway Act, 1844.
1845	February	Resigned over the Maynooth Grant (see Chapter 4).
1846	June	REPEAL OF THE CORN LAWS (see Chapter 4).
1847	August	Elected 'Peelite' MP for Oxford University.
1852	December	Became Chancellor of the Exchequer under Aberdeen. Whig–Peelite coalition.
1853	April	FIRST FREE TRADE BUDGET: tariffs on 123 articles removed.
1855	February	Palmerston became Prime Minister. Gladstone resigned as Chancellor.
1859	June	Meeting at Willis's Rooms (formerly Almacks) where Whigs, Peelites and Radicals agreed to work together for Italian unification. Foundation of the parliamentary Liberal Party.
1860	April	GLADSTONE'S budget left only 43 articles on the tariff. COBDEN'S FREE TRADE TREATY with France.

1861	April	REPEAL OF THE PAPER DUTIES: made him popular with provincial press. Resisted Palmerston's demands for increased military expenditure.
1863	May	POST OFFICE SAVINGS BANK established.
1864	May	SPEECH IN FAVOUR OF FRANCHISE REFORM.
1865	July	Defeated at Oxford University; elected MP for South Lancashire.
1866	March	REFORM BILL INTRODUCED; defection of Lowe and 'the Adullamites'. Bill defeated.
1867	August	Disraeli's Second Reform Act.
1868	December	Gladstone became leader of the Liberal Party; succeeded Lord John Russell. Elected MP for Greenwich. BECOMES PRIME MINISTER OF THE FIRST LIBERAL GOVERNMENT; 112 majority.
1869	July	IRISH ANGLICAN CHURCH DISESTABLISHED (see Chapter 9).
1870	March	IRISH LAND ACT (see Chapter 9).
	June	CIVIL SERVICE REFORM: all public offices (except Foreign Office) open to public competition.
	July	Franco-Prussian War.
	August	ELEMENTARY EDUCATION ACT introduced by Forster. Elected School Boards were to 'fill in the gaps' left in the system. Nonconformists objected to increased rate aid for voluntary Anglican schools. The Act aggravated religious strife.
1871	June	ARMY REGULATION ACT: completed Cardwell's measures to modernise the British Army. UNIVERSITY TESTS ACT: teaching posts at Oxford and Cambridge open to non-Anglicans. TRADE UNION ACT introduced by H A Bruce. Made unions legal, protected their funds and allowed the right to strike. CRIMINAL LAW AMENDMENT ACT: forbade all picketing.
1872	July	BALLOT ACT: introduced the secret Ballot.
	August	LICENSING ACT: tightened control of licences and fixed the hours of closing for public houses at 11 pm for the country and 12pm for London.
1873	April	JUDICATURE ACT: consolidated and rationalised the administration of justice.
1874	February	Gladstone defeated in general election. He said of this: 'We have been borne down in a torrent of gin and beer.'
1875	January	Gladstone retired from leadership of the Liberal Party.
	September	Gladstone's book THE BULGARIAN HORRORS AND THE QUESTION OF THE EAST published.
1878	July	TREATY OF BERLIN.
1879	November	THE MIDLOTHIAN CAMPAIGN: electoral campaign against Disraeli's Eastern and imperial policies. Gladstone came out of retirement for this 'pilgrimage of passion'.
1880	April	Gladstone again Prime Minister: his second ministry; majority of 46. MUNDELLA ACT: compulsory elementary education.
	May	Charles Bradlaugh, newly elected MP (and atheist) refused to take the oath.
1881	August	IRISH LAND ACT: conceded 'the 3Fs' – fair rents, fixity of tenure, and free trade – to Irish tenants.
1882	May	MARRIED WOMEN'S PROPERTY ACT: granted married women the same rights over their property as single women.
1883	August	CORRUPT PRACTICES ACT: fixed a limit for election expenses in proportion to the number of voters.
1884	December	THIRD REFORM ACT: adult manhood suffrage added two million voters to the electorate.
1885	June	REDISTRIBUTION ACT: single-member constituencies established. Chamberlain's 'Unauthorised Programme' published. Salisbury's first administration.

1886	February	Gladstone again Prime Minister; his Third Ministry.
	April	IRISH HOME RULE BILL defeated; defection of Chamberlain and 93 Liberal Unionists (see Chapter 9).
	July	Salisbury's Second Ministry.
1891	October	THE NEWCASTLE PROGRAMME: Liberal manifesto, radical in tone; advocated Home Rule, triennial parliaments, disestablishment of Welsh and Scottish Church, 'one man, one vote', House of Lords reform.
1892	August	Gladstone yet again becomes Prime Minister; his fourth ministry.
1893	September	SECOND IRISH HOME RULE BILL was defeated. Lords reject it 419–41.
1894	March	Gladstone retired; succeeded by Lord Rosebery.
	April	Harcourt's budget introduced death duties.
1895	June	Salisbury's Third Ministry.
1898	May	Death of Gladstone.

Illustrative questions and answers

1 Why was Gladstone able to emerge as unchallenged leader of the Liberal Party by 1868?

Tutorial note

The question is slightly misleading in so far as it implies that the Liberal Party existed and that Gladstone rose to power within it, prior to 1868. In fact, though certain elements of Liberalism existed before Gladstone, the Party and the leader rose to prominence together.

You need to know about

An understanding of Gladstone's early career and the evolution of his political beliefs. The influence of Peel, and his downfall, on Gladstone's career after 1846. The emergence of provincial, middle-class, non-conformist liberalism in the 1850s and 1860s. Gladstone's fusing of the newly founded parliamentary Liberal Party and grass-roots liberalism prior to 1868.

Suggested answer plan

1   After Peel's downfall, Gladstone became the main keeper of the Peelite conscience (sound administration, free trade, moral rectitude, internationalist approach to foreign affairs) in the 1850s; this 'conscience' became the core of the new Liberal Party. Gladstone held aloof until 1859 because Palmerston went against all these tenets (except free trade). But Gladstone was already the dominant political figure by the mid-1850s, and his inability to choose between Tory, Whig and Peelite factions mainly accounts for the political confusion of those years, as no one else cared to commit himself until Gladstone had.

2   Gladstone finally joined the Whigs (despite Palmerston) because there was really no alternative; also he could not bear Disraeli; even so, his inclinations were mainly Tory in 1859; once in office he dominated Palmerston's cabinet, and forged his own Liberal Party out of the Whig-Liberal, radical-Peelite coalition of the 1850s; the 1861 budget crisis finally established his dominance.

3   Although socially conservative, Gladstone managed to put himself at the head of the radical-liberal grassroots crusade, by keeping politics focused on political and not social issues, and on rather symbolic political issues at that (Church rates, Italy, America, Eyre); friendship with Bright and Newman Hall helped him, though a high churchman, to cement an alliance with dissenting radicals; the paper duties repeal led to his adulation by the popular press, and especially by the *Daily Telegraph*; he became the first politician to speak extensively outside parliament; by attacking privileges he managed to become the 'People's William'; by taking up temperance, nonconformists' rights, anti-jingoism and franchise reform, he became the idol of respectable, moralistic, middle-class Liberals.

4   By the time of Palmerston's death in 1865, Gladstone had defined the issues in such a way that only he could lead the Party. Besides, with Newcastle's death in 1864, the last of Gladstone's contemporaries had disappeared; apart from Russell, Gladstone was now by far the senior politician on the Liberal side, and quite without any rival.

5   Gladstone's adoption of Irish Church disestablishment in 1868 finally made him indispensable; he was motivated by the need to pacify Ireland and by genuine conviction (see his book, *Chapter of Autobiography*), but also by a desire to thwart his rival, Disraeli. He won the premiership, but only by putting himself at the head of forces (radical and dissenting) which would want to go much further than him on education, the Church, the land and on other reform issues. Nemesis came in 1874.

6   As Vincent says, the Liberal Party was mainly formed out-of-doors, and Gladstone came to lead it because he was the only politician who conde-scended to appeal directly to extra-parliamentary forces.

2   'The differences between Gladstone and Disraeli in colonial and foreign policy were real and important: their differences on domestic issue were largely a matter of emphasis.' Discuss.

Tutorial note

'Discuss' means that you may consider this (very broad) question from any angle you please. You can agree with the quote and substantiate it with evidence; or disagree with either of the two points made, or even with the whole quote. In fact, one could argue that both were pursuing similar policies abroad (though by different methods) and that it was their domestic policies that were fundamentally different.

You need to know about

A general understanding of the foreign policies of the governments of Gladstone and Disraeli, 1868–86. The domestic policies and legislative enactments of both governments, 1868–86.

Suggested answer plan

1   It is hard to believe that either Disraeli or Gladstone took external policy seriously. Pandering to the country gentlemen, Disraeli called colonies 'mill-stones round our necks', an expensive irrelevance; but when Palmerston died he seized the opportunity to take over the 'patriotic card' and to play on the expanded electorate's innate jingoism. Gladstone spoke about the rights of small nations and the duties of large nations to sacrifice their own interests, but in office he found himself bombarding Alexandria and annexing territory nonetheless. Both found themselves helpless in the face of economic forces and of the 'men on the spot' (Sir Bartle Frere, General Gordon).

2   The point is that the Schleswig-Holstein affair, the Indian Mutiny and the rise of Prussia shattered the 'Pax Britannica'. Britain felt vulnerable. For 20 years she pursued a diplomacy of fantasy. Disraeli's fantasy was to go on behaving (over Afghanistan, Treaty of Berlin, etc.) as though Britain were still the strongest

power; Gladstone's fantasy was to make a virtue of weakness and pretend it was self-abnegation (neutrality between France and Prussia, the Alabama claims). Not until Salisbury did anyone work out a coherent diplomacy or strategy. So, yes, Gladstone and Disraeli differed sharply on external policies, but both were play-acting.

3   On domestic policy it is true that Disraeli and Gladstone shared a similar vision of society. Both believed in a hierarchical and organic society, in which property both acknowledged its duties and asserted its rights. Both preferred the agricultural to the industrial mode of life. Despite their bitter opposition, both were arguing within fairly prescribed limits; especially both opposed constructive radicalism, and disliked bureaucratic centralisation. Many of their reforms were being pressed by civil servants (licensing, judicature reform, artisan dwellings) and it would have made no difference which government was in power.

4   And yet the domestic policy differences were fundamental. Gladstone was an individualist, believing in equality of opportunity, meritocracy, and self-help; society would 'progress' as the aspiring, respectable, industrious members of society worked hard to improve their situation. Disraeli genuinely disliked respectability, hard work, social aspiration and the sort of improvement which made barriers between people. He preferred people to be lazy, gregarious, community-oriented, unambitious, hard drinking, immoral and happy. If not a philosophy, it was a basic intuition of his, and distinguishes him from Gladstone.

5   So, while the two men complemented each other – Gladstone reformed the law and the institutions, Disraeli took more constructive action in social policy – their domestic differences were more than just a matter of emphasis.

3   What were the main features of Gladstone's Liberalism?

Tutorial note

Once you have defined Gladstone's Liberalism this becomes a straightforward question; the problem is to define it.

You need to know about

An understanding of Gladstone's political philosophy. The reasons why this philosophy appealed to the Victorian middle classes. The liberal philosophy in practice in domestic, Irish and foreign affairs.

Suggested answer plan

1   First it is necessary to define Gladstone's Liberalism. The definition should centre on Gladstone's political philosophy from the time that he became a Liberal politician, say 1860. He did not articulate a political philosophy himself, but you might refer to Mill's *On Liberty* and Morley's *On Compromise* as coming closest to Gladstone's own beliefs.

2   Obviously some classes were more likely to support Gladstonian Liberalism than others (the archetypal lower-middle classes, superior and respectable artisans, dissenting shopkeepers, self-educated craftsmen, the more earnest, self-righteous, and 'philanthropic' of the upper classes); also Gladstonian Liberalism can be defined in terms of policies.

3   But in fact Gladstonian Liberalism was not really based on a class appeal or on a programme. It appealed rather to a particular mentality which might be found among all classes; in this sense it was above class, and spawned vertical rather than horizontal loyalties (hence the importance of nonconformity). Also, it was more a political style – a particular way of looking at problems – than a set-piece political programme.

4   The four main elements in the Liberal canon were: that it was possible to achieve appropriate institutional arrangements for the exercise of individual initiative within a minimalist state; that free trade would reconcile classes and nations to each other; that men must stand on their own feet and earn their own comforts by labour and prudence; that progress (mainly of the moral sort, but also material progress) was both possible and indeed inevitable, as individuals learned to behave *conscientiously* in public and private matters.

5   In practice this meant, so far as domestic policies were concerned, securing an equality of opportunity in which merit could be rewarded. Reform of the Civil Service in 1870 thus appealed more for its moral and social aspects than for its effects on bureaucratic efficiency. All special privileges (such as the Anglican monopoly of Oxford and Cambridge, the purchase of Army Commissions) should be removed. And everyone, potentially, had the right to a vote, though in practice he believed in some qualification to ensure respectability (say a £5 franchise).

6   In foreign affairs Gladstone believed in Britain's duty to set an example of self-denial (e.g. the Alabama claims), unlike Palmerston and Disraeli. He did not always achieve this in practice (e.g. the occupation of Egypt). But he also believed in nations as organic entities; hence he opposed ultramontanism, supported Italy, attacked the Irish church, and eventually adopted Home Rule for Ireland.

7   As Vincent has shown, Gladstone created a revolution in rhetoric and public expectation, but did little in policy terms to change society; believing as he did in strict retrenchment, his governments did not have enough money to make major practical reforms. But he thought men should improve their own lots and helped to fire his followers with a sense of their own moral worth and importance. He did not, however, aim to change a society which – Anglican and landed as it was in essentials – pleased him very much.

Question bank

1   Document question (Gladstone looks back): study the extract below and then answer questions (a) to (g) which follow:

Extract

…Within the half-century a new chapter has opened…I will refer as briefly as maybe to the sphere of legislation. Slavery has been abolished. A criminal code, which disgraced the Statute Book, has been effectually reformed. Laws of combination and contract which prevented the working population from obtaining the best price for their labour have been repealed… . The scandals of labour in mines, factories and elsewhere…have either been removed, or greatly qualified and reduced. The population on the sea coast is no longer forced wholesale into contraband trade by fiscal follies… . The entire people have good schools placed within the reach of their children, and are put under legal obligation to use the privileges and contribute to the charge. They have also at their doors the means of husbanding their savings…under the guarantee of the State to the uttermost farthing of the amount. Information through a free press, formerly cut off from them by stringent taxation, is now at their easy command. Their interests at large are protected by their votes, and their votes are protected by the secrecy which screens them from intimidation… . Nor are the beneficial changes of the last half-century confined to the masses… . Swearing and duelling have nearly disappeared from the face of society… . The sum of the matter seems to be that…we who lived 50, 60, or 70 years back, and are living now, have lived into a gentler time.

(From an article by Gladstone published in *The Nineteenth Century* in 1887)

(a) In what ways had the 'criminal code which disgraced the Statute Book' been reformed in the 70 years before 1887?   (5)

(b) What had Gladstone's own government contributed towards the repeal of the 'Laws of combination and contract which prevented the working population from obtaining the best price for their labour' and why had he not gone as far as Disraeli on this issue?   (5)

(c) What had Gladstone personally contributed to ending the state of affairs in which 'The population on the sea coast' was 'forced wholesale into contraband trade by fiscal follies'?   (4)

(d) What steps had he taken in the twenty years before 1887 to ensure that 'the entire people' had 'schools placed within the reach of their children'?   (4)

(e) Explain the phrase 'legal obligation to use the privileges and contribute to the charge'.   (2)

(f) What part did Gladstone play in giving the people 'the means of husbanding their savings' and in bringing about a 'free press'?   (6)

(g) What had Gladstone done towards enabling people to protect 'their interests at large by their votes' and to protect their votes 'by secrecy'?   (5)

2 What did Gladstone believe to be the fundamental principles of Liberalism and how completely did he apply them during his periods as Prime Minister?

(WJEC, June 1991)

3 Why did Gladstone lose the election of 1874?

(Cambridge, December 1988)

4 'We speak about 'a great political leader' but he is also 'the captive of circumstance'. In the light of this statement, compare any **two** of Peel, Disraeli and Gladstone.   (NISEAC, June 1990)

5 On the evidence of his career from 1868 to 1880, to what extent during these years did Gladstone pursue consistent objectives in his foreign policy?

(JMB, June 1989)

READING LIST

Standard textbook reading
R. Shannon, *The Crisis of Imperialism* (Paladin, 1976), chapters 4, 7, 8.
R. K. Webb, *Modern England* (Allen and Unwin, 1980 edn.), chapters 8, 10.
A. Wood, *Nineteenth-Century Britain* (Longman, 1960), chapters 11, 15.

Further suggested reading
P. Adelman, *Gladstone, Disraeli and Later Victorian Politics* (Longman, 1970).
M. Barker, *Gladstone and Radicalism* (Harvester Press, 1975).
E. J. Feuchtwanger, *Gladstone* (Allen Lane, 1975).
H. J. Hanham, *Elections and Party Management.*

Politics in the time of Disraeli and Gladstone (Longman, 1959, 1978).
P. J. Jagger (ed), *Gladstone, Politics and Religion* (Macmillan, 1985).
T. A. Jenkins, *Gladstone, Whiggery and the Liberal Party* (OUP, 1988).
P. Magnus, *Gladstone* (Murray, 1954).
H. G. Matthew, *Gladstone 1809–74* (OUP, 1986)
R. Shannon, *Gladstone* vol. 1 (Hamish Hamilton, 1982).
J. Vincent, *The Formation of the Liberal Party 1857–68* (Constable, 1966).
M. Winstanley, *Gladstone and the Liberal Party* (Routledge, 1990).

JOSEPH CHAMBERLAIN

Units in this chapter

8.1 *The social and political background*
8.2 *The New Imperialism*
8.3 *Radical and imperialist*
8.4 *Chronology*

Chapter objectives

❶ Chamberlain was the first of the new provincial, nonconformist, professional politicians; he was a self-made millionaire, and his non-conformist commitment and passion soon transferred into politics. He joined the National Education League to campaign for universal, compulsory, free education and led the nonconformist campaign against Forster's 1870 Education Act; the campaign's failure led him to advocate Church disestablishment.

❷ Radical reputation was made in the Education revolt and the Birmingham Liberal Association which won the local council, school board and mayoralty for Chamberlain in 1873; ostensibly democratic organisation of local Liberal politics – called the caucus – soon extended into the National Liberal Federation of local associations (1877), which threatened to run the Liberal Party. Chamberlain's municipal crusade as mayor; civic gospel at work backed by nonconformist determination and conscience. Birmingham was made into a 'model municipality'.

❸ Chamberlain stood as a Radical MP for Sheffield in 1874; he offered as a platform the 'Four Freedoms': free church, free schools, free land and free labour – but was defeated. He threw his energy into Birmingham Liberalism and the NLF; he was aided by Schnadhorst. The Whigs feared the NLF as a movement to radicalise the Party; Chamberlain argued that its aim was to enable the Liberals to discuss policy and make policy. Gladstone and the caucus triumphed in the 1880 election: Chamberlain entered the cabinet as president of the Board of Trade.

❹ Chamberlain campaigned vigorously for the Franchise Bill of 1884 (which sought justice for the agricultural labourer). This was held up by the Lords; Chamberlain condemned this hold-up as an 'insolent pretension of an hereditary caste'. Salisbury negotiated a compromise – plus the Redistribution Act. Chamberlain expected the Acts to revolutionise English urban politics and boost radicalism in the Commons (in fact the towns voted Tory in 1885).

The main problem was Ireland, to which Chamberlain was prepared to offer generous powers of local government but would not countenance severance of the Union. He offered his Central Board scheme, which Parnell dismissed as 'a harmless reform'. Neither Parnell nor Gladstone sought to win him over to Home Rule. Backed by the NLF he campaigned for his 'unauthorised programme' in the autumn of 1885. In the election he predicted that 'the Tories will be smashed and the Whigs extinguished'.

❺ After Parnell's abortive flirtation with the Conservatives in 1885, Chamberlain joined the new cabinet but resigned when Gladstone presented his Home Rule Bill. With him went Gladstone's chance of carrying the Liberal Party on the issue. The Liberals split; Chamberlain and 92 Liberals voted against the Bill. The reasons for his stand must be conjectural – a combination of injured pride, principle, ambition and resentment. Gladstone hoped to reunite the Liberals, Chamberlain hoped to found a new, more national, Party. In fact Chamberlain's future role was to be in the Conservative Party.

❻ Chamberlain had sensed the possibilities of Empire in the 1880s; he chose the post of Colonial Secretary in 1895. He saw the colonies, like Birmingham, as areas to be improved and developed by careful concern and investment; his was a positive, constructive approach. Social reform at home was linked to imperial development; he hoped for imperial federation through an imperial customs union (or Zollverein) and imperial defence; he advocated these policies in colonial conferences. On the negative side, Chamberlain was involved with Rhodes in the Jameson Raid, which led to the Boer War and the denigration of Chamberlain's ideal.

❼ After the Boer War, Chamberlain announced his conversion to imperial preference – income from tariffs would pay for much-needed social reforms. On this the Conservatives split. Chamberlain founded the Tariff Reform League and resigned from the government. The Tariff reform campaign and the landslide defeat of the Unionists at the 1906 election. A stroke ended his political career.

❽ Chamberlain's achievements were major at a local and personal level – he became an influential civic leader and an astute political organiser – but much more slight at a national and imperial level, where he split both political parties in turn – a victim perhaps of his own progressive ideas and impatient ambition.

'Radical Joe' Chamberlain was one of the ablest and most colourful politicians of the late Victorian period. His family had built an industrial empire on an American screw patent allowing Chamberlain, at the age of 37, to begin his career in politics as the Lord Mayor of Birmingham, the city he loved. Throughout his career his strength was his Birmingham base and he built a following there which never deserted him.

A man of vigour, originality and imagination, he proved a dedicated social reformer and a great imperialist. Like C J Fox, he had talents and ability that exceeded those of many a Prime Minister but, though he never attained the highest office himself, he did achieve the unhappy distinction of splitting the two major political parties of the day.

In many ways, however, the man proved greater than his work and, despite his failure to reach the top, nonconformists of every class and working men of every creed found him a champion peculiarly their own.

8.1 THE SOCIAL AND POLITICAL BACKGROUND

The 'Great Depression' (1873–96) cast its shadow over late Victorian Britain. It hit agriculture particularly hard, stimulated fears about Britain's industrial performance, produced areas of high unemployment and strained relations between management and men.

Many leaders of the 'new.unionism' were avowedly socialist, militant and active in politics. Meanwhile the old aristocracy and the new industrial wealth began to merge while the lower middle classes often moved closer to labour.

Politicians during this period were forced to respond to the advent of more national class-based, politics. They did so either by seeking to control, pacify or exploit this new democracy. The Second and Third Reform Acts destroyed the old structure of politics – a new structure had to be made.

Early radicalism

Joseph Chamberlain was one of the new politicians who attempted to adapt politics to these changed circumstances. His career presents one of the most remarkable transformations in England's political history. He began as a self-made republican radical, became an aggressive imperialist and ended as the idol of protectionist Tories – in Winston Churchill's (exaggerated) comment, 'first fiery Red, then True Blue'.

A Birmingham manufacturer and prominent Dissenter, he gained his first experience of public affairs as Lord Mayor of Birmingham from 1873–76. Using Disraeli's legislation, he made the city 'a model municipality' and had it 'parked, paved, assized, marketed, gas, watered and improved' – all as a result of three years' dedicated work. The performance of this city-bred, nonconformist, provincial businessman gained him, in 1876, a seat in parliament, where he soon became the champion of the new radicalism.

Earlier, his interest had been stimulated by the lack of a national education system. He founded the National Education League in 1869, led the Nonconformist revolt against Forster's Education Act in 1870 and campaigned for a system of 'free, national secular education.'

He also took over the Birmingham Liberal Party organisation in 1872, tightened discipline, organised speakers, fund-raised and canvassed on behalf of candidates and threw open membership of the caucus (as it was called) to the newly enfranchised artisans. To coordinate the work, a National Liberal Federation was founded in 1877 and was soon propagating its famous radical slogan: 'Free Church, Free Schools, Free Land.'

Find out what you can about these early political interests and policies of Chamberlain and assess their political importance.

Ireland

The NLF played an important part in the Liberal victory of 1880 and, despite Gladstone's misgivings about 'Radical Joe', he was obliged to admit him into his cabinet in 1880. His apprehensions proved well-founded. Chamberlain continued to champion the cause of new radicalism, resented the preponderance of landed Whigs in the Party hierarchy and attacked the Tory Lord Salisbury and his class as those who 'toil not, neither do they spin.' He played a major part in pushing through the Third Reform Act of 1884 and, when the Lords resisted, impatiently echoed Morley's phrase 'mend them or end them'.

The big question of the day, however, was Ireland, and here Chamberlain (who helped Gladstone oppose coercion in cabinet) offered his limited 'Central Board' scheme. In his 'unauthorised programme' of 1885, however, he insisted that the interests of the British electorate be given priority over Irish affairs. When Gladstone unveiled his Home Rule scheme, Chamberlain and 92 others – mostly Whigs – defected and split the Party.

Gladstone was not upset. He believed that Home Rule offered a better platform for uniting the Party and that his continued leadership would prevent it from losing its soul to Chamberlain's collectivist outlook. This was Gladstone's bid to bind the future. Find out what you can about Chamberlain's 'unauthorised programme' of 1885. Note how he wanted more state power and was willing to use it to effect social reforms. It is also important that you know the reasons why he opposed the Home Rule Bill of 1886.

Liberal-Unionism

Chamberlain's defection appears to have been a mixture of tactics and principle. His long-term hopes still centred on Liberalism. Gladstone, he believed, would soon retire and then he – Chamberlain – would return to lead the Party. The Conservatives, meanwhile, were happy to work with the Liberal-Unionists, who had the advantage of possessing a popular reform programme.

The alliance was fruitful and produced the Local Government Act of 1888, free education in 1891 and the Workmen's Compensation Act of 1897.

Although Gladstone feared the new radicalism – and its creature the NLF – it was not a revolutionary or a socialist creed; nor was it as dangerous as he supposed: Chamberlain was simply attempting to provide a programme which, by answering some of the legitimate demands of the lower classes, would retain their support for upper-class Parties and politicians. He had a social conscience but also realised that the appeal of Socialism as a mass movement was in the current facts of economic deprivation, not political ideology.

He believed that the working classes could be bought, or at least persuaded, by the offer of much-needed social legislation, to accept the continued rule of the established orders. His defection in 1886 ended the first stage of his political career but it did not mark the end of his radicalism.

8.2 THE NEW IMPERIALISM

Chamberlain waited in vain for Gladstone to retire but – when he finally did so in 1893, after the defeat of his second Home Rule Bill – the leadership passed to Lord Rosebery. Meanwhile, Chamberlain had discovered imperialism. In 1895, when the leading Liberal-Unionists took office with the Conservatives, he rejected the offer of the Exchequer and to the surprise of many contemporaries chose instead the Colonial Office. The Queen's Jubilee and Colonial Conference of 1887 had captured his imagination and, after the second Colonial Conference at Ottawa in 1894, he was determined to exploit the possibilities of the new imperialism.

Between 1884 and 1900 Britain acquired a new empire, and as it grew so did the sense of 'imperial mission' among politicians. So also did the belief that somehow the empire was necessary as a means to social reform at home. It was argued that it could provide an outlet for surplus population, for new markets and for new jobs. There was a noticeable and growing tendency for reformers to be imperialists.

The question of why Britain went into empire-building in the late nineteenth century is an important one. Research the main reasons. Finally, try to discover what was 'new' about the 'New Imperialism'.

Chamberlain's imperial policy

Chamberlain's view of empire marked the end of the old laissez-faire attitude to the

Fig. 8 The partition of Africa 1880–1914

colonies. His was to be a new, positive policy of intervention and reconstruction, combined with an acceptance of the economic importance of empire.

His first few years at the Colonial Office were devoted to the tropical colonies, which he regarded as estates to be developed by careful planning and expenditure. He was ready to invest capital in any worthwhile scheme – railways in Nigeria, imperial steamship lines, the modernisation of sugar production in the West Indies. He also encouraged the founding of Schools of Tropical Agriculture and Medicine at London University.

He saw the British Empire as a force for peace and for the expansion of trade and the development of civilisation but there was also an aggressively defensive side to it. Faced by British economic decline and the rise of dangerous European rivals, Chamberlain was determined to hold on to England's imperial dominions, including Ireland, and – something which marked him as a dedicated imperialist – extend them where possible.

In Africa he gave Cecil Rhodes the land on which to build a Cape-to-Cairo railway, he checked French expansion in Nigeria and got involved with the Rhodes-organised Jameson Raid. The latter poisoned Anglo-Boer relations for some considerable time and was one of the reasons for the outbreak of the Boer War in 1899. This event (and especially the British use of 'concentration camps') undermined the heady confidence and sense of duty involved in early attitudes to imperialism and eventually made it a dirty word. Find out as much as you can about Chamberlain's contribution to the Empire during this period. How different was it from Disraeli's imperialism?

Imperial preference

Although the Boer War showed the strength of the Empire, Chamberlain wanted more. The fourth Imperial Conference, called in 1905, convinced him of the impossibility of achieving imperial unity on the basis of Free Trade. His imperial vision was to be realised by the continuation of imperial conferences, by imperial preference in trading, by a new imperial Navy and by new, imperial political institutions to bind the mother country and the Empire together.

After a visit to South Africa in 1903, Chamberlain shocked his cabinet colleagues by suggesting a policy of protection with imperial preference. Tariff reform would also provide the revenue for much-needed social reforms – in particular old-age pensions. The cabinet split and Chamberlain resigned, determined to fight the next election on the issue. He founded the Tariff Reform League and vigorously publicised the policy he hoped would win the working classes to Conservatism.

To the Liberals, squabbling and divided in the wilderness of opposition, Chamberlain's decision was a godsend. It not only bitterly divided the Conservative Party, it provided the Liberals with an issue that they could unite on. H H Asquith (a champion of Gladstonian economics) was appointed to dog Chamberlain's heels, challenge his protection arguments and remind the electors of the benefits of free trade – a task he successfully accomplished.

You must find out the main points in these two opposing arguments. Note how Chamberlain's is the more idealistic; Asquith makes it an issue of practical politics – the 'big loaf' of Liberalism versus the 'little loaf' of Conservatism. Asquith's arguments proved the more convincing and the divided Conservative Party was overwhelmingly defeated by the Liberals in the 1906 election.

Chamberlain held Birmingham and some argue that he may even have succeeded Balfour as leader of the Conservatives. On his 70th birthday, however, he had a stroke and, though he lived until 1914, his political career was over.

8.3 RADICAL AND IMPERIALIST

In parliamentary and platform strength Chamberlain was the equal of Gladstone and Disraeli. He was also closer in touch than either of them with the spirit of the age. Against the old aristocratic order he pitted the growing confidence and egalitarian spirit of the new provincial towns. Capable of imagination and vision, he found, like Gladstone, that it was dangerous for politicians to move faster than public opinion; and, like Gladstone, he was often seized by a sense of mission in politics, with a non-conformist rectitude underlying much of what he did.

He was not lacking in ideals. He believed in the extension of democracy, in the sweeping away of inherited privilege in the Church of England and in the countryside, in the extension of the franchise, in the destruction of the old Whigs in the Liberal Party and their replacement in the towns by a more democratic party machine – the caucus and the National Liberal Federation.

A second ideal was his belief in the 'civic gospel' – progress and improvement for the citizens of England – better housing, sanitation, education and welfare benefits: 'I would reform and remove ignorance, poverty, intemperance and crime at the very roots.'

His imperial vision was that of a great statesman. It was paradoxical that his Boer policy marked both the apex and the beginnings of decline of the new imperialism. He failed to understand the self-government ambitions of the Boers, of the Irish or of the other dominions. Perhaps, like the Elder Pitt, he came too late in the history of the Empire to hold together those parts which preferred to break away. He did, however, herald the new post-1919 British Commonwealth with its emphasis on unity through common interest.

Assessment

Chamberlain is the greatest 'might-have-been' in modern political history. His character and career will always be something of an enigma. Despite his professional dedication, his vigour, originality and imagination, he failed to get to 'the top of the greasy pole.' He was tough and ruthless, and indeed made some mortal enemies, but then so did Gladstone, Disraeli and Lloyd George; they, however, were not stopped from achieving their ambition. According to Peter Jay, Chamberlain's career can be seen as 'a study in failure'. Many of his acclaimed successes and his ideals are now treated less sympathetically. He set out to change the structure of politics, democratise the Party, held great office, effected major legislative changes – all subsequently abandoned or brought to nothing. Salisbury dismissed him as the 'Prince of opportunists'.

The main reason for Chamberlain's lack of success is clear. He was the victim of Ireland. If he had been prepared to accept Gladstone's Home Rule Bill he could not have failed to inherit the leadership from Gladstone. However, as a staunch believer in the United Kingdom, he could not stomach the thought of Irish separation. What Ireland needed, he believed, was good government. Because of the failure of his 'unauthorised programme' of 1885 to be a vote-winner, he was unable to lead an enlarged, radical Whig group in an assault on the moderate Whig majority. The most he could do in the circumstances of 1886, therefore, was to manoeuvre as best he could. Only his exceptional energy and ability as a politician saved him from oblivion. His break with the Party, then, was due more to tactics than to idealism. Note that the majority of those who voted with him were Whigs, a group long dissatisfied with the way things were going in the Party. The Liberal revolt in 1886 was, in fact, a 'centrist' revolt similar to the earlier revolt over Irish Disestablishment. This split, however, proved permanent.

As Colonial Secretary after 1895 he again displayed remarkable ability and, when Salisbury retired in 1902, many people expected him to succeed as Prime Minister. Salisbury saw to it that he did not. His policy of tariff reform must have seriously damaged his chances with the Conservative Party and certainly split them as disastrously as Home Rule had split the Liberals in 1886. Again, was it a question of conviction or a calculated effort to oust Balfour and become Prime Minister?

It is unlikely that it will ever be possible fully to explain Chamberlain's change of allegiance, outlook and policy. It is quite probable that he could not explain it himself. Fundamentally, as Robert Blake points out, there was something about him that made others suspect and dislike him. Many found him too aggressive, too ambitious, too restless, too racist, too much 'on the make'. Lord Salisbury is supposed to have said: 'Mr Gladstone was greatly hated, but he was also greatly loved. Who loves Mr Chamberlain?' Who, indeed? Perhaps in the end that is why he failed to get to the top.

8.4 CHRONOLOGY

1836	July	Chamberlain was born in London.
1868		CHAMBERLAIN ORGANISED THE BIRMINGHAM LIBERAL ASSOCIATION; from it grew the Liberal 'caucus' which developed and extended in the years that followed.
1869	October	HE HELPED FOUND THE NATIONAL EDUCATION LEAGUE to campaign for free, national, secular education.
1870		He led the 'nonconformist revolt' against Forster's Education Act.

1873	November	Chamberlain became LORD MAYOR OF BIRMINGHAM: he introduced a policy of 'gas and water Socialism' and preached the 'civic gospel' of improvement.
1876	June	He became MP for Birmingham.
1877	May	National Liberal Federation founded by Chamberlain to control the work of local Liberal caucuses. The NLF was dedicated to radicalism and to overthrowing the power of the landed Whigs in the Liberal Party.
1880	April	Chamberlain joined Gladstone's Second Ministry as President of the Board of Trade.
1883	March	Attack by Chamberlain on Lord Salisbury 'and his class'. The CORRUPT PRACTICES ACT rigorously curtailed election expenses.
1884	December	THIRD REFORM ACT: Chamberlain was the driving force behind this law, which conceded adult manhood suffrage.
1885	June	REDISTRIBUTION ACT established single-member constituencies; when the Lords temporised, Chamberlain argued that they should be 'mended or ended'.
	September	CHAMBERLAIN LAUNCHED HIS 'UNAUTHORISED PROGRAMME': this included Church disestablishment, land and local government reform, better housing, improved social services, etc.
1886	June	CHAMBERLAIN OPPOSED GLADSTONE'S HOME RULE BILL; he resigned in March and defected with 92 other Liberals – including Lord Hartington and John Bright. This split the Liberal Party. Parnell said of him, 'there goes a man that killed Home Rule'. Liberal-Unionists then became a separate group in the Commons, giving their support to the Conservatives.
1887	April	FIRST COLONIAL CONFERENCE: economic cooperation and imperial defence were discussed.
	June	Queen's Jubilee celebrations.
1888	August	Local Government Act established 62 County Councils to discharge all local administrative duties; councillors to be elected by household suffrage.
1891	April	Education Act made elementary education free.
1894	June	SECOND COLONIAL CONFERENCE AT OTTAWA: imperial trade discussed.
1895	August	CHAMBERLAIN MADE COLONIAL SECRETARY in Salisbury's Third Ministry.
1896	December	JAMESON RAID: Chamberlain was accused of being involved but exonerated by a parliamentary Select Committee.
1897	June	THIRD COLONIAL CONFERENCE in London under Chamberlain, who put forward a policy of imperial federation.
	August	WORKMEN'S COMPENSATION ACT extended compensation to workmen but excluded agricultural labourers.
1899	October	The Boer War began.
1902	May	Peace of Vereeniging ended the Boer War.
	June	FOURTH COLONIAL CONFERENCE: imperial trade and federation were discussed.
1903	May	CHAMBERLAIN DECLARED FOR PROTECTION AND IMPERIAL PREFERENCE.
	September	Chamberlain resigned from the cabinet, founded the TARIFF REFORM LEAGUE and vigorously campaigned in favour of imperial preference. The CONSERVATIVE PARTY SPLIT on the issue.
1906	January	Conservatives routed at the general election. Chamberlain held Birmingham.
	July	Stroke ended his political career.
1914	July	Chamberlain died.

Illustrative questions and answers

1   Discuss Joseph Chamberlain's policies and achievements.

Tutorial note
An uncomplicated question. The only difficulty lies in the use of the word 'achievement' and the need to decide what aspects of his work merits that description.

You need to know about
It is essential to know the details of his work as Mayor in Birmingham and as the founder of a new form of political organisation (the National Liberal Federation). His achievement in giving Liberalism a new social content. The redefining of the importance of the Empire and also of the Colonial Office.

Suggested answer plan
1   Chamberlain was a new type of professional politician; an industrialist who challenged the leaders of the two great Parties and left his mark upon them both. It is questionable whether he had in the end the circumspection and political tact necessary for a Prime Minister or a leader of one of the great Parties.
2   He emerged as a Birmingham city councillor in 1869 and became famous outside the city council as an Education League spokesman and founder of the Birmingham Liberal Association. He became Mayor in 1873 and began by putting the 'civic gospel' of Birmingham nonconformists into practice; the era of 'gas-and-water Socialism' arrived in his two measures to take 'regulated monopolies' out of the hands of private enterprise; he had a great dream to build a rival to the Champs Elysée in Birmingham; Corporation Street, built by clearing the slum dwellings of the city centre, was the result. Birmingham city politics moved (literally) from the age of local public house meetings (the Woodman) to the city hall.
3   Chamberlain took over from the local radical, George Dixon, the leadership of the Education League, which became an engine for challenging the Gladstonian party leadership on education. The Birmingham Liberal association took advantage of the 1867 Reform Act, which enfranchised the working-class voter and ostensibly established a democratic organisation; in reality this was run by Chamberlain and his friends; it was the forerunner of the National Liberal Federation, set up in Birmingham as a means of selecting candidates and controlling MPs: this was to become the model for other Parties. Chamberlain failed to defeat Gladstone (the Party leader) in the Home Rule crisis of 1886 but the NLF remained a powerful institution.
4   Chamberlain advocated a social content to Liberalism – in particular as the voice of Birmingham nonconformity and the 'civic gospel'. His 'unauthorised programme' argued for better housing for the working-classes; the doctrine of 'ransom' (society owed compensation to the poorer classes); free schools; 'three acres and a cow'; and a graduated property tax. His abandonment of the Liberal Party left this work undone (although this was in part taken up by the Liberals' Newcastle Programme of 1891) but gave to Victorian Liberalism a new direction. Chamberlain's own achievement in this direction is (as a member of the Salisbury Conservative government) the Workmen's Compensation Act, 1897.
5   Chamberlain's imperial policies led directly not only to the South African war – hardly an achievement – but also to the Colonial Conferences (forerunners of the Commonwealth conferences) and to the doctrine of imperial preference established in 1932. His other ideas included an imperial parliament and an imperial Navy (both rejected by the colonies, which were anxious to preserve

their new-won independence) but his concept of aid to undeveloped colonies (realised with subsidies to shipping lines and for new crops) became a common coin of colonial policy.

His main achievement was to make the Colonial Office of fundamental importance in government. Chamberlain was effectively co-Prime Minister. His Tariff Reform programme split the Conservative and Liberal-Unionists (as his Irish policy had split Liberals) and his negative achievement was to make possible the Liberal landslide in 1906.

6 Chamberlain could never be regarded as negligible. He was often wrong-headed (e.g. over Ireland), but his policies were based upon considerable analysis and were expounded in great and noble speeches. His achievements as a politician, as a Midlands mayor, as a social reformer and as an imperialist are all quite remarkable set against the normal inertia of English politics.

2 Compare the imperial policies of Chamberlain and Disraeli.

Tutorial note

This calls for a straightforward comparison which requires that you also identify the major differences. Note that, because of the rise of new Powers in Europe, both men felt that Britain was vulnerable and their policies were a reaction to this fact.

You need to know about

An understanding of Disraeli's policies: his Crystal Palace speech, the Suez Canal shares, the defence of the Mediterranean (acquisition of Cyprus), his forward policy in Afghanistan and in West and South Africa; and of Chamberlain's policies: the Colonial Conferences and the imperialist concept, his 'forward policy' in Southern Africa, his concept of undevelopment, the Imperial tariff, his 'new imperialism.'

Suggested answer plan

1 Both politicians had much in common – they were 'outsiders' who dominated the Conservative Party; both were capable of advocating original ideas on policy. The imperialism of both was not restricted to Conservative Party or Liberal Imperialists of the period. Both gave a new direction to British imperialism.

2 The concept of Empire was expounded by Disraeli in his Crystal Palace speech in which he put forward a most important idea – an imperial parliament; this idea was taken up and developed by Chamberlain at the Colonial Conferences; it met resistance from dominions such as Canada, who were anxious to maintain their own independence and had no wish to become again a part of the British Empire. Chamberlain developed this concept of Empire to propose an imperial Navy and a *Zollverein*, an imperial free trade plan, neither of which aroused much enthusiasm among colonial statesmen. His Colonial Conferences did in themselves create a new informal imperial institution, which was to develop in our own day into the Commonwealth Prime Ministers' conferences.

3 Disraeli has traditionally been described as the architect of a new expansionist policy in empire-building, and as one who made a final break with the old Liberal policy of inertia. Such a view cannot be maintained. Not only did the Empire keep developing in the mid-Victorian years in the Far East but even in Africa Disraeli's transformation of the Fanti protectorate into a Crown Colony in 1874 had already been decided on by the previous Gladstone government. In Southern Africa, Disraeli supported a federation of all four states (Chamberlain's war in South Africa produced this result which Chamberlain approved of and Chamberlain's own Commonwealth of Australia Act of 1900 set up a federation of the Australian colonies).

Both Disraeli and Chamberlain fought wars in defence of African policy – Disraeli against the Zulus (and therefore to protect Boers), and Chamberlain against the Boers. Both were aware of the extent of British economic interests in the area but Chamberlain, as an ally of Rhodes, was committed to a 'forward' policy which led to the Jameson Raid and the South African war.

4   Chamberlain and Disraeli were each involved in different areas. Disraeli's spectacular purchase of the Suez Canal shares in 1875 (his comment to Victoria: 'you have it, Madam', was misleading, as his purchase was only 45%, with no voting rights) involved Britain in Egypt – leading to occupation – and to Fashoda in 1898, when Chamberlain and his French counterpart Hanotaux hovered near conflict. It was India, however, which was *the* Empire under Disraeli, (symbolised by Victoria becoming Empress of India in 1876). Chamberlain was associated with the last stages of the 'scramble for Africa', the great partition of the African continent by the European Powers; these involved ambitious schemes such as the Cape-to-Cairo railway.

5   In economic matters, Chamberlain went beyond Disraeli in seeing the mutual advantages of the Empire for trade and development: these included subsidies to shipping lines and for new crops, and to schools of tropical medicine; the importance of the gold and diamond reserves in South Africa. He was very conscious of the decline in Midlands industries and, when *Zollverein* became a non-starter, he modified the policy into one for an imperial tariff as a means of furthering British economic interests. Chamberlain was working within a new imperialist mood and his thinking was symbolised by Birmingham's recommendations to the Royal Commission on the Depression of Trade and Industry, 1885–6, i.e. tariffs and the development of colonial markets.

6   Both Chamberlain and Disraeli show similarities in institutional thinking but Chamberlain, coming at a later stage in the development of the imperial mood and the decline of British industries, pushed imperial policies towards the revival of an eighteenth-century type of Empire. He urged, however, that they should run it more in the common interest of all the partners than had been the case with the pre-1776 Empire.

Disraeli sketched out the ideas for change; Chamberlain tried to put them into practice. Disraeli developed imperial forward policies within the newly evolving orthodoxy. Chamberlain pushed beyond, in the headiness of his vision and the weight of his armies. In South Africa this aroused for Britain the kind of hostility in Europe that American policies were to do in Vietnam in a later age. In short, an informal empire was replaced by a formal Empire.

3   To what extent was the 'New Imperialism' of the later nineteenth century a product of economic and social factors?

Tutorial note

This question calls for an understanding of the various explanations of imperialism and asks the student to relate the theories and Britain's economic situation to the policies followed by Chamberlain (and to some extent by his predecessors). The words 'To what extent' urge some consideration of the political and diplomatic content of the new imperialism.

You need to know about

An understanding of Hobson's theory of imperialism, first published in 1902 (*Imperialism, a study*) which attempted to relate the new expansionist policies to the social and economic situation. The Great Depression and the rise of the 'Fair Trade' movement; the Royal Commission on Depression and the Birmingham arguments; the rapid industrialisation of Germany and the USA. Chamberlain's imperial policies and their purpose; and of the European political background, i.e. the threats posed by Russia to the route to India, and by France and Germany in Africa.

Suggested answer plan

1   According to Robinson and Gallagher (*Africa and the Victorians*) the scramble for Africa was initiated by Britain's invasion of Egypt in 1885; and her

withdrawal from a steadily weakening Turkey to an Eastern Mediterranean base in Cairo, from which she could protect the route to India. From thence she was drawn reluctantly into central and southern Africa and, feeling isolated and vulnerable in Europe, bargained away potential interest in many parts of the new continent to placate her European adversaries. Chamberlain, however, reversed this defensive approach and, in the 'nineties, was determined to consolidate British gains.

2   A change of mood from the mid-1880s onwards. There was the growth of a sense of imperial mission to carry civilisation to underdeveloped parts of the world, and to end slavery, the slave trade and other barbarous practices in Africa. This was paralleled by a sense that the existing Empire was not fully deployed to maintain living standards in England; that the problems of competition could perhaps be solved by protectionism (practised by most other countries). Do these factors explain the new imperialism?

Contemporaries talked of a need to make full use of the Empire to offset adverse trade conditions. Hobson, writing in 1902, advanced the view (a) that imperialism was partly a response to the existence of surplus capital – i.e. when capital cannot profitably be invested in England, it will be invested abroad, (b) that the existence of this surplus capital was due to underconsumption, (c) that this state was produced by low wages, and (d) that imperialism was therefore of benefit only to capitalists and capitalism, and not the nation as a whole. These conditions in later nineteenth century England – declining industry, the reappearance of the cycle of depressions and underconsumption – were a cause for concern. Rowntree's survey revealed that an estimated 25% of the population were below the level of subsistence. Chamberlain, looking at the economic and social situation, argued, however, that imperialism could benefit the working classes by providing new markets for British products.

3   Even before Chamberlain, the informal empire was giving way to the formal Empire; there was more talk of 'trade following the flag' as mapped out by explorers and missionaries in central, East and West Africa – e.g. the arguments for making Zanzibar a protectorate turned upon an analysis of trade. Chamberlain was to give the whole process a new drive and form: in particular, Rhodes's development of Rhodesia and Chamberlain's involvement in forward policies in Southern Africa, and the invasion and conquest of the Ashanti kingdom on the Gold Coast in 1895. But was Africa, potentially, a good market for British goods?

4   The new imperialism: Chamberlain's concept of a *Zollverein* – a free-trade Empire, protected against foreign competition – makes clear the general economic context of his imperialism. Its development-tariff reform, the argument about employment produced by tariff reform, a higher standard of living and an end to declining trades such as sugar-refining, iron and cotton. As early as 1895, Chamberlain had called on all colonial governors to buy British. Equally, his approach to the South African problem was largely concerned to make the Transvaal safe for British investors. However, if there had been no Rand gold, could Britain have afforded to ignore the scramble?

5   Britain was feeling isolated and vulnerable in the last quarter of the nineteenth century. Her economy was declining from the heights of mid-Victorian prosperity; her politicians (and businessmen in government) were forced to develop new policies to meet new times. Her imperialism was a complex affair which included (as A P Thornton shows) strands of Socialism, humanitarianism and Christian evangelicalism, but was also rooted deep in the new economic situation of the United Kingdom. Hobson and Chamberlain represent two different economic approaches to the same phenomenon: one, a theory to explain it; the other, practical measures, to a large extent determined by economic forces, to root out the problem.

Question bank

1 Document question (Chamberlain's imperial dream): study the extract below and then answer questions (a) to (g) which follow:

Extract

> 'My... proposition is that a <u>true Zollverein</u> for the Empire, that a free trade established throughout the Empire, although it would involve the imposition of duties against foreign countries, and would be in that respect a derogation from the high principles of free trade, and from the practice of the United Kingdom up to the present time, would still be a proper subject for discussion and might possibly lead to a satisfactory arrangement if the colonies on their part were <u>willing to consider it</u>...it would undoubtedly lead to the earliest possible development of <u>their great natural resources</u>, would bring them population, would open to them the enormous markets of the United Kingdom... .'

(a) What did Chamberlain mean by a 'true Zollverein'? (3)
(b) What practical steps had Chamberlain already taken to develop the 'great natural resources' of some of the colonies? (3)
(c) Did Chamberlain's imperial dream as reflected in this passage rest squarely on the economic needs of the Midlands? (4)
(d) What measures did Chamberlain put to the Colonial Conference of 1902 to further his imperial policy? (4)
(e) Were the colonies, for their part, 'willing to consider it'? (4)
(f) What effect did Chamberlain's imperialism have on his subsequent career? (6)
(g) ...and upon the Conservative and Unionist Party? (6)

2 'Both constructive and destructive.' Discuss this view of Joseph Chamberlain's impact on the Liberal and Conservative parties.
(Cambridge, November 1990)

3 What light does the career of Joseph Chamberlain throw upon the development of British politics between 1880 and 1906?
(Oxford and Cambridge, June 1990)

4 'Chamberlain promised much but achieved little.' Comment on this view of his political career up to 1895. (JMB, June 1990)

5 How far did British imperial expansion 1871–1902 represent 'a struggle for profitable markets of investment'? (AEB, June 1989)

READING LIST

Standard textbook reading
R. Shannon, *The Crisis of Imperialism* (Paladin, 1976), *passim*.
R. K. Webb, *Modern England* (Allen and Unwin, 1980 edn.), chapters 8, 10.
A. Wood, *Nineteenth-Century Britain* (Longman, 1960), chapters 15, 17, 19, 20.

Further suggested reading
M. Bentley, *The Climax of Liberal Politics 1868–1918* (Arnold, 1987).
H. Browne, *Joseph Chamberlain: Radical and Imperialist* (Longman, 1974).

M. E. Chamberlain, *The New Imperialism* (Historical Association, 1970).
R. Jay, *Joseph Chamberlain: a Political Study* (OUP, 1981).
A. Jones, *The Politics of Reform, 1884* (CUP, 1972).
D. Judd, *Radical Joe* (Hamish Hamilton, 1977).
W. R. Louis (ed.), *Imperialism: The Robinson and Gallagher Controversy* (New Viewpoints, 1976).
R. Robinson and J. Gallagher, *Africa and the Victorians* (Macmillan, 1961).

GLADSTONE AND IRELAND

Units in this chapter

9.1 *Irish nationalism*
9.2 *Major issues*
9.3 *Gladstone's measures*
9.4 *The Home Rule Bill, 1886*
9.5 *Chronology*

Chapter objectives

❶ The Irish problem: the importance of the Act of Union; the abject standard of existence for the mass of the people; underdevelopment, complications of tenure and landholding; high rents, evictions and outrages; rule by a small, largely absentee, Anglo-Irish Protestant landlord class; English ignorance of conditions in Ireland combined with religious and national prejudice; the fear that 'Home Rule would mean Rome Rule'.

❷ Rise of nationalism in Ireland; the impact of Young Ireland; the Famine; the Fenians; Fenian links with America; the rising in 1867; the outrages in England, in Manchester and Clerkenwell emphasised the immediacy of the problem to English politicians and people. The Irish problem was a combination of economic, religious and nationalist factors.

❸ Gladstone's liberalism and sense of justice encouraged him to take up the Irish problem: the pacification measures of his first ministry 1868–74; the effect of the Ballot Act on the Irish Parliamentary Party, the emergence of Parnell, and the policy of obstruction – 'stepping on English toes'.

❹ The agricultural depression of the late 'seventies; evictions, outrages, coercion; Davitt and the Land League, Devoy and the Clan na Gael in America; policy of the New Departure. Gladstone concedes the 1881 Land Act; the problem of rent arrears; the Kilmainham Treaty emphasised Parnell's acceptance of constitutionalism; Parnell's tactics; the Phoenix Park murders destroy the possibility of further progress; Parnell's liaison with Kitty O'Shea; pacification removed grievances but the Irish then demanded Home Rule. The Phoenix Park murders, however, convinced the English that the Irish were not ready for self-government.

❺ Parnell and the Irish National League; Davitt abandoned; new goal to be Home Rule won from Liberals or Conservatives; the effect of the third Reform Act on the IPP; Parnell's negotiations with the Conservatives in 1885, denounced by Chamberlain as 'flagrant political dishonesty'; the Conservatives drop Parnell after an inconclusive election result and the 'Hawarden Kite'.

⑥ Gladstone's conversion to Home Rule; the consequences of his tactical secrecy; resignation of Whigs and Radicals – Hartington, Bright, Chamberlain. The Home Rule Bill introduced – limited measure with no Irish MPs at Westminster – provoked violent reaction; Churchill's 'concern' for Ulster ('Ulster will fight and Ulster will be right'), Chamberlain's for Empire; Liberal Party split, Bill rejected. Home Rule henceforth a party political question. The Irish Party was now dependent on the Liberals.

⑦ Parnell and the *Times*; the divorce scandal breaks but Parnell was re-elected as leader by the IPP; Gladstone's letter made it clear that it had to be Parnell or Home Rule; IPP rejected Parnell but, aided by some followers, he campaigned against the decision; he married Kitty O'Shea but died shortly afterwards (October 1891). Although he had set the Home Rule argument on its legs and made it the major issue in British politics, yet effectively it seemed to die with him.

⑧ Gladstone's final effort; the second Home Rule Bill, 1893, (providing for Irish MPs to remain at Westminster) was passed by House of Commons but rejected by the House of Lords by the largest majority recorded. Home Rule was Gladstone's unhelpful legacy to a divided Liberal Party.

⑨ Gladstone had progressed from coercion and conciliation to Home Rule; he was convinced that Irish nationalism was not a transitory objective but an inextinguishable passion; Britain's safety and natural justice demanded that the problem be solved. According to Hammond, 'he had spent on Ireland strength, health, power and popularity, as no politician had ever done'; his struggle for Home Rule was a gallant attempt but a noble failure.

As Professor Mansergh rightly observes, 'the condition of Ireland in the middle years of the nineteenth century, or at least all of it outside Ulster, dismayed and distressed those who saw it – from Italian nationalists to Communist internationalists, to Frenchmen, Germans, Americans and by no means least, to Englishmen, whether economists, officials or more ordinary voyagers'. English rule in Ireland, whether of coercion or conciliation, had been a failure – illustrated above all in Irish eyes by its unsympathetic response to the tragedy of the famine.

Some Englishmen, like John Bright, sought to right Ireland's wrongs but most politicians, like Disraeli, saw Ireland as a problem best avoided or ignored. Gladstone, imbued with a strong moral as well as European sense, proved the exception. He sought to remove Irish grievances primarily to pacify the Irish but also so that Englishmen might be able to look their fellow Europeans in the face.

According to Dr Hammond, Gladstone alone had the breadth of vision and ability 'to change the English temper towards Ireland, to shake fundamental views of property and economics, to overcome all the prejudices that estrange men divided by race, religion and history….' Despite Gladstone's efforts, Home Rule proved unacceptable to the majority of the English people. English politicians failed to offer an alternative solution and the fall of Parnell convinced many Irishmen that the opportunity for a constitutional solution had gone for ever.

9.1 IRISH NATIONALISM

The belief in Irish separatism and Irish nationalism developed throughout the nineteenth century. O'Connell began the process in 1829 with his success in organising peasant Ireland to achieve Catholic emancipation. The literary men of Young Ireland continued it in the 1840s. Yet, although the leaders of this movement made a cultural impact, politically they proved ineffective.

Despite their propagation of the romantic glories of ancient, Gaelic Ireland, for most Irish the famine of 1845–49 was the reality. One million died; another million emigrated. The famine became a dividing line in Irish history – above all in the attitude to England that it engendered in the mass of the people of Ireland and their kin in America. Irish policy was henceforth to be one of attack; and in the 'sixties the Fenians, spurred on by US money, opened a new chapter of violence in Ireland and England.

Gladstone's concern

Gladstone fought the general election of 1868 on the Irish issue. Although it was his interest in Italy that aroused his sympathy for Ireland, Gladstone first became aware of the gravity of Irish affairs in 1845, when, in a letter to his wife, he described Ireland as 'that cloud in the West, that coming storm.'

The famine, Fenianism and continued disorder convinced him that a solution to the Irish question was the greatest problem facing the next administration. When he was told in 1868 that he was to become Prime Minister for the first time, he declared, 'My mission is to pacify Ireland.'

Clearly, Ireland was in a distracted state. Reforms were long overdue; but most Englishmen contended that the problem was incapable of solution. We can now see that the root of the problem was nationality.

Ireland wished to be free, but England could not allow freedom to a country strategically vital to her own security. Furthermore, by the Act of Union, England was committed to safeguarding the privileges of the Protestant ascendancy in Ireland. Thus, a passionate and growing Irish nationalism was baulked by an equally determined English imperialism.

9.2 MAJOR ISSUES

The Irish question in the nineteenth century revolved around three issues:
❶ The political and constitutional relations between the two countries.
❷ The existence in Ireland of an established Anglican (Protestant) Church. This represented only a tenth of the population but sought to claim goodwill and tithes from the overwhelming Catholic majority.
❸ Almost all the land of Ireland (gradually confiscated since the sixteenth century) was owned by Anglo-Irish Protestant landlords. They introduced a system of landholding alien to the Celtic Irish. Furthermore, they were often absentees whose sole interest in their estates appeared to be to maximise their income from rents. Peasant resistance led to eviction, violence, disorder and the introduction of innumerable Coercion Acts by an English government determined to maintain law and order. The resultant conflict between landlord and peasant was eventually translated by nationalists into a conflict between England and Ireland. Nationalist policy oscillated between constitutional demands for some form of Home Rule and revolutionary activities for separation.

Attitudes

The origin of the conflict was English rule in Ireland in accordance with English ideas. Her attitude to Ireland was blinded by her own agricultural and industrial progress. Ireland was blamed for her economic backwardness whereas, in fact, it was the economic backwardness of English government in Ireland that was at fault. Irish nationalists felt that the English government was ignorant of Irish conditions and contemptuous of her legitimate aspirations. They did not accept that England had an Irish problem – rather that Ireland had an English problem. In vain, therefore, did the English government seek to conciliate, civilise or coerce the Irish.

By the 1870s all had been tried and found wanting. Initially it was Gladstone's commitment to Italian freedom from Austria that made him consider the Irish question, but it was also an essential part of his belief in liberalism, which, as it matured, convinced him that Home Rule was the only just and honourable solution. But how would this decision be received at Westminster? How far did Ireland really matter to English politicians?

9.3 GLADSTONE'S MEASURES

At first, Gladstone felt that the desire for separation was merely symptomatic. He recognised that Ireland had two outstanding and genuine grievances – religious and agrarian – and believed that if he could solve these, the Irish would stop agitating for repeal of the Union. Fenian outrages in Ireland and England prepared parliament, during his first ministry, for his policy of pacification.

In 1869, despite much opposition, he disestablished the Anglican Church of Ireland and put it on the same footing as the dissenting and Catholic churches in Ireland. Disraeli argued that this weakened the Protestant supremacy, threatened the union of church and state and undermined the rights of property. Although disestablishment pleased the Irish Catholic bishops it did little to pacify the rest of the population in Ireland.

In 1870 Gladstone passed his first Irish Land Act. This gave some protection to tenants and began (with the Bright clause) the process of land transference which, by 1914, had solved the land question. You should know the main provisions of the Land Act and be able to explain why it proved ineffective. It did, however, manage to frighten the English landowning class who, in an age of laissez-faire, regarded property rights as sacrosanct and feared that Gladstone's Irish reforms might 'cross the water.'

In 1870 also Isaac Butt founded the Home Government Association which proposed a federal solution to the Irish problem. At the time, this seemed a fantastic proposal – Gladstone himself denouncing the idea as absurd. Instead, Gladstone proposed his third measure to pacify Ireland – the Irish University Reform Bill – a complicated attempt to set up a non-denominational state university system in Ireland. The Bill was defeated. Gladstone dissolved Parliament but lost the general election that followed.

The agricultural depression

Three events of major importance occurred in Ireland while Gladstone was out of office. The first was the onset of economic depression (primarily owing to American competition) which had disastrous results on Irish agriculture. For the first time since the famine, there was starvation in some Western counties. Thousands were evicted for non-payment of rent; inevitably there were outrages – 2,600 in 1880 alone.

Meanwhile, Michael Davitt had founded the Land League to prevent evictions and boycott those who dared take over vacant tenancies. This was a truly original development in that it organised for the first time a secular mass movement to challenge landlordism in Ireland. Fuelled by newspaper propaganda and radical ideas, and aided by American dollars, it proved a remarkably successful pressure group. By 1881 it had landlordism in retreat.

The emergence of Parnell

The second event was the emergence of Charles Stewart Parnell, a Protestant landowner and MP for Wexford – under whose leadership Irish power was deployed in the House of Commons as never before. Parnell was an unlikely leader of Catholic nationalist opinion in Ireland. He knew little of Irish history, lacked a political philosophy and his political instincts were conservative. Yet his ability for political organisation and shrewd use of parliamentary tactics quickly enabled him to wrest power from the kindly but inefficient Butt.

Parnell realised that the key to Ireland's future lay at Westminster. A disciplined and united Irish Party in the House of Commons might come to hold the balance of power and thereby wring concessions from one of the two English Parties as the price of its support. By using obstructionist tactics he had, by 1880, made his presence felt in the House of Commons. He convinced Gladstone that Ireland needed reforming and eventually that she needed liberty. It was one of the great political performances of the nineteenth century.

The New Departure

The third event was the 'New Departure'. This was fashioned by Michael Davitt, who persuaded John Devoy, the leader of the Irish-American Fenians, to throw the full support of Irish Fenianism behind the Land League. The next step was to convince Parnell that the Land League could be 'the engine that would drag the Home Rule movement in its train.'

Though Parnell rejected the violence of the Fenians (even though he exploited their emotional appeal), and also Davitt's policy of social revolution through land nationalisation, he realised the enormous popular support that the land question was capable of generating. He therefore became President of the League in 1879. His involvement in the movement was purely tactical, but it made him more powerful in the House of Commons, lending him some of the magic of extremism.

According to MacDonagh, the New Departure allowed the three great forces of Irish nationalism to be brought together for the first time – the revolutionary, the civil and the parliamentary. Their masterful deployment by Parnell in parliament presented the strongest threat to date to English government in Ireland.

The Irish Land Act, 1881

The New Departure was a clever and highly efficient instrument of agrarian agitation. Circumstances, however, militated against its success. The severity of the economic depression prevented any quick solution to the land question; and the 'racist' opposition of Chamberlain and the Unionists, coupled with the sectarian bitterness

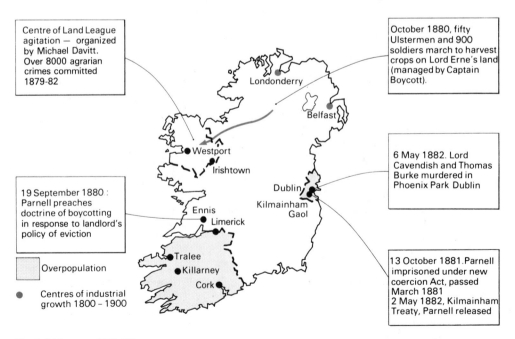

Fig. 9 Irish unrest 1879–82

of Ulster Protestants, made a reasoned political solution unlikely. Against this unpromising background, Gladstone strove to find a constitutional solution short of separation.

In 1881 he passed a second Land Act which conceded the '3Fs' – fair rents, fixity of tenure and free sale. It was a generous Act which, in the long run, made stable tenant farming possible in Ireland. But its timing was wrong. It did nothing for the enormous and increasing burden of rent arrears and it was accompanied by a Coercion Act. Parnell, therefore, publicly denounced it, while privately he encouraged Irish tenants to test it in the courts. The English ruling class viewed the Act with apprehension. It marked a sharp break with laissez-faire and threatened to undermine one of the most basic of Victorian beliefs – the sanctity of private property.

In the short run, the repressive Coercion Act created a vicious circle of popular unrest, evictions, boycotts and violence, which in turn led to more stringent measures. Check carefully the details of the Kilmainham Treaty of 1882, which resolved this phase of the struggle. You should also assess the significance of the Phoenix Park murders that followed.

Note that Parnell considered that the land question had been settled. He severed his connections with Fenianism and replaced the banned Land League with the National League, now avowedly dedicated to securing Home Rule.

9.4 THE HOME RULE BILL, 1886

By 1885 Gladstone had come to accept that the Irish problem was basically a question of nationality. The election of the same year gave Parnell 86 seats, the overwhelming majority of Irish seats in the Commons. Gladstone was convinced that Ireland had spoken. He determined, therefore, on a Home Rule Bill, but because Parnell was currently negotiating with the Conservatives, he kept his decision secret. When his son Herbert divulged it, most Conservatives and some Liberals – especially Chamberlain – were outraged.

A dispassionate and objective approach to the problem was now out of the question. Randolph Churchill decided that 'the Orange card was the card to play.' Against a background of religious prejudice and political partisanship, Chamberlain, who was prepared to offer local, but not self-government to Ireland, attacked the Bill on three grounds: (a) Ulster's rights, (b) the dismemberment of the Empire and (c) his belief in the inability of the Irish to rule themselves. The Party split, the Bill was defeated and, in an era of growing imperialist feeling, Gladstone's appeal to the electorate was rejected. Henceforth, Irish MPs always cast their vote for the Liberals, and Home Rule now became a Party issue. This was a tragic development.

Thus, in 1886 a great opportunity for solving the Irish Question was lost. A modified Home Rule Bill passed the Commons in 1893, only to be rejected by the House of Lords. The matter was then shelved by the Liberals until the constitutional crisis of 1909–11 brought it to the forefront of politics once more.

Motives

During the last fifteen years, interpretations of the 1886 crisis have been much influenced by Cooke and Vincent's argument in *The Governing Passion* (1974) that it was neither the moral nor ideological crisis that Gladstone claimed. It was, they argue, purely a tactical battle in the power struggle at Westminster, where Gladstone and Salisbury strove to keep control of their respective parties in the face of potential threats from the mavericks, Chamberlain and Churchill. They may have overstated the case, but there is no doubt that there were many other reasons besides Home Rule for party divisions in that year.

It would appear that Gladstone knew precisely what he was doing when he declared for Home Rule in 1886. It was a carefully calculated and a righteous decision. Having tried coercion and conciliation without success, he felt that *limited* separation was now the only alternative. He was also aware of the feeling that England had much to gain and nothing to lose by devolution. He knew that some Whigs and Radicals in the Party would reject this solution, and there is little doubt that his tactical handling of these groups can be faulted. However, like his political master Peel, he was determined to follow a policy which he regarded as just and righteous, regardless of Party feelings.

Aware that in the 'seventies and 'eighties sectionalism had been a major weakness of the Party, Gladstone hoped that Home Rule might provide an issue around which the majority of Liberals could now unite. Chamberlain, though, knowing that the election of 1885 had shown that the Liberals could no longer rely on the urban working-class vote, sought to rally the Liberals around the more relevant issue of social reform.

Gladstone's Peelite outlook would not allow him to countenance such a programme. His belief that the Party could be reconstructed around the single issue of Home Rule was finally dashed in 1893. His legacy to the Party on his retirement, therefore, was not unity but personal rivalry, divisions over policy and a further decade in opposition. Gladstone may have miscalculated about the future of Liberalism. In terms of electoral appeal, the Party probably needed Home Rule *and* social reform.

Parnell's achievements

Meanwhile, for all his apparent success as leader of the Irish Party in the Commons, Parnell was eventually caught in a web of his own making. By uniting the main strands of Irish agitation, he had fashioned a powerful weapon for political action. But in the end extremism, which he rejected, triumphed. He was neither a separatist nor a revolutionary, as he demonstrated in his discarding of both the Land League and the Fenians as soon as he was safely able to do so.

By establishing a disciplined Party tightly bound to the policy of Home Rule, however, he created a series of situations in the Commons in which he appeared to be indispensable. The policy of the New Departure, coupled with his shrewd tactical use of power, allowed him to treat with English politicians on an equal footing and brought him tantalisingly close to his ultimate goal of Home Rule.

Despite the drama and intrigue of his final years, and the suddenness of his fall, his career was not without achievements. He changed the Anglo-Irish balance of power and substantially modified English imperial attitudes to Ireland. Gladstone's Land Acts brought tangible gains in terms of tenant right and land purchase schemes, policies which the Conservative Party under Salisbury continued. After 1886 the Liberals pledged themselves to Home Rule. The discipline and effectiveness of the Irish Parliamentary Party showed that, despite Chamberlain's misgivings, the Irish were capable of self-government.

Parnell's failure

According to Professor Lyons, Parnell was, in the end, largely responsible for his own downfall. His methods and speeches made him many enemies, not least among the ordinary English electors whose feelings he disregarded. He knew what the consequences of his clandestine relationship with Katherine O'Shea would be and, when the divorce scandal made it public, he refused to withdraw from the Party under sympathetic terms. He now appeared to be putting his own career before Home Rule (the Liberal Party – largely Nonconformist – having made it clear that they would not work with him). Despite his achievements, it was too high a price to pay for his leadership. His insistence on total Party subservience finally split the Party itself. The Catholic Church then decided against him and his influence steadily slipped away. Determined, and with a certain tragic desperation, he fought against the decision of the Party. Though unwell, he contested a series of by-elections in Ireland, contracted pneumonia and died in October 1891.

Assessment

Unquestionably, Parnell was the greatest Irish leader since O'Connell and he exercised in the House of Commons a far greater authority than O'Connell ever had. Yet in the end he failed. To some extent, the failure lay in himself. With typical Parnellite obstinacy, he had insisted throughout those final months that he alone was right and incurred martyrdom to prove it.

9.5 CHRONOLOGY

1867	March	Fenian Rising in Ireland. Fenian outrages in England – Manchester and at Clerkenwell Prison, London.
1868	December	Gladstone's first administration.
1869	July	DISESTABLISHMENT OF THE IRISH CHURCH. Broke the connection between Church and State Irish Church also partially disendowed, nearly half its income being allotted to relief. The Bill met strong opposition in the Lords – partly overcome through the intervention of the Queen, who counselled moderation.
1870	March	FIRST IRISH LAND ACT. Gave the force of law to tenant-right, provided compensation for unjust disturbance and improvements, and under 'the Bright clause' sought to facilitate land purchase by the tenant. Coercion Act to control crime and agrarian disturbances.
	May	HOME GOVERNMENT ASSOCIATION founded by Isaac Butt in Dublin. The Irish University Reform Bill was defeated by three votes. Parliament was dissolved.
1874	February	Home Rule League won 59 seats in the Commons.
1877	July	Policy of obstruction began. IRISH AGRICULTURAL DEPRESSION deepened as prices for farm produce continued to fall.
1879	October	IRISH LAND LEAGUE founded by Michael Davitt. Parnell became President. THE NEW DEPARTURE; joint programme of action agreed by Davitt, Devoy and Parnell.
1880	April	Gladstone's second administration.
	September	Parnell preached the doctrine of 'boycotting' at Ennis, Co. Clare.
	October	Fifty Ulstermen, protected by 900 soldiers, march to Lord Erne's lands in Co, Mayo (managed by Captain Boycott) to harvest his crops. Parnell met and fell in love with Mrs Katherine O'Shea, sister of General Wood, VC, and niece of Lord Chancellor Hatherley.
1881	February	Irish obstruction lasted 41 hours. The 'closure' motion introduced.
	March	Coercion Act. Imprisonment without trial for those suspected of agrarian outrages.
	August	SECOND IRISH LAND ACT conceded the 'three Fs': fair rents, fixity of tenure and free sale. Ignored the problem of rent arrears.
	October	Parnell and other Nationalist leaders imprisoned in Kilmainham Gaol. Land League proclaimed illegal.
1882	April	KILMAINHAM TREATY. Government agreed to pay rent arrears – Parnell to dampen agrarian violence.
	May	PHOENIX PARK MURDERS. Lord Cavendish, younger brother of Lord Hartington and Burke, Irish Under-Secretary were stabbed to death in Phoenix Park, Dublin by a gang of assassins called 'the Invincibles'. All were eventually captured and five were hanged. Crimes Act introduced.
	October	National League founded by Parnell to replace the banned Land League.
1885	June	Salisbury's first administration.

	August	Ashbourne Act extended the state-assisted scheme of land purchase. The Coercion Acts withdrawn by the government.
		Parnell entered negotiations with the Conservatives – hoped for some form of devolved government for Ireland.
		'CENTRAL BOARD SCHEME': Local, but not self, government advocated by Chamberlain for Ireland. Gladstone was converted to Home Rule but he kept the decision secret.
	November	Encouraged by the government's attitude, Parnell told the Irish in England to vote Conservative. Conceded 30 seats to the Conservatives at the election. Result of election: Liberals 335, Conservatives 249, Irish Party 86.
	December	Herbert Gladstone revealed his father's conversion to Home Rule before Parliament met. Conservatives now decided to abandon Parnell.
1886	January	Conservatives were defeated on the Royal Address – the famous 'three acres and a cow' amendment moved by Jesse Collings.
	February	Gladstone's third administration. Hartington and others refused to serve; Chamberlain and Trevelyan resigned from the cabinet on the Home Rule proposal.
	April	FIRST HOME RULE BILL introduced by Gladstone. Established an Irish parliament in Dublin to deal with all Irish affairs except reserved subjects such as peace and war, defence, foreign affairs, customs and excise. Irish MPs no longer to be present at Westminster.
	June	HOME RULE BILL DEFEAT: 343 votes to 313. 93 Liberals vote against.
	August	Salisbury's second administration.
	October	'PLAN OF CAMPAIGN': Irish tenants to offer what they considered to be fair rents which, if refused, were to be put in a 'war chest' to fight evictions and aid its victims.
	December	'Plan of Campaign' declared illegal. Balfour takes stringent measures to restore law and order.
1887	April	'PARNELLISM AND CRIME': a series of articles in the *Times* alleging that Parnell approved of the Phoenix Park murders. A Special Commission of three judges was appointed to examine the charges.
1889	February	Richard Pigott admitted that letters alleging Parnell's involvement were forged; he fled the country.
1890	November	Captain O'Shea granted a *decree nisi*, with Parnell cited as the co-respondent.
		Gladstone, owing to strong pressure from Liberal nonconformists, decided that he could no longer cooperate with Parnell.
	December	SPLIT IN THE IRISH PARLIAMENTARY PARTY; the majority accept the leadership of Justin McCarthy.
1891	June	Parnell married Katherine O'Shea.
	October	Parnell died, aged 45.
		Land Purchase Act introduced by Balfour: widened the scope of the Ashbourne Act. The state advanced to purchasers of land the total price – to be repaid in 49 years.
	December	Congested Districts Board set up in the western counties to encourage investment and employment in these overpopulated areas.
1892	August	Gladstone's fourth administration.
1893	February	SECOND HOME RULE BILL: made provision for the presence of Irish MPs at Westminster. Involved 85 sittings of the House. Passed the Commons with a majority of 34.
	September	Lords reject the Home Rule Bill by 419 votes to 41.
1894	March	Gladstone resigned from the Liberal Party.

Illustrative questions and answers

1 Why did Ireland need pacifying in 1868?

Tutorial note

The question is a reference to Gladstone's famous comment in 1868: 'My mission is to pacify Ireland' and is asking what grievances Ireland had which required redress and also if there was any additional bitterness and urgency given to those grievances by recent events.

You need to know about

An understanding of the Act of Union, 1800. The position of the Catholic Church in Ireland. The effect of the Famine and emigration on Irish landholding and social structure. The nature of English government in Ireland. Fenianism in 1867.

Suggested answer plan

1 British statesmen were well aware of Irish problems: these were summed up by Disraeli as 'a starving population, an absentee aristocracy and an alien church, and in addition the weakest executive in the world'. The extent of Irish bitterness was revealed by the Fenian outbreaks of 1867. In the election campaign it was clear to Gladstone, and to England, the minimum needed to pacify Ireland. Note, however, that Gladstone ignored Fenian demands for total separation.

2 The alien church: the Church of Ireland was guaranteed by the Act of Union, representing pockets of Protestantism around the great houses, around Dublin and in Ulster; the mass of the population was Catholic, owing allegiance to the Catholic hierarchy but with education, particularly higher education, firmly under Protestant control. Initiative begun by the 1829 Catholic Relief Bill not followed up; the Catholic Church was a bastion of Irish nationalism, giving special urgency to the need for disestablishment.

3 Absentee aristocracy: the land settlement dates back to 17th century, particularly to post-1688; fundamentally it was a transfer of most of Ireland's land to the English and Dutch conquerors; it created the Protestant ascendancy, akin to the Norman aristocracy in England after 1066. Social centre and political centre: London and the shires; usually land holdings in both countries. Pockets of aristocratic society were Protestant, with a lifestyle similar to that of the English aristocracy, surrounded by oppressed and resentful Irish Catholic tenantry; the situation was worsened by famine, emigration and the consolidation of landholdings, with depopulation of parts of the western counties and a standard of living very near absolute destitution.

4 Weak executive: the union with England had not been a true union between two countries; Dublin Castle basically was still an outpost of colonial government, with an inefficient aristocratic court. Bills passed through parliament at Westminster were not automatically law in Ireland (e.g. the Poor Law Amendment Act, 1834). This could occasionally be beneficial, e.g. the setting up of the National Board of Education in 1831 in Ireland, not in England. Fundamentally, however, instrument of anglicisation; it was double-edged in that Celtic nationalism was later to reject the whole process. The analogy was with English practice in India: the argument advanced by Irish constitutional nationalists like O'Connell was that Ireland was a colonial appendage justified by the separation of control.

5 Fenianism: Fenians were revolutionary nationalists strongly supported by their kin in America. The rising in March, 1867 was followed by widespread arrests (but no death sentences were carried out); the rescue attempt in Manchester (September): the three Manchester Martyrs; the explosion at Clerkenwell prison in December 1867; this brought the Irish question into the heart of England; the problem now had to be faced. This could lead either to tougher measures or, as in the case of Gladstone, to a search for improvements.

6 Conclusion: New dimension to Irish problem in 1868; American support from Irish-Americans; revival of 1798 tradition of revolutionary nationalism. What was needed were policies which would reduce the legacy of bitterness and the sense of calculated neglect (particularly strong as a result of England's attitude to Irish poverty and her policy towards Ireland in the famine years). The grievances were widely known and acknowledged: Gladstone believed that Ireland had just grievances and that prompt action on these would undermine Fenianism and preserve the Union. Hence his attempt to bring in the healing balm of his Irish policies.

2 'In Irish affairs, Gladstone always did too little, too late'. Discuss.

Tutorial note

A straightforward question asking for an assessment of Gladstone's policy in Ireland, relating his policy to Ireland's needs. Was this policy ungenerous, grudgingly conceded and tardily implemented?

You need to know about

The Act of Union, 1800. Gladstone's disestablishment of the Irish Church, 1869; the Land Act, 1870; the Land Act, 1881; the Kilmainham Treaty, 1882. The treatment of Parnell, 1885; the Home Rule Bill, 1886; the Home Rule Bill, 1893.

Suggested answer plan

1 'Too little, too late' is a comment often made on England's Irish policy as a whole. In general, this is apt and true but when applied to Gladstone's Irish policy it breaks down as an overall generalisation. Gladstone came late to Irish affairs but in the next 25 years he addressed himself to all the main aspects of the Irish problem, with effect and dispatch in some areas and disaster and delay in others.

2 Disestablishment: the Act of Union had guaranteed the Protestant ascendancy in the Church, in property and in the state. Gladstone set about each of these problems in turn. The position of the Church was eroded by the Catholic Emancipation Act; English nonconformists through the British Liberation Society pushing for general disestablishment, as was the Irish Catholic hierarchy. Gladstone made this his first task; he vigorously piloted the Bill through parliament; severed the link between the Irish Church and the state; sought justice for Irish Catholics and a fair settlement for Irish Protestants. This measure was in no sense too little and could be regarded as too late only if the whole span of nineteenth-century policy in Ireland is included. Certainly not late in Gladstone's achievements.

3 Agrarian reform: England's great achievement in Ireland was to carry out a profound revision of the structure of landed property without revolution. Completed by the Conservatives in Wyndham's Act (1903), it was Gladstone's pioneering work which set the policy in motion. The basis of the Protestant ascendancy in land goes back to the seventeenth century and essentially created an occupying power throughout the land, acting through the normal means of civil government. To tamper with this was to undermine the English position in Ireland. Certainly the 1870 Act was too little – clauses were evaded and tenants were still evicted for the non-payment of rent – but it was a further example of the sense of urgency which Gladstone brought to Irish affairs; it was revolutionary in its implications. The 1881 Bill established the novel principle of co-partnership in the soil between landlord and tenant.

4 Gladstone and Parnell. The wisdom of the Kilmainham Treaty; which gained Irish, Liberal support; the Irish worked within the constitution until 1916; Gladstone failed to give Parnell a firm commitment on Home Rule in 1885 (potentially difficult with the Liberal Party) but decision in 1886 brought Gladstone into power to try to rectify the last of Ireland's grievances. The Home Rule Bill was too little in two respects: the lack of Irish MPs in the Commons and the limitation on the Dublin parliament's powers, but it would have been a precedent. Its failure may have been due, in part, to Gladstone's tactless handling of Chamberlain, the new power in the Liberal Party. Liberals were now committed to Home Rule. In 1893, and again in 1912, Home Rule was carried in the Commons. In 1886, or even 1893, Home Rule would have been neither too late nor, on the whole, too little.

5 Conclusion. Gladstone's major achievement in Irish policy was to set course in the right direction: towards a free Church, towards agrarian reform, towards political autonomy. The judgement 'too little, too late' might be the comment

expected from extreme Irish nationalists such as the Fenians, and may to some extent be justified in the details of his policy, but not in the grand sweep of his inspiration.

3   Assess the strengths and weaknesses of Parnell as a leader of the Irish cause.

Tutorial note

The question calls for an understanding of Parnell's personality, character and private life – in so far as they affected his leadership of the Irish Party. It also requires an understanding of what the Irish cause was, how Parnell led it and, finally, an assessment of the tactics he used to achieve his objectives.

You need to know about

A knowledge of Parnell's character and personality. His involvement in the Land League; the 'Boycott' initiative; Parnell's insistence on the priority of political, i.e. constitutional, methods – as in the Kilmainham Treaty (1882). The negotiations with the Conservatives and Liberals (1885–86) over Home Rule. The year 1890 and the crisis, personal and political, which led to Parnell's loss of the leadership.

Suggested answer plan

1   Parnell emerged in the 1870s as a great Irish leader to stand with O'Connell in the Irish imagination; he advocated Irish self-government, and impressed English politicians. By his style and appearance, he was cast in the mould of a leader but basically he was a diffident, nervous man, driven by passion and a commitment to master all the public arts of politics and to accept all the necessary tedium of political life. What were his strengths and weaknesses as an Irish leader?

2   His major strength was his commitment to a single goal: self-government. He took over from Isaac Butt, replacing the latter's unsatisfactory federalism with a policy of Home Rule for Ireland. This commitment was of great importance in the agrarian disturbances of the period (1879–82). Parnell became President of the Land League (seeing it as useful in 'laying the foundation in the movement for the regeneration of legislative independence'); this allowed him to share in some of the excitement of extremism and violence but did not, despite the Coercion Bill and Davitt's arrest, tempt him to secede from Parliament to lead a potentially violent agrarian campaign in Ireland.

Parnell accepted the 1880 Land Act and the Kilmainham Treaty, promising an end to 'outrages' in return for a settlement of the rent arrears question. Parnell made an important promise to co-operate with the Liberals; from then on, the Irish Party worked strictly within the constitutional context to achieve the political ideal of Home Rule. His unwillingness to support the Plan of Campaign (after 1886) demonstrated that his association with the Land League was tactical.

3   Parnell's strength was also seen in his astuteness, flexibility and political insight. Sometimes he was seen as obdurate, by reason of his obsessive commitment to his political goal; the other side of the coin was his shrewd political insight coupled with flexibility used for tactical purposes. His call to send to a 'moral Coventry like a leper of old' anyone who moved onto a farm from which a tenant had been evicted highlighted the campaign against the evictions of the late 'seventies. The same political insight and flexibility showed in his willingness, in 1885, to negotiate with the Conservatives (through Caernarvon) with an offer to support them if they would introduce Home Rule. Parnell knew that the Conservatives could more readily get a bill through the House of Lords – as did Gladstone, who refused therefore to commit the Liberals. Parnell's instructions to the Irish in England to vote Conservative lost perhaps 30 seats to the Liberals. Gladstone's conversion in 1886 swung Irish MPs behind the Liberals.

4   Parnell's weakness: the impact of his private life on his political life. Neither Catholic Ireland nor nonconformist England could overlook Parnell's co-

habitation with a married woman; this misalliance (despite the personal comfort it brought to him) proved fundamentally injurious to his leadership when revealed publicly in 1890. Although his health was failing, yet he refused to see that his only course was resignation – for (as Morley and Gladstone saw) a Liberal Party based on English nonconformity would not be able to accept an Irish leader who was involved in a divorce case.

Parnell's intransigence put at risk the Liberal/Irish alliance and the Home Rule policy which Liberals had adopted. His unwillingness to accept the logical consequences of his action split the Irish Parliamentary Party and reduced the strength of the powerful machine he had created.

5   Irishmen, like the editor D P Moran, were to criticise Parnell for ignoring Irish civilisation in the pursuit of the principle of Home Rule. However, not all goals may be pursued at the same time with success. Parnell made all England conscious of the Irish problem, created a great parliamentary Party and set Irish politics on the road of constitutionalism where they remained until 1916. A combination of charm, passionate conviction, political skill and astute parliamentary tactics took Parnell (and with him the Irish cause) to the forefront of British politics. Protected by his bitter anti-Englishness from the danger of being won over by the English establishment, he was defeated in the end by his pride and his failure to see where his duty to Ireland lay.

Question bank

1   Document question (Gladstone and Ireland): study the following extract and then answer questions (a) to (g) which follow:

Extract

'Today's *Times* throws back Mr Gladstone's recent conduct into the perspective of history, saying: "The first Minister of a great nation, having just admitted to political rights a great mass of voters entirely unpracticed in political affairs, appealed to the country as a whole for power to deal independently with a conspiracy which he had himself denounced in the strongest language, the leaders of which he had put in prison, and against which he had repeatedly employed exceptional powers. No sooner were the elections over than that Minister allied himself closely with the leaders of that conspiracy, accepted their traitorous plans for the disruption of the empire, and fought 'shoulder to shoulder' with them in Parliament and afterwards in the country, a desperate battle for the attainment of their ends. In the interests of his new allies he turned ruthlessly against all the men who had done most to build up the party from which he derived his power, and whose single offence was that they guarded the great interests which he betrayed. The most elementary right of the nation was to have the whole question laid before it with the most scrupulous fairness and the most absolute clearness; but this Minister, on the contrary, resorted to every trick, device and stratagem to conceal from the people the nature, cost and consequences of submission to the conspiracy he had joined. The touching confidence reposed in him by the masses of his countrymen was by this Minister deliberately used without stint or scruple to blindfold, mislead and betray the nation which had made him the chief guardian of its interests. Great as is Mr Gladstone's fall measured by numerical standards, it is altogether eclipsed by the tremendous moral descent, which we venture to think cannot be paralleled in English history."'

(From *The St James's Gazette*)

(a)   From the information and accusations contained in this extract, in what year do you consider that it first appeared in print?   (2)

(b) Explain to what 'having just admitted to political rights a great mass of voters' refers. (3)

(c) Show clearly to what each of the following refers:
  (i) 'conspiracy';
  (ii) 'leaders of which he had put in prison';
  (iii) 'repeatedly employed exceptional powers'. (6)

(d) What 'traitorous plans for the disruption of the empire' did Gladstone accept from 'the leaders of that conspiracy'? (2)

(e) Of which individuals and groups is the writer thinking when he refers to 'all the men who had done most to build up the party from which he derived his power'? (6)

(f) What is meant by saying Gladstone 'fought shoulder to shoulder with them in Parliament and afterwards in the country'? (4)

(g) The writer accuses Gladstone of acting in a manner calculated to 'blindfold, mislead and betray the nation'. Discuss the bias shown in the report and the real reasons why Gladstone acted as he did. (8)

2 Did Parnell help or hinder the cause of Home Rule for Ireland?
(Cambridge, June 1990)

3 Why had Gladstone failed to solve the Irish Question by 1894?
(AEB, June 1989)

4 'Irish nationalism excited widespread popular appeal in the second half of the nineteenth century'. How do you account for this? (NISEAC, June 1990)

5 'Gladstone himself must bear the major responsibility for the failure of his Irish policies after 1880'. How far would you agree with this statement?
(JMB, June 1988)

READING LIST

Standard textbook reading
R. Shannon, *The Crisis of Imperialism* (Paladin, 1976), chapters 4, 8, 10.
R. K. Webb, *Modern England* (Allen and Unwin, 1980 edn.), chapter 8.
A. Wood, *Nineteenth-Century Britain* (Longman, 1960), chapters 15, 17.

Further suggested reading
P. Adelman, *The Decline of the Liberal Party* (Longman, 1989).
J. C. Beckett, *The Making of Modern Ireland 1603–1923* (Faber, 1966).
M. Bentley, *The Climax of Liberal Politics, 1868–1918* (Arnold, 1987).
D. A. Hamer, *Liberal Politics in the Age of Gladstone and Rosebery* (Clarendon Press, 1972).
K. Laybourn, *The Rise of Labour* (Arnold, 1988).
J. Lee, *The Modernisaton of Irish Society 1848–1918* (Gill and Macmillan, 1973).
F. S. L. Lyons, *Ireland Since the Famine* (Collins, 1971, 1973).
F. S. L. Lyons, *Charles Stewart Parnell* (Collins, 1977).
G. Morton, *Home Rule and the Irish Question* (Longman, 1980).
A. O'Day (ed), *The Edwardian Age, 1906–1914* (Macmillan, 1984).
M. J. Winstanley, *Ireland and the Land Question 1800–1922* (Methuen, 1984).

THE LIBERAL GOVERNMENTS, 1906-14

Units in this chapter

10.1 *The end of an era*
10.2 *The 1906 election*
10.3 *The elections of 1910*
10.4 *Chronology*

Chapter objectives

❶ Problems of the Liberal Party to 1914: the Party's split on Home Rule in 1886, and Boer War divisions; the loss of middle-class business support weakened Party finances; it could not, therefore, afford to adopt working-class candidates as MPs; the Party's severe organisational weaknesses, despite the efforts of Herbert Gladstone.

❷ Progress of the Labour Party to 1914: never a single unified body – mixture of elements such as SDF, Fabians, Socialist League, etc. Grew out of poor social conditions of the late 19th century: rise of 'New Unionism'. Hostility led to coalition and then union of separate interests under the leadership of Keir Hardie and Ramsay MacDonald (ILP and LRC). Party wins 29 seats in 1906. Labour's problem: should they try to permeate or replace the Liberals?.

❸ The Liberal landslide victory of 1906 occurred on issues like free trade, Chinese labour, nonconformity and education; was this a last flicker of the 'old' Gladstonian Liberalism or an indication of future political strength? Efforts to revitalise the Liberal Party: the 'New Liberalism', evolving from the 'Liberal Imperialism' of Asquith, Rosebery and Grey, was then taken further by Churchill, Lloyd George and Scott's *Manchester Guardian*; demands for purposive intervention in the economy to achieve greater 'national efficiency'.

❹ Campbell-Bannerman and Asquith governments ushered in a period of Liberal reforms – old age pensions, national insurance, etc; there was also the bitter constitutional dispute over the 'People's Budget' and the Parliament Act – this was instigated by Unionist determination to retain their monopoly of power despite the 1906 defeat. Why did Balfour adopt these tactics? To appease his critics? Or was he a victim of the prevailing mood of political extremism?

⑤ The Parliament Act marked the zenith of Liberal success; the Party had already exhausted its programme, and now its radical energy in the struggle; the Unionists under Bonar Law were more disaffected than ever. The Irish question was reopened due to the Parliament Act; the Liberal Party in the 1910 general election advocated Home Rule – in return for Irish Party help in the constitutional crisis. The prospects seemed good but Liberal and Nationalist hopes were dashed by Ulster's intransigence under Carson; openly encouraged by Bonar Law's Conservative and Unionist Party ('there are things stronger than parliamentary majorities', Blenheim, July 1912).

⑥ The Ulster 'rebellion' undermined government confidence during the years 1911–14. There were other problems, too – e.g. the tense situation in foreign affairs and, at home, industrial unrest, syndicalism, the 'Triple Alliance'. Askwith and Lloyd George occasionally rescued the government here but militant labour (i.e. the Shop Stewards' Movement) were clearly disenchanted with Liberal efforts to tackle the economic and social problems of the day.

⑦ Positive in their handling of labour unrest, the government was weak, irresponsible and divided in their treatment of women's suffrage. Asquith's procrastination discredited the constitutional approach and encouraged WSPU militancy. On the other hand, the suffragettes' unwillingness to compromise, and the violence of their campaign, was ultimately self-defeating.

⑧ Assessment of the Dangerfield thesis. Were the Liberals in the throes of a 'a strange death' during the years 1906–14? Were they ceasing to govern? Was their replacement by Socialism and the Labour Party inevitable? The answer must be negative but the Liberals were clearly on the defensive during the period 1911–14 and the omens were not good.

The Edwardian age often conjures a colourful, nostalgic image of an apparently stable and happy society soon to be shaken by the horrors of the Great War. Yet although the Liberals laid the foundations of the welfare state and righted many political wrongs, it was conflict which characterised almost every aspect of Edwardian life. Feminist frustration, labour unrest, a rebellious House of Lords and Ulstermen in revolt – all this made the Edwardian period an epilogue of political violence, confusion and pessimism.

Fervently held beliefs – in laissez-faire and free trade, in capitalism and in Empire – were being challenged as never before. Everywhere unwelcome change was in the air; to contemporaries the future looked troubled and unpredictable; Victorian certainty had slipped away.

10.1 THE END OF AN ERA

The death of the Queen on 22 January, 1901, marked the end of an era in British politics. Laissez-faire, British economic supremacy, imperialism – all were under attack; and the conviction was growing that to solve the industrial and social problems of England the state must accept more responsibility for the welfare of the people.

During their period of dominance (1886–1905) the Conservatives had failed to come to terms with this development. In 1906, for the first time in English history, there was a government which not only represented the majority of the people but which consisted largely of men drawn from the middle and even lower ranks of society. The pre-eminence of the landed classes was successfully overthrown. It was now the turn of a Liberal government and its Labour allies to confront these problems.

The rise of Labour

The early Labour Party was never a homogeneous body, more 'a coagulation of incompatible elements' such as the Social Democratic Federation, the Fabians, Trade Unions and Labour Churches. Also, although the word 'Socialist' was used to describe all these elements, it meant very different things to each group.

In the early 1880s a number of important developments took place and a number of factors began to converge, e.g. the rise of the 'new' (more militant) unions and the employers' and judges' hostility to them – culminating in the Taff Vale decision of 1901.

Some important Socialist groups such as the SDF and the Fabians also emerged, inspired by books such as Henry George's *Progress and Poverty* (1881), and to a lesser extent Marx's *Das Kapital* (English translation 1887). The crusading, popular Socialist Keir Hardie, the 'member for the unemployed' was the man who unified these disparate groups and helped found the ILP in 1893 and the LRC in 1900. The Taff Vale case led to a renewed surge of Trade Union support and after Ramsay MacDonald's pact with the Liberals in 1903, the new Labour Party won a parliamentary foothold in 1906, gaining 29 seats.

10.2 THE 1906 ELECTION

The election of 1906 was one of the most dramatic in British history. It gave the Liberals a landslide victory and an absolute majority in the Commons. But it would be a mistake to interpret this as a massive vote of confidence in the Liberal Party and its electoral programme.

A vote against Conservatism reflected, in particular, nonconformist fury against the Education Act of 1902. Labour supporters were angry at the Taff Vale judgement, 'Chinese slavery' and growing unemployment. But above all it was a vote against protection. The electors were punishing the Conservatives, who had to some extent neglected the middle ground, rather than positively supporting the Liberals. It is important to remember this when one examines the difficulties which the Liberal Party encountered during the next eight years.

Old Liberalism or new?

The Party which took over government in 1906 loosely represented this mixed force of Liberal, Labour and nonconformist dissidents. Would the Lib–Lab electoral pact endure? Could the government satisfy the demands and hopes of its many supporters? Would the Labour Party replace a Liberal Party unable to cope with the divisive politics of class?

The new administration was certainly talented but was by no means united – nor could it clearly see the way ahead. Churchill and Lloyd George wanted the Party to adopt the cause of the working classes and, by introducing valuable social reforms, show them that the Liberals and not the Labour Party could best be relied upon to advance their interests.

Despite the misgivings of some Right-wing members, they seized the initiative in the field of social policy and introduced government measures on trade unions, wages and conditions of work, health insurance and old age pensions – the latter to be paid for by increasing income tax, death duties and land taxes. Clearly these were policies designed to adapt to the increasing importance of class, steal the thunder of the new Labour Party and re-emphasise the progressive and reforming nature of Liberalism. 'Socialism,' Churchill declared, 'seeks to pull down wealth; Liberalism seeks to raise up poverty.' Many in the Party were reluctant, however, to sanction more state interference or agree to any further taxation for social reforms. Instead, they reiterated their dedication to the fundamental principles of laissez-faire and the capitalist economy. Despite Lloyd George's efforts, therefore, many Liberals were still committed to the policies of 'Old Liberalism' – Cobdenite free trade, Gladstonian economy and nonconformist conscience.

The origins of the reforms

The social policies of Churchill and Lloyd George were not original. They were able to draw on much creative social thought generated since the 1870s by Chamberlain, the Fabians, the Liberal academics JA Hobson and LT Hobhouse, philanthropists, administrators and civil servants. Reforms were long overdue. The social surveys of Booth and Rowntree showed that in England, ruler of the world's richest empire, a third of the population could be living below the breadline.

Recruiting statistics in the Boer War appeared to confirm the findings of these surveys. Social reform – in the interests of 'national efficiency' and British military power – was suddenly more respectable. German strength also seemed to emphasise the benefits of Bismarckian social welfare which, incidentally, provided Lloyd George with a model for his National Health Insurance scheme. There were also other continental social reform systems to emulate.

Nevertheless, it still needed authority and stamina to get things done and Lloyd George and Churchill, well endowed with both, were determined that the Liberal Party, and not Labour, should make full use of the 'new mandate' to improve the conditions of the working class.

Lloyd George believed that the main social purpose of the New Liberalism was 'to draw a line below which we will not allow people to live and labour'. In the attainment of this humane purpose, Gladstonian ideas of self-help had to be modified or discarded: Booth and Rowntree had documented circumstances – of childhood, sweated trades and old age, for example – in which it could not conceivably operate.

You will need to know the details of the social reform legislation of the Liberal governments from 1906 to 1912. Note that this legislation, though at first narrow in its application, laid the foundations of the post-1945 welfare state. And do not overlook the fact that these reforms were carried out only because progressive and enlightened administrators, such as Morant and Beveridge, were prepared to challenge Civil Service traditionalism. Note also that little of this legislation was introduced because of Labour Party pressure.

Labour support

If the policy of the Liberals was meant as an antidote to Progressivism by Socialism it would appear to have been effective. The Labour Party in the Commons during these years was content to support the programme while concentrating its efforts on attaining measures for the trade unions. The Liberal victories in the elections of 1910 also demonstrated the ability of the New Liberalism to win working-class votes while converting the new Labour Party in the Commons to a piecemeal approach to poverty, sickness and unemployment.

By 1914, the Labour Party – out-trumped by the social reforms of Lloyd George and Churchill – was, according to Brand, 'dependent on the Liberals, dissatisfied with its achievements, unsure of its aims and apparently in decline'. Other historians, however, emphasise the growth of trade-union membership and increasing Labour representation in local government during these years and insist that these developments indicate a growing 'future' threat to Liberalism. Up to 1914, therefore, the Liberals successfully contained the Labour Party – electorally and psychologically.

The House of Lords

Labour supporters appeared to have been satisfied with this programme of social reforms. But could the same be said of Liberal supporters? The Unionists, dismayed at their overwhelming defeat at the polls in 1906, decided to use the House of Lords as a second Conservative opposition, selectively savaging proposed Liberal bills, while at the same time carefully refraining from antagonising Labour. They had, since 1906, been in a most nervous and defensive mood. The new Liberal Government was denounced, privately and publicly, as a Home-Rule-Pro-Boer-Little Englander-Socialist party unfit to govern Britain or her empire.

Impotent in the Commons, Balfour was using the House of Lords as a means of perpetuating Conservative rule and appeasing his own critics. The Liberal cabinet was alarmed by this policy. Accordingly, before Asquith became Prime Minister, they agreed that if the legitimate aspirations of Liberal supporters were to be satisfied the power of the Lords would have to be reduced to a suspensory veto.

By 1908 the Liberals were frustrated and in disarray. They needed a popular issue on which to challenge the Lords. Home Rule and Welsh Church disestablishment clearly were not popular; defence spending and social reform were proving more expensive than many Liberals wanted but all were agreed that these policies at least were vital.

In the event it was Lloyd George's search for the £15 million to cover the cost of old age pensions and the new naval programme which was to provide the issue – the 'People's Budget' – on which to challenge the 'unconstitutional' actions of the Lords. Thus it was that the policy of defence and social reform precipitated a fundamental constitutional conflict which dominated the years 1909–11.

The People's Budget

Lloyd George designed a budget which infuriated the Unionist peers. It increased income tax, death duties and the introduction of a new Land Tax, coupled with the Chancellor's biting invective against the peers (e.g. at Limehouse in July), goaded them into rejecting the budget. Whether this was the intention or not, the trap was now sprung on 'Mr Balfour's poodle'.

In the ensuing events the worst fears of the more moderate Unionists in the Commons were confirmed. There followed two electoral defeats in 1910, the passing of the budget, the curtailment of the Lords' power, the prospect of more social reform and, even worse, Home Rule for Ireland.

According to Dangerfield, the struggle with the Lords was a triumph for Asquith, both as a Party leader and constitutional lawyer, who had treated the King with consideration. Lloyd George also had reason to be pleased.

Study carefully the details of the contest and the main provisions of the Parliament Act of 1911. Note that although the Liberals won a great victory over the aristocracy, the loss of their overall majority in the elections of 1910 marked the end of their Commons' supremacy. From then on they were dependent on Labour and the Irish Party – and the price of Irish support was Home Rule. It was now no longer possible to keep the Irish Question out of English party politics.

10.3 THE ELECTIONS OF 1910

Why was the Liberal majority reduced in 1910? Despite their legislative successes, they antagonised many sections of the community. First of all, wages were falling behind rising prices. Dissatisfied workers were beginning to lose faith in the Liberals' ability to look after their interests. And they insisted that the Liberal social reforms did not go far enough and were simply palliatives designed to ease, but not cure, poverty and unemployment. They also felt that, because of opposition in the Party, this was as far as the Liberals were prepared to go.

On the other hand, industrialists, manufacturers and farmers felt that these social reforms had gone too far and began to fear 'Socialism by the back door'. They had also lost faith in free trade and, encouraged by the prospective benefits for all classes, were beginning to look more favourably on the Conservative and Unionist policy of protection. Right-wing Liberals were alarmed at the size of government expenditure on the Army, Navy and social reform – policies hardly in keeping with the Liberal tradition.

Note that although Haldane's spending was stringently limited, he brought the Cardwell system up to date so that, when war broke out in 1914, Britain was militarily better prepared than she had ever been in her long history.

The Ulster Question

The year 1910, then, was a watershed and after this date the Liberal momentum appeared to slow down. A growing estrangement between the Liberals and Labour became noticeable as the government failed to contain, or to satisfy, a series of challenges made to parliamentary democracy itself. The Parliament Act of 1911 had solved the constitutional crisis, but the Irish Party in the Commons now demanded that Home Rule be implemented.

The Conservatives, having discarded Balfour, took a militant stand under Bonar Law and, in resisting the Bill, identified themselves with Ulster loyalist preparations for civil war. The actions and speeches of Carson and Bonar Law began increasingly to seem treasonable – 'there are things stronger than parliamentary majorities'.

Asquith seemed unable to face the Ulster situation squarely. He saw the impossibility of coercing Ulster but did not know how to deal with the implications. Faced with this 'grammar of anarchy', he adopted a policy of 'wait and see'. In the end, the Liberals' nerve failed but the outbreak of the First World War rescued them from the immediate consequences of their failure.

Votes for women

The Irish problem also complicated the issue of women's suffrage, for the Irish Party refused to consider any measure of electoral reform (presuming that the Liberals were willing to introduce such a measure) before Home Rule was conceded.

Meanwhile, the suffragettes, having failed to gain their objectives by persuasion in parliament, began to appeal, like the Unionists, to the argument of force outside it. They therefore waged a campaign of violence from 1912 to 1914. The Liberal leaders opposed the extension of the suffrage for party political reasons, believing that women, being naturally 'conservative', would vote for the opposition. Frustrated by a combination of Liberal male chauvinism and selfish political calculation, suffragette militancy added to the atmosphere of social crisis in the years before the war.

Labour and Labour unrest

The most serious challenge to Liberal power, however, came from the working class. In one industry after another, strikes dominated the scene from 1911 to 1914. Unofficial strikes also became more common. Union membership doubled during these years and with it there developed a new awareness of the power of trade unionism. Though the government made considerable progress in introducing techniques of industrial conciliation under George Askwith, syndicalist ideas continued to spread. These encouraged the belief that national strike action, especially when strengthened by industrial rather than craft organisation, would force the Liberals to intervene more positively on behalf of the workers.

The unrest also threatened to undermine the stability of the Lib–Lab pact (on which the future of Liberalism now depended) and precipitate a split between Liberals and Labour which would open the way for a Conservative victory at the polls. The depth of labour unrest, however, convinced many Liberals that a more independent, socialist Labour party would soon emerge, whatever measures the Liberals adopted.

Strange death?

George Dangerfield claims that these events turned a gradual Liberal decline into a rout from 1911–14. He alleges that the Liberal leaders, handicapped by an outdated philosophy, were 'airy, remote and irresponsible' and had lost the ability and the will to govern. This inability, he argues, provoked much of the violence of Unionists, workers and women.

Recent research suggests that this argument is now hopelessly exaggerated, As outlined above, the Liberal governments coped well with the rise of Labour, the industrial unrest and the suffragettes. They can hardly be condemned for not solving the Irish problem. Asquith's leadership remained strong (not one minister resigned before 1914). The programme of New Liberalism continued under Lloyd George and working-class support for these social reforms prevented Labour from achieving any important electoral gains.

Trevor Wilson argues that it was the 'rampant omnibus' of the First World War, with its massive programme of state intervention, and the ending of peace, retrenchment, reform and free trade, that destroyed Liberalism as a philosophy – quite apart from the split between the rival factions of Asquith and Lloyd George.

It may be, however, that events after 1918 may offer a better explanation for Liberalism's decline and two in particular may provide the key. First, the Reform Act

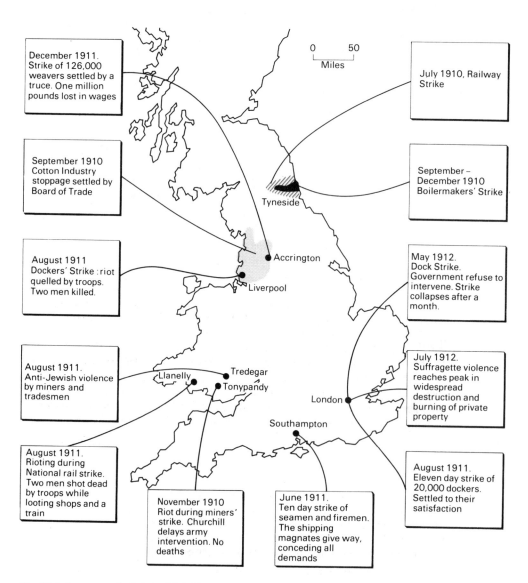

Fig. 10 Labour unrest in Britain 1910–12

of 1918 which trebled the electorate from roughly seven to twenty-one million, and gave the industrial workers a voting majority for the first time; and secondly, as a consequence, the Labour Party was able, finally, to achieve an electoral breakthrough.

This was in the future and though the future for the Liberals in 1914 looked uncertain, much had been achieved. They had laid the foundations of the Welfare State, modernised the Army and Navy, curtailed the powers of the House of Lords, tackled the wrongs of Labour and introduced an Irish Home Rule Bill. For some it was not enough, for others, too much. Dissatisfied Ulstermen and suffragettes, peers and trade unionists continued to agitate, but hardly sought to overturn the existing order as Dangerfield maintained. They did, however, ensure that the prewar years of Liberal rule would be turbulent ones.

10.4 CHRONOLOGY

1906	January	Campbell-Bannerman's first administration.
	February	First Dreadnought built.
	December	TRADE DISPUTES ACT reversed the Taff Vale decision of 1901. Trade Union funds not liable to actions for damages. WORKMEN'S COMPENSATION ACT: made compensation payable for accidents arising out of and in the course of, the workman's employment. SCHOOL MEALS ACT introduced in a Labour initiative, allowed local authorities to arrange for school meals. Education Bill rejected by the Lords. Plural Voting Bill rejected by the Lords. Land Bill rejected by the Lords.
1907	January	ARMY REFORMS begun by Haldane. Size of the Regular Army reduced but an Expeditionary Force set up under a new General Staff and backed up by a Territorial Army at home. Officers Training Corps also founded. In August 1914, some 26 divisions were quickly mobilised. SCHOOL MEDICAL INSPECTION introduced.
	December	Port of London Authority established by Churchill.
1908	April	Asquith's first administration.
	November	Licensing Bill rejected by the Lords.
1909	January	OLD AGE PENSIONS ACT implemented: pensions of 5s. per week to persons over 70 years of age, 7s.6d. to married couples. Royal Commission on the Poor Law: report published. The majority wanted to retain a reorganised Poor Law; the minority, headed by Beatrice Webb, wanted to abolish it. Both accepted the need to extend the state machinery to help the poor and the unemployed.
	March	COAL MINES ACT: limited the working day of coalminers to eight hours. TRADE BOARDS ACT: fixed minimum wages in the sweated trades, e.g. tailoring and lacemaking.
	April	THE PEOPLE'S BUDGET: a bold measure introduced by Lloyd George to raise £15 million for defence and old-age pensions. He also wanted fresh sources of revenue to finance social insurance. The Budget also increased income tax and death duties, as well as licensing, tobacco and spirit duties; there were new taxes on cars, petrol and land – the latter being the most contentious because it necessitated an inquisitorial valuation of land. CHILDREN'S ACT: forbade child begging, children in public houses or the sale of alcoholic liquor to children under 16.
	August	Labour Exchange Act passed.
	November	PEOPLE'S BUDGET REJECTED by the House of Lords by 350 votes to 75.
	December	OSBORNE JUDGEMENT: forbade the trade unions to raise a political levy. Asquith dissolved parliament. General election scheduled for January.
1910	January	Asquith's second administration. Liberals lost their overall majority in the Commons.
	April	PEOPLE'S BUDGET passed by the House of Lords.

	May	PARLIAMENT BILL introduced. The Lords to lose control over money Bills, but allowed the power to delay legislation for two years. Death of King Edward VII. Accession of George V.
	June	Constitutional Conference – to resolve the deadlock between the Lords and the Commons (over the Parliament Bill) – began but failed, after five months' negotiations in October, 1910.
	December	General election.
1911	February	Asquith's third administration.
	August	PAYMENT OF MPs introduced: £400 a year. Railway strike.
	November	PARLIAMENT ACT passed by the Lords, 131 votes to 113. Cambrian miners' strike against wage cuts. Troops used at Tonypandy; two fatal casualties; miners blamed the Home Secretary, Winston Churchill.
	December	NATIONAL INSURANCE ACT (introduced by Lloyd George) provided insurance for the poor against sickness for a contribution of 4d.; employers paid 3d. and the state 2d. Unemployed workmen (in certain trades) were to receive 7s. per week for 15 weeks. By 1914, thirteen million people were insured.
1912	February	Coal strike: 2 million men now unemployed.
	March	MINIMUM WAGES FOR MINERS. Dockers' strike in London.
	April	IRISH HOME RULE BILL introduced: similar to the 1893 Bill; attacked for its injustice to Protestant Ulster.
	September	Ulster Covenant pledged resistance to Home Rule.
1913	January	Home Rule Bill passed by the Commons, rejected by the Lords. Plural Voting Act prohibited an elector from voting in more than one constituency. TRADE UNION ACT: nullified the Osborne Judgment of 1909. 'Cat and Mouse Act': passed to deal with the suffragette hunger-strikers.
	July	Ulster Protestants founded the Ulster Volunteers to resist Home Rule by force of arms if necessary. Home Rule Bill again rejected by the Lords.
1914	May	Home Rule Bill passed the Commons.
	August	BRITAIN DECLARED WAR ON GERMANY.
	September	HOME RULE ACT passed but suspended until after the war, when the question of Ulster's exclusion from the Act could be further discussed. The Act never came into operation – it was replaced by the Home Rule Bill of December 1920. Welsh Church Disestablishment Act passed but suspended for the duration of the war.

Illustrative questions and answers

1   Explain the origins and development of the Labour Party down to 1914.

Tutorial note

This is a straightforward narrative question but you must remember to include all aspects of the Labour movement and support – not just the narrowly organisational development of the parliamentary Party; remember to point out the weaknesses of the rival parties.

You need to know about

Social and economic developments c. 1870–1914 and their effect on politics at grass-roots level. The history of trade unionism and the development of socialist organisations. Political history c. 1890–1914.

Suggested answer plan

1   The 'great depression' of the 1880s ends the long mid-Victorian boom; the effect on living standards and employment levels; middle-class observers and social theorists 'discover' unemployment as a structural problem; the poverty surveys (Booth, Rowntree) and propaganda awakens sensitive middle-class consciences; anger at the absorption of politicians with 'human rights' issues (Home Rule especially) instead of social reform and reconstruction.

2   The influence of socialist writers like Morris; the rise of middle-class socialist societies; the Social Democratic Federation (Hyndman) develops the Marxist critique; the Fabian Society (the Webbs) advocates 'permeation' (Lib–Labism) and piecemeal reforms; the Labour churches; the Co-operative movement; Socialism on the LCC and in the provinces (Blatchford in Manchester, Jowett in Bradford, etc.); the foundation of the Independent Labour Party (1893) under Keir Hardie; the Colne Valley by-election.

3   The rise of trade unionism 1825–1880, the effects of Disraeli's 1875 legislation; the growth of the 'new' unionism among unskilled labourers, starting with the gas workers (Will Thorne) and the dockers (Ben Tillett); the impact of the 1889 dock strike. Many unionists, however, still hoped that the traditional Parties (especially the Liberals) would attend to their interests.

4   The 1890s undermined the newly won trade-union confidence; few gains were made *despite* full employment; the employers fought back with the Free Labour Associations; judge-made law supported the employers (Lyons v Wilkins, Allen v Flood) culminating in the trauma of the Taff Vale decision; the decline of real wages after 1900, and the development of syndicalism.

5   The trade union crisis led to the foundation of the Labour Representation Committee (1900); the role of MacDonald in its policies; the Gladstone/MacDonald pact (1903) gave Labour 53 MPs in 1906 (including 24 Lib–Labs); the 1906 Trades Disputes Act enabled the rapid rise of trade unionism during the period 1906–14; the failure to make parliamentary headway, in 1910 (40 MPs) and the Osborne judgement (1908–9) encouraged more direct action (e.g. sydicalism; the Triple Alliance); the Liberals contained Labour in 1910–14 by-elections; even the Irish Home Rulers had more MPs than Labour.

6   The long-term forces favouring Labour against the Liberals; the rise of unionism, the greater industrial concentration, the new management structures, the increased geographical mobility of labour – all this led to the gradual break-down of the old 'vertical' deference politics, based on community relationships, places of worship, and paternalist employers, and to the arrival of 'horizontal' class-based politics looking for an extension of workers' power and comforts. The affiliation to Labour of the Miners' Federation in 1909 was a milestone; in this light, the rise of Labour was inevitable and awaited only the increased electorate (achieved in 1918) for its consummation.

7   And yet, Labour continued much of the ethos of the old Liberalism: free trade, a League-of-Nations type of pacifism, a secularised revivalism, teetotalism, the dignity of man and of labour, the old nonconformist conscience; Hardie and Snowden both preached a 'come-to-Jesus' type of evangelical Socialism, which had little in common with the collectivism of the unions or the full-blooded Socialism of the ILP; and since, down to 1914, the Liberals proved to be capable of responding to specific working-class needs, it is possible that, without the tumult caused by the war, the Liberals would have held off the Labour challenge.

2   Account for the crushing defeat of the Conservatives in the general election of 1906.

Tutorial note

The general election of 1906 saw one of the greatest electoral transformations in modern British political history. The question asks for a discussion of the reasons which lay behind the Conservative defeat and the remarkable recovery of the Liberal Party.

You need to know about

The election results in the 1895–1906 period. The changes in the position of the Conservative, Liberal and Labour political parties in the years before 1906. An understanding of the main issues in early twentieth-century politics.

Suggested answer plan

1 The 1906 general election brought an end to a long period of Conservative dominance in British politics. The Liberal split over Home Rule, together with the rise in imperialist sentiment, ensured a string of Conservative electoral victories, punctuated only by the weak Liberal government of 1892–5. The 1900 general election, held at the height of the Boer War and with British armies sweeping to victory in South Africa, brought only a slight diminution of the government's majority.

2 A major cause of Conservative success was the continued disarray in the ranks of their opponents. The Liberal Party had formed strong, successful governments in the heyday of Gladstone's political career; it was not clear, however, where the Party was to go thereafter. Gladstone had nailed Irish Home Rule (never an electoral winner in Great Britain) to the Party's banner; there were also serious disagreements between Liberals who favoured, and those who opposed, further government intervention in society. From the late 'eighties the Conservatives, with their Liberal Unionist allies, seemed a more united bloc, being anti Irish Home Rule and pro maintenance of the Empire.

3 In the early twentieth century this situation was transformed by the re-emergence as a major political issue of the question of tariff reform. Free trade, since the struggle over the Corn Laws, was almost an ingrained dogma of national belief; efforts to move away from free trade (the Fair Trade movement of the 1880s) made little impact. In 1903 Joseph Chamberlain, the main spokesman for the Liberal Unionists, came out openly in support of a policy of selective tariffs with these twin objectives: (1) the cementing of imperial bonds by strong economic links, and (2) helping British industries hard-hit by foreign competition in an unprotected home market. Chamberlain's tariff reform crusade broke the unity of the governing Party. Some Conservatives eagerly embraced this new doctrine, others refused to drop free trade, while Balfour and a middle group strove unconvincingly to paper over the cracks and preserve unity within the Party. On the other hand, almost all Liberals – however much they might differ on imperialism and on the role of government – happily came together in defence of free trade, to which Britain's increase in wealth and power was attributed. This issue was the biggest single factor in the Conservative catastrophe in 1906.

4 This was not, of course, the only factor tending towards a Conservative defeat; it was always easy for a government, especially in a very prolonged office, to accumulate enemies. The long-drawn-out last stages of the Boer War – the lack of spectacular victories impaired the patriotic fervour; the 'Chinese slavery' arising from the postwar settlement in South Africa – all this played a part in the 1906 electoral propaganda. Militant nonconformists expressed a strong dislike of the 1902 Education Act, with its increased aid to Anglican schools. The government could not point to a wide range of popular and exciting reforms for which it could claim credit.

5 Developments in the Labour area of politics also played a part, though it is important not to exaggerate the position of the infant Labour Party in these years. The creation of the Labour Representation Committee in 1900 provided a new basis which to build, while the Taff Vale judgement recruited important new trade union support. The electoral pact between the Liberal and Labour parties gave the new Party a chance to increase the number of MPs, while doing much to prevent competition for votes among opponents of Conservatives.

6 Although many subsidiary factors played a part in determining the result of the 1906 election, the principal cause of the Conservatives' disaster was that the

free trade v tariff reform debate arrived on the scene as the major political issue of the day, effectively smashing Conservative unity and credibility while allowing the Liberals to unite in defence of a popular traditional policy.

3   Why, and with what consequences, did the Conservatives oppose the People's Budget?

Tutorial note

Why did the Conservatives dislike the provisions of the budget? What did they think the Liberals were aiming to do in the budget, and why did they disapprove? What were the political repercussions of the Tories' stance?

You need to know about

The provisions of the 1909 budget and narrative of the events following the Conservative rejection. The Parliament Act crisis (1909–11).

Suggested answer plan

1   The best way to explain this Conservative opposition is to consider Liberal motivation: perhaps Lloyd George was deliberately setting a trap for the Lords, hoping for their rejection of the budget as an excuse for him to attack them on a 'Peers v People' basis and so, by emasculating the Lords, pave the way for Home Rule, which the upper House had blocked. If so, Conservative opposition is easily understandable.

2   Home Rule had created a sense of apprehension and bitterness in the Conservative *and Unionist* Party, and the Lords seemed to be the only weapon with which to preserve the union; there was a feeling that the whole Empire depended on 'confidence' in British strength and that, if Ireland could 'opt out' against imperial wishes, India and the rest would soon follow; Balfour's 1906 boast was: 'The Conservative Party still controls the destinies of the nation through the Lords.'

3   But there is little evidence that Lloyd George *was* setting a trap; Asquith, the previous Chancellor and the then current Prime Minister, also wanted a strong budget to bolster Liberal morale as well as intimidate the Lords.

4   The long battle between the Commons and Lords for constitutional supremacy: Lloyd George exploited the Commons' rights to exclusive cognisance of finance bills by tacking on blatantly *social measures* (especially the taxation of land values) to an ostensibly financial bill. Seen in these terms the Lord's opposition can be explained as a defence of their own powers.

5   Lloyd George was anxious to show that it would be possible to pay for social reforms like OAPs (and dreadnoughts) out of *direct* taxation without recourse to tariffs – a vital tenet of the 'new liberalism'. If so, many Conservatives may have opposed the budget in order to demonstrate that tariff reform really was essential to national efficiency and social reconstruction.

6   Perhaps Lloyd George genuinely saw the budget as socially reformist, especially the principle of graduation and the taxation of land values. If so, Conservative opposition may have been equally genuine. However, the radical element in the budget was limited, since it was to be balanced by increased taxation of such working class 'luxuries' as tobacco and alcohol.

7   Conservative opposition made no difference to the outcome of the budget, which passed in 1910 and set a trend towards increased direct taxation – and also (eventually) towards greater fiscal graduation.

8   The political and constitutional consequences of rejection: the Parliament Act, the elections of 1910, the action of George V, the threat to create peers, the 'last-ditchers' stand and the Conservative surrender. The Parliament Act reduced the power of the Lords to a suspensory veto; this was a triumph for the democratically elected Liberal government in the Commons. Asquith and Lloyd George had revitalised Liberal morale; the Party could now embark on further reforms – including Home Rule.

9   The Liberal victory was deceptive – the government's reforming energy was exhausted; the Lords could still delay legislation for two years. Defeat made the Unionist Party even more irreconcilable; Balfour was forced to resign, and Bonar Law initiated a new generation of professional businessmen-politicians, like Baldwin and Neville Chamberlain. The Party of law and order now also supported extra-parliamentary activities, like gun-running in Ulster, and encouraged plans by Ulster extremists for civil war in Ireland if Home Rule were allowed through the Commons.

10   The crisis still left unsolved the exact constitutional role of the reformed Lords. Reforms since 1911 have reduced the suspensory veto to one year and have widened the upper chamber's membership by the nomination of life peers. The Lords still await their true constitutional reformation.

Question bank

1   Document question (The Powers of the House of Lords): Study the extract below and then answer questions (a) to (g) which follow:

Extract

'...What meaning does the supremacy of the House of Commons convey to the minds of the House of Lords? In the first place, it is a matter of common knowledge that its working varies according to circumstances. <u>When their own Party are in power</u>...there is never a suggestion that <u>the checks and balances of the Constitution</u> are to be brought into play; there is never a hint that this House is anything but a clear and faithful mirror of the settled opinions and desires of the country, or that the arm of the executive falls short of being the instrument of the national will....

'...Witness the transition that takes place the moment a Liberal House of Commons comes into being. A complete change comes over this constitutional doctrine of the supremacy of this Chamber.... Now they challenge it; and it becomes <u>a deferred supremacy – a supremacy which is to arrive it may be, at the next election, or the election after that, or may be never at all</u>.... I have never been able to discover by what process the House of Lords professes to ascertain whether or not our decisions correspond with the sentiments of the electors; but what I do know is that this House has to...carry on its existence in a state of suspense, knowing that our measures are liable to be amended, altered, rejected and delayed. It is a singular thing, when you come to reflect upon it, that the representative system should only hold good when one Party is in office, and should break down to such an extent that the non–elective House must be called in to express the mind of the country whenever the country lapses into Liberalism....

'...Let the country have the fullest use in all matters of the experience, wisdom, and patriotic industry of the House of Lords in revising and amending and securing full consideration for legislative measures; but, and these words sum up our whole policy, <u>the Commons shall prevail</u>.'

(Extract from a speech by Sir Henry Campbell–Bannerman on 24 June, 1907)

(a) Why did the House of Lords habitually behave in the manner referred to 'when their own Party' were 'in power'?   (2)

(b) What is the meaning of 'the checks and balances of the Constitution'?   (3)

(c) Explain the passage from 'a deferred supremacy' to 'or may be never at all'.
                                                                                      (5)

(d) What evidence from the previous half-century could Campbell-Bannerman draw on to support his view of how the Lords behaved towards Liberal administrations?   (5)

(e) Explain how conflict between the Lords and the Liberal government developed into a major political conflict during 1909–10.   (6)

(f) What legislation did the Liberals pass to ensure that 'the Commons shall prevail'? (5)

(g) What is the connection between the passage of that legislation and the conduct of the Conservatives in the years 1912–14? (5)

2 How far did the social reforms of 1906–1914 inaugurate a Welfare State in Britain? (London, June 1990)

3 Explain why Liberal governments between 1906 and 1914 faced opposition from trade unionists, suffragettes and Ulstermen. (Cambridge, June 1987)

4 How far was the 'socialist revival' of the 1880s responsible for the emergence of the Labour Party? (WJEC, June 1991)

5 Why, and to what extent, did a 'New Liberalism' develop between the resignation of Gladstone in 1894 and the outbreak of the war in 1914? (AEB, June 1990)

READING LIST

Standard textbook reading

T. O. Lloyd, *Empire to Welfare State* (OUP, 1970), chapters 1, 2.

R. Shannon, *The Crisis of Imperialism* (Paladin, 1976), chapters 16, 17, 18.

R. K. Webb, *Modern England* (Allen and Unwin, 1980 edn.), chapters 10, 11.

Further suggested reading

P. Adelman, *The Rise of the Labour Party 1880–1945* (Longman, 1972).

M. Bentley, *Politics Without Democracy* (Fontana, 1984).

C. Cook, *A Short History of the Liberal Party 1900–1976* (Macmillan, 1976).

G. Dangerfield, *The Strange Death of Liberal England* (Paladin, 1936, 1970).

J. R. Hay, *The Origins of the Liberal Welfare Reforms* (Longman, 1975).

R. Jenkins, *Mr Balfour's Poodle* (Heinemann, 1954).

K. O. Morgan, *Lloyd George* (Weidenfeld and Nicolson, 1974).

K. O. Morgan, *The Age of Lloyd George* (Allen and Unwin, 1971).

M. Pugh, *Women's Suffrage in Britain 1867–1928* (Hist. Assoc., 1980).

D. Read, *Edwardian England* (Harrap, 1972).

P. Thompson, *The Edwardians* (Paladin, 1975).

BRITAIN'S INTERWAR ECONOMY

Units in this chapter

11.1 *Effects of World War I*
11.2 *Economic problems*
11.3 *Unemployment*
11.4 *Recovery*
11.5 *Chronology*

Chapter objectives

❶ The effects of the 1914–18 inflation and monetary depreciation on the economy and on the different social groups; the loss of markets and increased foreign competition; the reasons for the difficulties of the staple industries, especially cotton, coal, shipbuilding, and iron and steel; the wage cuts and their effect on industrial relations.

❷ The 'new' industries of the 1930s – especially vehicles, chemicals, electrics, synthetic fibres, housebuilding and the service industries – were made possible by cheaper money after 1931, by greatly increased industrial concentration (mergers, trade associations, etc.) in the 'old' and 'new' industries alike, and by modest improvements in technology, productivity, and scientific research during the 1930s.

❸ It is difficult to discern whether these 'new' industries amounted to an industrial 'recovery' or merely to a cyclical upswing; the problem of distinguishing short-term fluctuations (the 1918–20 boom and inflation, the early 1930s consumer boom, the late 1930s rearmaments-led boom) from underlying structural trends; the good industrial growth rate of 1924–39 and the improved per capita income; but reasons for seeing the recovery as a mainly defensive retreat from the nineteenth-century international economy to the protected home and commonwealth markets, which often fostered inefficient production.

❹ Britain's position in the world economy: the depression was less sudden and severe than elsewhere, which perhaps inhibited a thorough revitalisation in the 1930s; the dependence on America and the effects of the Wall Street Crash; the export trades were hit by the reduced purchasing power of the world's primary producers, in whose economic system the Victorian economy had become entwined.

❺ The depressed areas and patterns of unemployment: the distribution of wealth and condition of the unemployed; the policies on unemployment insurance, pensions and other welfare provisions; one-third of British families were near the official poverty line in 1939, while the remainder enjoyed an unprecedentedly high standard of living; the contrasts in the 1930s between the depressed areas (Scotland, Wales, Northern England)

and the prosperous South and Midlands, which benefited from the domestic consumer boom.

❻ The pressure for retrenchment and for prewar normalcy or 'decontrol', especially from Liberals and Conservatives but also from Snowden, who repealed the McKenna Duties in 1924; this undermined 'War Socialism' or government intervention in industry; the establishment in 1926 of the BBC and the CEB merely highlighted a lack of centralised planning elsewhere; the Geddes' Axe undermined Lloyd George's and Addison's plans for social reconstruction (Homes Fit for Heroes, the Fisher Education Act); Party disputes over fiscal and financial policies, 1926–30.

❼ Civil Service (Niemeyer) and banking (Norman) pressure for a return to gold at the old parity raised interest rates and aggravated industrial difficulties; the decision to abandon gold and reintroduce protection (especially the Ottawa agreements) contributed to the economic upturn in 1930s; invisible earnings remained high but were not now (unlike before the war) sufficient to compensate for visible trade deficit.

❽ An analysis of the 'balance of power' within the economy – was, for example, the Macmillan Committee right in saying that industry was being sacrificed to the financial sector? The influence of 'The City' and also of the Chambers of Commerce in policy-making circles, compared with National Employers' Confederation (but note the increased role of NEC and the TUC in the 1930s); the 1920s revival of agriculture was not maintained in the 1930s.

❾ The 'Keynesian' policy alternative called for public works, deficit financing and counter-cyclical controls; the work of the 1930 Economic Advisory Council began the process of the gradual conversion of official thinking to such economic planning; there is reason for believing that senior Treasury and Bank of England officials (e.g. Phillips and Hopkins) were converted from classical economics to 'Keynesianism' before the publication of the *General Theory* in 1936 – but the government machinery and the political will to implement the new policies were both lacking before the 1939–45 war; anyway, the size of the budget was still too small in the 1930s for deficit financing to have had much immediate impact. In short, 'recovery' (if that is what it was) took place without a 'New Deal', but benefited from cheap money, protection and increasingly favourable terms of trade.

The First World War made obvious Britain's relative decline as an industrial nation. The war put an enormous strain on her resources. She emerged with much of her export trade lost, her capital equipment depleted and an industrial structure clearly outdated. The structural roots of the interwar crisis lay in the prewar inheritance of a narrowly based and increasingly archaic export trade. This was exacerbated by the general decline in world markets between the wars.

Britain now paid the price for her businessmen's preference for underdeveloped and imperial markets since 1870 and her failure to encourage the more technologically advanced industries such as motor cars, machine tools, electrical goods and so on. Unemployment was the result – over 9% throughout the period and reaching 23% in August 1932. The politicians had no effective remedies.

Economic orthodoxy triumphed over Keynesian and socialist alternative policies. Large-scale government expenditure and public works were rejected as possible solutions. Meanwhile politicians argued, irrelevantly, about the benefits to be gained from protection as opposed to those which might accrue from the continuation of the prewar policy of free trade.

Introduction

The First World War stimulated wartime industries and agriculture and ensured full employment. It also caused inflation with a consequent rise in prices and profits. The war cost the Exchequer £9 000 million, and dictated economy for the remainder of the interwar years. After the brief postwar boom, which lasted until 1920, came the inevitable slump, as wartime demands and contracts for industrial goods and agricultural produce fell.

Optimism, however, prevailed and most people still hoped for a return to pre-1914 'normalcy'. Paradoxically, the difficulties of the 1920s, including the General Strike, simply strengthened this feeling. Britain returned to the Gold Standard in 1925 at the prewar parity of pound to dollar. Even in the early 'thirties, after the onset of the world economic depression occasioned by the Wall Street Crash in the US, most voices still maintained that Britain's difficulties were mainly temporary, caused by external events and forces outside her control.

The uncomfortable truth was that Britain had been in decline for some considerable time – the First World War had simply emphasised this fact. This decline had begun in the 1870s when Britain was first challenged by Germany and the US in foreign markets. The latter had considerable advantages over Britain – bigger home markets, modern technology and up-to-date equipment. Their entrepreneurs could produce on a large scale and reap the benefits of economies of scale primarily through lower costs.

Britain's early start left her with outdated plant and technology, and dependent on industries (coal, iron and steel, textiles and shipbuilding) which reflected the past rather than the present. The future lay with the newer industries (chemicals, electrical, petro-technology and motor cars) which formed an insignificant part of our Gross National Product.

11.1 EFFECTS OF WORLD WAR I

Britain's decline in the world economic league was seriously hastened by the Great War. During the period 1914–18 our overseas customers had to buy from other nations (Japan and the USA), develop the commodity themselves, or learn to use a substitute. Wartime allies also borrowed heavily from Britain (£1825 million) and from the USA, and in order to repay these debts after the war they reduced their imports – imports which Britain relied on selling to them. They also protected their new industries with tariffs and subsidies, thereby further undermining Britain's vitally important exports – a trade on which rested the viability and prosperity of her basic industries.

The staple industries

Other factors accentuated these changes. The nature of demand changed. Britain had won her industrial supremacy in the nineteenth century by selling, primarily, producers' goods. After the Great War, demand for these staple goods was not so great and consequently our export trade of coal, iron, shipping and textiles suffered. This decline could, of course, have been offset by the rise of new industries (and to a limited extent it was) but we were slow to develop these and had not made as much progress as had our nearest competitors. The result was a decline in our export trade, accompanied by a fall in the National Income, a rise in unemployment and a growth of depressed areas where the old staple industries were concentrated.

The chief of these depressed areas (or, as they were euphemistically called, 'special' areas) were Lancashire, the North-East, South Wales and South-West Scotland. They contained only one-quarter of the population but nearly one-half of the unemployed. The emergence of those depressed areas emphasised the continued existence of the division of the people of the United Kingdom into 'two nations' – the rich and the poor – soon to be joined (in Ernest Bevin's words) by the 'third nation', the unemployed. One of the main early reasons for this, as Mowat explains, was that throughout the 'twenties, 'Britain's industrial machine was throttled down; the world's workshop worked only on short time'.

The return to gold

This situation was compounded by the effects of the revaluation of the dollar in 1925 at \$4.86 to the pound. This was largely a political decision – people wanted to see the pound 'look the dollar in the face' but the effect was to *increase* the price of Britain's exports and further weaken her position in markets in which she was already struggling to retain a much diminished share. Equally, this decision *lowered* the price of one of our major competitor's imports into the United Kingdom, with disastrous effects on certain home industries now unable to compete.

It is clear that circumstances were against Britain's export trade anyhow – the world needed less of what she had to sell – but overvaluation, by keeping export prices artificially high, only made matters worse. It called forth an enormous volume of criticism. In a pamphlet, *The Economic Consequences of Mr. Churchill*, Keynes had clearly warned what the result would be, but economic orthodoxy died hard. In 1930 Montagu Norman continued to insist that the subsequent depression in industry was simply due to bad luck! Coal miners in particular, the first to suffer the inevitable wage cuts, would have had little sympathy for such a convenient analysis.

The Coal industry

The coal industry is a good example of an industry which was suffering acutely from the onset of depression. Because Britain had been the first nation to industrialise, her pits were older and deeper, and geological formations often meant that in many areas mechanisation was impossible. British miners were also paid higher wages than their German and Polish counterparts and, consequently, our exports dropped.

Furthermore, in the home market substitutes for coal, such as electricity and oil, were being increasingly used. Improved industrial techniques also provided output from a smaller input of coal, as did newer and more economical grates in the homes of domestic consumers. Finally, the switch from coal to oil fuel in the Navy and merchant marine further exacerbated an already difficult situation. Consequently, after the war the British coal industry found itself with a large surplus of coal for which no market existed.

These circumstances, made even more intractable by poor management, to a great extent explain the problematical political and social nature of the industry in the 'twenties. Remedies were, of course, proposed – nationalisation, the amalgamation of pits, the closing of uneconomic mines, reorganisation and so on – but the owners usually resorted to the more traditional methods of wage cuts and longer hours, methods which defeated the miners in 1926.

Apart from the coal industry, it is essential that you have a good understanding of the comparative strengths and weaknesses of the staple industries between the wars.

11.2 ECONOMIC PROBLEMS

The word *depression* needs defining. There are many criteria which economists may use to interpret it. Some will emphasise long-term figures, others concentrate on whether the depression is continuous or cyclical. For example, examination of growth rates during the period reveals a much healthier picture than concentrating on cyclical down-swings or on unemployment figures.

Some sectors of the economy were growing – chiefly the consumption goods industries such as motor cars, bicycles, aircraft, man-made fibres (rayon), plastics, electrical goods and so on. The tertiary (or service sector) was also expanding but, as yet, these newer industries only accounted for around 16% of Britain's exports in 1930, while the staple industries still accounted for over 60%.

This development was a welcome one but employing, as it did, only 8% of the workforce, it was hardly a substitute for the declining staple giants. (Note that there remains the occasional extra problem of separating old and new industries – for example, are chemicals and textiles old or new? Both had experienced important changes over a long period of time.)

Another difficulty for economic historians is to define precisely what is meant by the interwar years. Because of the postwar boom they rarely wish to begin with 1918 or end, because of rearmament, with 1939. The choice of the base year is vital. If, for example, we were to choose the period 1920 to 1937, one would get a different picture than by taking the years 1921 to 1937 because, whereas 1920 was a boom year, 1921 was a year of deep slump. Growth statistics, in particular, would inevitably be affected by the choice of the base year.

There is also the problem of what statistical criteria to use to measure the depression – industrial production, per capita productivity, Gross Domestic Product, or unemployment? Finally, when we use the word *depression* are we simply referring to the interwar period in comparison to Britain's previous economic performance, or are we comparing Britain with other countries during the same or earlier periods?

Modern research shows that Britain's industrial growth and productivity performance (1924–39) vis-a-vis other countries was above average. Even old industries, such as shipbuilding and textiles, had a high output per capita in the 'thirties – but, of course, at the cost of shedding labour and thereby creating pools of unemployment. Ironically, many of the older industries performed well in productivity terms and could not be defined as depressed but, in terms of overall growth and employment, they were obviously in 'depression'.

Recently researched data shows that output and employment fell less in Britain during the 1929–32 depression than in most other countries, and, amazingly, most people in Britain did not suffer a fall in their standard of living. This was primarily due to two factors. First, Britain was the world's largest importer of food and raw materials, the price of which fell sharply in the early 'thirties. Second, there was no financial collapse in England – as there was in Germany and the US. Britain's recovery was also relatively fast. The depression bottomed-out in late 1932 and output reached its 1929 level by 1934. So the depression was very serious for many people, but not for the majority. It was the unfairness that made it difficult to bear.

11.3 UNEMPLOYMENT

It is not surprising that unemployment is regarded as the critical problem of the interwar period. The average unemployment rate over the whole period was above 14% of the insured population, varying from 395,000 in 1920 to 3.4 million in 1932. Note that these are figures for those insured – 12 million out of a working population of 19 million. These tend to exaggerate the percentage of those unemployed because there was a lower rate of unemployment amongst the uninsured. It has been calculated that the insured unemployment rate in 1931 was 21%, but only about 15% if one includes the uninsured. Whatever figures one uses, the two main types of unemployment between the wars were structural and cyclical in nature.

Structural unemployment occurred where entire industries contracted due to economic or market change. This was the case with the old staple industries which were export-orientated and labour-intensive. Technological and productivity improvements often merely aggravated these structural problems by causing more unemployment. Cyclical unemployment, on the other hand, was caused by major downturns (or slumps) in the economy, the two most notable being in 1921 and (much the more severe one) in 1932. The latter was largely the result of the Wall Street Crash of 1929 and led to unemployment figures of the order of 46% in coal, pig-iron and shipbuilding in 1932. Unemployment was not equally distributed throughout the country. The rate varies from 67% in an old staple town like Jarrow to a mere 3% in a new industry town such as High Wycombe. Those industries not tied to export markets, therefore, fared much better. In the consumption goods industries (irons, vacuum cleaners, refrigerators, wireless sets, washing machines, etc.) and in the distributive trades, unemployment averaged 12–14%.

Suggested remedies

Certain historians have argued that the migration of labour, underemployment and an acceptance of lower wages might have reduced the numbers of unemployed still further. There was considerable voluntary internal migration from the depressed areas towards the South Midlands and outer London, but hardly on the scale required to solve such a massive problem. Furthermore, in the face of such profound structural and cyclical problems it is doubtful if this would have had much effect – especially during a period of enforced technological and industrial change, during which time the population between the ages of 15 and 65 increased by over 4 million.

To have solved the unemployment problem it would first have been necessary to generate sufficient industrial growth to absorb the increasing number of new people coming into the labour market. Interwar governments failed, however, to realise the need for a positive labour policy, embracing overall unemployment, labour migration and planned location of industry, and appeared content to extend unemployment benefits and accept a situation of maintaining in enforced idleness a large section of the country's most highly skilled workers.

Benefits dulled the pain of economic distress but did little to cure the widespread despair caused by long-term unemployment. Demonstrations by the unemployed, hunger marches, deputations to Downing Street, etc. all showed that what the unemployed wanted was not state maintenance but work.

Government response

As stated earlier, the governments' economic policy reflected Britain's position in the world economy and was biased, quite understandably, towards the international context. Despite the more direct involvement by these governments in the domestic economy during the Great War, they carried this outlook into the 'twenties and 'thirties, often with disastrous results – as in the case of the revaluation in 1925. In budgetary and fiscal policy, their stance was basically orthodox and they refused to consider Keynesian (or 'Mosleyian') reactionary policies.

The Labour Government of 1929–31 accepted Snowden's view that public works were mere 'palliatives' and that deflation was the correct response to the depression. There was to be no 'New Deal' in Britain. However, even if they had implemented these reflationary policies, structural economic problems of the magnitude Britain was experiencing (compounded by cyclical downturns) would have been almost impossible to solve in such a relatively short period of time.

What did governments do? They imposed tariffs, made bilateral trade agreements (e.g. with Scandinavian countries), lowered the Bank rate, encouraged schemes for rationalisation and made some attempt to create employment in depressed areas. At best these measures enjoyed only limited success. However, it is also important that these governments did not make any disastrous policy mistakes – as happened in several other countries. Find out what you can about the drawbacks which resulted from the implementation of each of these policies.

11.4 RECOVERY

Britain's recovery in the 1930s has been the subject of much research in recent years and certain points have been stressed. Some recovery was inevitable as the world moved out of the 1929–32 slump. (Nevertheless, this recovery was by no means a complete one). The abandonment of the gold standard and the imposition of tariffs in 1932 by the National government certainly helped. The former encouraged a cheap-money policy while the latter aided some of the older industries such as iron and steel.

Rearmament was an important stimulus to growth in the 1930s, but it came very late. Not until 1938 did it reach 9% of national income. Unlike many other countries, rearmament played little part in Britain's actual recovery from the slump.

The main stimulus, however, was given not to the protected industries but to the building, distribution and new industries, such as motor manufacturing and electrical – all based on a home demand activated by the introduction of 'hire-purchase' buying. This increase in demand in turn stimulated the older, staple industries. Furthermore, the housing boom was critical, as this was a labour-intensive industry (note in particular the extraordinary growth of the middle class suburbs and their stimulus to the development of both public and private transport).

The governments' role in the upswing, therefore, was permissive rather than positive. The partial economic recovery that occurred may have occurred in any case, and owed little to the deliberate actions of the state. It would appear that the main political debate on economic policy between the wars was irrelevant, concentrating as it did on the issue of free trade versus protectionism.

The alternative of progressive capitalism or Socialism (Keynes and Mosley) were never clearly posed at the centre of the political debate. It took the Second World War to put these alternatives seriously on the political agenda.

In conclusion, it is important to note that the interwar years, for all their tragic unemployment and distress, were not years of unrelieved economic stagnation and decline. In spite of mass unemployment, hunger marches, etc., there was a substantial rise in the volume of industrial production, (both from old and new industries), a fall in the cost of living (cheaper imports due to more favourable terms of trade), a decline in the number of families below the poverty line and a welcome expansion of the social services by governments who were not allowed to discontinue the work begun by the Liberals from 1906–14.

11.5 CHRONOLOGY

1917	July	MINISTRY OF RECONSTRUCTION, headed by Dr C Addison, set up to consider postwar schemes for demobilisation, health, housing, education and employment insurance.
1918		Wartime price controls abandoned.
1919	February	TRIPLE ALLIANCE (miners, railwaymen, transport) resurrected. The miners demanded a 30% pay increase and a seven-hour day; the government offered a Royal Commission under Mr Justice Sankey. National Industrial Conference to promote better relations between employers and employees.
	March	SANKEY COMMISSION recommended partial nationalisation of the mines and a 20% increase in pay; this was rejected in September by Lloyd George. Government control continued.
	July	Army demobilisation was completed; most of the 4 million men released were absorbed into industry. HOUSING ACT (Addison Act) gave powers and subsidies to local government for the building of council houses. 170 000 houses were built by 1923.
	September	RAILWAY STRIKE against a threatened wage reduction; settled by Lloyd George in favour of the railwaymen.

Gold Standard was suspended.

Ministy of Health created; included the Poor Law, Housing and Local Government Boards.

1920	February	Government decided to ignore the recommendations of the Sankey Commission; the coal mines were to be returned to the owners, who immediately reduced wages.
	October	Miners Strike. The 'Slump' began.
		UNEMPLOYMENT INSURANCE ACT: extended to cover all insured men.
	November	Agriculture Act, to deal with postwar problems in agriculture, included a guaranteed price for wheat and oats, but was later to be repealed, due to the slump, in 1921.
1921	April	MINERS STRIKE/lockout: the railway and transport unions refused to strike in sympathy (Black Friday, 15 April).
	July	Miners were defeated and returned to work.
	November	Unemployed Workers Dependents Act: gave relief for wives (5s. per week) and children (1s. per week).
		Safeguarding of Industries Act: selected import tax to prevent dumping.
1922	February	GEDDES AXE: aimed to save £75 million by economies. Cuts in the Army and Navy, education, housing, public health and teachers' salaries were recommended by the Geddes Committee on Government Expenditure.
	November	UNEMPLOYMENT INSURANCE ACT: this consolidated the Acts of 1920 and March 1921. It made the dole general for an unlimited period for all unemployed, and recognised the responsibility of central Government to help the unemployed.
1923	July	CHAMBERLAIN'S HOUSING ACT: £6 million subsidy, primarily for private housebuilding; produced 362 000 houses.
1924	September	WHEATLEY HOUSING ACT, designed to meet the needs of working-class tenants, increased the government subsidy to house builders (who built to rent only) to £9 million per annum; 504 000 houses were built by 1933.
		Dawes Plan, for the payment of German reparations, encouraged period of economic recovery.
1925	April	RETURN TO THE GOLD STANDARD by Churchill, ending the wartime and postwar prohibition on the export of gold; J M Keynes opposed the proposals in his pamphlet *The Economic Consequences of Mr Churchill*. He argued that the return would lead to further deflation and unemployment.
	May	Widows, Orphans and Old Age Pensions Act passed by Chamberlain; provided (contributory) widows' pensions of 10s. per week.
	September	Samuel Commission set up to investigate coal industry problems; government subsidy of £23 million.
1926	March	SAMUEL COMMISSION reported: advocated the nationalisation of royalties, the amalgamation of smaller pits, etc. Also called for wage reduction. The Commissions recommendations were rejected by the miners.
	April	MINERS LOCKED OUT (30 April). The government declared a general emergency.
	May	GENERAL STRIKE began (3 May) in support of the miners. The strike ended (12 May). The government brought back the eight-hour day for miners.
	November	MINERS RETURNED TO WORK on the owners' conditions, i.e. longer hours and lower wages.
1927	May	TRADE DISPUTES AND TRADE UNION ACT: made *general* strikes illegal; forbade civil servants to form trade unions; made it necessary for a trade union member to 'contract-in' in order to contribute through his union to Labour Party funds.
1928	January	Mond Committee met to investigate ways of improving the efficiency of British industry.
1929	April	CHAMBERLAIN'S LOCAL GOVERNMENT ACT: its main measures were the abolition of the 1834 Poor Law Act; the transfer of poor relief powers to county and borough councils; and derating to help industry and agriculture.
	October	WALL STREET CRASH: markets collapsed, unemployment grew to almost 3 million by 1932.
1930	August	Coal Mines Act: cut half-hour off the miners' working day; also set up a scheme to close inefficient pits.
		GREENWOOD HOUSING ACT continued subsidised housebuilding.
1931	July	May Committee Report recommended public expenditure cuts, including unemployment relief.

	August	Cabinet failed to agree on the May Committee cuts. The Labour government resigned. MacDonald formed the National Government.
	September	BRITAIN ABANDONED THE GOLD STANDARD: the pound fell from $4.86 to $3.40. Means test introduced to determine eligibility for unemployment benefit.
1932	February	IMPORT DUTIES ACT: imposed a general tariff of 10% on all except imperial imports.
	June	Bank rate reduced to 2%. The recovery began as world trade improved, but its effects were uneven.
	August	Ottawa Agreements established imperial trade preference for the Dominions.
1933	June	Children and Young persons Act passed: 'a landmark in the history of child protection'.
1934	May	UNEMPLOYMENT ACT: restored the 10% benefits cuts but retained the means test.
	December	UNEMPLOYMENT ASSISTANCE BOARD set up with a staff of 6000 to help relieve the pressure on Labour Exchanges. Special Areas Act: aimed to stimulate investment in depressed areas.
1935		HILTON YOUNG'S HOUSING ACT: obliged local authorities to clear slums and end overcrowding.
1936		Public Health Act: a major consolidating measure.
	March	Rearmament began, especially aircraft production.
1937	July	Factory Act: a major consolidating measure.
1938	July	COAL ACT: nationalised coalmine royalties, with compensation given to the pit owners. The Act brought full nationalisation nearer.

Illustrative questions and answers

1 To what extent did government policies help Britain's economic recovery in the 1930s?

Tutorial note

This question demands a knowledge of the various economic policies which the government used to influence the economy between 1929 and 1939. It requires an assessment of whether the policies were specifically aimed at recovery and also whether such policies were capable of success, given the structure of the British economy in the 1930s.

You need to know about

An understanding of the National government's role in restoring confidence by abandoning gold (1931) and introducing tariff protection (1932). A brief analysis of the government's fiscal and monetary policies in the 1930s. Other factors influencing this limited economic recovery – often irrespective of government policy, e.g. Britain's improved terms of trade position.

Suggested answer plan

1 The problem of the 1929–32 world depression led Britain to abandon the gold standard and introduce tariff protection. These two factors may have restored confidence in the British economy, as it was now possible to let rates of interest fall from the higher levels of the 1920s; the pound fell to $3.40, thus reducing the price of British goods and boosting our export trade. The introduction of the tariff helped some industries, e.g. steel, but some retaliatory action and diversion of trade occurred. Also, the economic recovery of the 1930s was not based solely on these newly protected industries.

2   The introduction of 'cheap money' meant that investors could now borrow money at lower rates of interest (2%). The figures of bank advances in the 1930s, however, do not show a substantial increase as much business investment was still derived from reinvested profits. The policy of cheap money was, in general, a passive factor in the recovery of the 1930s. The government's fiscal policy was still orthodox in the sense that attempts at balancing the budget were paramount in the minds of successive Chancellors. They favoured public expenditure cuts and new taxes (viz. the May Committee). There was no real counter-cyclical government fiscal policy during the depression.

3   Britain's recovery in the 1930s was due to more specific circumstances. This country had not suffered such a severe economic downturn as had the US and Germany; confidence was not so low. Even at the trough of the cycle, real incomes and consumption were relatively high; this gave a greater chance for a reasonably quick recovery. In 1932 there was a distinct shortage of housing: also scope for the growth of the 'new' industries. The basis of recovery was to be seen more in the growth of these two areas than in specifically designed government policies. Nevertheless, cheap money and low interest rates (especially through building society loans) encouraged the private building boom which stimulated other sectors of the economy through the multiplier process. Tariff reform signalled a retreat from competitive international markets to protected imperial and home markets; it encouraged recovery but also inefficient production.

4   Some government assistance was given to depressed industries; attempts were also made to rationalise industry, e.g. textiles, and alleviate unemployment, e.g. the dole. Unlike the US, Britain did not attempt to reflate the economy by budget deficits and preferred deflation; therefore there was no increase in state interference in, or control of, the economic system. This was left to private enterprise, aided only by protection and cheap money. The government failed to take advantage of the cheap money to introduce a national public works programme of the kind that occurred in the US, or to raise the school-leaving age; what was attempted (roads, public buildings, etc.) was totally inadequate. The government was aided, however, by a temporary revival of world trade in the mid-thirties and by rearmament which proceeded rapidly after 1936.

5   To conclude: recovery from the world depression was expected as the economy naturally moved out of the recession phase. Government policy may have been a contributory factor but, in some cases, was not particularly beneficial (e.g. the fiscal stance). The recovery was also incomplete in the sense that the growth of the new industries could not compensate for the decline of the old industries. Structural problems reflected in unemployment levels of 13.8% in 1938, could not be alleviated by the government's policy. Most of the time the government reacted to international factors rather than to internal needs, to orthodoxy rather than to active economic management.

2   Account for the high rate of unemployment in Britain between the world wars.

Tutorial note

This is a reasonably straightforward question which requires an analysis of the various types of unemployment which Britain experienced between the wars and an assessment of the main reasons for this depressing phenomenon.

You need to know about

The decline in Britain's relative share of world trade and production in the interwar period and the particular role of World War I in disguising pre-1914 trends. An analysis of structural unemployment and its causes. The emergence of regional, technological, cyclical unemployment and their effects. Government attitude to these varying levels of unemployment.

Suggested answer plan

1   Britain's share of world trade, particularly in manufactured goods, declined during the interwar period; this set an overall constraint on the growth of production and on the maintainance of employment. The experience of World War I at first hid the unemployment problem, but after 1918, to some extent, exaggerated its effects. Even in the best interwar years the volume of exports never again exceeded 80% of the 1913 level. The trend after 1918 should have been away from the international market, with more concentration on potential domestic demand, because the international market was in depression. The return to gold (1925) further undermined Britain's competitiveness in the staple industries.

2   The major reason for Britain's unemployment problem was the slow pace at which the structure of the economy adjusted to meet the changing demand pattern of British and world economies. Most 'new' industries (using new fuels like oil and electricity) were demand-orientated (i.e. geared to consumer wants) and were less labour-intensive, but they could not compensate adequately for the decline of the old labour-intensive staples which produced capital goods for export. Even by 1937, the old industries still accounted for most of Britain's industrial capital. Industrial adaption to new conditions remained incomplete and the result was severe structural unemployment on Tyneside, Merseyside and in South Wales, etc.

3   Many of the traditional staples – coal shipbuilding, textiles – were concentrated in specific areas of Britain, basically near sources of raw materials and power. Hence, the effect of structural unemployment was exaggerated. The fact that unemployment in the coalfields was twice the average for other areas illustrated the problem of regional unemployment. The presence of regional unemployment meant that frictional unemployment frequently resulted. Often, short-term unemployment can be caused by workers moving from job to job. But the difficulties created by strong ties to a specific area greatly inhibited mobility and thereby increased longer-term frictional unemployment during the interwar period. Government measures sought to deal with symptoms rather than the cause of unemployment and although they adopted a cheap money policy, the government refused to adopt Keynesian reflationary schemes, having an unrealistic desire to maintain prewar policies.

4   The emergence of the 'new' industries, which made good use of labour-saving techniques, sometimes meant further redundancies as capital was increasingly substituted for labour. Ironically, old industries often increased their productivity and streamlined their production by adopting new techniques, but only at the cost of shedding labour. Thus, structural change during the interwar years involved technological changes which often further increased unemployment.

5   In conclusion, unemployment arose because of decreased demand, accentuated by government unwillingness to adopt certain policies that might have alleviated the situation. Not all was depression, however. Recovery was uneven (until rearmament, post-1937) and technological advances were patchy but the overall growth record of the economy was better than before 1914; there was a marked increase in per capita industrial production. By the mid-thirties, real income per head had increased by about 30%. The middle classes, and those in employment, made the greater gains but the trend towards smaller families and a shorter working week, plus the growth of social services, ultimately benefited all. It was only with the coming of the Second World War that the problem of high unemployment was solved.

3   'A period of economic gloom and increasing prosperity?' Is this a good description of Britain in the 1930s?

Tutorial note

This question requires an analysis of the paradoxical nature of the interwar economic experience characterised by depression and gloom but, after our abandonment of the gold standard, also by symptoms of dynamism and increased prosperity.

You need to know about

An understanding of why the period has been designated as one of gloom – i.e. of high unemployment, slow industrial transformation, inadequate change in the distribution of income, a high incidence of poverty, and problems of international trade. An analysis of the positive features of the period – faster growth in Britain than the average of the other major countries, rising real incomes and consumer expenditure, an increased emphasis on housebuilding, the rapid introduction of electricity, an extension of statutory holidays, the gradual involvement of the state in providing help for the unemployed, increased expenditure on entertainment and holidays, and the introduction of the motor car.

Suggested answer plan

1   The 1930s are often described as 'gloomy' because of the waste of resources involved in unemployment – which ranged from a high of 22% in 1932 to just under 11% in 1937. This high unemployment rate was intimately bound up with the structural problems of the staple industries during the interwar period, which the upswing in the economy in the 'thirties could not totally alleviate. This created a mood of despair and disillusionment. Successive governments appeared unable to cure the unemployment problem.

2   The gloomy description of the period is also linked to the comparatively slow change in the distribution of wealth towards the lower-income groups and to the persistence of poverty in the depressed areas. The overall nature of the depression was exaggerated by Britain's relatively poor international trade performance and her inability either to reduce imports or to increase substantially her invisible earnings.

3   However, it is important to note that the symptoms listed above underestimate Britain's real progress during the 1930s. Britain's overall growth rate was higher than the average of other industrialised countries. There was an increase in GDP; also, rising real incomes and consumer expenditure created a demand for the products of the new consumer-orientated industries. The increase in housebuilding and the spread of electricity contributed to improving the general standard and quality of life. Unemployment insurance was widened and the government became more generous in the provision of welfare facilities. There was also a gradual increase in the length of holidays, and greater expenditure on leisure (e.g. Butlin's Skegness holiday camp opened in 1937). At the outbreak of World War I, the average working-class family spent 60% of its income on food and 16% on rent and rates. By 1935 only 36% was spent on food and 9% on rent and rates – leaving more to spend on other goods. This resulted in the growth of consumer stores such as Woolworths, Marks and Spencers, Sainsbury's, etc. Furthermore, new technologies, plus economies of scale, meant cheaper prices for consumer goods in the shops.

4   Finally, both assessments of the 'thirties are valid but the experience of that part of the population living on unemployment benefit/dole was not similar to that part of the workforce in constant employment – e.g. in the 'new' industries, the rapidly growing consumer-goods industries and in the distributive trades. It has been estimated that three-quarters of Britain's population benefited significantly from a rising standard of living in the 1930s, but a quarter still lived on the bread-line – some experiencing abject poverty.

Question bank

1 Document question (The General Strike): study the extract below and then answer questions (a) to (h) which follow:

Extract

'The miners were greatly heartened by the support of the TUC. On 4 May jubilation in the mining village was at its height, though all knew the going would be tough. The Government had already indicated that it had plans in preparation to oppose the TUC's efforts in their support of the miners. Glowing speeches of support for the miners from TUC leaders, from Bevin, Ramsay MacDonald (the traitor), Thomas (another one) were good for sustaining morale…since the Government had now declared a State of Emergency. My family deduced correctly that troops would be used to break the strike.

'Councils of Action were set up in our area…to set up at strategic points barriers to be manned by pickets to control the movement of any vehicle in and out of the village.

'The news media were already blazing out unprincipled lies about breakaways from the strike and denunciations against the strikers…. There was total paralysis of the mines, railways and factories. But at this vital stage, grave doubts given great publicity by the TUC leaders, began to appear. Meetings behind the scenes of the union leaders supporting the miners became common. It was no secret that the way was being prepared for retreat. Warrants issued for the arrest of several trade union leaders in the North aroused fierce opposition. The Council of Action in Newcastle were dealing quite effectively with the Government's Commissioner…. It was the same elsewhere. Boards of Guardians, long hated for their means-test manner of doling out food to the sick, injured and miners' families, were the target of many demonstrations…. We had our share too of the Specials and Volunteers…the press played its usual role. Through it I learned first about…'Moscow reds' and 'alien workshy agitators' who were supposed to have infiltrated our British way of life….

'The collapse of the General Strike, while disheartening to the miners, did not lead to any weakening of resolve…. As strike funds dried up, a growing number of men did return to work…. By November…the Government offered what they thought were reasonable terms as conquerors: (a) immediate resumption of work (b) longer hours to be discussed at district level, (c) rates of pay temporarily at pre-strike level (but conditional on acceptance of longer hours), (d) no guarantee against victimisation…. On November 29 it was all over.'

(From an account of the General Strike of 1926 by Bill Carr in
The General Strike ed. J. Skelly, 1976)

(a) Which Prime Minister of which party was in power this time? (2)
(b) What light does the first line throw upon the origins of the General Strike? (2)
(c) In what ways does this extract illustrate differences in attitude between the ordinary mineworkers and the official leaderships of the TUC and of the Labour Party? (5)
(d) What distinctive view of the General Strike does the extract offer? (3)
(e) Who were 'Boards of Guardians', and what was meant by 'their means-test manner'? (4)
(f) What light does the extract throw on the reasons for the failure of the General Strike and for the prolongation of the coal strike? (4)
(g) Comment on the terms which were accepted by the miners in November, 1926. (5)
(h) What steps were taken by the Government in 1927 to prevent a repetition of the General Strike? Comment on the political significance of the fact that such steps were taken. (2)

2 How depressed was the British economy between 1919 and 1939?
(Oxford and Cambridge, June 1992)

3 'The effect of economic developments in the interwar period was to sharpen the differences between the prosperous and depressed areas of the country.' In what ways and why? (AEB, June 1989)

4 'A period of rising prosperity and living standards.' How accurate is this description of Britain during the 1930s? (Oxford, June 1991)

5 Assess the impact of 'economic depression' on Britain between 1929 and 1939. (JMB, June 1988)

READING LIST

Standard textbook reading
T. O. Lloyd, *Empire to Welfare State* (OUP, 1970), chapters 4, 5, 6, 7.
L. C. B. Seaman, *Post-Victorian Britain* (Methuen, 1966), chapter V.
R. K. Webb, *Modern England* (Allen and Unwin, 1980 edn.), chapter 12.

Further suggested reading
D. H. Aldcroft, *The Interwar Economy: Britain 1919–39* (Batsford, 1973).
M. Booth and M. Pack, *Employment, Capital and Economic Policy 1918–1939* (Blackwell, 1985)
S. Constantine, *Unemployment in Britain Between the Wars* (Longman, 1980).
R. Floud and D. McCloskey (eds), *The Economic History of Britain since 1700*, Vol II (CUP, 1981).
S. Glyn and J. Oxborrow, *Interwar Britain: A Social and Economic History* (Allen and Unwin, 1976).
J. Lovell, *British Trade Unions 1875–1933* (Macmillan, 1977).
K. Nicholas, *The Social Effects of Unemployment in Teeside 1919–39* (MUP, 1986).
C. L. Mowat, *Britain Between the Wars* (Methuen, 1955).
R. Skidelsky, *Politicians and the Slump* (Macmillan, 1967).
J. Stevenson, *British History 1914–45* (Penguin, 1984).
J. Stevenson and C. Cook, *The Slump* (Cape, 1977).

BRITISH POLITICS IN THE 1920s

Units in this chapter

12.1 *A new political stage*
12.2 *The Lloyd George coalition, 1918–22*
12.3 *The first Labour Government, 1924*
12.4 *The second Labour Government, 1929*
12.5 *Chronology*

Chapter objectives

① The consequences of the First World War; the intrigues leading to the formation of the coalition and to Lloyd George's replacement of Asquith; Labour Party divisions (over pacifism) healed in time for 1918 election, but divisions within the Liberal Party were emphasised by the use of the coupon; the Conservatives, in a demoralised state before the war, were revitalised by participation in government and by the patriotic mood in the country.

② The structure of politics: the 1918 Reform Act nearly tripled the electorate; the likely social composition of new voters; the effects of the female franchise; the frequency of elections (1918, 1922, 1923, 1924, 1929) heightened tension: in voting terms, England now had a genuine three-party system which, without proportional representation, led to the gradual elimination of the weakest party, the Liberals.

③ The heightened tension and the polarisation of politics: the Spen Valley by-election (1919) and postwar industrial unrest (the Triple Alliance, the 1921–3 strikes, the General Strike) made 'the impact of Labour' or 'Labour versus Capital' or 'the Bolshevist menace' the major factors in politics and contributed to the elimination of the middle party, the Liberals.

④ Weak political leadership, composed mainly of prewar survivals: the 'sale of honours' by Lloyd George typified the smell of corruption in postwar politics.

⑤ The Conservative Party: backbench opposition to and overthrow of Lloyd George in 1922; the struggles for leadership, 1922–3, and the return of the Coalition Unionists, 1924; the accession of Churchill; disputes on fiscal and imperial (especially Indian) policies; the 'Empire Free Trade' group attacks Baldwin; the nature of the latter's leadership in the 'twenties – especially his 'astute' or 'feeble' role in the 1931 crisis.

⑥ The eclipse of the Liberal Party: the 'coupon election' confirmed the split; MacDonald saw the Liberals as a more immediate threat than the Tories; the 1923 reunification and Lloyd George's accession to the leadership in 1926 both came too late; the Liberals' poor organisation; the Summer School initiatives and 'We Can Conquer Unemployment' create a modest but temporary Liberal revival in the 1929 election; reasons for thinking that Liberal economic policy would have been inadequate to deal with unemployment.

⑦ The Labour Party became the alternative 'party of government', which had been MacDonald's main objective; the major electoral advances in 1922; the 1918 Constitution confirmed trade union dominance (the block vote, etc.) in return for a vague ideological commitment to Socialism; the establishment of a General Council and of relations between PLP and TUC (weakened by the general strike); the declining position in the Labour movement of the ILP and the socialist societies; the influence of the *Daily Herald* and improved organisation; the Party was outflanked on the Left by the Communist Party (1921); MacDonald succeeded Clynes, his qualities of leadership and his socialist philosophy – which was of the organic evolutionary, 'one-step-enough-for-me' type of gradualism; the attitudes of Snowden, Thomas, the Webbs, Henderson, etc.; the desire for social spending, to be paid for by a capital levy on rentiers.

⑧ Party policies and attitudes in the 1923 election; no party majority: Asquith decided to back Labour because of the danger of Liberal absorption by the Conservatives; Labour established its competence to govern – the Party's achievements were modest at home but more impressive in foreign affairs. A *Workers Weekly* article brings the government down, impact of Zinoviev letter.

⑨ Baldwin returned to office; the eclipse of the Liberals; the return to the gold standard exacerbated the depression; the Liberal public works proposals and 'proto-Keynesianism'; the effect of revaluation on coal-mining. The causes and course of the general strike of 1926; the political consequences for the trade union and Labour movements. Chamberlain extended Welfare provision; the Conservatives' public enterprise measures – establishment of the BBC and the CEB; parliamentary duels between Churchill and Snowden.

⑩ The 1929 election: the growing problem of unemployment; the 'safety first' policy of Labour and the Conservatives; the election result was inconclusive but the Liberals again backed MacDonald; Labour was unable to deal with unemployment, to balance the budget or to maintain the external value of the pound. The economic crisis, the May Committee recommendations, the divisions in party and in the cabinet; and did MacDonald's behaviour 'betray' the Labour Party?

⑪ Foreign policy and politics: the Anglo-Irish war and Lloyd George's 'settlement' of the Irish problem by partition; his pacific attitude towards Germany alienated Tory backbenchers, and was anyway undermined by Chanak, which made him appear a warmonger. MacDonald's successful and pacific foreign policy – his handling of Franco-German relations and the reparations problem; the Geneva Protocol and Locarno; the Zinoviev letter and its part in the Labour government's downfall; the Kellogg Pact and the Hague Conference marked an easier foreign situation; imperial politics were more important than foreign in the later 1920s.

The first World War and the Reform Act of 1918, which trebled the electorate, had a profound effect on British politics and society. It was a severe test of Britain's social stability and brought about major political changes, the most important being the eclipse of the Liberals as a major party of government and its replacement by a reunited and reconstructed Labour Party committed in theory to implementing a comprehensive programme of Socialism, but in fact to implementing the broad policy of progressivism begun by the Liberals before 1914.

During this period, the three-cornered nature of the political struggle (plus the number of elections) kept party politics alive, exciting and unpredictable. For some time it appeared that Lloyd George would resist the challenge of Labour and establish a centre party with progressive goals. His downfall in 1922, however, encouraged Baldwin, in the electoral stalemate of 1923, to give Labour its chance.

The failure of direct action appeared to suggest that Labour could be trusted; MacDonald could be relied on to control the militant class-conscious forces of labour and, in the process, perhaps destroy Liberalism. While the collapse of the General Strike in 1926 confirmed MacDonald's position on the former, the rout of the Liberals in 1924 seemed to indicate the success of the latter.

Though beset by challenges from Right and Left, Baldwin and MacDonald restored the two-party pattern of prewar government and, in doing so, contained the working-class challenge to the established order.

12.1 A NEW POLITICAL STAGE

British politics in the immediate aftermath of the war were characterised by a heady optimism about the future. As early as 1919, however, the Lloyd George coalition's taste for social reform was disappearing, and working-class unrest only convinced the Conservatives that firmer government was needed. By 1921, furthermore, the post-war boom had ended, and politicians, though coming to terms with a three-party system, were baffled by the onset of an economic depression whose effects were to dominate interwar politics.

The traditional parties had also to recognise the threat posed by the rapidly growing Labour Party, a threat given particular edge by a new political style which drew heavily on class-based rhetoric to foment party unity.

How are we to explain Labour's successful emergence after 1918? First to a growth in working-class consciousness which demanded its own party, and secondly to an upsurge in Trade Union membership which provided the new party with organisation and funds. Finally, it had a flexible, attractive, pragmatic set of policies (largely inherited from the Liberals) which could appeal to all classes of society.

In the event, the main consequence of the rise of Labour was political, not economic: it killed off Liberalism as a political force, without finding any way out of the economic tangle in which the country found itself, with the problems of ageing industries, mass unemployment and international indebtedness throughout Europe.

The reaction to these events was overwhelmingly political. In five general elections the major Parties disputed who should have power, but had nothing to offer on the economic questions which faced the country, except caution and financial orthodoxy. Only the Liberals, by then a fading force, came up with a comprehensive alternative economic policy (inspired by Keynes) in 1929, and they were brushed off by the voters.

Following Lloyd George's departure in 1922, politics were dominated by two men whose policies were, in practical terms, almost indistinguishable; Ramsay MacDonald and Stanley Baldwin. Both wanted England to recover, and neither had the slightest idea how she might. Baldwin offered political stability and, although MacDonald stood against him in Parliament, what he sought for Labour was a share in maintaining that stability, not a mandate for revolution or class war. The limited vision of Baldwin and MacDonald was the price England had to pay for maintaining its political freedom and stability at a time when, everywhere else in Europe, these things were fast disappearing.

12.2 THE LLOYD GEORGE COALITION, 1918-22

The general election of December, 1918 (the 'Coupon Election') returned to power the Lloyd George coalition, which had made extensive promises of social improvement. These were never fulfilled, for both economic and political reasons. The cost of the war had been enormous, far beyond what anyone had imagined, and the House of Commons was obsessed with the need to reduce expenditure.

Lloyd George had only a small political following in Parliament. He was dependent for survival on his coalition allies, the Tories, who increasingly demanded the decontrol of industries taken over by the government during the war and resisted proposed expenditure on social reform. The Labour Party and the trade unions, on the other hand, wanted to extend the more egalitarian aspects of war collectivism. Lloyd George himself was by now prepared to trade principles for power, and he went along with the Tories' arguments. As a consequence, retrenchment, not reconstruction, dictated government thinking, and inevitably it was the newest areas of state activity which suffered most.

The cause of social improvement was not helped by Lloyd George's failure to make it a cabinet priority. The commitment to social improvement through vigorous government action was eventually abandoned in 1921, when the Geddes Committee was appointed to recommend cuts in expenditure. The Tories, after the Chanak crisis, finally ditched Lloyd George in October 1922, and won decisively the election which followed in November 1922, but this was largely a consequence of his personal unpopularity and of resentment of the Irish treaty. He had cast aside social reform long before then.

Baldwin's adoption of Protection as a cure for the country's economic ills in May 1923 at once polarised politics. It was the signal for a Liberal reunion after the electoral drubbing in November 1922 and, indeed, they gained 67 seats from the Conservatives, but still ended up in third place. Asquith, hoping for a Labour débâcle, accepted their minority government. Thus, factionalism caused the Liberals to miss their best opportunity to restore Liberalism as an independent party. Baldwin sensed that a MacDonald-led government could be trusted. Rather a short period of 'responsible' Labour rule than to drive them back to supporting 'direct action' by the trade unions. Labour was indeed 'contained', and resentment of, and policy of non-cooperation with, the Liberals, hastened the latter's now rapid decline. Between them, Baldwin and MacDonald crushed the Liberal revival and engineered a return to the two-party system, offering the electorate a choice between 'decent' Conservatism and 'respectable' Labour.

12.3 THE FIRST LABOUR GOVERNMENT, 1924

In March 1923, a Conservative peer told a friend: 'I think that people are rather sick about the King and Queen going to dine…to meet a lot of Labour bounders'. Within a year, and to the dismay of many, the 'bounders' took office in the first Labour government under Ramsay MacDonald. He chose an ineffective political team; his cabinet was almost totally inexperienced.

Dependent on the Liberals, 'Labour were in office but not in power'; this goes some way to explain their modest performance (and also their growing resentment of the Liberals). MacDonald was anxious, above all, to rebut Churchill's sneer that Labour was not fit to govern. He succeeded and, as Prime Minister and Foreign Secretary, he made a considerable personal impression both in Britain and abroad. But, like Baldwin's Conservative administration, his government was devoid of ideas on how to remedy Britain's deep-rooted economic problems.

In the circumstances of the time, with many Tories still paranoiac about the dangers of Bolshevism, MacDonald's caution was understandable. It did, however, cause some resentment among the TUC and Left-wing Labour MPs. Apart from his own success in foreign affairs, and some improvements in social policy, his government's record was uninspiring; it was notable chiefly for the fact of its existence.

Labour had made remarkable progress in a very short time, from being largely the spokesmen for the trade unions (who favoured direct action) to being a major parliamentary and national force now campaigning to gain political power so that they might change (constitutionally) the political system. MacDonald's major intentions were to consolidate these gains by making Labour an acceptable party of government, and to destroy the Liberal Party as a party of the Left. According to one historian, 'he had tried to prove that Labour was fit to govern; all he did in the end was to prove that MacDonald was fit to be Prime Minister'.

Consider now some fundamental problems of interpretation: did Socialism replace Liberalism, or was it merely that Labour replaced the Liberals and continued much of the old Liberal policy (free trade, little Englandism, etc.)? Was the triumph of Labour the inevitable consequence of long-term trends – the growth of class politics, the rise of organised labour, the decay of old Liberal laissez-faire values – or was it the fortuitous and chance result of war and of personality differences among the Liberals in the Liberal leadership? (See Chapter 10). Now is the time also to attempt an assessment of the career of Lloyd George: crusader, opportunist or charlatan?

Baldwin

Baldwin's air of good-humoured laziness was misleading. He appreciated the fragile nature of postwar politics where dynamic forces like Lloyd George and Churchill could prove liabilities. Mediocrity also had its function; hence Baldwin stood for conciliation all round. He had a clear sense of how Britain should develop, and made political stability a key objective at a time when much of Europe was experiencing political and economic upheavals. He appreciated that Labour had become part of the political system and determined to resist their effort to make class conflict a main factor in politics.

He strove to make himself the acceptable leader of all non-Labour opinion. His success is reflected in the fact that his severest critics were in his own Party. On occasion he could act with speed and decisiveness – see for example how effectively he led the revolt against the Lloyd George coalition. As Prime Minister in 1923 and from 1924 to 1929, he aimed to preserve a balance in the country's affairs. Despite economic difficulties and the general strike, in political terms he succeeded. His style of leadership, however, did have repercussions on the Conservative Party – note in particular the disputes on fiscal and imperial policies.

Where the economy was concerned, however, his government had nothing to offer except traditional remedies. Unemployment and depression were regarded as unalterable facts of life; Baldwin lacked political imagination and took the line that the country could only wait until things got better. His government fell, not because it did not come up with the right answers – but because it failed to come up with new ideas to tackle the problems. Its only positive economic action was the return to the gold standard in 1925, a decision which made things even worse for Britain's export industries. Apart from Neville Chamberlain (the real driving force behind government reforms) at the Ministry of Health, his cabinet had few achievements to record in their five years in office. But politics remained orderly and broadly consensual, which was Baldwin's particular aim.

The General Strike of 1926

The General Strike was not the climax of postwar political, ideological or even industrial confrontation and tension. It was something which few people wanted to happen. In the end it was forced on the TUC by Baldwin's decision to suspend negotiations. Basically, he was not prepared to back down from a confrontation with the labour movement either by enforcing a fair settlement on the mine owners or by continuing to subsidise wages while negotiations went on.

The government had learnt the lesson of 'Red Friday', when it had been forced to give way in the face of the threat of widespread industrial action. By May 1926 adequate preparations to combat a general strike had been made. The trade unions, by contrast, had done little to prepare for action. In the event, once the labour movement blundered into open conflict with the government, both sides had reason to be pleased: the government's plans to maintain essential services worked almost without a hitch, while nearly all trade unionists unhesitatingly obeyed the strike call.

The strike was generally an orderly affair: there was little serious violence and no bloodshed. Nevertheless, for the TUC it was a traumatic episode. They insisted that the reasons for the strike were economic and they did in fact fear a general wage-cutting onslaught by the employers: however, the object was to get the government back to the negotiating table. Their problem was that in order to do this they had to defeat the government in the strike. The government regarded it as a political action designed to usurp the authority of Parliament (the constitutional issue was always uppermost in Baldwin's mind), and took the line that it could not possibly negotiate at the point of a gun.

Neither the TUC nor the vast majority of the strikers had any wish to bring the Government down, and the unions had no clear idea of what to do if the dispute dragged on for any length of time. In the end, faced by the government's intransigence, the weakness of their own policy, the fear of permanent Communist domination of local trade councils (which had run the strike) and by the miners' obstinacy, the TUC called off their action in response to a vague promise of intercession from the Liberal MP, Sir Herbert Samuel, who had led an earlier enquiry into the coal industry. The miners stayed out, but eventually were forced to go back to work for more hours and less pay.

How well did Baldwin handle the strike? Left-wing historians argue that he acted in his usual indolent manner and failed to restrain hotheads like Churchill. The sympathetic view is that he played a clever, ameliorative, waiting game, knowing that the TUC would not tolerate a prolonged strike.

The outcome of the strike has often been portrayed as a massive weakening of the trade union movement, which persisted throughout the interwar years. As A J P Taylor points out, however, it was 'a warning to other employers not to push their workers too far'; in fact, wages in Britain held up well in the difficult years that followed. Although the cost for the unions in terms of money, membership and employment was great, it was at least a positive response to the country's economic problems. During the protest they also demonstrated how responsible and law-abiding they were – no longer could they be accused of fomenting revolution every time they took industrial action. According to Lloyd 'a whole cycle of working class militancy...had come to an end... . For the next five years, immobility reigned triumphant and almost unchallenged'.

12.4 THE SECOND LABOUR GOVERNMENT, 1929

MacDonald's Second Government brought few changes for Britain. Although interesting alternative economic policies were advocated by the reunited Liberals under Lloyd George, they managed to win only 59 seats. Baldwin, because of his detestation of Lloyd George, refused the Liberals a coalition with his 260 MPs. So Labour, with 288 seats took office, but once there, regarded the Depression with the same fatalism which had characterised Baldwin's government. Skidelsky has described Labour's failure to adopt Keynesian policies as 'the major missed opportunity of the interwar period'. But would they have worked?

The Labour Government was more innovative in foreign policy, with Henderson, the Foreign Secretary, pushing for disarmament and winning French confidence. The question of European security, however, was tied up with the complex problem of reparations. MacDonald and the Treasury believed that only when the tangle of

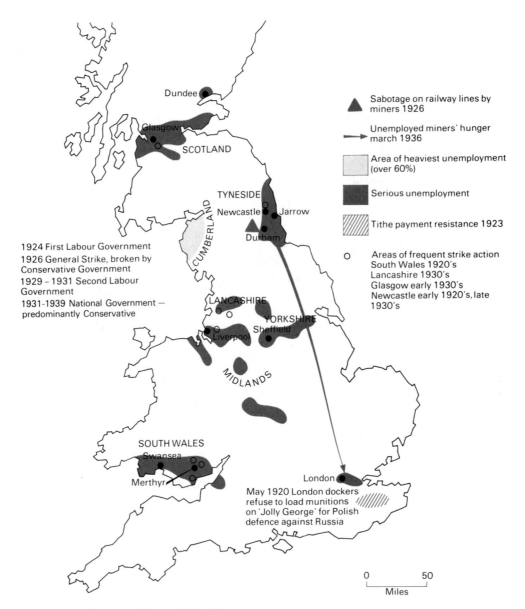

1924 First Labour Government
1926 General Strike, broken by
Conservative Government
1929–1931 Second Labour
Government
1931–1939 National Government —
predominantly Conservative

▲ Sabotage on railway lines by
miners 1926

→ Unemployed miners' hunger
march 1936

Area of heaviest unemployment
(over 60%)

Serious unemployment

Tithe payment resistance 1923

○ Areas of frequent strike action
South Wales 1920's
Lancashire 1930's
Glasgow early 1930's
Newcastle early 1920's, late
1930's

May 1920 London dockers
refuse to load munitions
on 'Jolly George' for Polish
defence against Russia

0   50
Miles

Fig. 11 Unemployment and unrest during the interwar years

international indebtedness was finally cleared away should a settlement of the political tension between France and Germany be attempted. Henderson took the contrary line that Germany's economic problems represented an opportunity to force her into political concessions and thereby ease French fears.

The 1931 crisis

Unemployment in Britain, which had been over a million, had shot up to 2.5 million by early 1931, but the government took no action to reduce it. Things were made far worse in August, 1931 by the dramatic collapse of the pound; Henderson and his followers refused to accept the proposed drastic economies. These included cuts in unemployment relief, and were held to be necessary to balance the budget – thus restoring the confidence of holders of sterling and preventing a financial collapse. As the cost of living had fallen substantially, some argued that the cuts were not entirely unjustified. MacDonald, who undoubtedly liked office and who was tired of his perpetual battle with Henderson, split decisively with his Party by staying on as Prime Minister of a 'national' government formed to see out the immediate crisis. The shocked surprise of his colleagues indicated his isolation in the Party and demonstrated in their eyes his love of power. Equally, however, it could be argued that their actions during the crisis demonstrated their fear of exercising it. In considering this emotive episode, two questions should be borne in mind. First, why did the government of 1929–31 not take up interventionist economic policies such as those put forward by Oswald Mosley from their own party or Lloyd George from the Liberals? Second, given the conventional wisdom of the day, what other course could the Government have taken in August, 1931 if a financial collapse was to be avoided?

Macdonald's rule

Did MacDonald betray his party in 1931? The majority of the party certainly thought so. There is, however, little solid evidence to support this view. According to David Marquand, MacDonald was persuaded by George V and Baldwin to put nation before party as the best way of restoring national confidence. Skidelsky argues that MacDonald's betrayal occurred earlier, in 1930, when he ignored good advice and thereby failed to take action which might have averted the monetary crisis of 1931. Perhaps the main actors in the drama were right to gauge that only a National Government would be able to carry out policies such as the abandonment of the gold standard and free trade, without precipitating widespread national panic

12.5 CHRONOLOGY

1918	August	FISHER EDUCATION ACT raised the school-leaving age to 14.
	November	Armistice ended the fighting in the Great War. REPRESENTATION OF THE PEOPLE ACT introduced full manhood suffrage and gave the vote to women aged 30 and over.
	December	Lloyd George Coalition won the 'Coupon Election'. First vote for more than 6 million women. Sinn Fein won 73 seats in Ireland and decided to boycott the Westminster Parliament.
1919	January	Sinn Fein set up their own assembly, the Dail, in Dublin. A guerrilla war between the IRA and the Royal Irish Constabulary (the British armed police) followed.
	June	Allies concluded the world war with a peace treaty at Versailles. The huge reparations demanded of Germany created immense problems in international finance during the following years.
1920		The breakdown of law and order in Ireland: Lloyd George sent supplementary British forces (the Auxiliaries and the 'Black and Tans') to Ireland to enforce a policy of coercion.
	August	War between Poland and Russia: the British government was deterred from intervention by the threat (at home) of a general strike.
	December	GOVERNMENT OF IRELAND ACT: provided for Ireland to remain in the UK, but for Southern Ireland and the Six Counties each to have their own elected assemblies. This was ignored by Sinn Fein.
1921		Postwar boom ended; the onset of economic depression.
	March	UNEMPLOYMENT INSURANCE ACT: introduced the 'dole'.
	April	Black Friday; the railway and transport unions refused to support the miners by coming out on strike.
	July	Truce declared in Ireland.
	December	IRISH TREATY signed between the government and Sinn Fein representatives; gave substantial independence to Southern Ireland, now to be called the Irish Free State, but not the republican status desired by De Valera. The Six Counties were allowed to contract out. De Valera denounced the Treaty and a civil war followed between the pro-treaty (Free Staters) and the anti-treaty (IRA) parties.
1922	February	GEDDES COMMITTEE called for major cuts in public expenditure.
	October	Conservative backbenchers rebelled against the coalition at a Party meeting, rejecting the advice of most of their leaders. Lloyd George resigned; he was replaced by his former colleague, Andrew Bonar Law.
	November	Conservatives won the general election.

1923	January	The war debt with the US settled by the Chancellor, Baldwin, on what were regarded as unfavourable terms.
	May	Baldwin became Prime Minister, succeeding Bonar Law.
	October	TARIFF REFORM: Badwin announced his conversion to protectionism.
	December	Conservatives lost their overall majority at the general election. Baldwin declined to continue in office.
1924	January	FIRST LABOUR GOVERNMENT: a minority administration formed under James Ramsay MacDonald.
	June	Dawes Plan: new proposals for the payment of German reparations.
	August	*WORKERS' WEEKLY*: offices raided. Editor charged with incitement to mutiny.
	October	ZINOVIEV LETTER, apparently from the Comintern and signed by Zinoviev, called on English Communists to overthrow the Labour government; published by the Foreign Office. Conservatives returned to power under Baldwin.
1925	April	BRITAIN RETURNED TO THE GOLD STANDARD at prewar parity of $4.86 to the pound.
	July	RED FRIDAY: the government backed down in the face of the threat of a general strike over problems in the mining industry.
	September	SAMUEL COMMISSION set up to investigate the problems of the coal industry. Baldwin bought time by granting a subsidy of £23 million.
	October	Treaty of Locarno: began an era of tranquility in international affairs.
1926	March	Government failed to persuade the miners and the mine owners to accept a compromise on pay and reorganisation of the coal industry.
	1 May	Miners locked out.
	3 May	GENERAL STRIKE began.
	12 May	General strike ended; miners decided to stay out – and did so until December.
1927	May	TRADE DISPUTES and TRADE UNION ACT: reduced the income of the Labour Party by forcing trade unionists to 'contract in' to the political levy raised by the unions. This was resented by the Labour movement as an attack upon fundamental union rights and as a breach of faith by Baldwin and the Conservatives.
1928	April	REPRESENTATION OF THE PEOPLE (EQUAL FRANCHISE) ACT: gave the vote (dubbed the 'flapper vote') to women on the same terms as men.
	August	Kellog-Briand Pact: Britain, as one of the signatories, renounced war as an instrument of national policy.
1929	April	LOCAL GOVERNMENT ACT, introduced by Chamberlain, abolished the 1834 Poor Law Act.
	May	Labour won most seats in a three-party general election; Liberals seats were reduced to 59.
	June	SECOND LABOUR GOVERNMENT formed.
	October	WALL STREET CRASH: securities at market value crashed by almost $16 000 million; this immediately affected world trade and investment. British exports began to fall from a current £839 million to a 1931 low of £461 million; growing unemployment was the result.
1930	May	Cabinet rejected the Mosley reflation scheme.
	August	COALMINES ACT: reduced miners' working day by a half-hour.
1931	July	MAY COMMITTEE recommended public expenditure cuts. Foreign investors withdrew funds. Bank of England lost £2½ millions per day.
	August	Cabinet failed to agree on the cuts. Labour government resigned. NATIONAL GOVERNMENT FORMED by MacDonald.
	September	Naval mutiny at Invergordon; caused a run on the pound. BRITAIN ABANDONED THE GOLD STANDARD; the pound fell from $4.86 to $3.80.

Illustrative questions and answers

1   Why did the Second Labour Government fail to solve the problems posed by the Depression?

Tutorial note

You must review the ways in which the problems might best have been solved, and also the restraints imposed on the government, both from within the Labour movement and from without.

You need to know about

The causes and course of the economic depression of the 1920s and 1930s. The response of the Labour Government. Alternative policies proposed for dealing with it.

Suggested answer plan

1   Causes of the depression: the loss of traditional markets in wartime; the difficulties of staple industries in the cost-price squeeze of the 1920s; dependence on world trade meant Britain could only recover in the wake of a general world recovery; this restricted the freedom of manoeuvre in dealing with the domestic economy, since Britain dared not take measures (e.g. competitive devaluation) which might impede world recovery; the 1925 return to gold aggravated the depression; the course of the depression, with unemployment figures, etc.

2   The long-term constraints on economic policy: the unrealistic desire to return to the favourable conditions of Edwardian England; hence the gold standard and the 'politics of nostalgia'; free trade as an article of faith with the electorate (cf. the 1923 election), which hampered all governments' attempts to deal with the economic problem.

3   External constraints on the Labour Government: pressure from bankers like Norman ('Bankers' ramp') and civil servants like Maybury, who were both in collusion with Tories like Chamberlain to undermine ministers; the Government's minority position and dependence on the Liberals.

4   The internal constraints on the Government: the indecisiveness of MacDonald; Snowden was rigidly locked into the orthodox Treasury view (balanced budgets, free trade, sound money); Thomas was irresponsible and lazy (and responsible for severe cabinet leaks); the PLP was indisciplined; the ILP was alienated from the government; the TUC was suspicious since the General Strike; Henderson was hostile to MacDonald; ultimately the cabinet divided on the question of unemployment benefits; the Labour Party had inherited the old Liberal/Cobdenite free-trade/ League-of-Nations tradition, which further hampered its freedom of action.

5   Was there really a better alternative? Sweden, New Zealand and Australia do not provide satisfactory analogies; the small size of the English public sector made an interventionist policy hard to operate; there were legal and administrative difficulties in the way of public works; 'Keynesianism' became the great alternative, but it was not codified until 1936; advisers Keynes and Hubert Henderson were both very confused and self-contradictory throughout 1930/1 – they did not realise until 1931 that protection and devaluation were required; in 1929 the Liberal Party, under Lloyd George, proposed public works but was against protection and against cuts in the dole, so reflecting only a feeble grasp of 'Keynesianism'; reflation without protection would merely have sucked in imports; TUC policy under Bevin and Citrine (to suspend the national debt and to tax rentiers) would have been dangerous; only Mosley had a properly worked-out alternative strategy, and it was unacceptable to the Party.

6   So, while the government may be blamed for its policy of 'drift' when *either* full-blooded deflation or reflation might have been preferable, the problems it faced were immense; and it did do some positive things (e.g. the Economic Advisory Council began industrial reconstruction).

2 Examine the causes and consequences of the General Strike in 1926.

Tutorial note

This is a straightforward question on a single event in political and working-class history; remember that, while its causes were mainly local and industrial, its consequences may be traced over a wide area of British life.

You need to know about

The economic, social, industrial and political events of the interwar period. A fairly detailed narrative of the general strike itself.

Suggested answer plan

1   The General Strike has given rise to a most consolatory myth – i.e. one in which both parties to the dispute (establishment *and* workers) can look back on it as a moment of supreme triumph (for 'individualism' and for 'collective solidarity' respectively); as such it had a usefully purgative effect on the bitter politics of the 1920s; indeed, all except the miners could derive some comfort from the event.

2   The fundamental causes of industrial unrest in the 1920s: the rise of the trade unions, 1914–20, and the rise of shop-floor power; the increase of Syndicalism in the union movement; the establishment of the TUC General Council (1920) and the Communist Party (1921); the depression and unemployment, 1922–5, put trades unions on the defensive, starting with 'Black Friday'; the losses of membership 1920–5, and concentration within the movement (Triple Alliance); the increasing power of national officials vis-a-vis the rank and file; wage-cuts caused a wave of disputes, 1921–3; then in 1925 the return to gold at old par made further wage cuts seem necessary.

3   The specific problems of the mining industry: the workers desired nationalisation; the Sankey Report and Lloyd George's decision to decontrol (leading to Black Friday and to great bitterness); renewed competition from Polish and German coal hit the market in 1924; A J Cook led the resistance to the projected wage cuts; Bevin and other unionists were anxious to show that direct action could accomplish more for workers than could 'woolly' Labour politicians (even when in government), so the General Council took up the miners' cause; Red Friday and the Samuel Commission; cabinet 'hawks' like Joynson-Hicks and Churchill finally provoked the general strike by breaking off negotiations after an 'overt act' on the part of *Daily Mail* compositors.

4   A brief narrative of the events of the General Strike, of volunteer strike-breaking and the subsequent miners' lock-out.

5   The political consequences: the alienation of the TUC from Labour Party over the attitude to the strike of MacDonald and others; Baldwin threw away his reputation for fairness with the Trade Disputes and Trade Union Act (1927); membership of the Communist Party collapsed in 1926; the Conservatives looked for recovery through planning rather than renewed confrontation.

6   The consequences of the strike for the mining industry: the miners were demoralised by the General Council's decision to end the strike and did not recover their former power within the movement (until 1972–4); the large wage cuts and consequent bitterness led ultimately to nationalisation in 1947.

7   The consequences of the strike for the trade union movement: membership was falling anyway (1920–5) and the General Strike merely reinforced the trend (1925–8) – especially on the railways and in printing, which had done relatively well during 1921–5; except in mining, membership (and funds) were to recover, 1933–9; there was a decline of Syndicalism and in use of the strike weapon generally – which may have occurred anyway during the depression – but it must be significant that the main strikes in 1929–33 were in an industry largely unaffected in 1926 (textiles); shop stewards lost in influence to the national officials; the General Council (under Bevin and Citrine) turned against

the Communist Party, and agreed to participate in industrial rationalisation and planning (or state monopoly capitalism), instead of trying to overthrow capitalism completely; the Mond-Turner talks paved the way.

8   So the General Strike marked a transition in the Labour movement towards a more willing cooperation with capitalism – but it was probably happening anyway; more significantly, it made employers (except the mineowners) more moderate in the future – there was little wage-cutting (except according to negotiated sliding-scales) in the 1929–33 depression.

3   Consider the achievements and limitations of Baldwin as Conservative Party leader.

Tutorial note

This is a question about the Conservative Party's political success in the interwar years and Baldwin's contribution to it. Do not waste time discussing Baldwin's qualities as a national leader.

You need to know about

The party-political history of the 1920s and 1930s.

Suggested answer plan

1   The considerable success of the interwar Conservative Party, compared with its demoralisation and disarray before 1914; the benefits to the party from the 1918 and 1928 franchise extensions and from the Liberal decline; the divisions within the Party.

2   Baldwin's industrial background and swift political rise; his career at Board of Trade and Exchequer; the settlement of the war debt to America brings him prominence at a critical time; his part in the Carlton Club's rejection of Lloyd George (1922); he was preferred to Curzon as Party leader in 1923.

3   Baldwin's leadership was constantly challenged by apparently cleverer men, who could never understand his success, and who chafed at his 'masterly inactivity'; his deliberate rejection of Lloyd George's 'dangerous dynamism' – such opposition culminated in the 'Empire Free Trade' group's (Rothermere, Beaverbrook, Churchill) attack on his Indian and fiscal policies in 1930–1; in thwarting this group, Baldwin showed himself to be a master of political tactics; his handling of the abdication crisis revealed the same.

4   Yet he himself mendaciously claimed: 'I am not a clever man. I know nothing of political tactics.' His greatest contribution as leader was to project and personify the Conservative image of morally serious, commonsensical, anti-intellectual, unflappable, honest, pipe-smoking, rural-utopian decency; this 'Salisbury-style' of Conservatism, an effective antidote to Lloyd George's flippant insincerity, attracted many middle-class and female voters, and some deferential worker voters; through association with Reith's BBC, Baldwin became the first modern media politician.

5   As leader, Baldwin made many apparent blunders: he threw the 1923 election away 'needlessly' by espousing protection, squandered a reputation for social 'fairness' by agreeing to the Trade Disputes and Trade Union Act (1927), misjudged the electorate's mood in 1929 by relying on 'Safety First' and his own persona, and he might have done better, from a party viewpoint, to have refused support to MacDonald's National government, since the Conservatives would certainly have won handsomely in 1931 on their own; his only really successfully managed election was that of 1935.

6   Yet, looked at in a longer perspective, all these actions revealed his tactical astuteness; protection provided a clear line of demarcation between the Conservatives and the Coalition Liberals, prevented Chamberlain and Birkenhead from joining Lloyd George, and so helped to heal old party wounds; it was probably a wise move to 'lose' in the depression of 1929, and by supporting

a National government Baldwin was able to settle the protection issue – the Conservative's biggest albatross – in a non-party-political way.

7   But, in longer terms still, Baldwin's homely image worked against the Party, making it seem too stupid for the dangerous 1930s, and also dishonest (e.g. the 1935 election and rearmament); his failure to encourage younger moderates and reformers (Macmillan, Boothby, Stanley) was also costly; Baldwin's Party collapsed in bitterness in May 1940; he had managed to keep it together for a decade, but had associated it too closely with his own personal political 'style'.

Question bank

1   Document question (Labour and Liberalism in 1924): study the extract below and then answer questions (a) to (h) which follow:

Extract

'My difficulty about the Liberal Party lies further back than yours. I doubt if it any longer stands for anything distinctive. My reasons are on the one side that moderate Labour – Labour in office – has on the whole represented essential Liberalism, not without mistakes and defects, but *better* than the organised party since Campbell-Bannerman's death. On the other side the Liberal party, however you divide it up, never seems any better agreed within on essentials. Of the present fragment, part leans to the Tories, part to Labour, part has nothing distinctive, but is a kind of Free Trade Unionist group. The deduction I draw is that the distinction between that kind of Labour man who does not go whole hog for nationalisation on the one side, and the Liberal who wants social progress on the other, is obsolete. I myself have always felt it was unreal and that if we divided parties by true principles the division would be like this

Communist	ordinary Labour	Bad Liberal	Diehards
Theoretical Socialist	Good Liberal	ordinary Tory	

'But tradition and class distinction kept many good Liberals outside Labour. Now Labour has grown so much that it tends to absorb them and to leave only the 'bad' Liberals who incline to the Tories and a mass of traditional Liberals who can't desert a party of that name... .

'For a moment fate seemed to be avoided by the decision of the Liberals on the *Manchester Guardian* lead to support Labour. Labour responded badly, and the Liberals then drew away and inevitably gravitated to the other side. They failed to present a third view because outside the extremists there is really no third view. Liberals may be full of fight, but as against the main body of Labour, what have they to fight for? Internationalism? Free Trade? Ireland, India, any particular kind of Social Reform? No, on all these there is agreement. There is really nothing, till you come up against doctrinaire Socialism, which is really outside 'moderate' Labour.'

(J A Hobhouse to C P Scott, 7 November, 1924)

(a) Who was Prime Minister in the Labour Government of 1924? Who was Campbell-Bannerman; and who was leader of 'the other side'?   (3)
(b) Explain the comment 'Labour responded badly'.   (2)
(c) To what extent had the 1924 Labour Government's policies 'represented essential Liberalism' ?   (7)
(d) Comment on the division of 'parties by true principles', laid out above.   (4)
(e) How apt is the writer's assertion that there was 'no third view', in the light of the party politics of the 1920s?   (3)
(f) Why had Labour 'grown so much' since 1918?   (2)

(g) The writer suggests that the Liberals' main problem was the common ground between Labour and Liberal policies. What other factors are relevant to Liberal decline up to 1924? (4)

(h) The writer clearly found little 'doctrinaire Socialism' in the First Labour Government. How much would he have found in the second? (6)

2 How skilful and constructive a statesman was Stanley Baldwin?

(London, June 1990)

3 Did Ramsay MacDonald serve his country better than his party?

(Oxford and Cambridge, June 1992)

4 Why did the 1926 General Strike occur, and why did it fail?

(Cambridge, June 1991)

5 'To understand the rise of the Labour Party between the wars, one need look no further than the fortunes of the Liberal party.' How far do you agree with this assessment? (WJEC, June 1991)

READING LIST

Standard textbook reading

T. O. Lloyd, *Empire to Welfare State* (OUP, 1970), chapters 4, 5, 6.

L. C. B. Seaman, *Post-Victorian Britain* (Methuen, 1966), chapters III, IV.

R. K. Webb, *Modern England* (Allen and Unwin, 1980 edn.), chapter 12.

Further suggested reading

P. Adelman, *The Decline of the Liberal Party 1910–31* (Longman, 1981).

R. Blake, *The Conservative Party from Peel to Thatcher* (Fontana, 1985).

S. Constantine, *Lloyd George* (Routledge, 1992).

C. Farman, *The General Strike* (Hart-Davis, 1972).

J. Hinton, *Labour and Socialism: A History of the British Labour Movement* (Wheatsheaf, 1983).

D. Marquand, *Ramsay MacDonald* (Cape, 1977).

R. K. Middlemas and A. L. Barnes, *Baldwin, a Biography* (Weidenfeld, 1969).

K. O. Morgan, *Consensus and Disunity 1918–22* (OUP, 1979).

G. A. Phillips, *The General Strike* (Weidenfield and Nicholson, 1976).

M. D. Pugh, *The Tories and the People 1880–1935* (Blackwell, 1985).

J. Ramsden, *The Age of Balfour and Baldwin* (Longman, 1978).

R. Skidelsky, *Politicians and the Slump* (Macmillan, 1967).

A. J P. Taylor, *English History 1914–45* (OUP, 1965).

THE NATIONAL GOVERNMENTS, 1931-9

Units in this chapter

13.1 *The emerging danger*
13.2 *National politics ,1931–5*
13.3 *The National government, 1935–9*
13.4 *Chronology*

Chapter objectives

❶ The formation of the National Government: background to the financial crisis of 1931; the collapse of the Vienna Credit Anstalt (May), and the May Committee Report (August) led to a run on sterling and to a cabinet split over the budget; the role of opposition leaders (especially Chamberlain) and of the King in helping to 'persuade' MacDonald.

❷ The composition of the National Government: Conservatives predominated at ministerial level and overwhelmingly so at the parliamentary level; the failing powers and political weakness of MacDonald, the nominal premier, and the growing dominance in cabinet of Chamberlain; the National Liberals increasingly submerged within the Conservative coalition; the exclusion of Churchill and Amery; Baldwin's succession, then Chamberlain's.

❸ The electoral history of the National Government: the abusive nature of 1931 and the scare campaign against Labour's 'Bolshevism run mad'; the essential dishonesty of MacDonald's demand for a 'doctor's mandate', since a protectionist solution to the economic problem was already intended; the divergent nature of the manifestos of the different parties to the Coalition; the reasons for its enormous victory; a class and regional analysis of the 1935 election; Baldwin's astute handling of it, again on the somewhat dishonest slogan, 'Collective Security through the League'. Labour's recovery in London, Yorkshire, Scotland and Lancashire, and the collapse of the Liberals.

❹ Political opposition to the National Government: the lack of government dynamism stemmed in part from the weakness of the opposition; the problems of the Labour Party under Henderson and Lansbury; the latter's pacifism and resignation over Mussolini; the recovery under Attlee and the likelihood by 1939 that Labour would win the next election. Samuelite Liberals (and Snowden) quit the National Government over the Ottawa Agreements in 1932, leaving the Simonite

National Liberals inside; bleatings of 'the Goat in the Wilderness' (Lloyd George), mainly for public works and 'Keynesianism', could not prevent a further squeeze of the Liberals in 1935.

❺ In the absence of political opposition, most attacks on the government came from outside the Commons; the hunger marches, demonstrations and growth of political violence, especially from Mosley's Blackshirts (BUF, founded in 1932) and the Communist Party; this enabled the government to pose as the bastion of law and order, by restoring general warrants in 1934 and by the 1936 Public Order Act.

❻ The domestic policies of the National Government: the abandonment of gold and free trade; the Imperial Economic Conference revealed little accord but did lead to the Ottawa Agreements; the protective tariff and colonial preference played an important part in 1930s economic recovery; note also the importance of rearmament (from 1934, seriously from 1936); Chamberlain as Chancellor, balancing rearmament against social spending, and the influence here of Horace Wilson. There was some very modest deficit financing (1932–3) and cheap money (a low Bank rate), but few public works; there was some economic regulation (marketing boards) and nationalisation (London Transport, BOAC); the school-leaving age was raised to 15; the 1934 Unemployment Act regulated relief and created political controversy. There was a steady, unnoticed, growth of Treasury influence in government decision-making during the 1930s, especially under the Treasury-minded Chamberlain. The TUC was also playing a more independent role in the developing 'corporate' state and was less reliant on the Labour Party.

❼ For foreign policy and 'appeasement', see *A-level European History*, Chapters 12 and 13, and Chapter 14 of this book, but note the domestic political aspects of appeasement: opposition to the National government inside the Conservative Party grouped round Churchill and focused on appeasement; note the roles of Eden, Amery and Boothby; Churchill's shortcomings as leader of this opposition – his rhetoric was splendid but he lacked credibility; he was personally discredited by his stand on Indian nationalism and the abdication; look at the pivotal role of Halifax in supporting this Churchillian opposition in 1939; the events leading to the collapse of the National Government in May 1940, and its replacement by a more genuine, less Conservatively dominated coalition.

The starting point for an understanding of British politics in the 1930s is the political crisis of 1931, which led to the formation of the National Government dominated by the Conservatives. The way was now open for them to introduce their favoured policies of tariff reform and imperial preference in the Ottawa agreements of 1932. In practice, the Ottawa agreements fell a long way short of Empire free trade but at least they had implemented prewar Tory aspirations without splitting the Party.

Both the domestic and foreign policies of the 1930s were influenced by this victory of Empire free trade over prewar Liberal internationalism. Political opposition to the National Government was weak. The only challenge to the government, such as it was, came from outside Parliament – from Oswald Mosley's British Union of Fascists and, to a lesser extent, from the Communist Party.

The main problem faced by the Conservatives in the general election of 1935 was still unemployment and the need to justify their policy of appeasement – which Baldwin cleverly accomplished by stealing Labour's 'collective security' approach for the purposes of electioneering.

Though the Munich agreement in September 1938 was greeted with much pacifist relief, and some popular approval, it became clear – as Czechoslovakia was dismembered in the months that followed – that appeasement as a policy was doomed. Winston Churchill, who had led the opposition to appeasement within the Party throughout the 'thirties, finally became Prime Minister in May 1940 on the downfall of a government whose every move 'had seemed stamped with futility and failure'.

13.1 THE EMERGING DANGER

The 1930s were at first characterised by the same economic problems which had dominated politics in the 'twenties. The rise to power in Germany of Hitler, however, was a turning point; from then on, the government was increasingly concerned with questions of foreign policy and defence. As the economic situation gradually improved for Britain, so international relations steadily deteriorated.

Until 1937 the public was largely unaware of the danger to Britain posed by German expansionism. Pacifism and disarmament were popular. These were, nevertheless, unrealistically combined with the belief that Britain should support the League of Nations against those countries which broke their pledges to the international community. Yet no one could explain how the League's supporters could defeat military aggression without themselves rearming.

Defence spending was, therefore, politically unpopular – although a national necessity – and so the government had to begin rearmament slowly and cautiously. The result was that foreign policy evolved from a position of weakness in relation to the dictator states; the temptation for the government was continually to buy time by making concessions.

This process culminated in the Munich agreement in 1938, widely welcomed in Britain at the time, but soon to be regarded as a national disgrace. It is correctly associated with the Prime Minister of the day, Neville Chamberlain, and it is for this policy that he is now chiefly remembered and vilified.

What should be borne in mind, however, is that in its best sense appeasement was a popular preference for peace and conciliation and was a policy for which the nation as a whole bore considerable responsibility. After all, no one of importance had publicly aired a realistic alternative foreign and defence policy in the mid-thirties and it was not until 1939 that Churchill, Eden and the Labour Party began to emerge as a credible opposition to Chamberlain.

13.2 NATIONAL POLITICS, 1931–5

The General Election of 1931 was a triumph for the Conservative Party (disguised as the National Government), a disaster for Labour (52 MPs) and a humiliation for the Liberals who won just 72 seats. The 'National' Government, formed in August, 1931, failed in its immediate object of protecting the pound – after a brief revival of confidence, the Invergordon mutiny panicked the market and forced Britain off the gold standard. (According to Seaman, the Navy saved the country from 'the economic consequences of Mr Churchill' !) Despite this, the government continued in office, and grew in strength as its overwhelming electoral victory of October 1931 testified.

In considering why it was so successful politically, it should be noted that, in general, people trusted the National Government. It contained well-known political figures from all three Parties. This emphasised the gravity of the crisis; it also meant that alternative policies lacked prominent spokesmen; Henderson, who led the split against MacDonald, lost his seat. It meant, too, that opposition to the government came from Parties themselves split by its formation.

From the start, the government was predominantly Conservative in outlook, and grew more so as the immediate crisis receded. It was a Conservative Party, however, which had been manipulated slightly to the left of centre by Baldwin in the 'twenties. By 1932 its leaders, having emasculated the right wing of the Party, were sufficiently confident to introduce measures for tariff reform and imperial preference.

Protectionism

Since 1903, the central demand of progressive Conservatives had been for tariff reform. In the 'twenties this proved impossible but, after the collapse of Churchill's attempt to return to a policy of Liberal internationalism, the way was now open for a policy of imperialist protectionism. The collapse of the Labour Government in 1931 allowed the Tories to get their protective tariff in 1931, and the Ottawa agreements that followed in 1932 moved Britain nearer the concept of Empire free trade.

This victory for the 'new imperialists' explains much of the domestic and foreign policies of successive governments in the 'thirties, but especially their conciliatory responses to the colonial nationalisms in Ireland, India and the Middle East. It was also their starting point for dealing with Hitler, for it emphasised the defence of overseas empire, which Germany did not threaten, but which Japan, for example, did. Fearing Japan more meant that confrontation with Germany *had to be* avoided. Eventually many Conservatives, including Chamberlain, came to believe that such a clash *could* be avoided.

Snowden and two Liberals resigned from the cabinet in protest at this protectionism, but their departure had no effect on the government's standing. The sheer size of its majority made parliamentary opposition appear futile, and on Right and Left, reaction against it became focused in political movements which took their inspiration from the supposed achievements of Fascism and Russian communism.

Electorally these movements were insignificant, but they were a source of continual worry to those in power. Mosley's Fascists were hampered by their own absurdity as much as by government action, but the intellectual challenge from the Left was much greater. Nevertheless, its popular appeal, even in areas of mass unemployment, was slight. The Labour Party recovered from the shock of 1931, and in the election of 1935 won 154 seats, mainly at the expense of the Liberal Party whose total of seats now slumped to 20.

The politics of unemployment

Since the collapse of the postwar boom in 1921, unemployment had been a permanent feature of British economic life. But the rapidity with which it increased in 1930 was entirely unexpected. Although the country recovered slowly from the shock of the 1931 crisis, the numbers of unemployed remained obstinately high. They never fell below 1 400 000 and reached almost 3 million in 1932.

In studying this phenomenon and its effect on national politics, it is important to look at the figures region by region; while South Wales and parts of the North had huge numbers of unemployed for most of the decade, much of the country was relatively unscathed, especially London and the South-East. This may explain why, in spite of the scale of the problem and of considerable political agitation, the unemployment situation never threatened to split the government or to produce an electoral revolution against its cautious and rather limited policies.

There were some suggested remedies for unemployment. J M Keynes argued that the government should spend its way out of the Depression by introducing a massive programme of investment in new industries while organising the contraction of the old. A group of young Conservative MPs, led by Harold Macmillan, set out in 1935 a detailed scheme for investment in public works such as road building, electrification and so on. Some Labour MPs, inspired by John Strachey, argued in 1936 that what was needed was not a laissez-faire but a controlled economy which a policy of nationalisation could provide and which would, through planning, limit production and thereby eliminate unemployment.

The National Government, like the Labour Government before it, ignored most of the advice offered. Its remedies were traditional. By the 1934 Unemployment Insurance Act they accepted responsibility for looking after the unemployed and tried to establish for them a minimum standard of existence. This was their chief policy. Apart from this, they reintroduced tariffs and encouraged bilateral trade agreements, left the gold standard and lowered the Bank rate, encouraged all reasonable schemes

Dates of departure for
arrival in London on
Oct 27

Glasgow
Sept 26

Newcastle
Oct 2

Burnley
Oct 9

Sheffield
Oct 14

Manchester
Oct 11

Liverpool
Oct 11

Mansfield
Oct 15

Stoke
Oct 15

Birmingham
Oct 18

Hereford
Oct 17

Norwich
Oct 16

Cardiff
Oct 15

London

Bristol
Oct 16

Canterbury
Oct 21

Plymouth
Oct 10

Brighton
Oct 23

Southampton
Oct 21

Fig. 12 The National Hunger March on London, 1932

for the rationalisation of industry and made some attempts to create employment in the depressed areas. The expenditure allowed, however, was meagre and the results, therefore, were predictably disappointing.

Two other factors kept unemployment figures high. First, the continual influx of school-leavers into industry and second, the rise in the number of immigrants (especially Jews) from Europe during the 'thirties.

The failure to adopt a more positive attitude to the problem of unemployment – for example, by raising the school-leaving age or attempting a wider scheme of public works, as Roosevelt did in the US – did not affect the government's general popularity very much. The depressed areas were by now probably safe Labour seats and it is a fact that, for those in jobs, real wages increased. For them, the National Government's timid policies brought tangible improvements, all the more valued because of the well-publicised plight of those out of work. (For a further discussion of the government role, see Chapter 11.)

Rearmament

It may seem surprising in view of Chamberlain's later commitment to appeasement, that planning of rearmament began as early as the winter of 1933, in reaction to Hitler's rise to power, but it was not until March 1935 that a White Paper on defence gave a cautious warning to the public. Pacifist feeling was very strong in the country, and the opposition was critical of all arms expenditure. The minister most enthusiastic for rearmament against Germany was the Chancellor, Neville Chamberlain. He urged Baldwin to fight the 1935 election on this issue; Baldwin refused. The consequence was that the public remained very ignorant of the danger from abroad.

In July, 1936 a Labour MP wrote in his diary: 'The Hitler rearmament races on. Few people in the Labour Party seem to know or care anything about it'. By 1937, when the first major programme was announced, opinion had shifted decisively: now the government was criticised for proceeding too slowly.

Rearmament was, however, a huge undertaking, not a tap which could be turned on at will. Industry had to re-equip itself, and Britain's manufacturing output could not be switched overnight to making arms, since it produced the wealth which financed government spending. Ironically at a time of mass unemployment, there was also an acute shortage of skilled workers, and the unions were understandably reluctant to abandon established working practices for what might be only a temporary boom.

Finance was an additional constraint, although this has been exaggerated. Each service department saw their own needs as paramount, whereas only the Treasury had an overview of the whole financial and industrial situation and was in a position to impose priorities on the three services. In fact, it was only due to the Treasury (and Chamberlain) that in 1938 a reluctant RAF was forced to give higher priority to fighter production.

By the time war broke out, Britain had just enough arms to secure her survival. Note that rearmament was essentially defensive. No expeditionary force was planned before 1939. The development of air power was concentrated on fighters, not on bombers. Britain was equipping herself for national defence – not for resistance to German aggression on the Continent.

13.3 THE NATIONAL GOVERNMENT, 1935-9

In June 1935, Baldwin took over as Prime Minister from the ailing MacDonald, now merely a figurehead. It was Baldwin's centrist, liberal, conciliatory brand of politics that had triumphed since 1925 and had kept the Conservatives in power. His ability to reassure rather than provoke had also won over most of the uncommitted. In November, his Party won a majority in this important general election. Within a few weeks, his new government was attacked from every side because of the Hoare-Laval pact. The storm blew over, however, once the scheme was abandoned. Baldwin's personal stock had never been lower: his public image of decency and honesty was badly undermined. Nevertheless, he recovered his prestige in 1936 with his masterly handling of the abdication crisis, and early in 1937 announced his intention to retire.

His departure in a blaze of glory brought Chamberlain to No 10. He was unlike his predecessor in almost every respect: hard-working, efficient, aloof. Contemptuous of Labour, he aimed to succeed by accomplishment, not by amiability. He had been waiting a long time for his chance, but was already an elderly man. Furthermore, the talents which had made him a good Minister of Health and Chancellor of the Exchequer were not those required of a party leader. Chamberlain failed to realise that in the volatile sphere of foreign policy, different rules applied. Ironically, his greatest mistake, the Munich agreement, at first brought him mass adulation; ultimately it totally discredited him, obscuring his earlier support for rearmament and the general rise in the standard of living for which he deserved some credit.

Fascists and Communists

One of the effects of Baldwin's attempts to dominate the central ground of British politics was the risk of driving his opponents towards alternative parties outside the National Government. During this period, a number found a more coherent and exciting alternative was on offer in the British Union of Fascists. Its leader was Sir Oswald Mosley, aristocrat and ex-Conservative; he had also been a cabinet minister in the Labour government, but had resigned in protest at his colleagues' passivity in the face of the economic crisis. He eventually came to argue that only drastic political action, on the lines followed by Mussolini in Italy, could save the country and give employment to all. Thus he drifted into Fascism, and moulded the hitherto insignificant Fascist groups in Britain into a relatively organised movement.

It soon became clear, however, that the electorate had no taste for Italian-style corporatism, and Mosley's party resorted more and more to anti-Jewish propaganda, to marches and to public meetings intended to provoke a response from the Left and thus to force the government to act against what he saw as the dangers of Communism. The climax was a mass meeting held at Olympia in June, 1934, when Fascist stewards treated hecklers with un-English brutality. Deliberately provocative Fascist marches in the East End of London later resulted in some violent rioting but the only important consequence was a further diminution of the movement's credibility.

Yet it was not until 1936, with the economy reviving and clear evidence of the BUF's growing unpopularity, that the government felt confident enough to pass an act forbidding the wearing of political uniforms and granting the authorities power to ban public marches and displays which were judged a threat to public order. This straightforward measure was enough to kill off the BUF as a political force. Denied their black shirts and parades, Mosley's supporters melted away.

Communism was intellectually much more respectable than Fascism, and in the 1930s evoked admiration in some circles – as demonstrated by the success of the Russians (through the Cambridge connection) in penetrating British intelligence. Its working-class support, however, was never strong, despite the influence of some front organisations, such as the National Unemployed Workers Movement.

The problem both for Communism and for Fascism was that the weakness or unpopularity of the government was never serious enough to threaten the downfall of the existing political order.

Another difficulty for both was that they were identified with foreign powers – the Fascists with Mussolini's Italy and the Communists with Soviet Russia. The Communists in particular took their line from Moscow, with the result that their policy on international events changed (often dramatically) whenever Stalin's did. This was particularly marked when the Germans and the Russians signed their non-aggression pact in August, 1939, after which the British Communists opposed the war until 1941, when Hitler suddenly invaded Russia.

In the long term it was Socialism, not Communism, which was the main beneficiary of the intellectual ferment of the 1930s in Britain. This bore fruit in the radical programme of the Attlee government elected in 1945.

Conclusion

Until recently the National governments have usually been subjected to adverse criticism by historians for their failure to solve Britain's economic problems and their willingness to accept unemployment and its social consequences. Furthermore it is alleged that they were Tory dominated, complacently middle class in outlook and feeble in action both at home and abroad. Recent research has tended to modify this picture. Unemployment and industrial decline was never widespread in the 'thirties while economic recovery and a return to full employment had been achieved by 1937. Nor was the government ungenerous in its response to the plight of the unemployed – there was a marked increase in expenditure on the social services. These governments may have appeared feeble in action, but they preserved political stability and if they excluded talent (e.g. Churchill and Lloyd George) they also excluded extremists (e.g. Mosley and Maxton). European Fascist and Communist governments could hardly be regarded as attractive alternative propositions, while the benefits ascribed to Keynesian policies (like the New Deal in the United States) were hardly impressive. Clearly, it would be unjust to see the ministers of the National governments as the only failures during the 'thirties while their impressive election victories in 1931 and 1935 demonstrated that they enjoyed enormous popular support.

13.4 CHRONOLOGY

1931	August	NATIONAL GOVERNMENT formed under MacDonald; the cabinet included Baldwin, Neville Chamberlain, Samuel, Snowden, Thomas and Lord Sankey.
	September	Naval Mutiny at Invergordon. GOLD STANDARD abandoned; the pound fell from $4.86 to $3.80.
	October	The Government won a huge victory in the general election.
1932	February	IMPORT DUTIES ACT: the Government abandoned free trade; a general tariff of 10% on all except imperial imports. BRITISH UNION OF FASCISTS founded by Sir Oswald Mosley. Four hundred branches by 1934: 20 000 estimated membership.
	July	ILP disaffiliated from the Labour Party.
	August	Ottawa Agreements: imperial trade preference meant that Britain obtained more of her food imports from the Dominions.
1933	January	Adolf Hitler became Chancellor of Germany. Children and Young Persons Act.
1934	May	UNEMPLOYMENT ACT took the issue of unemployment out of the political arena by removing it from local control and putting it under an Unemployment Assistance Board from December 1934.
	June	BUF meeting at Earls Court.
	August	Government of India Act: gave dominion status to India.
	October	Peace Pledge Union formed by Canon Sheppard.
	December	SPECIAL AREAS ACT: to stimulate investment in depressed areas; a grant of £2 million allowed. UNEMPLOYMENT ASSISTANCE BOARD set up to administer unemployment relief on a national level.
1935	March	Government White Paper, *Statement Relating to Defence*, was published; this emphasised the nation's inadequate defences.
	May	MacDonald resigned as Prime Minister; succeeded by Baldwin (June).
	June	Peace Ballot result published; high-water mark of postwar pacifism.
	October	Italy invaded Abyssinia.
	November	Conservatives won the general election with 432 seats; Labour recovered with 154 seats; the Liberals won 21 seats.
	December	Hoare-Laval Pact provoked an outcry against the government by a public newly devoted to the aims of the League of Nations.
1936		Beginning of serious rearmament. Left Book Club founded. (Between 1935 and 1937 nearly one million Communist pamphlets were sold in Britain).
	July	Spanish civil war: the British Government adopted the controversial policy of non-intervention.
	October	Jarrow hunger march.
	December	ABDICATION OF EDWARD VIII because of his love for (twice-divorced) Mrs Wallis Simpson. The crisis was handled brilliantly by Baldwin; Edward's only prominent supporter was Churchill. Edward was succeeded by his brother, George VI. Public Order Act, prohibiting the wearing of political uniforms was aimed at the BUF. Irish Dail removed the King from the Constitution.
1937	May	Neville Chamberlain became Prime Minister on Baldwin's retirement. He adopted a policy of rearmament and conciliation (appeasement) toward the dictator states.
	December	Irish Free State adopted its Gaelic name, Eire, but did not yet formally contract out of the Commonwealth.
1938		International affairs dominated domestic politics.
	February	Anthony Eden resigned over the policy of appeasement.
	July	COAL ACT: brought nationalisation of the coal industry nearer.

	September	MUNICH AGREEMENT: Chamberlain visited Hitler and then met him at the Munich Conference. He conceded most of his demands; Czechoslovakia was dismembered; the agreement at first was warmly welcomed by the British public; but it was soon seen to have bought time but not peace, and at a very high price.
1939	March	Poland's territorial integrity was guaranteed by Britain after Germany had seized the remainder of Czechoslovakia.
	September	Germany invaded Poland. WAR DECLARED by Britain on Germany. 'Phoney War' began (September–April 1940).
1940	May	Chamberlain lost the support of the Commons. Churchill became Prime Minister.

Illustrative questions and answers

1   Why was a National Government formed in 1931?

Tutorial note

You have mainly to consider the motives of those individuals most responsible for setting up the National Government; look also at the long-term problems which precipitated a crisis in the old Party system.

You need to know about

A detailed knowledge of the Second Labour Government and of the political crisis of the summer of 1931. A general knowledge of political events between the wars.

Suggested answer plan

1   A brief narrative of the Labour Government up to the divisions of August, 1931: its inadequate attempts to solve the unemployment problem; the collapse of Credit Anstalt and the run on sterling; the financial crisis and the May Committee Report; the demand by Opposition leaders for cuts in the unemployment fund as the price of their support for the budget, and Snowden's willing compliance; Bevin and Citrine, on the TUC General Council, demanded the suspension of the national debt and the sinking fund, and also called for a tax on rentiers, instead; this prompted Henderson and eight other ministers to withdraw their agreement to Snowden's cuts, leading to a cabinet deadlock (22–23 August).

2   A brief narrative of the events leading from here to the formation of the National Government: the meetings between MacDonald, Snowden, Baldwin, Chamberlain, Samuel, McLean and George V; the decisive role of the latter in persuading MacDonald.

3   The government's immediate rationale was the overriding national need for orthodox financial policies to restore foreign confidence in sterling; in this respect Snowden was central – he was an ardent free trader (the only man in the Labour cabinet who had opposed a revenue tariff) and was a believer in balanced budgets; he was not disloyal to his class and sincerely believed in inaugurating Socialism by confiscating the profits of successful capitalism; but, first, capitalism had to be made to succeed, which required orthodox policies leading to a restoration of confidence among capitalists.

4   Snowden, and probably MacDonald, genuinely believed this rationale for the National Government, but as a defence it was undermined by the fact that the new government quickly abandoned orthodox policies (the gold standard and free trade).

5   The central and most enigmatic figure was MacDonald: perhaps he *did* betray the movement he had so much shaped, as opponents alleged; his vanity made

him susceptible to royal flattery and the 'aristocratic embrace'; but there is no evidence that he deliberately planned a National Government before the cabinet deadlock; yet he undoubtedly relished the role of national saviour, and by now regarded nearly all his Labour colleagues with contempt.

6 The possibility that MacDonald was deliberately playing the role of martyr, knowing his career was nearly over anyway, in order to save the Labour Party: there is some (albeit flimsy) evidence that he discouraged young Labour politicians like Morrison from joining him in the National government; certainly MacDonald's act enabled Labour to maintain its essential unity and to be spared further unpopularity for the Slump, and after the 1931 electoral disaster it quickly began to recoup; but that this was MacDonald's motive seems unlikely in view of his vitriolic attacks on his former colleagues in the October 1931 election.

7 There is little evidence of a Bankers' ramp (either by Norman and the City bankers, or by the New Yorkers who imposed conditions on further credits to Britain); the City was genuinely alarmed by the possibility of devaluation – needlessly, as it turned out.

8 Baldwin, perhaps, was happy to form a National Government (though he would have won the next election anyway) because of his recent difficulties with Empire Free Trade Conservatives; his affection for MacDonald; Snowden also had been cooperating with Chamberlain for some time – the latter, especially, helped to sow the seeds of the 'coalition' idea, perhaps even in George V's mind; did the Conservatives see a National government as the only way of pushing fiscal reform (protection) past the electorate?

9 The Liberals saw it as a way of getting a toe-hold back on power; in fact it marked their virtual absorption by the Conservatives; they were crushed in 1935.

10 To conclude: the National Government was really a Conservative government in disguise; the national divisions and economic crisis, however, demanded a veneer of non-partisan respectability, and this MacDonald provided by consenting to lead it.

2 How 'national' was the National Government, 1931–39?

Tutorial note
You must first consider how much general public support there was for the National Government, both in geographical and class terms; secondly, how far its policies were in the national interest.

You need to know about
The political history of the 1930s and the policies of the National Government.

Suggested answer plan
1 Two opposing views have dominated the historiography of the National Government: one – that it was a thinly-disguised cover for Conservative rule which, by pursuing deflationary policies (reduction of public salaries and unemployment benefits) and an ungenerous social welfare policy (especially the hated 'means test') at a time of between two and three million unemployed – was clearly acting in a partisan and sectional (i.e. pro-middle class) way; the other – the 'official' view – is that its policies were in the national interest and were broadly correct, and that, by attracting widespread support, it managed to heal the bitter sociopolitical divisions of the 1920s.

2 A brief account of the circumstances leading to the formation of National Government; of the composition of the government and of its parliamentary support in terms of previous Party allegiance.

3 The October 1931 election showed overwhelming national support for the Government (67% of votes on a 76.3% turnout); but note that Conservative

voters made up 55.2% out of this 67%, Liberals 10%, and National Labour only 1.6%, while there were no *non*-national Conservatives and (at this stage) very few *non*-national Liberals; Conservative voting strength was reflected in the number of MPs (473 out of 554 supporting the government, out of 615 altogether); 1935 gave the government 55% of the vote, an impressive victory but hardly one of 'national' dimensions.

4   Regional analysis of the elections: Durham and South Wales were persistently hostile to the government, but otherwise in 1931 it had some claim to be called 'national'; Clydeside, Tyneside, West Riding, Lancashire and London showed a considerable Labour revival in 1935, however; there was now support for the government concentrated in prosperous Southern England and the Midlands, reflecting the economic division of Britain into 'two nations'; the professional middle classes and many white collar workers probably had 'never had it so good', and provided the backbone of the Government's support.

5   Also, the two individuals most conspicuously excluded from the Government (Lloyd George and Churchill) were, of all politicians, the ones who had most hankered after coalition or consensus politics, and the only two with the stature to embody (the one previously, the other in the future) the national will; therefore in retrospect the National government, in its rejection of Churchill and his timely warnings against Hitler, seemed to be anything but national.

6   In standing for compromise, the Government undoubtedly reflected the rather lacklustre national mood; Baldwin skilfully exploited George V's Silver Jubilee to capitalise on the patriotic sentiment and devotion to the Monarchy; the BBC and Dawson's *Times* contributed to the Government's image here.

7   Beneath the Party battle, somewhat attenuated anyway because of the one-sided 1931 election, the 1930s saw the silent advance of the 'corporate state'; the Civil Service, the TUC and the FBI probably counted for more in decision-making than did the cabinet and politicians; this was especially noticeable under Chamberlain, who strictly controlled the flow of information to the cabinet; in so far as this burgeoning bureaucracy reflected a national, rather than Party, viewpoint, the 1930s probably marked an advance in 'national' solutions.

8   MacDonald, on forming the National Government, denied an intention of holding an election under 'national' auspices, but Conservative backbenchers forced him to hold an early election; the different elements in the Coalition issued different manifestos, so that the Government could claim no mandate to do anything; what it did was, of course, Conservative policy (especially protection); Snowden's Land Valuation policy, for example, was discarded. One may defend the National Government's policies, but there can be no doubt that they were more Conservative than 'national'.

3   'The National Government solved the immediate problems but left the fundamental ones unsolved.' Discuss.

Tutorial note

One is tempted to point out that most governments leave most fundamental problems unsolved, since such problems are often insoluble – this is really a straightforward question on the achievements of the National Government.

You need to know about

The social, economic and political difficulties facing Britain in the 1920s and 1930s. The policies of the National government.

Suggested answer plan

1   Perhaps the main immediate problem of the 1920s was political: how to fit three Parties into a two-party, 'first-past-the-post', political system. This had led to

weak governments and frequent elections, which meant a lack of continuity in policy at a time when the economic slump made such a thing highly desirable; the Second Labour Government merely took a decade of 'drift' and 'wait-and-see' policies to extremes.

2 At least the National Government solved this problem; it was formed as a short-term emergency administration which would not even fight an election – but in the event it stayed in power for a decade, and at least provided more consistent, if hardly more decisive, policies.

3 A more fundamental political problem in the 1920s was the bitter polarisation of politics; to some extent the National Government, by reflecting a national mood (perhaps exaggerated by Dawson's *Times* and Reith's BBC), contributed to national reconciliation.

4 In terms of policy, it is perhaps not true to say that the Government even solved the immediate crisis, which was financial. Ostensibly it was formed to save the gold standard, yet it went off it almost immediately after the Invergordon mutiny (September 1931); moreover, this short-term 'failure' – i.e. devaluation and cheap money – probably contributed as much as anything that the Government did, or could do, to 'fundamental' economic recovery in the 1930s; the lesson was, of course, that only a government which has the confidence of investors can, in a free enterprise capitalist system, *dare* to follow unorthodox policies.

5 Again, the National Government was formed to balance the budget; yet the 1932/3 Chamberlain budgets were mildly inflationary with modest deficits; this was hardly full counter-cyclical economic control, but it was pragmatic and a sensible response to a fundamental problem of public finance.

6 By 1931 it was clear to many, including Keynes, MacDonald and Hubert Henderson, that the fundamental problem of economic policy lay in the electorate's refusal (see 1923) to countenance an abandonment of free trade; by laying this particular nineteenth century ghost, the National Government made it possible for the British economy to enter the twentieth century.

7 It is true that the absence of a strong parliamentary opposition made the National Government more supine in dealing with new dangers (like Nazism) as well as with old sores like unemployment; but it seems unlikely that a more energetic government with the provision of public works could have reduced the dole queues, given the small size of the British public sector – and it is unlikely that public opinion would have allowed a much less craven attitude to Hitler.

8 The history of the National Government was in many ways one of decline after a relatively successful beginning. Its economic policies – given ministerial beliefs in palliatives rather than government cure (i.e. that there was little that government, as opposed to natural economic forces, could do) – were modestly successful. The worst of the unemployment was over by 1933. Economic recovery, however, had little to do with government action. The ultimate failure in foreign affairs lost the government whatever credit it deserved for its earlier modest successes – as Mowat remarks, Neville Chamberlain 'succeeded to a barren inheritance' when he became Prime Minister in 1937.

Question bank

1 Document question (Crisis in 1931): study the extract below and then answer questions (a) to (f) which follow:

Extract

'At 10 a.m. the King held a Conference at Buckingham Palace at which the Prime Minister, Baldwin and Samuel were present. At the beginning, the King impressed upon them that before they left the Palace some communiqué must be issued which would no longer keep <u>the country and the world in suspense</u>. The Prime Minister said that he had <u>the resignation of his Cabinet in his pocket</u>, but the King replied that he trusted there was no question of the Prime Minister's resignation: the leaders of the three Parties must get together and come to some arrangement. His Majesty hoped that the Prime Minister, with the colleagues who remained <u>faithful to him</u>, would help in the formation of a National Government, which the King was sure would be supported by the Conservatives and the Liberals. The King assured the Prime Minister that, remaining at his post, his position and reputation would be much more enhanced than if he surrendered the government of the country at such a crisis. Baldwin and Samuel said that they were willing to serve under the Prime Minister, and render all help possible to carry on the Government as a National Emergency Government until an emergency bill or bills had been passed by Parliament, which would <u>restore once more British credit and the confidence of foreigners</u>. After that they would expect His Majesty to grant a dissolution. To this course the King agreed. During the Election the National Government would remain in being, though of course each Party would fight the election on its own lines.

'At 10.35 a.m. the King left the three Party leaders to settle the details of the communiqué to be issued. About 11.35 the King was glad to hear that they had been able to some extent to come to some arrangement. His Majesty congratulated them on the solution of this difficult problem and pointed out that in this country our constitution is so generous that leaders of Parties, after fighting one another for months in the House of Commons, were ready to meet together under the roof of the Sovereign and sink their own differences for a common good and arrange as they had done this morning for a National Government to meet <u>one of the gravest crises that the British Empire had yet been asked to face</u>.'

(Memorandum by Sir Clive Wigram, Private Secretary to King George V,
24 August 1931)

(a) Who was the Prime Minister at the time of this meeting and why were 'the country and the world in suspense' ? (6)

(b) Why did the Prime Minister have the 'resignation of his Cabinet in his pocket' and why, apparently, would only some of his colleagues remain 'faithful to him'? (5)

(c) What possibility was so greatly feared at the time that it should cause the king to speak of 'one of the gravest crises that the British Empire had yet been asked to face'? Why was fear of this possibility so great? (4)

(d) What was the National Government (i) able to do and (ii) unable to do, when taking steps to 'restore once more British credit and the confidence of foreigners'? (6)

(e) What aspects of their characters and policies would make the three Party leaders at this meeting unusually ready to be influenced by the King's assurance in the first paragraph and his congratulations in the second? (5)

(f) What were the effects of the decision arrived at by this meeting on the position of the three main Parties during the rest of the 1930s? (5)

2 'The restoration of prosperity'; 'A divided nation'. Which of these comments better describes the domestic achievements of the National Governments from 1931 to 1939? (Cambridge, June 1991)

3 What was the contribution of Ramsay MacDonald and Stanley Baldwin towards the stabilisation of British political life in the 1920s and 1930s? (NISEAC, June 1991)

4 Why did Winston Churchill's standing as a politician sink so low during the 1930s? (Oxford and Cambridge, June 1990)

5 Assess the effectiveness of the economic and social policies of the National Governments in the period 1931–1939. (AEB, June 1990)

READING LIST

Standard textbook reading

T. O. Lloyd, *Empire to Welfare State* (OUP, 1970), chapters 6, 7.

L. C. B. Seaman, *Post-Victorian Britain* (Methuen, 1966), chapter V.

R. K. Webb, *Modern England* (Allen and Unwin, 1980 edn.), chapter 12.

Further suggested reading

S. Constantine, *Unemployment in Britain between the Wars* (Longman, 1980).

D. Dilks, *Neville Chamberlain* (CUP, 1985).

K. Feiling, *The Life of Neville Chamberlain* (Macmillan, 1946, 1970)

C. L. Mowat, *Britain between the Wars* (Methuen, 1955).

B. Pimlott, *Labour and the Left in the 1920s* (CUP, 1977).

M. Pugh, *The Making of Modern British Politics 1867–1939* (Blackwell, 1982).

H. W. Richardson, *Economic Recovery in Britain 1932–39* (Weidenfeld and Nicolson, 1967).

R. Skidelsky, *Oswald Mosley* (Macmillan, 1975).

J. Stevenson, *British Society, 1914–45* (Penguin, 1984).

J. Stevenson and C. Cook, *The Slump* (Cape, 1977).

A. J. P. Taylor, *English History 1914–45* (OUP, 1965).

R. Thurlow, *Fascism in Britain 1918–85* (Blackwell, 1986).

BRITISH FOREIGN POLICY IN THE 1930s

Units in this chapter

14.1 *The question of defence*
14.2 *Rearmament*
14.3 *Chronology*

Chapter objectives

❶ As background: the Versailles Settlement, particularly the territorial, disarmament and reparations clauses; criticisms of these terms, especially those of J M Keynes; and British relations with France, Germany and the Soviet Union, 1918–30.

❷ Public opinion and pacifism: the mood of 'never again' after the First World War; the League of Nations Union; the East Fulham by-election; the Peace Ballot; the Oxford Union 'King and Country' debate; the hostility of the Dominions to the prospect of involvement in another European war.

❸ Britain and the problems of defence: the 'twin pillars' of home and imperial defence; the Ten-Year Rule; the difficulty of preserving both the Empire and the home islands from attack – the respective threats of Germany, Italy and Japan to British interests and the insistence of British military planners that Britain could not defend herself against these powers simultaneously – the concept of 'limited liability'.

❹ Rearmament: priority given to the Royal Air Force; the Defence White Paper of March 1936; the two-power standard for the Navy; the rejection of the idea of a field force as involving a continental commitment that was too expensive, given Britain's limited resources, and unacceptable to British public opinion.

❺ British conduct of foreign policy during (a) the Manchurian crisis, (b) the Abyssinian War, and (c) the Spanish civil war. Note particularly the Hoare-Laval Pact and the role of public opinion during the Abyssinian war; on the Spanish civil war, special attention should be given to the reasons for the British policy of non-intervention *and* the unofficial involvement of British volunteers in the war; note also the attitudes of the political Right and Left in Britain to the Spanish conflict.

❻ The significance of (a) the German reoccupation of the Rhineland; (b) the Anschluss; (c) the crisis over Czechoslovakia, 1938, and the German occupation of Bohemia and Moravia, 1939; and (d) the guarantees of the British government to Poland, Greece and Rumania.

❼ The reasons for the mutual distrust between the British and Soviet government and the failure to reach an understanding to resist Hitler in 1939; the Molotov-Ribbentrop Pact; the immediate prewar crisis over

Danzig and the course of events leading to the outbreak of war.

⑧ An overall assessment of the foreign policy of Neville Chamberlain: a comparison of his approach with that of Stanley Baldwin; Chamberlain's view of the Powers and his meetings with the dictators.

⑨ The justifications offered for the appeasement of Italy and Germany, particularly at the Munich Conference; the role of the anti-appeasers, especially Churchill and Eden; the revulsion against appeasement after the final collapse of Czechoslovakia in March, 1939.

⑩ The circumstances of Chamberlain's resignation and of Churchill's assumption of power.

British foreign policy in the 1930s must be understood in the context of public opinion, which was intensely opposed to any repetition of the horrors of the 1914–18 war and which was demoralised by the severity of the world economic depression. At government level there was an acute awareness of the limitations of British power – of the fact that the burdens of imperial and home defence were increasingly more than resources could meet.

Practical considerations of strategy and finance, and of the likely impact of a future major war, combined with a public mood resistant to the idea of war to produce the policy of appeasement. The three 'revisionist' Powers – Germany, Italy and Japan – presented the greatest threat to British interests during this period, which saw the progressive destruction of the Versailles Settlement and the discrediting of the notion of collective security under the League of Nations. Though the Munich Conference was popularly applauded as a vindication of appeasement, Chamberlain's hopes of long-term peaceful coexistence with Germany collapsed with the dismemberment of Czechoslovakia in March, 1939 and the German invasion of Poland in September of that year.

Background

The British policy of appeasement in the 1930s has often been portrayed in simple terms, with the cowardice and wrong-headedness of the 'guilty men', Chamberlain, Halifax and Hoare – who failed to stand up to the dictators until it was too late – contrasted with the courage and vision of Churchill. This is, in fact, a very simplistic view and fails to take into account the extremely tight constraints on British policy-makers in these years.

Britain during the 1930s was strongly influenced by the fear of war and looked to governments to ensure that the horrors of 1914–18 would never recur. The League of Nations Union, which advocated the renunciation of war and campaigned in favour of collective security, helped to organise a 'peace ballot' in June, 1935: over 11½ million people demonstrated their support for the League and about 10 million voted to reduce armaments and abolish military aircraft. This last vote reflected the universal terror of bombing, expressed in the statement by the Prime Minister, Stanley Baldwin, that the 'bomber would always get through'.

The East Fulham by-election convinced politicians that the public would not tolerate a massive rearmaments programme. The general mood, however, was not one of out-and-out pacifism, which was a minority cause, but a rejection of the idea of national war for King and Country in favour of collective security through the League of Nations.

Another sentiment, which was quite widespread, was regret over the treatment of Germany in the Treaty of Versailles – something bitterly attacked by J M Keynes in his book *The Economic Consequences of the Peace*. The German people themselves never accepted the postwar Eastern boundaries, nor the scale of disarmament imposed upon them. And though the deeply resented reparations payments were effectively abolished at the Lausanne Conference, Hitler was able skilfully to exploit the British sense of injustice at the settlement. He also set out to convince the West that a strong Nazi Germany was the only bulwark against the spread of Soviet Communism.

14.1 THE QUESTION OF DEFENCE

Britain's defence policy was based upon the 'twin pillars' of home and imperial defence. This was a period in which the power of the Empire as a military bloc was being undermined by the development of air and submarine warfare and by the relative decline of the British Navy itself. Although Britain had always concerned herself with the balance of power in Europe, she had traditionally avoided involvement unless that balance was endangered by the dominance of a single major Power.

In the 1920s Britain had reverted to non-involvement as far as was practicable. This was encouraged in the interwar years by the growing independence of the Dominions, which was recognised in the 1931 Statute of Westminster. They made very clear their resistance to being drawn into a future European war, thereby powerfully reinforcing British hostility to European entanglements.

Urged on by Churchill, (then Chancellor of the Exchequer), Britain drastically reduced her armaments under the Ten-Year Rule. Later, the slump made increased arms expenditure even less attractive. The Chiefs of Staff, as well as the Treasury, were strongly opposed to burdening Britain with commitments greater than her resources could bear. Foreign and defence policies were dominated by the concept of 'limited liability'.

It was regarded as self-evident that Britain could never successfully combat three major enemies simultaneously – and yet Germany, Italy and Japan all posed a threat. Some experts, like Hankey and Chatfield, considered Japan to be the main threat to Singapore and other Far East interests. However – to give one instance – the Navy would find itself unable to guarantee the safety of British possessions in the Far East if we had to withdraw ships from Far Eastern waters to combat Mussolini in the Mediterranean. Consequently, reasonable relations with Italy appeared essential.

Appeasement was, among other things, a reflection of Britain's defence weakness. There was a further reason for appeasing Mussolini – the realisation that Germany posed the greater long-term threat to British interests. The Stresa Front – between Britain, France and Italy – was brought into existence in 1935 in order to contain growing German power.

The Abyssinian crisis

The unity of Stresa, such as it was, was broken by the Abyssinian crisis. Mussolini's invasion of Africa in quest of Italian empire led the Abyssinians to appeal to the League of Nations – but the League was more preoccupied with Hitler's renunciation of the disarmament clauses of the Versailles Treaty and his reintroduction of conscription.

In June 1935, Eden visited Rome to explain Britain's signing of the Anglo-German Naval Treaty, which permitted Germany's Navy to reach 35% of Britain's, and Eden added a suggestion that Abyssinia make Italy some small concessions. When war broke out, the League, including Britain, imposed sanctions on Italy – though these excluded the crucial item of oil, which could have halted Mussolini.

The British Foreign Secretary made a pact with the French Prime Minister, Laval, whereby Abyssinia would have to cede much of its territory to Italy. This deal entirely contradicted the principle of collective security which Hoare had recently, and openly, upheld at Geneva. There was uproar, followed by Hoare's resignation.

In March 1936, partly encouraged by this international distraction, Hitler reoccupied the Rhineland. The British government offered no firm opposition to this and many shared the view of Lord Lothian that it was hardly reprehensible for Germany to re-enter 'her own back garden'. Eden did add that Britain would support France and Belgium if Germany invaded them.

Subsequently, many shared Churchill's view that this was a missed last chance to stop Hitler before he began his major rearmament programme. At this time, however, there was no likelihood that British public opinion would have supported a war against Germany over the Rhineland.

14.2 REARMAMENT

The British government began a major rearmament programme after the 1935 general election. Defence expenditure rose from £103 million in 1932/3 to £186–7 million in 1936/7. Chamberlain tried to raise a national defence contribution from business in 1936, though this scheme failed.

The Defence Requirements Committee had, in November, 1935, recommended a programme that included 1736 front-line aircraft by 1939 and a two-power standard Navy. The suggestion that there should be a field force for the Army was squashed, Chamberlain arguing that the public would not tolerate 'continental adventures' and that national resources could not sustain increased expenditure in all the Services. Britain's opposition to the idea of a 'continental commitment' was very deeply entrenched.

The Labour Party, which – under its pacifist leader Lansbury, who resigned in 1935 – had opposed all military increases, slowly moved towards support for rearmament in the later 1930s. This was strongly encouraged by the Spanish civil war, which broke out in 1936. Many socialists supported, or (in the International Brigades) fought for, the Republic against the Nationalists under Franco, who were supported by Hitler and Mussolini. The British Government's policy was one of non-intervention, one which the French followed reluctantly and the dictators ignored.

Britain's policy of rearmament in the later 1930s was essentially defensive. The RAF expansion, for instance, was concentrated on fighters, not bombers. Britain was equipping herself for national defence, narrowly defined, but not for resistance to German aggression on the Continent.

The Anschluss and Munich

In 1937 Neville Chamberlain succeeded Baldwin as Prime Minister. He set out, in contrast with his predecessor, to pursue an active foreign policy. He believed in the value of personal talks with the dictators. He wished, at all costs, to avoid the division of Europe into ideological blocs. War, in his view, would mean the end of the British Empire. He had little trust in the US, which – with her two Neutrality Acts of 1935 and 1937 – seemed gripped by a public mood of profound isolationism from European concerns.

In March, 1938 Hitler invaded Austria in what, to Sir Winston Churchill, was only part of a 'programme of aggression…unfolding stage by stage'. This very seriously weakened the position of Czechoslovakia, a pro-Western democracy with an army of 35 divisions. Hitler's demands from Czechoslovakia centred on the 3½ million ethnic Germans living in the Sudetenland, which he wished to see incorporated in the Reich. The issue endangered the general peace since France had an alliance with Czechoslovakia and, since 1935, had had a pact with the Soviet Union.

On 15 September 1938, Chamberlain flew to see Hitler at Berchtesgaden, where the dictator made it quite clear that he was prepared to go to war over this issue and demanded the annexation of the Sudentenland. The French ministers, Daladier and Bonnet, were persuaded by Chamberlain to agree to a peaceful transfer of territory – in return for which Britain would guarantee the new Czechoslovak frontiers.

Though this concession to Hitler meant France reneging on her treaty commitment to Czechoslovakia, Chamberlain was confronted by even more extreme demands from Hitler at Bad Godesberg. War seemed imminent and the British Navy was mobilised, but Chamberlain was determined to avoid armed conflict – at least at this stage.

Appeasement in this crisis meant discouraging East Europeans from resisting Hitler's expansion and thus preventing the French from getting themselves embroiled in a war to defend their Eastern allies.

This was the essence of his policy at the subsequent Munich Conference. This, despite the criticisms which can be levelled against it, won Britain a breathing-space in which to rearm, and Chamberlain's declaration of 'peace in our time' was accorded very wide public support at home.

From Munich to the outbreak of war

When Hitler marched into Prague in March 1939, Chamberlain was not at first alarmed, for he had not believed that the guarantee to the remainder of Czechoslovakia would prove durable – but this event marked a turning-point in public opinion, which now increasingly turned against the policy of appeasement.

The Government had now to declare its opposition to any further German expansion and a guarantee was given to Poland, followed by undertakings to Greece and Rumania. Negotiations were also begun with Russia. Chamberlain was highly distrustful of Russia and harboured an intense dislike of Soviet Communism. But what also complicated the discussions with Russia was the deep fear and hostility towards her of Britain's new allies, Poland and Rumania. Furthermore, Chamberlain still hoped for a basis of agreement with Hitler.

These Anglo-Russian negotiations ended when the Nazi-Soviet Non-Aggression Pact was signed. This was the immediate prelude to the German-Polish crisis and the German invasion of Poland on 1 September, 1939. Any hope of further appeasement was ruled out by the robust stand of the House of Commons; Chamberlain admitted that everything he had worked for had 'crashed in ruins'.

He remained Prime Minister, however, until May, 1940. Then – following the Norway disaster – many Conservatives voted with the Opposition, as a result of which he was obliged to resign. As Chamberlain had anticipated, the war exposed the vulnerability of the British Empire and accelerated its end. It marked the end of Britain's role as a really major world Power.

14.3 CHRONOLOGY

1931	November	MacDonald's Second National Government.
1932	February	Second Disarmament Conference opened in Geneva under Arthur Henderson; Germany made claim to equal status.
	March	The Cabinet dropped the TEN-YEAR RULE.
1933	January	Hitler became German Chancellor.
	February	THE LYTTON REPORT ON JAPANESE AGGRESSION AGAINST MANCHURIA: endorsed by the League of Nations; Japan rejected it and left the League. THE 'KING AND COUNTRY' DEBATE at the Oxford Union: interpreted abroad as a sign of British unwillingness to resort to war.
	October	Germany left the League. EAST FULHAM BY-ELECTION: victory of a pacifist candidate convinced many politicians, including Baldwin, that the British people would not support large-scale rearmament.
1934	July	Baldwin announced a major increase in expenditure on the Royal Air Force, which from now on took priority in rearmament.
	December	Clash between Italian and Abyssinian troops at Wal-Wal.
1935	April	Britain, France and Italy formed the STRESA FRONT against German expansion.
	June	Baldwin became Prime Minister. ANGLO-GERMAN NAVAL AGREEMENT: the Germans agreed to limit their navy to 35% of the British. THE PEACE BALLOT: 11½ million supported the League and 10 million voted for disarmament, but 6¾ million supported military action to prevent aggression.
	September	Hoare pledged Britain to collective action against aggression.

	October	Italy invaded Abyssinia. Britain joined in League sanctions against Italy – but no sanction on oil.
	December	THE HOARE-LAVAL PACT: a substantial reduction of Abyssinian territory suggested, leaving her 'a corridor for camels' to the sea. Hoare resigned as Foreign Secretary; succeeded by Eden.
1936	March	HITLER REOCCUPIED THE RHINELAND. DEFENCE WHITE PAPER: substantial construction of British front-line aircraft proposed.
	May	Italy formally annexed Abyssinia.
	June	Chamberlain denounced sanctions as the 'very midsummer of madness' and Britain withdrew them.
	July	THE SPANISH CIVIL WAR BEGAN: Britain and France adopted a policy of non-intervention.
1937	May	Chamberlain succeeded Baldwin as Prime Minister.
	November	Halifax visited Hitler at Berchtesgaden.
1938	February	Eden resigned as Foreign Secretary; succeeded by Halifax.
	May	FIRST CZECH CRISIS: Britain and France stood firm over German threats.
	July	Runciman visited Czechoslovakia as mediator.
	September	Hitler called for self-determination for Sudetenland.
	15	Chamberlain visited Hitler at Berchtesgaden: Hitler stated he would annex the Sudetenland.
	18	Daladier, the French Premier, and Bonnet, his Foreign Minister, visited London: it was agreed to ask the Czechs to accept the terms in return for a guarantee of the new frontiers.
	22	Chamberlain visited Hitler at Bad Godesberg, where Hitler made extreme demands.
	27	Royal Navy mobilised.
	29	Chamberlain flew to the MUNICH CONFERENCE: Britain, France, Italy and Germany signed agreement.
	1 October	Duff Cooper, First Lord of the Admiralty, resigned.
	10	German forces occupied the Sudetenland.
1939	January	Chamberlain and Halifax visited Mussolini.
	February	Britain recognised the Franco regime in Spain.
	March	GERMAN TROOPS OCCUPIED BOHEMIA AND MORAVIA: Czechoslovakia ceased to exist. THE BRITISH GUARANTEE TO POLAND.
	April	THE BRITISH GUARANTEE TO RUMANIA AND GREECE. Britain introduced conscription.
	May	Anglo-Turkish Mutual Assistance Pact signed. Germany and Italy signed the 'Pact of Steel'.
	23 August	Molotov and Ribbentrop signed NAZI-SOVIET NON-AGGRESSION PACT in Moscow.
	27	Chamberlain warned Hitler that Britain would stand by Poland.
	1 September	HITLER INVADED POLAND.
	3	BRITAIN AND FRANCE DECLARED WAR ON GERMANY: SECOND WORLD WAR BEGAN; Churchill was made First Lord of the Admiralty.
1940	10 May	CHAMBERLAIN RESIGNED AS PRIME MINISTER, following the Norway debate: Churchill became Prime Minister and Minister of Defence.

Illustrative questions and answers

1   Examine the rapid rise and fall in the popularity of Neville Chamberlain 1938–40.

Tutorial note

You must be willing to enquire into Neville Chamberlain's policy in the light of public opinion and its expectations. Do *not* simply record the course of his foreign policy and its reverses – explain why the consensus of opinion running strongly in his favour at the time of the Munich Conference progressively deserted him over the next 18 months.

You need to know about

Neville Chamberlain's foreign policy objectives and his style of diplomacy. The course of events from the first Czech crisis to Churchill's assumption of power. The changing attitudes of public opinion and the political parties towards appeasement.

Suggested answer plan

1 Introduction. Neville Chamberlain's skills as a politician were essentially those of an administrator who was most at home in matters of finance or local government. When he succeeded Baldwin as Prime Minister, however, he found political debate increasingly dominated by foreign affairs, with which he had far less familiarity. Moreover, he had to deal with demagogic dictators whose style and ambitions and political systems were totally alien from his own.

2 In contrast to Baldwin, he intended to pursue an active foreign policy, with personal discussions with the dictators. He had encouraged British rearmament and he hoped that an armed peaceful coexistence would provide the basis for long-term détente with Germany. He continued to believe this (quite unrealistically, which helps to explain his later unpopularity) even *after* the Second World War had broken out. He was acutely aware of British vulnerability. His desire to preserve peace was fully in harmony, in 1938, with British public opinion. Those who opposed appeasement at this stage neither had the consensus, nor did they appear to be entirely consistent amongst themselves.

3 The Czech crisis and Munich: The problem was to prevent war breaking out over German ambitions in Eastern Europe – primarily to prevent the French from blocking Hitler in such a way as to provoke a general war – hence the strategy of appeasement. Munich was the peak of Chamberlain's popularity. The policy of appeasement, with which he was identified, *seemed* to have succeeded. The popular acclaim for his announcement of 'peace in our time' expressed immense public relief. So long as Hitler's policy could be interpreted simply as one of putting right the 'wrongs' of the Versailles Treaty, of which one was the situation of the Sudeten Germans, then Chamberlain's missions to Berchtesgaden, Bad Godesberg and Munich could be seen to have been vindicated. In any case, Chamberlain was seen as having prevented war; 'justice' had been done to Germany, and if, as Hitler maintained, Germany had no more territorial claims, peace would be maintained.

4 After Hitler's occupation of Prague in March 1939, there was a marked revulsion against appeasement, which was now seen to be a craven retreat in the face of force, rather than magnanimous. Hitler's ambitions now seemed to be much more far-ranging than redressing Versailles. The British government was now forced to declare resistance to any further German expansion: Chamberlain, in a Birmingham speech, announced that the 'democracies would resist'. The guarantee to Poland was an unprecedented alliance for Britain to have with an Eastern European state, and was intended to incline Hitler to moderation. The Labour Party opposed appeasement and Halifax informed Chamberlain that no government which continued to pursue appeasement – *in public* – could hope to win the next election.

5 While openly taking a firm stand, Chamberlain still hoped for success from appeasement after the fall of Prague. As public opinion became more and more impatient, his foreign policy in 1939 seemed increasingly characterised by failure – in A J P Taylor's words, the Government 'drifted helplessly'. Note the unenthusiastic pursuit of an understanding with the Soviet Union – e.g. the Prime Minister's unwillingness to send a senior statesman to negotiate; the Molotov-Ribbentrop Pact. The Polish crisis and the unpopularity of Chamberlain's continued attempt to find a compromise after the German invasion of Poland; the revolt of the House of Commons against any further appeasement, and Chamberlain's confession that his policy had 'crashed in ruins'.

6   His war policy: The 'phoney war' – the uncertainty of purpose, with no sense of forceful direction. The German attack on Norway and Denmark and the British failure, due to lack of air cover rather than to Chamberlain. However, he is now seen as the discredited figure of a failed strategy of appeasement, while Churchill is regarded as the prophet of the 1930s and the courageous man of the moment. Leo Amery's appeal: 'In the name of God, go.' – though note that the Conservative Party preferred Halifax (another appeaser) to Churchill.

2   Why did British governments of the 1930s follow a policy of appeasement towards the dictators?

Tutorial note

Note that this is about the policy of British governments. Ensure that you give a full and reasoned account of the practical power-political constraints on policy, such as defence strategy, as well as of the influence of public opinion.

You need to know about

Government foreign policy in the 1930s. The course of international relations over the same period. The arguments offered in favour of appeasement.

Suggested answer plan

1   Britain in the 1930s was slowly climbing out of a very grave economic depression and was faced, at the same time, with worldwide defence commitments. Strategic thinking was based on home and imperial defence and on the need to preserve the balance of power on the Continent – i.e. the need to prevent any single power (in the later 1930s, Germany) from dominating Europe. Given the resources available, these objectives imposed extremely burdensome demands; this was particularly so since the Dominions had made clear their reluctance to become drawn into any European entanglements. Note that the estimated cost of a major rearmament programme presented a slowly-recuperating economy with great difficulties.

2   The national mood of 'never again', after the horrors of the 1914–18 war, found expression in the League of Nations Union, the Peace Ballot, etc. and in the literature of the interwar period, e.g. *Journey's End* and *Testament of Youth*. Note the influence of this on governments.

3   Another factor influencing British attitudes was the view (forcefully advanced by J M Keynes in *The Economic Consequences of the Peace*) that Germany had been unjustly treated in the Versailles Settlement; hence Hitler's moves to revise the treaty in the German interest were regarded with some sympathy.

4   Many in governing circles took the view that the greater long-term danger was the spread of Soviet Communism, which, Hitler claimed, only a strong Nazi Germany could resist. Chamberlain was deeply distrustful of Russia – something which was intensified by the purges of the 1930s under Stalin. Mussolini, Hitler and Franco found support for some of their objectives (if not for their methods) among Right-wing parliamentarians.

5   Anglo-French relations: the background of mutual distrust in the 1920s; Britain was unwilling to be dragged into a war as a result of French commitments in Eastern Europe. The Rhineland crisis of 1936: the French wanted sanctions against Germany but the British were unwilling to support them. This was also the case, during the Spanish Civil War, with the policy of non-intervention – Britain indicating to France that she would not support her in a war with Germany arising out of French involvement in Spain.

6   Illustrate the strategy of appeasement by examining two crises: (a) Abyssinia; and (b) Czechoslovakia. In (a) the traditional policy of friendship with Italy was endangered. Britain did not want naval confrontation in the Mediterranean – her priority at this stage was defence of her Far Eastern interests against the

possibility of Japanese attack. Hence the Hoare-Laval Pact with its major concessions to Mussolini was the logical outcome of this priority of imperial defence.

7 The Czech crisis – Hitler claimed the Sudetenland to be his 'last territorial demand'. German economic interests and territorial expansion in this area could be seen as legitimate and as posing no threat to British interests ('a far away country of which we know nothing.'). But if the East Europeans resisted Hitler's expansion and France became embroiled in a war with Germany, Britain would not be able to stand aside – hence a policy of active appeasement, 'Munich sprang from a mixture of fear and good intentions' (A J P Taylor). Note that the Cabinet's military advisers at this time drew up the balance of advantage of war in 1938 or a year later: a crucial consideration was that British air defences would be radically improved within a year.

8 To conclude: the turning point, with public opinion abandoning appeasement, came with the German invasion of Prague and the British guarantee to Poland. It was now clear that Hitler's ambitions went far beyond any justifiable revision of Versailles – but note that Chamberlain still pursued a policy of appeasement, believing that a major war would involve the end of the British Empire and, quite probably, bring about the Soviet domination of Eastern Europe.

3 Why did Britain go to war in 1939 over Poland but not over Czechoslovakia?

Tutorial note

You should avoid offering *simply* a narrative account of the Czech and Polish crises and the course of events leading to war. Consider how far the circumstances of September 1939 differed from those of September 1938 and be prepared to assess the change in public opinion towards appeasement and the reasons for it.

You need to know about

The course of British foreign policy since 1933, particularly during the crises over Czechoslovakia and Poland, and the events leading to the outbreak of war. The considerations underlying the policy of appeasement. The attitude of British public opinion towards German demands in this period.

Suggested answer plan

1 View the later 1930s as a period of continuous crisis, with Germany and Italy seeking to expand and Britain and France making concessions to them. If Hitler's demand for the Sudetenland in 1938 had been his 'final territorial demand', then the Munich Conference could have inaugurated a new period of international cooperation. But with his occupation of Prague in March 1939, his ambitions were proved to be more extensive than a mere revision of the Versailles Treaty. Thus British opinion rapidly hardened against him.

2 Give a brief account of the motives underlying the policy of appeasement: (a) strategic necessity – possible aggression (from Japan, Italy and Germany) dictated conciliation wherever possible; British policy in Europe was concerned to avoid a war for which she was not prepared in terms of home air defence of the homeland; (b) the prevalent mood of 'never again' after the First World War; (c) the 'justice' of the German case against the Versailles Settlement; and (d) the fear of Soviet Communism, which was seen in some quarters as a far greater danger than Nazi aggrandisement, led to the rejection of the idea of collective security with Russia.

3 The Munich Conference and the Czech crisis: Both Britain and France were fundamentally unsympathetic towards the Czechs over the Sudetenland. It was not Hitler's claims, but his brutal, threatening presentation of them which affronted Chamberlain, who supported a *peaceful* revision of Versailles. He was eager at all costs to prevent a general war breaking out over France's commitments in Eastern Europe; a further practical consideration was the British

need for more time in which to build up its air defences. Also, there was no enthusiasm among the Dominions for a war on behalf of the Czechs. The public response to Munich one of great relief – but note that Chamberlain nevertheless took the precaution of speeding up the armaments programme.

4 The 'final settlement' of Munich was broken by the annexation of Czechoslovakia: independence had been guaranteed by the four signatory Powers, but there was no question of Britain making this guarantee an occasion for war. The British government took the view that, as the Czech state no longer existed, the guarantee was invalid. However, in the light of Hitler's clear betrayal of the previous understanding, public opinion shifted to one of opposition to further concessions; the 'triumph' of Munich was now regarded by British people with a degree of self-disgust.

5 Opposition to further German expansion now became the first principle of *declared* British policy: Chamberlain's speech and the guarantee to Poland. Britain did not, however, succeed in bringing the Soviet Union into a European system to make the Polish guarantee a military reality (Chamberlain confessed to 'the most profound distrust of Russia'); here note the Molotov-Ribbentrop Pact.

6 Hitler invaded Poland on 1 September 1939, expecting British acquiescence. As at Munich, Mussolini was ready to act as the middle man, but Britain insisted on German withdrawal from Poland. Despite the cabinet's agreement to the sending of an ultimatum, the Government continued to seek a negotiated agreement to a conference. In the end, the House of Commons revolted against any further procrastination and the ultimatum was sent. The British Government went unwillingly to war; the ultimatum flowed both from the guarantee to Poland and from the pressure of public opinion, as represented by the House of Commons, and Hitler failed to assess the British reaction accurately.

Question bank

1 Document question (Britain and Europe in the 1930s): study Extracts I, II and III below and then answer questions (a) to (g) which follow:

Extract I

'The Members of the League undertake to respect and preserve as against external aggression the territorial integrity and existing political independence of all Members of the League. In case of any such aggression the Council shall advise upon the means by which this obligation shall be fulfilled.'

(The Covenant of the League of Nations, Article 10)

Extract II

'Should any member of the League resort to war in disregard of its covenants under Article 12, 13 or 15 it shall *ipso facto* be deemed to have committed an act of war against all other Members of the League, which hereby undertake immediately to subject it to the severance of all trade or financial relations, the prohibition of all intercourse between their nationals and the nationals of the covenant-breaking State, and the prevention of all financial, commercial or personal intercourse between the nationals of the covenant-breaking State and the nationals of any other State, whether a Member of the League or not.

'It shall be the duty of the Council in such case to recommend to the several Governments concerned what effective military, naval or air force the Members of the League shall severally contribute to the armed forces to be used to protect the covenants of the League.'

(The Covenant of the League of Nations, Article 16, paragraphs 1 and 2)

Extract III

'In October 1934, the so-called 'Peace Ballot' was held, and the results were made known in June 1935. It consisted of six questions. Over 11 million people 'voted'. The questions and the approximate number of 'yes' votes for each were as follows:
1. Should Great Britain remain a member of the League of Nations? (*over 11 million*).
2. Are you in favour of an all-round reduction in armaments by international agreement? (*over 10 million*).
3. Are you in favour of an all-round abolition of national military and naval aircraft by international agreement? (*just under 10 million*).
4. Should the manufacture and sale of armaments for private profit be prohibited by international agreement? (*over 10 million*).
5. Do you consider that, if a nation insists on attacking another, the other nations should combine to compel it to stop by
   (a) Economic and non-military measures? (*over 10 million*);
   (b) If necessary, military measures? (*under seven million*).
   (G. M. Gathorne Hardy: *A Short History of International Affairs 1920–39*)

(a) What comment, in the light of the European situation in the autumn of 1934, would you make on the large majority who answered 'yes' to question 2 of the 'Ballot'? (3)

(b) What may be deduced about general opinion at the time from the inclusion of question 3 in the 'Ballot'? (3)

(c) From an examination of Extracts I and II, to what extent do you think there is inconsistency in the fact that there was a large majority in favour of question 1 of the 'Ballot' and a considerably smaller one in favour of question 5(b)? (4)

(d) In what way did Stanley Baldwin's pledges during the 1935 election campaign suggest he was influenced by the size of the 'yes' vote to most of the questions in the 'Peace Ballot'? (2)

(e) What did the policy of the British government in 1935 towards Mussolini's invasion of Abyssinia reveal about the application in practice of the principles of Extracts I and II? (6)

(f) It is often claimed that the voting in the 'Peace Ballot' of 1934 showed that the British people were 'pacifist' at that time. How far do the figures given in Extract III justify this claim? (5)

(g) What other evidence from the 1930s is used to support the claim that the British people were 'pacifist', and why do you think they nevertheless supported war against Nazi Germany in 1939? (8)

2 How strong was Britain's commitment to the League of Nations between 1919 and 1939? (WJEC, June 1991)

3 When, and why, did British governments finally abandon the policy of Appeasement? (Oxford and Cambridge, June 1992)

4 'Britain's declaration of war on Germany in 1939, though inevitable, was ill-timed: it should have happened sooner'. Discuss. (London, June 1990)

5 In the years 1935 to 1938 there was no effective alternative policy for Britain to that of appeasing the European dictators.' Discuss this view. (JMB, June 1989)

READING LIST

Standard textbook reading

T. O. Lloyd, *Empire to Welfare State* (OUP, 1970), chapters 7, 8.

L. C. B. Seaman, *Post-Victorian Britain* (Methuen, 1966), Part VI.

R. K. Webb, *Modern England* (Allen and Unwin, 1980 ed.), chapter 12.

Further suggested reading

Lord Avon, *Facing the Dictators* (Collins, 1962).

P. M. H. Bell, *The Origins of the Second World War in Europe* (Longman, 1986).

W. S. Churchill, *The Gathering Storm* (Cassell, 1948).

P. Hayes, *The Twentieth Century 1880–1939* (A & C Black, 1978).

M. Howard, *The Continental Commitment* (Temple Smith, 1972).

W. N. Medlicott, *British Foreign Policy since Versailles* (Methuen, 1968).

K. G. Robbins, *Appeasement* (Blackwell, 1988).

W. R. Rock, *British Appeasement in the 1930s* (Edward Arnold, 1977).

A. J. P. Taylor, *The Origins of the Second World War* (Penguin, 1964).

C. Thorne, *The Approach of War 1938–39* (Macmillan, 1967).

D. Weigall, *Britain and the World 1815–1986: A Dictionary of International Relations* (Batsford, 1987).

LABOUR IN POWER, 1945–51

Units in this chapter

15.1 *The 1945 General Election*
15.2 *Labour's domestic policy*
15.3 *Foreign and defence policy*
15.4 *The defeat of Labour, 1951*
15.5 *Chronology*

Chapter objectives

❶ Background to the 1945 election: the Labour 'broad church' of the 1930s, taking in Cripps's ethical Socialism and Morrison's pragmatic 'Fabianism'; the development of agreed policies based on 'planning', nationalisation and government intervention; the participation of Attlee, Bevin, Dalton, Morrison and others in the wartime coalition; the 'Left Book Club' and other intellectual socialist organs contributed to the wartime socialist mood.

❷ Reasons for Labour's 1945 victory: the evidence of Mass Observation; *Let us Face the Future* appealed to the progressive, vaguely Left-wing, consensus in the nation; Attlee's quiet competence contrasted favourably with Churchill's scaremongering; the Service vote (influenced by the Army Bureau of Current Affairs) and a general pro-Russia sentiment probably helped Labour; younger voters also supported Labour, and Labour's emphasis on such issues as housing (while the Tories were trying to emphasise foreign policy) also contributed to victory.

❸ Even so, the 1945 election result was not the popular mandate for Socialism that it was often supposed to be; despite a huge popular vote, Labour benefited mainly from Tory defections, a massive protest vote against the economic and foreign policy record of the Tories in the 1930s; it was especially the middle-class white-collar vote in the south and east which deserted the Conservatives.

❹ The 'balance of power' within the Attlee government: the efficient but unassertive leadership of 'chairman' Attlee; the general dislike of Morrison; the domination of the Right-wing in the cabinet isolated Bevan; the use of cabinet committees and of standing committees of the House (with powers of delegated legislation) to push through the government's crowded programme.

❺ Economic policy and performance: full employment, an 8% rise in industrial production, and a 25% rise in exports during 1945–51 could not compensate for the widespread feelings of deprivation and austerity, especially among the middle classes who had voted Labour in 1945; the suspicion that Cripps even relished and welcomed such austerity did not help; the impact of food rationing; difficulties caused by dependence on American loans; the financial crises, the cheap money policies, and the 1949 devaluation; Wilson's 1948 'bonfire of controls' and moves towards deregulation.

⑥ Foreign policy under Bevin: his patriotic imperialism and close relationship with Foreign Office officials; he moved towards support of America in the 'Cold War' against Russia, leading to a 'Keep Left' reaction (Foot, Mikardo), and supported the policy of American defence of Western Europe (leading to NATO, 1949); the reluctant commencement of decolonisation in the Indian subcontinent (Mountbatten and Partition) and in Palestine; despite Bevin's 'Western Union' speech (1948), Labour used imperial commitments as an excuse not to participate in plans for European unity; Britain opposed the 1950 Schuman Plan.

⑦ Social policies: Bevan's policies on housing and the struggles with SMA over the National Health Service; Griffith's National Insurance policies; the Trade Disputes and Trade Unions Act (1946) reversed Conservative legislation of 1927; town and country planning.

⑧ The piecemeal and uncoordinated nature of the nationalisation programme; Morrison's influence, and the decision to provide fair compensation; Dalton's nationalisation of the Bank of England, Shinwell's of coal; then the nationalisation of civil aviation, gas, railways and road haulage; finally, the controversy and political complication roused by the bills to nationalise iron and steel.

⑨ The developing splits in the government and in the Labour Party: the loss of morale following the 1947 winter, the coal crisis, and the disastrous 'groundnuts' scheme; the Cripps and Dalton intrigue to replace Attlee by Bevan; Dalton was forced to resign over budget leaks.

⑩ The Conservatives in opposition: organisational improvements under Lord Woolton; also sensible enough not to oppose the more 'defensible' parts of Labour's programme; the emergence of progressive young Conservatives like Butler, Macleod and Macmillan.

The Second World War brought about fundamental changes in the nature and structure of British politics and society. Labour had made a notable contribution to the Churchill coalition government and, in 1945, won its first parliamentary majority in a landslide victory. War had stimulated collectivist ideas and government intervention in every aspect of social and economic life.

A White Paper in 1944 had accepted government responsibility for maintaining full employment in the future, and in 1943 the predominantly Conservative government had agreed to implement the main principles of the Beveridge Report after the war. Nevertheless, reconstruction promises had been made before and one reason for the Labour victory in 1945 was the knowledge that such promises were often forgotten once war was over. But, unlike 1918–22, this time there was no equivalent retreat from wartime collectivism.

The Labour Government continued the mixed economy through the policy of nationalisation and, through its social reforms in health, etc., established the welfare state. These reforms fell short of the socialist state the Labour Party, in theory, was committed to building, but at least the Labour Government did accomplish the extensive programme of reform that they had promised in *Let us Face the Future*. This was not an inconsiderable achievement.

Background

The Labour Government elected in 1945 was quite unlike those which had taken office in 1924 and in 1929. Attlee's government had a parliamentary majority, an abundance of talent and experience, and a definite and well-thought-out programme. Unlike the

Conservatives, the Labour Party in 1945 knew what they wanted to do and, when elected, they did it.

Although faced with economic problems far beyond what had been expected, the government did not sacrifice its policies in the difficult years after 1945. The things for which it is most remembered are the creation of the welfare state and the nationalisation of major industries, but other achievements should not be forgotten: the country came through crippling balance-of-payment difficulties, and the government repaid in a few years a huge proportion of Britain's vast overseas debts while maintaining full employment at home and putting through its domestic policy.

Britain's foreign policy under Ernest Bevin was also notably successful in achieving its aims, though there were divisions within the Party about what those aims should be.

The economic problems inherited by the Labour government were formidable and it was inevitable that, as time went on and hardship persisted, the government should lose popularity and, eventually, support. Nevertheless, the final defeat in 1951 came as a great shock to many Labour men, just as Churchill and the Conservatives had been stunned by the result of the 1945 election. In terms of positive action, Labour had promised and achieved far more than any other peacetime government, and it set the pattern for postwar politics in Britain.

15.1 THE 1945 GENERAL ELECTION

Labour's victory in 1945 surpassed all expectations. The King commented that Attlee arrived at the Palace 'looking very surprised indeed'. What was not a surprise was the complete eclipse of the Liberals – except outside England. The Conservatives had been confident that the electors would vote for Churchill, the man who had saved the nation. Instead, they turned him out and gave Labour a massive mandate for change. There were a number of reasons for this: Labour's programme as expounded in *Let us Face the Future* was more sweeping and better worked out than the Tories', though in fact, with the exception of nationalisation, its proposals were quite similar to those which the Conservatives offered.

To the public, however, it appeared that Labour had a positive commitment to social reform, whereas the Conservatives endorsed it, as they had in the 'coupon election' of 1918, only because they thought it politically necessary. In addition, although Churchill was personally popular because of his wartime leadership, his attitude towards the Labour movement in the decades before the war had not been forgotten or forgiven. Furthermore the Conservatives, as the principal party of government between the wars, were blamed for the failures of British foreign and domestic policy during the 1930s; as Lord Blake puts it, 'it was the Conservatives who were in' in the 'thirties, 'and they were bound to take the rap for what went on'.

There were other factors also: the experience of war had altered attitudes greatly. Evacuation, in particular, had revealed the deprivations of urban working-class life. People were unwilling to abandon what the war had brought about, such as the commitment to increased social and economic equality and the mobilisation of the country's resources by the government in the interests of all.

The egalitarian spirit built up in wartime, and the determination that the sacrifices of war should be worthwhile, naturally inclined the voters, even normally Conservative middle-class voters, towards Labour. As Bevan remarked, 'the British people have voted deliberately and consciously for a new world'. It had been the 'people's war'; now they wanted a people's peace, not a return to the prewar pattern of government. They could no longer be frightened by Churchill's spectre of collectivist, Socialist government, inseparably woven with totalitarianism. What Labour offered above all was a continuation of wartime egalitarianism and state intervention.

15.2 LABOUR'S DOMESTIC POLICY

In considering Labour's domestic record, therefore, the impact of war upon the expectations of the people must be remembered. They had seen the beneficial effects of state intervention in industry, in the labour market and in welfare, and they wished it to continue. The Beveridge Report of 1942 provided a blueprint for politicians to follow, and it was Labour which embraced its proposals most enthusiastically. New Liberals and progressive Conservatives had been associated with welfare provisions as well as Labour before 1945, but this was not so afterwards.

The creation of the welfare state was immensely popular, although the Conservatives objected to the structure of the National Health Service. It was, however, a pragmatic development of the state's responsibilities, not a revolutionary step into the unknown; that Labour's approach was not doctrinaire was shown by its introduction of contributions and charges for those who could afford them in 1950.

Labour also put a great deal of effort into housing, although their record was somewhat disappointing. There were acute shortages of essential building materials, and it was widely believed that progress was slow because of the insistence of Bevan, the Minister of Health, on quality rather than quantity in the housing programme. Although unemployment never became a major problem, unemployment benefit and pensions were greatly improved.

The other main element in Labour's domestic programme was nationalisation, and this was more controversial. Morrison, however, urged that nationalised industries should be managed not by civil servants but by public corporations, whose members would be appointed by the relevant minister. In this way, the State was kept out of management. It proved to be a succesful compromise. Schemes for public ownership were proposed, however, in terms more of efficiency than ideology. Its approach was piecemeal, uncoordinated and technocratic rather than socialist. The Bank of England and the airlines were taken over without much trouble: most Western countries already had state-run central banks, while it was generally agreed that a national airline could not operate satisfactorily without some form of government support.

It soon became clear that the two classic issues of nationalisation would be coal and the railways. Neither had been profitable before the war, and their workforces were

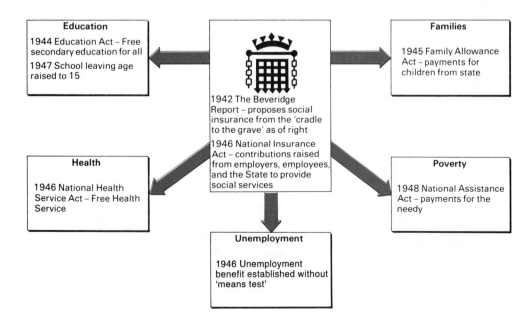

Fig. 13 Labour in Power 1945–51

heavily unionised and in favour of the abolition of private ownership. Yet, as Lloyd says, 'it was the performance of these two industries that did more than anything else to reduce enthusiasm for public ownership, and this played its part in weakening the Labour government'.

The coal industry's problems were deep rooted, and nationalisation could not work wonders overnight. The government was unlucky in that the takeover was followed by the severest winter for decades, creating a demand for fuel which could not be met. According to Dalton, the major casualty of the crisis, 1947 was Labour's '*annus horrendus*'. It was doubly unfortunate that the minister responsible had disregarded warnings about production levels and failed to take action to improve them.

The railways also had a bad public image, and in nationalising them the government took on their unpopularity. Electricity and gas, by contrast, were nationalised without much difficulty in 1948, though the takeover of steel provoked fierce controversy even within the government and was easily undone by the Conservatives when they returned to power. The problem with all these industries was that they had never been very profitable or rationally organised, and the state – in assuming responsibility for them – could do little to change this.

Clement Attlee as Prime Minister

When Attlee became leader of the Labour Party in 1935, in succession to the ineffectual Lansbury, his appointment was generally regarded as a temporary measure. Few people within the Party or elsewhere thought of him as a future Prime Minister. Attlee was seen as inoffensive, dull and uninspiring – yet his leadership was never seriously challenged. He sought to hold the various groups in the Party together, not to secure the supremacy of either Left or Right, and, because he could command trust on all sides, he succeeded. Like Morrison and Bevin, he had a preference for pragmatism rather than doctrinal purity.

As leader and Prime Minister he was as unlike Ramsay MacDonald as it was possible to be. His personal modesty was matched by his practical commonsense, something for which most of his challengers were not noted, and this made him an effective wartime minister and a good leader in the difficult postwar years. Despite his lack of personal charisma, he won his internal battles in the Party and in the cabinet against more forceful and colourful men.

He had, however, the defects of his virtues. He was not an exciting political figure, and as Prime Minister he conveyed an air of drabness which was in keeping with the difficult times in which Britain found herself, but which was not very cheering for the people. Even after Labour's extraordinary success in the 1945 election, he was regarded as a political pygmy, and despite the achievements of the following years this image has persisted.

While it is true that he was more the chairman of the Party than its leader, it is hard to see how another man would have done any better in the circumstances. Under Attlee's leadership, the Labour Government put through the radical legislation it had promised. Its economic record was good. That the voters (and especially the middle class) did not thank them for it by renewing their mandate was hardly surprising, given the inevitable economic hardship of the immediate postwar period.

15.3 FOREIGN AND DEFENCE POLICY

The economic problems inherited by the Labour government were enormous. As Keynes noted, they forced Britain into dependence on the Americans – who drove an excessively hard bargain, hence the sterling crisis of 1947. One price of the economic dependence was a foreign policy influenced by American susceptibilities and pressure.

Despite Labour's commitment to extensive social reform at home, Britain under Attlee began spending a larger proportion of her national income on defence than any other Western European country. This was the result, however, not merely of her overseas obligations, but of a belief that she remained a world power.

Clearly the government believed that England could still play a decisive role in any future war. Both Attlee and Bevin (like Churchill) accepted that the wartime alliance with America had to be retained, but they felt that a more satisfactory relationship could be worked out from a position of independence and strength: hence the decision that Britain should have her own atomic weapons.

In the wake of the Berlin blockade and the onset of the Korean War, two important developments occurred: in 1949 the North Atlantic Treaty Organisation was founded, an event which Bevin regarded as the crowning point of his career, and in September 1950 a massive rearmament programme was announced. These left Britain and Western Europe firmly aligned with the United States against the Soviet bloc, a pattern which has persisted ever since.

American pressure, together with a simple inability to hold on, also had more to do with Labour's decolonisation programme than any socialist belief in anti-imperialism. In general, Attlee's government handled the withdrawal from Empire in an entirely pragmatic, almost a ruthless, fashion. It refused to abandon Malaya (because of the Communist threat to the strategically and economically invaluable supplies of rubber and tin) but hastily abandoned India and Palestine to predictable post-colonial violence and unrest.

15.4 THE DEFEAT OF LABOUR, 1951

The 1950 election produced a victory for Labour – albeit a narrow one. Experts concluded that women and the suburbs had deserted the government – influenced, no doubt, by Conservative allegations that government by Whitehall was inefficient and expensive. The Liberals failed to gather in discontented Labour voters and the future for this party looked bleak. The Labour Left, now, inevitably, demanded a more Socialist policy. The Right and Centre favoured 'modernisation'. It proved an inconclusive struggle as, by late 1951, Labour was out of office.

The defeat of Labour in the 1951 election came in spite of its achieving the highest number of votes in its electoral history. Yet the defeat was not unexpected. The 1950 election had sapped the Party's strength and morale; the leadership appeared jaded; policy and personality differences in the Party were deep and plain to see. The closeness of the result offered little consolation; defeat was still a profoundly disillusioning experience.

Yet the achievements of the governmnent were not inconsiderable. It had set the scene for a new brand of postwar orthodoxy – policies based on the mixed economy, the creation of a welfare state at home, decolonisation and collective security abroad. It was not a revolutionary government. The welfare state was created, but the class system continued. Also there were limits to nationalisation – despite Clause IV. Eatwell points out that the major centres of private power were left untouched, and certainly those who in 1945 thought that they were about to witness the advent of Socialism were to be disappointed. Nevertheless, the government did seem to have an impressive unity of purpose and its record compared very favourably with previous postwar administrations.

The pattern of future British politics was firmly set by the innovations in peace-time state control and provision of welfare services – and, beyond the largely symbolic denationalisation of certain industries, there was little that the Conservatives could do to alter it. Labour could take satisfaction from the fact that the events of the 1940s had given rise to a profound and irreversible change for the better in the position of the working class in Britain.

15.5 CHRONOLOGY

1945	July	Labour won the general election with 393 seats (145-seat majority).
1946	February	BANK OF ENGLAND nationalised. Labour divided about the necessity of this measure. Dalton believed that power had been transferred from 'the City to the Exchequer'. Bevin and the TUC were sceptical. Trade Disputes Act of 1927 was repealed: restored the status quo. The Act's main result was the doubling of Labour Party income from the political levy.
	July	NATIONAL INSURANCE ACT: provided for compulsory payments to finance the new National Health Service; also provided various other benefits – e.g. unemployment, sickness, maternity, widows', retirement etc.
	August	COAL INDUSTRY nationalised (with compensation for the owners) and placed under National Coal Board, which was allowed to borrow £150 million during 1946–51 for modernisation. The Act was fervently welcomed by the unions. HOUSING ACT: Bevan began the task of rebuilding; but the record in 1946 was unimpressive; Conservatives accused Labour of 'socialist inefficiency'
	November	NATIONAL HEALTH SERVICE ACT: based on the Beveridge Report; the whole population was to be covered, regardless of income. Nationalisation of hospitals; free drugs on prescription; free dental and optical treatment. Doctors' resistance to the scheme was eventually overcome. The Act came into operation in July 1948. New Towns Act: sought to place housebuilding powers in public hands. New towns, such as Stevenage and Harlow, were built.
	December	Civil Aviation Act: BEA and BSAA were added to the existing corporation, BOAC.
1947	June	Marshall Plan: American financial aid for Europe.
	August	India granted independence, Britain to withdraw in 1948. ROAD, RAIL AND CANAL TRANSPORT nationalised (with compensation allowed) under the British Transport Commission. This was strongly supported by the unions – but fiercely opposed by road hauliers and the Conservatives. ELECTRICITY industry nationalised under the British Electricity Authority, with subsidiary Area Electricity Boards. This was vigorously opposed by the Conservatives. Fuel Crisis and the introduction of Labour's 'austerity programme'. The Conservatives had a slogan, 'Starve with Strachey and shiver with Shinwell'. Town and Country Planning Act: all development land was henceforth to be subject to planning permission. Agriculture Act: retained the wartime government control of prices and output by retaining subsidies and the Marketing Boards.
1948		NATIONAL ASSISTANCE ACT: complemented the National Insurance Act of 1946; the Poor Law was finally abolished. National Assistance Boards henceforth handled all cases of hardship, paid weekly subsistence rates, etc.
	May	Palestine mandate ended: the British withdraw; war between Jew and Arab followed.
	July	GAS INDUSTRY nationalised – an uncontroversial measure; Area Gas Boards were set up under the British Gas Council. Berlin Airlift began (ended May, 1949). British Nationality Act: all citizens of the Commonwealth made British subjects.
	August	India and Pakistan granted independence: Britain withdraws; followed by rioting and bloodshed between Hindu and Muslim. Local Government Act: introduced by Bevan; it regulated finance between central and local government; allowed the introduction of local Citizens Advice Bureaux.
	December	National Service Act: provided for compulsory military service for men aged 18 to 26. REPRESENTATION OF THE PEOPLE ACT: abolished university votes. Criminal Justice Act: abolished corporal punishment, and generally allowed for greater leniency towards criminals.
1949	April	Eire declared itself an independent Republic. Housing Act: sought to improve Labour's housebuilding programme.
	June	Dock Strike: led to a proclamation of a state of emergency.
	September	DEVALUATION of the Pound from $4.03 to $2.80. Legal Aid and Advice Act: allowed legal aid for the poor.

	November	IRON AND STEEL industry nationalised and placed under the British Iron and Steel Corporation; this controversial measure was strongly resisted by the Conservatives and the owners. It was Labour's final nationalisation measure.
1950	January	Britain recognised Communist China.
	February	Labour won the general election but its majority was reduced to seven.
	April	Britain recognised Israel.
	June	Korean War began: Britain supported the UN and the US; she subsequently contributed naval and ground forces.
	December	Bevan and Wilson resigned over the introduction of Health Service charges to meet the rise in rearmament spending proposed by the government (£4 700 million from 1951–4).
1951	April	Anglo-Iranian oilfields in Abadan taken over by Iran.
	October	Conservatives won the general election.
		Churchill became Prime Minister.

Illustrative questions and answers

1   To what extent was the Labour Government of 1945–50 an innovator in social policy?

Tutorial note

You must place the social policies of the Labour government in the context of twentieth-century thought and policy on social problems. You must consider especially how far prewar and wartime 'blueprints' influenced the legislation of 1945–48.

You need to know about

The domestic legislation of c. 1918–50. The intellectual and political forces which contributed to the development of theories of social welfare.

Suggested answer plan

1   It has often been claimed that Attlee's government established the 'welfare state'; its commitment to full employment, attempts (not wholly successful) to establish a coherent housing policy, its schemes for national assistance independent of a means test, and – above all – its establishment of a free National Health Service, contrast so greatly with the situation in the 1930s that the claim has much apparent validity.

2   An assessment of the Attlee government's commitment to social welfare – especially the attitudes of Bevan, and also of Chancellors Dalton and Cripps, who successively controlled the purse-strings on which social policy depended.

3   The fact that 'welfare state' legislation was put through by the first Labour Government to possess a parliamentary majority strengthens the claim that such a policy was innovatory; the fact that the Conservative opposition supported much of the legislation (though not the Health Service), perhaps undermines it; it is also the case that the government was only able to achieve full employment thanks to Marshall Aid.

4   In fact there was considerable continuity; even before the war the Treasury had been slowly adopting Keynesian ideas, though the first full-scale Keynesian budget was Kingsley Wood's of 1943. Despite the demand of armaments spending, Chamberlain had been developing policies on housing and insurance during the years 1937–9.

5   But the main anticipations of Labour's policy are to be found in wartime; though little (except Butler's 1944 Education Act) was actually *done* under Churchill, much was being prepared. In order to encourage support for the war, the government subscribed to the popular belief that it was being fought, not to beat the Nazis, but to 'build a better Britain'; Sir John Anderson directed Civil Service plans for social reconstruction, while Beveridge's 1942 Report popularised the idea of cradle-to-grave social insurance; despite the government's disapproval of its emotive overtones, the media took up its message, and by the time the war ended, the build-up of expectations was such that no government could have ignored it.

6   An analysis of the social legislation of 1945–8: Cripps and the Treasury maintained a high commitment to welfare and social spending, so there was no 'Geddes Axe' to undermine policies as after World War One; Bevan's National Health Service went beyond wartime blueprints in securing the public ownership of hospitals, which Bevan fought for in cabinet, but otherwise followed wartime precedents; thus Bevan accepted the policy of contributions which the Labour Party had long opposed; Attlee also accepted Butler's tripartite division of the schools; the 1947 Town and Country Planning Act followed the wartime Uthwatt Report closely; and though there was a great ethos of 'planning' during 1945–8, in reality it amounted to little more than the (necessary) continuation (and extension) of wartime controls.

7   Despite its achievements, the Attlee government lacked any carefully thought-out plans of social reconstruction, and so followed rather haphazardly along the lines which the wartime coalition had stumbled on during a national crisis.

8   Setbacks for Labour in the 1950 election; the impact of the Korean war on the foreign policy of the second Attlee government; Morrison as Foreign Secretary; inflation and balance of payments difficulties led to the Bevanite/Gaitskellite split over terms of the 1951 budget (especially the Health Service charges); Bevan, Wilson and Freeman resign.

9   An analysis of the election campaign and results of 1951: Labour's popular vote held, but the middle-class 'idealists' of 1945 reverted to Conservative allegiance; the defeat of the Labour Government provoked heart-searching in the Labour Party as to whether Attlee's government had failed because it had been too socialist or not socialist enough (Croslandite revisionism as against Bevanism). Despite its achievements, it had failed to capitalise politically on a golden opportunity (a large parliamentary majority, a pliant Right-wing TUC, etc.); probably, as in 1929–31, economic difficulties had proved decisive.

2   Why did the Labour Party win the election of 1945 and lose the election in 1951?

Tutorial note
This is a straightforward question on the political fortunes of both main Parties during the 1940s; remember to provide a background to the Labour victory of 1945.

You need to know about
The political and electoral history of the 1940s.

Suggested answer plan
1   Both the 1945 and 1951 election results were once thought surprising; that of 1945 seemed to Churchill, the war hero, to be one of outrageous ingratitude; the 1951 result seemed unfair on a government which had broadly carried out its popular mandate of 1945.

2   The 1945 result had, therefore, to be explained by special factors: perhaps there were naive people who voted for Labour not realising that Churchill would have to resign if Labour came in; perhaps the soldiers wished to register a protest against their commanding officers; perhaps Churchill's 'Gestapo'

speech and generally alarmist campaign alienated moderate and middle-class voters; perhaps the Conservative organisation had run down while its personnel were at the front, allowing Labour's more home-based activists (trade union officers, etc.) to 'steal a march'.

3   Recent historians have rejected these special factors, and see the 1945 result as unsurprising; many contemporaries thought Labour would have won an election in 1940 if there had been one; Conservative unpopularity seems to have peaked in 1940–41 (according to Mass Observation), and seems to have recovered thereafter, even during the course of the 1945 campaign.

4   Perhaps the main point is that by refusing to take Labour members (or even Conservative rebels) into his administration, Chamberlain ensured that his fall in May 1940 and replacement by a Churchill coalition, seemed to contemporaries to be a total replacement of the discredited Conservatives by their bitterest rebel; thus, though Churchill won credit for winning the war, the Conservatives did not; meanwhile Labour leaders (like Attlee, Morrison and Bevgin) participated in the government, mainly on the home front, and made themselves 'known' to the public; since Labour also provided the leader of the opposition, it gained the sympathy of both supporters and opponents of the coalition.

5   Reasons for the reversal of electoral fortunes, 1945–51: was it merely a 'swing of the pendulum' effect? Personal squabbles (often involving Morrison), and later the Bevanite/Gaitskellite split, gave the government an air of incompetence; Bevan's 'vermin' speech gave its image a veneer of class hatred hardly warranted by its policies, and frightened moderates; despite the government's accomplished economic policies (in the face of crippling financial difficulties), nevertheless the 1947 winter, the coal and food shortages, general austerity (rationing, etc.) and devaluation made it unpopular; meanwhile, Conservative organisation improved under Lord Woolton, and a fairer face of Conservatism (Butler, etc.) began to emerge; the 1948 Redistribution probably gave the Conservatives about 40 more seats.

6   But Labour's *popular* vote remained steady even in 1951. Despite its large popular vote, Labour won in 1945 because normally Conservative, middle-class, professional and white-collar voters in London and the dormitory suburbs of the south and east (Newbury, Dover) deserted the Tories; the Liberal vote (not seats won), and that of the minor parties, also improved, suggesting that it was as much a protest against Conservative rule in the 1930s as a mandate for radical change. However, it may be that a new mood of socialist idealism, fostered by wartime propaganda ('Fair Shares for All', the Left Book Club, J B Priestley, etc.), did infuse the middle classes with reformist ideals; if so, they were quickly disillusioned by austerity, and reverted to the Conservatives in 1950/51; by then, a BBC-inspired nostalgia for Churchillian glories (strengthened perhaps by indignation over the abandonment of India) helped to revive their conservatism.

7   Perhaps the most telling explanation is that both Parties went into the 1945 and 1951 elections saying the same things; in 1945 both were paying lip-service (at least) to social reforms, 'fairness' and full employment; by 1951 both parties were recommending deregulation and economic expansion (Wilson's 'bonfire of controls', Morrison's attack on further nationalisation); on each occasion (1945 and 1951), the electorate put its trust in the Party which was able to put the common message across most sincerely; in 1945 that was Labour – in 1951 it was not.

3   How 'socialist' were the policies of the Attlee governments?

Tutorial note

You must consider the various types of Socialism to be found in the Labour movement and assess the Attlee governments' record in the context of each.

You need to know about

The development of socialist ideology in the Labour movement down to 1945. The ideas, policies and subsequent recriminations of the Labour ministers of 1945–51.

Suggested answer plan

1   Morrison later defined Socialism as 'what Labour governments do'; since Labour, in 1945–51, carried out an extremely full manifesto, it could on this definition be regarded as extremely socialist. However, there was no agreed socialist tradition in the Labour movement, or socialist programme; Marxism had played an insignificant role (SDF), and the ILP, and later Cripps's Socialist League, had lost influence to the unprogrammatic and anti-ideological trade unionists; MacDonald's evolutionary gradualism and Lansbury's ethical Social-ism (best represented then by Cripps) survived to complicate the position.

2   The composition of Attlee's ministry, and the differences of opinion within the cabinet and the Party; his own social conservatism and 'moderate' approach to policy; despite a parliamentary majority and an apparent electoral mandate, constraints on policy were imposed by civil servants, by dependence on American aid, by financial difficulties, etc.

3   Socialism was enshrined in 1918 constitutional commitment to Clause IV: in this context Attlee's nationalisation programme seemed effective; 10% of all workers were in nationalised industries by 1951 – *but* they were mainly weak industries, not the 'commanding heights'. A brief account of the nationalisation of coal, gas, rail and road haulage, iron and steel, etc: despite the political controversy, the compensation provided was usually generous; no progress was made towards worker control or 'cooperatives', so that workers' positions in the industries involved did not improve; it was all done ad hoc, at the behest of trade union pressure, and without any planning.

4   Socialism can be defined in terms of welfare: Bevan introduced the National Health Service (conceding, however, the unsocialist 'dual system' or right to private practice by NHS consultants) and improved National Assistance. However, similar policies had been developed by the wartime coalition government, and were equally compatible with Liberalism (Beveridge Report) and with the Conservative determination to make the workers more contented with capitalism. Conservative opposition was muted; there was also a disappointing Labour performance (after high promises) on housing policy.

5   Likewise, increased state control and planning, Keynesian budgetary tech-niques, town and country planning regulations, etc., all followed imperceptibly from wartime precedent, when it had been undertaken out of necessity, not from socialist ideals; it had the full backing of the Treasury, and had more to do with 'efficiency' than with Socialism.

6   Attlee's government accomplished a modest redistribution of wealth through fiscal policy; but full employment and improved living standards for the working classes contrasted with a feeling of 'relative deprivation' among the middle classes, who perhaps suffered more austerity (food shortages, rationing, etc.) than in the flourishing black-market days of wartime. However, the tangible redistribution was limited, and far less than contemporaries supposed was taking place.

7   Under Bevin a 'socialist' foreign policy was lost sight of: there was an increasing identification with America against Soviet Russia. However, decolonisation was begun and hostility was shown towards the nascent 'capitalists' club' in Europe.

8   Perhaps Socialism is mainly about power? In 1918 the trade unions had accepted Clause IV in return for consolidating their constitutional position within the Party (the block vote); the Trade Disputes and Trade Unions Act reversed the interwar Conservative attack on the unions; close relations were maintained with a 'Right-wing' union leadership (Deakin, Lawlor, Williamson). However, both the government and the TUC fiercely opposed unofficial strikes, making

great use of strike-breaking emergency powers and sending troops to the docks and to the railways; this led to rank-and-file disaffection among trade unionists, which in turn led to a Bevanite revolt against the government (which was ironic, as Bevan personally was 'hawkish' on the subject of unofficial strikes).

9   Probably, then, Attlee should be seen as continuing the wartime consensus in favour of state-run capitalism and the mixed economy, plus a dash of welfare; it was later taken over by the Conservatives and called 'Butskellism'. Only in the 1950s did any serious rethinking of what Socialism means (Crosland's egalitarian version, Crossman's worker-power version) take place, though it split the Party in the process.

Question bank

1   Document question (Aneurin Bevan in 1951): study the extract below and then answer questions (a) to (g) which follow:

Extract

'Aneurin Bevan was born in 1897 at the mining town of Tredegar. The social setting in which his adolescent character...matured was the South Wales coalfield before and during the First World War. It was the grimmest part of the United Kingdom, the part that felt itself most disinherited, least connected with the war against the Kaiser. While the great North Welsh rebel, Lloyd George, was becoming the father of his country in its hour of need – taking confidence from the two thousand years of Celtic peasant history behind him – the young Aneurin, watching him with something of the ideology of an industrial "dead-end kid", was rejecting the ways of his fathers. He felt that he knew better what were the real needs of his like, and that patriotism was not a useful emotion.... .

'The only part of his father's outlook he adopted was that expressed by the Tredegar Workingmen's Medical Aid Society (a miniature National Health Service). His father was one of its founders, and Aneurin fought his first battle with a local outpost of the British Medical Association when they wished to <u>boycott</u> the miners' society. The only <u>ideas he accepted from Lloyd George</u> were those of his National Insurance Act.

'In the 'thirties he did not visit the countries threatened or seized by Fascism, as Ellen Wilkinson did, but consolidated his position in Monmouthshire and spoke in the House on coal. He will not be remembered for his warning speeches against Hitler, but for his violent wartime onslaughts on Churchill. And, since the war, his intensity has remained concentrated on domestic issues – despite the evident crisis of the world. The great totalitarian issue of our time has always seemed to be outside his ambit.

'There are only fairly exotic members of the Labour movement among those who have advised him to take his <u>recent decision</u> – it is the secession of a group that can be compared to the friends of the brilliant but ill-fated Lord Randolph Churchill (whom Bevan, in some respects, resembles).

'Much the most solid and constructive effort of his political career is, of course, the establishment of the National Health Service. It is easy to see how his <u>early training</u> had <u>equipped him to out-manoeuvre the doctors</u> – he turned their flank and captured them by playing to the calloused appetite for power and money of some great consultant physicians. And his driving motive was plain – his own experiences had given him ample reason to believe sincerely in the need for a free medical service for the poor.

'What is more surprising is his administrative success. He not only established the Service promptly, despite all obstacles, but earned the regard of his own civil servants. This may be the one episode in his career which justifies comparisons in stature between him and Lloyd George.'

(*The Observer*, 1951)

(a) Explain the meaning of 'boycott'. (2)

(b) What was the 'recent decision' which prompted the writing of this article? (3)

(c) How does the writer of the article show himself hostile to Bevan? (5)

(d) What 'early training', apart from that cited in the extract, 'equipped him to out-manoeuvre the doctors' ? (4)

(e) How far did Bevan extend the 'ideas he accepted from Lloyd George' in creating the National Health Service? (5)

(f) What light is cast, by the final paragraph, upon the relative roles of parliament and the Civil Service in modern Britain? (5)

(g) How does this extract exemplify the dilemmas of the Labour Party in the post-war period? (7)

2 How controversial was the nationalisation policy of the Labour administrations beween 1945 and 1951? (WJEC, June 1991)

3 How far was Britain's foreign policy after 1945 determined by the loss of imperial power? (Cambridge, June 1991)

4 How 'socialist' were the aims and policies of the Labour governments of 1945–51? (AEB, June 1989)

5 What motives underlay the creation of the Welfare State during this period? (NISEAC, June 1990)

READING LIST

Standard textbook reading

T. O. Lloyd, *Empire to Welfare State* (OUP, 1970), chapters 10, 11.

L. C. B. Seaman, *Post-Victorian Britain* (Methuen, 1966), chapter IX.

R. K. Webb, *Modern England* (Allen and Unwin, 1980 edn.), chapter 13.

Further suggested reading

P. Addison, *The Road to 1945: British Politics and the Second World War* (Quartet, 1977).

R. C. Birch, *The Shaping of the Welfare State* (Longman, 1974).

R. Eatwell, *The 1945–51 Labour Governments* (Batsford, 1979).

K. Harris, *Attlee* (Weidenfeld and Nicolson, 1982).

A. Marwick, *Britain in the Century of Total War* (Bodley Head, 1968; Penguin Books, 1970).

R. Miliband, *Parliamentary Socialism* (Merlin Press, 1964, 1973).

K. O. Morgan, *Labour in Power 1945–51* (OUP, 1984).

H. Pelling, *The Labour Government 1945–51* (Macmillan, 1984).

H. L. Smith (ed), *War and Social Change* (MUP, 1987).

R. Ovendale (ed), *The Foreign Policy of the British Labour Government 1945–51* (Leicester University Press, 1984).

L. J. Williams, *Britain and The World Economy 1919–1970* (Fontana-Collins, 1971).

TEST RUN

In this section:

Test Your Knowledge Quiz

Test Your Knowledge Quiz Answers

Mock Exam

Mock Exam Suggested Answer Plans

This section should be tackled towards the end of your revision programme, when you have covered all your syllabus topics, and attempted
the practice questions at the end of the relevant chapters.

The Test Your Knowledge Quiz contains short-answer questions on a wide
range of syllabus topics. You should attempt it without reference to the
text.

Check your answers against the Test Your Knowledge Quiz Answers. If
you are not sure why you got an answer wrong, go back to the relevant
unit in the text: you will find the reference next to our answer.

The Mock Exam is set out like a real exam paper. It contains a wide spread
of question styles and topics, drawn from various examination boards. You
should attempt this paper under examination conditions. Read the instructions on the front sheet carefully. Attempt the paper in the time allowed,
and without reference to the text.

Compare your answers to our Mock Exam Suggested Answer Plans. We
have provided tutorial notes to each, showing why we answered the
question as we did and indicating where your answer may have differed
from ours.

TEST YOUR KNOWLEDGE QUIZ

1   What were the main principles of the Tory Party in 1815?

2   What measures introduced by the Government between 1815 and 1820 made matters worse in the eyes of the Radicals?

3   How liberal were the Liberal Tories?

4   In what way does the 1832 Reform Act deserve the title 'Great'?

5   What was the principal driving force behind the Whig Reforms?

6   What were the main failures of the Whigs 1830–41?

7   Explain the rise of Chartism.

8   Who were the principal leaders of the Chartist movement?

9   Explain the success of the ACCL.

10 How did Peel restore his fortunes with the Tory Party after 1829?

11 Who opposed Peel's measures 1841–46, and why?

12 Was Peel a social reformer?

13 What were the main achievements of Castlereagh in foreign affairs?

14 How far did Canning change the foreign policy of Castlereagh?

15 Was there any consistency in Palmerston's foreign policy?

16 What was Disraeli's political philosophy?

17 Why did the Conservatives introduce a second reform act in 1867?

18 What were the main aims of Disraeli's foreign policy?

19 What were the main tenets of Gladstonian Liberalism?

20 Account for the legislative activity of Gladstone's First Ministry.

21 Why is the record of Gladstone's Second Ministry disappointing?

22 How 'radical' was Radical Joe?

23 What were the main tenets of Joseph Chamberlain's imperialism?

24 What was new about the 'new imperialism'?

25 Why did Joseph Chamberlain fail to become Prime Minister?

26 Why did Gladstone fail to gain Home Rule for Ireland in 1886?

27 How did Lord Salisbury deal with the Irish Question 1886–92?

28 What were the achievements of Parnell?

29 What was the origin of the Liberal social reforms of 1906–14?

30 Explain the emergence of the Labour Party after 1900.

31 Why was there a Budget crisis in 1909?

32 Why did the Liberal Government oppose votes for women?

33 Why was the British economy depressed between the wars?

34 Why did Britain go back on the Gold Standard?

35 What action did the Government take to deal with unemployment?

36 Why did the Liberals fail to form a government in the 1920s?

37 Why did MacDonald accept office in 1923?

38 Who was to blame for the outbreak of the General Strike in 1926?

39 Why did Baldwin lose the election of 1929?

40 What were the main measures taken by the National Government to promote recovery?

41 Account for the failure of the BUF to become a popular Party.

42 Why was political leadership in the 1930s so mediocre?

43 What was the significance of the Peace Ballot?

44 Explain the British policy of non-intervention in the Spanish Civil War.

45 What were the terms of the Munich Agreement?

46 Why did Britain fail to reach an understanding with the Soviet Union before the outbreak of the Second World War?

47 To what extent did government during wartime prepare the ground for post-war Labour policies?

48 Assess the impact of postwar economic problems on the Labour Government.

49 Explain Labour's policy of decolonisation after 1945.

50 What was the turning point in the fortunes of the postwar Labour Government?

TEST YOUR KNOWLEDGE QUIZ ANSWERS

1   The Tories stood for the Crown, the Anglican Church, the 1688 Constitution and the land. They believed in the preservation of the status quo and the firm maintenance of law and order. The more progressive were willing to encourage moderate humanitarian reform but in general were opposed to 'fundamental' reform.

2   The Corn Law of 1815, the abolition of the income tax and 1819 decision to return to the Gold Standard.

3   Reasonably liberal in economic matters and, to some extent, in foreign affairs under Canning, but immovable in matters they regarded as 'fundamental', e.g. reform of Parliament, the Corn Laws or religious change.

4   Despite its non-radical nature it did get rid of the worst of the rotten boroughs. It gave some of the middle classes the vote; it asserted the power of the elected Commons over the Lords and acknowledged the power of public opinion. Above all, it was the first change in the 1688 political system, opening the way to further (peaceful) change when necessary.

5   Benthamite utilitarianism – which provided a philosophy and a procedure for reform. Humanitarians and evangelicals also made a contribution, but it was far less influential.

6   They failed in finance and in Ireland but, more importantly, they failed to reform or repeal the Corn Laws. They upset the working classes by their lack of concessions in 1832, their suppression of Trade Unions and their introduction of the Poor Law in 1834. These failures led to the formation of three popular movements, the ACCL, the anti-Poor Law movement and Chartism.

7   Oppressive conditions in factories, mills and mines, poor living conditions and widespread unemployment during trade depressions, all fuelled general discontent among the lower orders. There was also political disillusionment at being excluded from the franchise in the 1832 Reform Act and anger over the Poor Law of 1834.

8   Among the moderates, William Lovett and Francis Place worked hard for what they called 'moral force' Chartism. Feargus O'Connor, J R Stephens, Bronterre O'Brien and G J Harney, 'who thought himself the English Marat', made more use of the 'mass platform' and the rhetoric of 'physical force'. Chartism only imperfectly fixed these two elements, e.g. 'peaceably if we may, forcibly if we must'.

9   Their message was simple and easily understood. Its leaders were united, skilful and persuasive. It was widely supported, brilliantly organised and well-funded. The strength of their arguments actually convinced Peel. The Irish famine brought matters to a head, giving Peel the opportunity to abandon the Corn Laws.

10 Peel worked hard at opposing the Reform Act from 1830–32 and supported the Established Church against Whig attacks after 1832. His Tamworth Manifesto sought to broaden the base of Tory support by advocating moderate, sensible reform in Church and State. Above all, he restored morale by his qualities as leader of the Opposition in the 1830s, and succeeded in portraying the new Conservative Party as the natural party of patriotism. This seemed to contrast favourably with the unholy alliance of Whigs, Irish and Radicals which made up the Lichfield House Compact in 1835.

11 Primarily the bulk of landed backbenchers in the Party. Peel earned their enmity by reducing the protection given by the Corn Laws, by easing the tax burden on the industrial classes, by favouring the philosophy of free trade, by seeking to help the Catholic Irish (the Maynooth grant) and by treating their own political and religious concerns with apparent disdain. Finally, he repealed the Corn Laws.

12 Peel's record in social reform is not good. He believed in laissez-faire and thought that a successful economy would solve the social ills of the day. Under pressure from Shaftesbury a Mines Act was passed in 1842 and a limited Factory Act in 1844. Under pressure from Chadwick a Royal Commission was appointed to enquire into urban conditions but no further action was taken.

13 Castlereagh played an important part in bringing about the eventual defeat of Napoleon at the Congress of Vienna and displayed a sound European sense, urging conciliation with France. After Vienna his primary concern was the maintenance of peace and a balance of power in Europe. He was a prime mover in the construction of the Quadruple Alliance and encouraged the introduction of the Congress System, a new departure in international cooperation, though he distanced himself from the interventionism of Metternich and Tsar Alexander I.

14 The contrast between the foreign policies of Castlereagh and Canning has been overplayed, partly because of well-documented mutual dislike. Fundamentally they were different in method and style. Castlereagh was more European in outlook, less overtly nationalistic, quieter in diplomacy and unwilling to explain high policy to the public. He was no upholder of absolutism, and was moving away from the Congress System at the time of his death. Canning also pursued England's interests, but as conditions had changed, did so in a more flamboyant, nationalist and popular fashion.

15 Like Castlereagh and Canning, Palmerston followed the basic principles of British foreign policy – in this he was consistent. Britain's interests always came first. Like Canning, he was prepared to improvise ('we have no eternal allies') and favoured the policy of a free hand for Britain. Like Castlereagh, he was prepared, when it suited Britain's interests, to discuss. He favoured Liberalism and Nationalism, peace and the balance of power, and protection for Britain's markets and sources of raw material, but he pursued them in ways which appeared inconsistent and idiosyncratic. This was mostly a matter of personality and style – the interests pursued remained consistent.

16 Disraeli did have a political philosophy but he was not always serious or consistent in applying it. It appears in his novels *Coningsby* and *Sybil* and in the slogans of Young England. It proclaimed the value of privilege and tradition – Crown, Church and aristocracy – but insisted that this privilege be used responsibly and for the good of the whole community – rich and poor alike. Disraeli outlines this communal, paternalistic approach for domestic politics in two speeches at Manchester and Crystal Palace in 1872. In foreign affairs, as an antidote to the Liberal offerings of Home Rule and Concert of Europe, he offered the heady brew of jingoistic imperialism.

17 The Liberal Party split over reform in 1866 and gave Disraeli and the Conservatives an opportunity to introduce a reform bill. Disraeli saw it as a gamble to get the Conservatives into power after years of opposition. Its motivation was to produce an electorate that would vote Tory. All parties now accepted that the 'labour aristocracy' could be entrusted with the vote. Driven by difficulties in his own Party and a minority position in the Commons, Disraeli was forced to pass a more radical measure than he intended – enfranchising all male householders in the boroughs. It is alleged that Disraeli saw the 'angel in the marble', i.e. the potential Tory working-class vote. His main objective, however, was to 'dish the Whigs' and get his Party into office.

18 Disraeli wanted to make British influence (weakened, he believed, by Gladstone's Ministry) supreme again in Europe and to consolidate and extend Britain's colonial empire. Though he had failed to maintain the integrity of Turkey, he succeeded at least in settling the Eastern Question. His imperial policy did little to strengthen the Empire though, and his critics alleged that under his administration imperialism was vulgarised by jingoism.

19 Gladstone's belief in Liberalism sprang from deep religious convictions, so civil and religious liberty were essential to him. This meant also that he upheld the idea of peace and the Concert of Europe in foreign affairs as well as the rights of lesser nations. Furthermore, liberty to Gladstone meant freedom in trade, individualism and laissez-faire in domestic policy. Gladstone did not advocate social reform, believing that people should learn to help themselves and not rely on the State. To encourage self-help there must be equality of opportunity and the abolition of all special privileges wherever they existed.

20 After the legislative inactivity of Palmerston's years, the time was ripe for many reforms. Disraeli began the process with the 1867 Reform Act. At the same time, Fenianism, the Franco-Prussian War and Trade Union disturbances all indicated the need for change. The Liberals were the Party of reform and progress and Gladstone's Cabinet was full of talent and ideas. There was obvious need for the secret ballot after 1867, and for public education. The Irish Question also called out for a solution. Radicals and special interest groups helped maintain the momentum for reform.

21 Compared to the legislative achievement of the First Ministry, this session does appear somewhat barren. Some important measures were introduced, e.g. the Married Women's Property Act, the Third Reform Act and a second Land Act in Ireland. This was a Ministry beset by difficulties, such as the Bradlaugh incident and the Dilke case. Gladstone's partiality to the Whigs upset the Radicals, and especially Chamberlain, who had his own ideas about social reform (his Unauthorised Programme), and how Ireland should be governed. Gladstone's foreign policy again proved unpopular while the Home Rule policy eventually led to a split in the Party and defeat in the election of 1885.

22 Chamberlain, a self-made industrialist, was a new type of professional politician who was determined to get things done. As Mayor of Birmingham he introduced radical measures to modernise the city, e.g. laid on gas and water and an improvement scheme to clear 90 acres of slum dwellings in the city centre. He became leader of the Education League (which challenged Gladstone's views on education), demanding that education should be free, national and secular. He also formed the NLF to democratise the Party and help Liberal candidates fight elections. Before the 1885 election he published his own 'Unauthorised Programme' of social reforms designed to benefit the working classes.

23 In the climate of late Victorian industrial decline Chamberlain believed that the best way of curing the trade depression was by developing and enlarging the British Empire. This would expand markets, make imports cheaper and reduce unemployment. He also believed in the British mission to civilise and modernise 'backward' peoples. He was an expansionist who was willing to fight wars to maintain and enlarge the British Empire and sought to institute a Zollverein and an imperial tariff as a means of cementing Britain and her empire's common interest.

24 British Imperialism was the belief that it was a good idea for Britain to control overseas territories, valuable both for trade and defence. At first, many accepted that this could be achieved without territorial occupation, i.e. 'informal empire'. Disraeli and Chamberlain were more interventionist in their desire to extend the benefits of British civilisation. This new, aggressive policy was later called 'formal empire'. The new Empire, acquired after 1884, would be vital to the economy of the home islands, providing an outlet for surplus population, new markets and new jobs.

25 Under the Liberals he was a victim of his convictions about Ireland. If he had accepted Home Rule he might well have succeeded Gladstone in the Premiership. Under the Conservatives he failed to overcome the opposition of Salisbury after the latter retired in 1902. Shortly afterwards, the adoption of the vote-losing policy of tariff reform ended whatever remaining chance he may have had with the Conservatives and Unionists.

26 After the famine what were needed were policies that would reduce the legacy of bitterness and neglect that eventually led to Fenianism and the attempt to subvert the Union. Gladstone tried Church disestablishment and land reform in 1870 and again in 1881. With these measures he achieved partial success. But through the tactical brilliance of Parnell and the pressure of the Land League in Ireland in the late 1870s the question had moved forward. By now, Parnell had made Home Rule the central demand which Gladstone eventually came to accept. He then immediately ran into difficulties with his own Party – with Chamberlain and Hartington and with the Conservatives who rejected Home Rule and saw an opportunity to defeat Gladstone by encouraging the fears of Protestant Ulster. The issue now became a party political one which reduced the possibility of an agreed solution. Gladstone pressed on but was clearly now in a minority. The Liberal Party split. Ulster threatened revolt; the Home Rule Bill was lost and the Liberals were roundly defeated in the election that followed. The English electorate had given its verdict – decisively against Home Rule, and once again Irish affairs brought down a British Government.

27 Salisbury was opposed to any form of Home Rule for Ireland and his government, which saw Irish unrest as a symptom of underdevelopment, set out 'to kill Home Rule by kindness'. First, law and order had to be restored because of the social unrest caused by the Plan of Campaign. A new Crimes Act was passed in 1887 and was rigorously enforced by Balfour, who earned the title of 'Bloody' for his efforts. With the political collapse and death of Parnell in 1891 the prospect of Home Rule receded and so the Conservatives turned from coercion to conciliation. A Land Purchase Act (1891) enabled many Irish tenants to buy their land and a Congested Districts Board Act helped overpopulated, depressed areas in Ireland by introducing government-funded improvements, from better farming methods to light railways. The steam had by now gone out of the Home Rule movement and so in the 1890s Ireland enjoyed a welcome period of comparative calm.

28 As President of the Land League, his pressure on Gladstone (who introduced the Land Act of 1881) revolutionised the approach of the British Government to the land problem and began the process that led to its solution with Wyndham's Act in 1903. He also developed Home Rule from a vague aspiration to being at the forefront of British parliamentary politics and won for it the support of the Liberal Party. His creation of a disciplined, efficient and powerful Irish Party in the House of Commons demonstrated that Ireland was ready for self-government.

29 The origins were many and varied. Each reform could be seen as an answer to a specific problem and the originators would have little thought of founding a 'welfare state'. Some measures were introduced for tactical reasons in inter-party parliamentary struggles. Key figures, however, such as Lloyd George, wanted not only a fairer, juster society but also to offer an antidote to the new Socialism. Liberal Unionists and the working classes also had proposals for social reform. A very important motive was to preserve the existing capitalist

economic system. Changing attitudes to poverty, 'class abatement' measures, humanitarian concerns – each contributed something. In a sense they were all aspects of a search for ways of preserving British imperial society in the early 20th century.

30 British politics 1906–14 was dominated by the Liberal Party. Many believed Labour would be absorbed or remain a small, isolated socialist group. Liberal strength was not as great as it appeared to contemporaries, however. Henry Pelling stresses its failures in local elections, its search for a policy after 1910, its organisational weaknesses and inability to capture working class votes. Labour, though apparently weak, was steadily recruiting Trade Union affiliations. The growing difficulties of the coal industry, industrial unrest and declining real wages all benefited Labour, as the Liberals had no apparent answers to these problems. Though the Parliamentary Party was small, the support of the Trade Unions in finance, membership and morale was vitally important for Labour's future.

31 After their humiliating defeat in 1906, the Conservative Unionists faced a bleak future in Opposition. At first they were reasonably restrained. Opposition to the Old Age Pensions Act was feeble and they were careful not to oppose essentially Labour legislation. However, under Balfour opposition gradually became reckless and even encouraged violence (as in Ulster). Soon he decided to use the House of Lords as a second Conservative Chamber to reject purely Liberal legislation, as Lord Landsdowne remarked: 'two separate armies in a common plan of campaign'. The Liberals saw the danger and Campbell-Bannerman in 1907 decided that the power of the Lords had to be reduced, at least from an absolute to a suspensory veto. All that was needed was an issue large enough to gain wide popular support. This issue was the People's Budget of 1909.

32 The Liberals believed that women, being conservative by nature, would vote Unionist. Backbench Liberals, believing in progressive change, favoured suffrage reform.

33 The structural roots of Britain's economic crisis lay in the pre-1914 inheritance of a narrow-based, increasingly outdated export trade. Interwar economic adversity hit such an economy hard, dependent as it was on the old staples – coal, iron and steel, textiles and shipbuilding – and on the ability of primary producing countries to buy these manufactured goods. Britain now paid the price for the businessman's preference for underdeveloped markets in the pre-World War I period. The prizes now went to nations best able to produce the new technologies – cars, machine tools, electrical goods, synthetic fibres, etc. Even in the staple industries, the persistence of relatively small units of production and the continuing inadequacy of scientific and technical education limited the competitiveness of British exports.

34 The First World War gravely damaged the international economy. The Gold Standard was suspended for the duration of the war. Postwar economic dislocation, with currencies floating freely and sometimes fluctuating wildly, did not encourage an immediate return. The depreciation of the German Mark in 1923 encouraged the view that gold alone could provide security. John Maynard Keynes was against the move, but in April 1925 Churchill announced a return to the Gold Standard at the old parity of $4.86 to the pound (which Keynes argued was 10% over value). The return to gold reduced demand for all British exports and, most especially, for coal which was also disadvantaged in June 1925 with the reopening of the Ruhr. What was wrong, therefore, was not the return to gold as such, but the return at too high a parity.

35 The National Government had few ideas on how to deal with unemployment. It consoled itself with palliatives rather than tackling the root of the problem. An Unemployment Benefit Act (1934) was set up to help the unemployed after their insurance ran out but it was to be 'means tested' and was bitterly resented. Some money was spent (to little effect) on depressed areas such as South Wales and Tyneside. Some investment was made in the iron and steel industry and

loans were offered to shipbuilders. Bank rate reductions helped stimulate housing. It was a piecemeal policy. Rearmament in the later 'thirties was more effective in reducing unemployment.

36 Many reasons may be advanced for this, from the Asquith/Lloyd George split to the advance of Socialism. Perhaps most important were the unpredictable effects of the First World War. The Liberals, believing in laissez-faire, watched from 1914–18 as the Government appeared to intervene in every aspect of commercial and industrial life. From DORA to military conscription, their ideas of liberty seemed to be in retreat. They lost heart and support. The 1918 Representation of the People Act also tripled the electorate and ensured that a return to a pre-1914 political world was now no longer possible.

37 With 191 MPs, the second-largest Party in the Commons, MacDonald grasped the opportunity to become Prime Minister in 1923. If he had failed to do so, the Liberals might have formed a government and Labour would have been forced off the Opposition Front Bench by the Conservatives. Also, he was eager to show that Labour could govern and that he could be an effective PM. Logically he should have sought Liberal help but his vanity and fear of the Left in his own Party prevented him from doing so. Having no Socialist programme and lacking policies for unemployment or the economy, he wished only to govern, respectably, for a short time. Helped by Baldwin, he achieved his aim.

38 It is easy to blame Baldwin (as many Left-wing historians have). There is no doubt that he could have been more positive about mineowner Alfred Mond's advice, and insisted that all sides accept the Samuel Report. He was also at fault in breaking off negotiations with the TUC at a critical stage in the talks. However, the miners themselves were not entirely blameless. Their demands appeared to be inflexible. The mineowners were equally at fault, insisting on local wage agreements and demanding longer hours and lower wages – whatever the consequences.

39 In the election the Conservatives polled most votes (8.6 million) and Labour most seats (288). Baldwin could hardly complain, however. He had done little to tackle the problems of unemployment or of the coal-mining industry. His Trade Disputes Act in 1927 was bitterly resented by the Trade Unions and the working class. The balance of payments was still unhealthy and apart from the efforts of the dynamic Neville Chamberlain (Minister of Health) who steered 21 bills through Parliament, the work of the Ministry was unexciting.

40 Snowden introduced emergency measures, raising income tax and reducing public employees' salaries by 10%. Soon afterwards, Britain went off the Gold Standard, but there was to be no sudden economic revival. After the election of October 1931, when MacDonald got his mandate, Free Trade was at last abandoned by Neville Chamberlain and a 10% duty placed on most imports. Some attempts to reorganise major industries and locate new industries in areas of high unemployment were tried but without much success. Stability was achieved but little progress was made as a result of government policies. Falling prices on the world market meant that real wages (and spending power) rose and this, together with rearmament, were the main reasons for economic recovery after 1935.

41 The major reason was the comparative lightness of the depression in Britain. The middle class were spared the hyperinflation of Germany and the better-off working classes survived reasonably comfortably. The BUF was too new to mount a successful challenge in the early 'thirties and economic recovery after 1935 deprived Oswald Mosley of the support of most uncommitted voters. Finally, by the later 'thirties Mosley's willingness to advocate Nazi German control of central and eastern Europe made him appear a Hitler sympathiser and agent. The BUF relied on marches and was involved in violent incidents. This alienated a number, including the press baron Lord Rothermere, originally a supporter of the movement. The Public Order Act of 1936 further undermined any appeal the movement might have by banning

the wearing of political uniforms and giving the police power to ban processions.

42 It is often alleged that British political life in the 'twenties and 'thirties was governed by mediocrities. It is true that Baldwin, MacDonald and Chamberlain were not imaginative political leaders of the ilk of Gladstone or Lloyd George. This, however, is no mere accident of personalities. 'Dynamic forces could be terrible things', as Baldwin said of Lloyd George. It was the relative weakness of British governmental power abroad as well as at home that placed dynamic political leadership at a discount. A realistic sense of the fragility of power promoted a quiet, cautious style that fitted eminently the abilities of Baldwin and MacDonald. Safety First, Peace in Our Time and appeasement, particularly the last, reflected the very great constraints which the economic situation and defence capability imposed upon decision-making.

43 The Peace Ballot was the popular name for The National Declaration on the League of Nations and Armaments and it followed the breakdown of the World Disarmament Conference and the occupation of Manchuria by the Japanese. It was organised by the League of Nations Union and other peace groups and was intended to elicit the support of British public opinion for the League and the idea of collective security. 38% of the adult population of Great Britain polled. There was very great support for the League and the idea of disarmament, but 10 million out of 11 640 066 endorsed the idea of imposing economic sanctions and nearly 7 million indicated a willingness to support military sanctions. The support for collective security influenced the tactics of the Government during the Abyssinian War of 1935–6. In the General Election of November 1935, Baldwin gave fulsome support to the League and this was exposed as plainly insincere when the details of the Hoare-Laval Pact became known.

44 The British were concerned that the conflict should be localised. Their greatest fear was that it would develop into a general European war. In the event, Italy and Nazi Germany assisted the Nationalist insurgents under Franco while the Soviet Union gave help, though on a smaller scale, to the Spanish Republic. Britain made it clear that she would not come to the rescue of France if the latter power involved herself in the conflict. The Non-Intervention Agreement, signed by 27 powers, called for an embargo on arms shipments to Spain. There were other considerations for Britain. She had considerable investments in Spain and was concerned about the strategic implications of Gibraltar and the Canary Islands. It was important that Spain should not be alienated, so that if a European war were to break out key bases would not come under enemy control.

45 This was agreed on 29–30 September 1938 and gave Nazi Germany the Sudetenland, an area of mixed population which contained 3¼ million ethnic Germans. It dictated that the area should be evacuated by the Czechs by 10 October and, further, that Czechoslovakia should cede territory to Hungary and Poland. It was agreed that the Four Powers – Britain, France, Germany and Italy – would guarantee the remainder of Czechoslovakia, but this promise was not fulfilled. Nor was the Anglo-German pact signed at Munich in which the two powers agreed to renounce war as a means of settling their mutual disagreements.

46 Neville Chamberlain had the deepest dislike and distrust of the Soviet Union. Ideological abhorrence of Soviet Communism was combined with a belief, encouraged by intelligence reports and the purge of the army by Stalin, that the Red Army was incapable of a successful offensive war. Britain sought to involve the Soviet Union in neither the Anschluss nor the Munich Agreement. Chamberlain believed any understanding with the Soviet Union would sabotage prospects for a lasting understanding with Hitler. All the Dominions, with the exception of New Zealand, were hostile to such an understanding with the Soviet Union. In the half-hearted negotiations with the Soviet Union in 1939, Britain was unwilling to force Poland to accept the Soviet demand

that her forces be allowed to cross Polish territory and Rumanian air space in the event of a Nazi attack.

47 Postwar policy was anticipated in a number of ways:
   ❶ Labour membership of the Coalition Government, and especially the contribution of Ernest Bevin at the Ministry of Labour;
   ❷ wartime labour legislation in which unions traded the right to strike for various benefits, e.g. minimum wages in some industries;
   ❸ wartime advances in welfare provision;
   ❹ introduction of food subsidies, price controls, rationing and taxation policy helped redistribute income – as, indeed, did full employment.

48 The economic problems inherited by the Labour Government were enormous. As Keynes maintained (and the Government accepted), they forced Britain into the arms of the Americans who, having attained global industrial and trading predominance, drove an excessively hard bargain. Hence the sterling crisis of 1947. In the long term, the leading objective of government policy had to be an export drive. Nothing took priority over this. Wartime controls were used to hold back domestic consumption and ensure high levels of capital investment. 'Austerity' was, in fact, responsible for laying the foundations of the long boom of the 1950s. Meanwhile, however, the Government had little alternative to dependence on the US and whatever terms could be obtained.

49 US pressure, together with a simple inability to hold on, had more to do with Labour's policy objectives than Socialist anti-imperialism. Let Us Face The Future had promised only self-government, not independence, to India. Events in Malaya and the Middle East strengthened this impression. India could be left to communal religious rioting because no vital strategic or economic interests were involved. Malaya could not, because the insurgents were Chinese Communists and threatened our invaluable supplies of rubber and tin. Similarly, the Government rejected withdrawal from the Middle East (Palestine excepted, because of the costs involved in the worsening situation there) because of the vital importance of Middle Eastern oil to Britain.

50 The fuel crisis, which led to 2 million unemployed in February 1947; the (unsuccessful) attempt by Herbert Morrison to abandon Labour's only controversial nationalisation pledge, steel, in 1947; and the sterling crisis in August of that year. These events marked the crisis of the Labour Government, the turning point between the mass of constructive legislation introduced in the years 1945–46 and the period of drift which led up to the final defeat in the election of 1951.

LETTS SCHOOL EXAMINATIONS BOARD
General Certificate of Education Examination

ADVANCED LEVEL
BRITISH HISTORY

Time allowed: 3 hours

Attempt question 1 and any 3 others

1 **Interpretations of the Chartist Movement**

Read the extracts below and then answer all the questions which follow.

Document A: From the report of a speech by G J Harney to fellow Chartists, January 1839.

> We have met here today to demand our rights…to tell our tyrants that they shall tyrannise no longer. We demand Universal Suffrage, because we believe that universal suffrage will bring universal happiness – for universal happiness there shall be – or our tyrants shall find to their cost that we will have universal misery. (Cheers). We will have happy homes and altars free, or by the God of our sires, our oppressors shall share the misery we have too long endured. (Cheers). My friends, we demand universal suffrage because it is our right, and not only because it is our right, but because we believe it will bring freedom…we believe it will give us bread and beef and beer. What is it that we want? Not to destroy property and take life, but to preserve our own lives, and to protect our own property – viz. our labour. We are for Peace, Law, Order; but…if our tyrants shall violate the law…then we will fall back upon the Constitution, and defend the few remaining of the blood-bought rights left by our fathers.
>
> …Again, I say, we are for peace, but we must have justice – we must have our rights speedily; peaceably if we can, forcibly if we must. (Loud cheers).

Document B: Adapted from *The Condition of the Working Class in England* (1845) by Friedrich Engels.

> Chartism was from the beginning in 1835 chiefly a movement among the working-men, though not yet separated from the radical petty-bourgeoisie. The Radicalism of the workers went hand in hand with the Radicalism of the bourgeoisie; adherence to the Charter was the shibboleth of both. They held their National Convention every year in common, seeming to be one party. The bourgeoisie then turned its attention to more practical projects, more profitable to itself, namely the Corn Laws. The Anti-Corn Law Association was formed in Manchester, and the consequence was a relaxation of the tie between the Radical bourgeoisie and the proletariat. The working-men soon perceived that for them the abolition of the Corn Laws could be of little use, while very advantageous to the bourgeoisie. The fruit of the uprising (the Plug Plot) was the decisive separation of the proletariat from the bourgeoisie. The Chartists had not hitherto concealed their determination to carry the Charter at all costs, even that of revolution; the bourgeoisie, which now perceived, all at once, the danger with which any violent change threatened their position, refused to hear anything further of physical force, the difference between Chartist democracy and all previous bourgeois democracy. Chartism is of an essentially social nature, a class movement.

Document C: From *What the Chartists Are: A Letter to English Working-Men by a Fellow-Labourer*, 1848.

> In speaking of the Chartists, of course I mean physical-force Chartists, as moral-force Chartists are only Reformers; but if any of the obloquy which I seek to attach to the name of physical-force Chartists should visit moral-force Chartists, let them remember that they have assumed a name which does not belong to them and be silent! It is their punishment, who are only reformers, for leaguing themselves with Revolutionists. Now that the speeches in the Convention have laid bare the designs of physical force, let moral-force dissolve the partnership.

Document D: From *A History of England during the Thirty Years' Peace* (1849) by Harriet Martineau.

> What was it all about? The difficulty of understanding and telling a story is from comprehending so vast a variety of things and persons. Those who have not looked into Chartism think that it means one thing – a revolution. Some who talk as if they assumed to understand it, explain that Chartism is of two kinds – physical-force Chartism, and moral-force Chartism – as if these were not merely an intimation of two ways of pursuing an object not yet described. Those who look deeper – who go out upon the moors by torchlight, who talk with a suffering brother under the hedge, or beside the loom, who listen to the groups outside the Union workhouse, or in the public house among the Durham coal-pits, will feel long bewildered as to what Chartism is, and will conclude at last that it is another name for popular discontent – a comprehensive general term under which are included all protests against social suffering.

(a) Using the evidence in Documents C and D and your own knowledge, distinguish between physical-force Chartism and moral-force Chartism. (3)

(b) Using Document B and your own knowledge, assess the validity of the explanation given by Engels for the collapse of the alliance between the working class and the bourgeoisie which had operated in the early years of the Chartist movement. (4)

(c) How far does the evidence in Document A confirm the analysis of Chartism provided in Documents B and D? (5)

(d) Compare and contrast the value to the historian of Documents A and D as evidence of the causes of Chartism. (6)

(e) Using Documents A C and D and your own knowledge, comment on Engels's definition of Chartism as 'a class movement'. (8)

2 Would you agree that Lord Liverpool's leadership is the basic explanation for the Tory Party's domination of politics between 1812 and 1827?

3 What did the Whigs achieve and what did they fail to achieve in the 1830s?

4 'More successful as a national statesman than as a party leader.' Comment on this assessment of Peel's achievements during his Second Ministry (1841–46).

5 'All bluff and bluster.' How fair is this criticism of Palmerston's handling of foreign affairs 1846–65?

6 'The domestic reforms of Gladstone's First Ministry were essentially administrative whereas those of Disraeli's Second Ministry were mainly social.' How valid is this view?

7 'Gladstone himself is largely to blame for the failure of his Irish policies after 1880.' How far would you agree with this statement?

8 Analyse the obstacles to the creation and development of a Labour Party between c.1880 and 1914.

9 How much did the Liberal welfare reforms do to improve the lot of the working classes in Britain between 1906 and 1914?

10 Why were the Conservatives so often in office in the interwar years?

11 Why were the governments of the interwar period unable to solve the problem of mass unemployment?

12 'The Labour governments of the period 1945 to 1951 broke little new ground in their social policies.' Examine the validity of this judgement.

MOCK EXAM SUGGESTED ANSWER PLANS

1 (a) This question specifically asks for a combination of textual analysis and your 'own knowledge'. Be careful, then, to use your own knowledge to infer from the sources what the main distinctions are between the types of Chartism.

   (b) The essential basis for a sound answer here is an understanding of Engels's argument, namely that the bourgeoisie, having initially favoured the Charter, later rejected it in favour of Repeal – which the workers regarded as irrelevant to their needs. You are asked to assess the validity (soundness, accuracy) of the argument.

   (c) Comparative evaluation is needed here, so it is vital that you refer to the arguments (and quote when necessary) from each of the sources given, e.g. the claim in extract B that Chartism was essentially violent is borne out by A's readiness to contemplate force.

   (d) Here is an opportunity for you to list the differences: e.g. A is an impassioned speech to the faithful, while D is a reflective passage in a book; A is a call to action while D is an analysis of motive – and so on.

   (e) Good answers here will grasp that all the sources suggested that Chartism was a working-class movement and that by 'class movement' Engels in particular meant a revolutionary force – an interpretation not necessarily implicit in A, C and D. A perceptive analysis of each source is called for, e.g. C explained as a direct rejection of 'the revolutionists' and D as stressing the fact that Chartism was not a monolithic class movement but an amalgam of various 'protests' against 'social suffering'.

2 You may be tempted to see the question as one on postwar distress – which it is not. It is about Lord Liverpool's leadership qualities during the period 1812–27 (note that the question begins in 1812). You need to comment on Liverpool's skills, e.g. persuasive, flexible, ameliorative, and then list the other reasons why the Tory Party stayed in power, e.g. the weakness of the Whigs, fear of revolution, the nature of the electoral system, etc. Was Disraeli's comment about Lord Liverpool, 'the Arch-Mediocrity', a fair description?

3 This is clearly a two-part question, the first part being the easier of the two. But beware of simply giving a list of reforms. Stress the aims of the Whigs as well as their achievements when dealing with their reforms. In the second part you must outline the main failures of the ministry, e.g., their failure to bring in Corn Law Repeal which upset the industrial middle classes, and led to the formation of the Anti-Corn Law League. Also the failure to extend the vote to the working classes which led to Chartism. Do not forget that they failed in finance, too, and in Ireland.

4 Here you must examine Peel's achievements both as a statesman and as a party leader. As a perceptive national statesman, Peel recognised that industrialisation had arrived and he encouraged it and showed his acceptance of it in his policies on cash and corn. He was also progressive on the Catholic issue: see Emancipation in 1829 and Maynooth in 1845. The Tories, however, rejected his brand of liberal Conservatism and reviled him for 'betraying' them on the '3 Cs'. Note, however, that Peel felt that these reforms would benefit the Tory Party and sustain it in power in the new industrial age. This is what the Tamworth Manifesto was all about — a sensible, pragmatic programme for the party. In Peel's eyes it was possible to be both a national statesman and an effective party leader.

5 The core of most questions on British foreign policy in this period demands an understanding of its basic principles. If you know these for Palmerston, for instance, then you can apply them to all his actions. How did his actions conform? Do not be tempted into giving a narrative list of his involvements abroad. Try to evaluate his aims. Show him pursuing these aims in different ways – conferences, gunboat diplomacy, etc. and then assess how much of this, if any, was simply 'bluff and bluster'.

6   Another two-part question, this asks you to consider the validity of the statement. It would be easy to describe the reforms of each ministry in turn, with a passing reference to 'administrative' and 'social', but there are pitfalls here. Note, for example, that Gladstone created opportunity by administrative reform, e.g., the Education Act of 1870, and showed here his concern for social issues. On the other hand, most of the legislation promoted by Cross was permissive and may have been mere vote-catching. Clearly the words 'administrative' and 'social' deserve thoughtful analysis in this context.

7   Be clear that this assessment of Gladstone's Irish policy begins in 1880. Do not be tempted to spend more than an introductory paragraph on events before that date. The question is asking you to evaluate why Gladstone's Irish policies failed and how great his own responsibility for this was. Note that the question asks you to consider the period down to 1894. Do not give short measure on, or ignore, the developments after 1886. Rather than getting trapped in a narrative run-through of events, it would be wiser to select the main reasons for Irish policy failure, e.g., the hostility of British public opinion, the Irish themselves – and especially Parnell's own mistakes, the House of Lords, Ulster's intransigence etc, ... and deal with them across the whole period from 1880 to the rejection of Gladstone's Second Home Rule Bill in 1893.

8   This question asks you to analyse the reasons for the limited political progress of the Labour party before 1914. The key word here is 'obstacles' and these must be carefully assessed. Labour activists (middle-class social reformers, socialists, trade union leaders) met formidable obstacles in the nature of the electorate, the persistence of Lib-Labism (not least within the trade unions), Liberal policies after 1906, lack of finance, and so on. Note that there is some scope for an assessment of the decline of Liberalism, but the question is largely about 'obstacles' to Labour growth. Note also that the question goes up to 1914 and so at least 40% of your answer must be on post-1906 developments.

9   This is a fairly straightforward question where an awareness of the main welfare measures introduced, and their limitations, could gain a high mark. However, it is vital to discuss in some detail the limitations of these welfare reforms. Do not be side-tracked into writing about the general aims of the Liberals, or about laying the foundations of the Welfare State. It would be better to assess the effects of the reforms on the living and working conditions of the working class. Obvious examples of welfare legislation are the Children's Charter, old age pensions, trade boards and labour exchanges, but do not neglect a detailed examination of the impact and importance of the National Insurance Act.

10 Avoid the temptation to write at length about the decline of, and splits in, the Liberal Party, or the weakness and inexperience of the Labour Party. While these are valid and important, they cover the negative aspect of the question only and should only form part of your answer. It is much more important that you examine the positive appeal of Conservatism, Baldwin's leadership qualities, the influence of electoral changes, for instance. While these factors were obvious in the 1920s do not forget that you must also explain the continuing appeal of Conservatism in the 1930s.

11 You must have a clear idea about government economic policy between the wars. Avoid the temptation to concentrate on the causes of the slump. Structural and cyclical problems must be isolated and commented on, the chronology of the Keynesian alternative to the Treasury view examined, the importance of regional factors and the general intractability of many problems analysed. Finally, do not forget to explain the constant interaction of politics and economics throughout the interwar years.

12 This question requires you to deal specifically with the social policies of the Labour Government. Avoid giving a general account of Labour policy, e.g. nationalisation, austerity, etc. Important as it is, it would also be unwise to

make too much of the introduction of the National Health Service to the exclusion of other social policies. Note also that you have been asked to examine whether these social policies were novel or not. So a successful answer would stress the importance of earlier social reforms in the 1920s and the influence of Beveridge. Although these were important precedents, there was also much that was novel in in Labour's policies on health, insurance, family allowances, housing, new towns and full employment. These should be given due weight.

INDEX

Aberdeen, Lord   62, 64, 66, 98, 104
Acts of Parliament (British):
  Act of Union (Ireland)   62, 124, 126, 133
  Agricultural Act   159, 212
  Army Act   101
  Army Regulation Act   105
  Artisan's Dwelling Act   88, 92, 94
  Ashbourne Act   132
  Ballot Act   105
  Bank Act   59, 68
  Bank Charter Act   61, 65
  British Nationality Act   212
  'Cat and Mouse' Act   146
  Children and Young Persons Act   160, 187
  Children's Act   145
  Civil Aviation Act   212
  Coal Act   160, 187
  Coal Mines Act   145, 160, 173
  Coercion Bills (Ireland)   63, 65, 129, 131, 135
  Combination Laws   18, 24, 25, 26, 39
  Companies Act   62, 65
  Conspiracy and Protection of Property Act   88, 92
  Corn Laws   16, 18, 20, 23, 34, 45, 50, 52, 52, 59,
    60, 63, 65, 66, 67, 80, 85, 91, 98, 104, 148
  Corrupt Practices Act   103, 105, 118
  Crimes Act   131
  Criminal Justices Act   214
  Criminal Law Amendment Act   105
  Education Acts   37, 88, 92, 94, 99, 101, 105, 111,
    113, 117, 140, 145, 147, 152, 173, 214
  Employer's and Workman's Act   88, 92
  Enclosure of Commons Act   88
  Factory Acts   23, 31, 35, 37, 39, 55, 62, 65, 160
  Franchise Bill   111
  Free Education Act   114
  Government of Ireland Act   173
  Great Reform Act (1832)   26, 30, 31, 33, 34, 37,
    39, 45, 48, 49, 56, 59, 60, 64, 68, 99, *See also:*
    Reform Acts (2nd) and (3rd)
  Home Rule Bill (Ireland)   106, 109, 112, 114, 117,
    118, 119, 130, 132, 133, 134, 146
  Housing Acts   158, 160, 212, 214
  Import Duties Act   160, 187
  Industries Act   159
  Game Laws   50, 159
  Irish Land Acts   99, 101, 103, 107, 127, 129, 131,
    134, 135, 145
  Irish Universities Reform Bill   102
  Land Purchase Act   132
  Law Act   101

Legal Aid and Advice Act   214
Licensing Act   101, 105, 145
Local Government Act   114, 118, 159, 173, 214
Married Woman's Property Act   105
Mines Act   62, 65
Municipal Corporations Act   31, 36, 39, 56
National Assistance Act   212
National Health Service Act   212
National Insurance Act   146, 212, 216
National Service Act   214
Navigation Acts   17, 16, 21, 22, 25
New Towns Act   212
Old Age Pensions Act   145
Parliament Act   139, 142, 146, 149
'People's Budget'   138, 142, 145, 149
Poor Law   31, 36, 37, 39, 40, 42, 43, 48, 56, 65,
  133, 159, 212
Public Health Act   62, 88, 92, 160
Public Order Act   181, 187
Public Worship Act   88, 92
Redistribution Act   92, 103, 105, 111, 118
Reform Act (2nd)   85, 87, 92, 101, 105, 119
Reform Act (3rd)   99, 103, 105, 113, 118, 124
Reform Act (1919)   167
Representation of the People Act (1918)   173
  (1948)   214
Sale of Food and Drugs Act   94
School Meals Act   145
Six Acts (1819)   18, 23, 61
Special Areas Act   160, 187
Statute of Westminster   196
Test and Corporation Acts   22, 23, 39
Town and Country Planning Act   212, 214
Trade Boards Act   145
Trades Disputes Act   145, 147, 212
Trades Disputes and Trade Union Act   159, 173,
  176, 177, 207, 216
Trades Union Act   101, 105, 146
Unemployment Act   160, 181, 187
Unemployment Insurance Act   159, 173, 183
Unemployed Worker's Dependents' Act   159
University Test Act   105
Widows Orphans and OAP's Act   159
Workmen's Compensation Act   86, 114, 118, 119,
  145
Wyndham's Act   134
Afghanistan   89, 103, 107, 120
Africa   115, 120, 121, 196
Alabama Claims   79, 102, 108

235

Albert, Prince   38, 71
Amalgamated Society of Engineers   88
Amery, Leo   181, 201
Anti-Corn Law League   31, 38, 45, 49, 50, 51, 52, 60, 67
Anti-Poor Law Movement   67
Asquith, Herbert Henry   116, 138, 142, 143, 145, 149, 166, 169
Attlee, Clement   181, 206, 207, 210, 214, 215
Attwood, Thomas   30, 33, 44, 47, 51, 56, 57, 59, 68
Australia, Commonwealth of   120, 175

Baldwin, Stanley   150, 166, 169, 170, 171, 173, 177, 178, 180, 183, 184, 187, 188, 192, 195, 196, 198
Balfour, A J   116, 138, 142, 143, 148, 150
Bank of England   34, 62, 153, 174, 207, 212
BBC   167, 177, 191
Beaconsfield, Lord Benjamin: *See:* Disraeli, B.
Beaverbrook, Lord   177
'Bedchamber Question'   31, 38, 42, 59, 65
Bentham, Jeremy   31, 32, 36, 58, 68, 88
Bentinck, Lord George   63, 64, 67, 86, 91
Berlin   211, 212
Bevan, Aneurin   188, 208, 214, 215
Beveridge, Sir William   141
  Report (1942)   207, 209, 212, 214, 216
Bevin, Ernest   154, 161, 176, 188, 206, 208, 211
Birkenhead, Lord   177
Birmingham Liberal Assoc.   111, 117, 119
  Political Union   31, 33, 45, 51
'Black and Tans'   173
Bonar Law, Andrew   139, 143, 173
Bright Sir John   45, 51, 53, 98, 101 107, 125, 131
British
  Electricity Authority   212
  Gas Council   212
  Iron and Steel Corporation   213
  Medical Association   217
  Union of Fascists (BUF)   181, 183, 185, 186
Brougham, Lord   34
Butler, R A   207, 214, 215
  (Butskellism)   217
Butt, Isaac   128, 131
Byron, Lord   81

Campbell-Bannerman, Henry   138, 145, 150, 178
Canada   120
Canning, George   17, 18, 21, 24, 25, 26, 30, 32, 37, 64, 67, 70, 71, 74, 75, 77, 80, 82
'Captain Swing' Riots   27, 32
Cardwell, Edward   64, 65
  (System)   143
Caroline, Queen   20, 23, 27
Carson, Sir Edward   139, 143
Castlereagh, Lord   17, 14, 23, 29, 70, 71, 73, 75, 78, 79, 80, 82, 89, 102
Catholic Association   60, 67

Catholics, Emancipation of   19, 22, 24, 26, 33, 38, 58, 60, 63, 64, 74, 80, 125, 133
Cato Street Conspiracy   20, 23, 27
Central Board Scheme   112, 132
Chadwick, Edwin   30, 36, 62
Chamberlain, Joseph   86, 92, 99, 103, 106, 111, 112, 114, 116, 117, 119, 121, 123, 129, 132, 141, 148
Chamberlain, Neville   150, 159, 167, 170, 173, 177, 180, 182, 184, 187, 188, 189, 192, 195, 197, 198, 199, 201, 203, 213, 215
Chanak Crisis   167
Chartism   27, 31, 40, 42, 44, 45, 47, 49, 54, 55, 56, 58, 60, 61 (*See also :* Kennington Common)
Chartist Convention   52
Co-op Land Society   48
Church of England   32, 38, 41
Church of Ireland   41
  (Disestablishment)   127, 131,133
Churchill, Lord Randolph   88, 125, 129, 217
Churchill, Winston   140, 141, 146, 159, 167, 170 176, 177, 180, 182, 188, 190, 195, 196, 199, 201, 206, 208, 211, 213, 217
Citrine, Lord   176, 188
Civil Service Reform   99, 101, 105, 108
Communist Party (Britain)   167, 176, 181
Cobbett, William   19, 21, 27, 32
Cobden, Richard   46, 50, 52, 53, 61, 98, 104, 141, 176
Complete Suffrage Union   44, 49
Congresses etc:
  Aix la Chapelle   77
  Berlin   88, 89, 92
  Colonial (GB)   114, 118, 119
  Hague, the   167
  Laibach   77, 80
  Lausanne   194
  London   75
  Munich   181, 182, 185, 195, 198, 200, 202, 203
  Troppau   74, 77, 80
  Verona   74, 77, 83
  Vienna   17, 70, 73, 77, 79
Conservative Party   85, 87, 89, 91, 92, 94, 103, 112, 116, 118, 123, 129, 139, 149, 167, 177, 181, 201
Co-operative Movement   147
Corporation St. (Birmingham)   119
Cripps, Sir Stafford   206, 207, 213, 214
  and Socialist League   216
Curzon, Lord   177
Cyprus   120
Czechoslovakia   181, 188, 195, 197, 199, 200, 202, 203

Dalton, Hugh   206, 207, 210, 212, 213
Danzig   194
Dawes Plan   159, 174
Defence Requirements Committee   197
Denmark   71, 79, 202

'Depressed Areas' (Britain)   154
Derby, Lord   91, 95, 96
De Valera, Eamonn   173
Devoy, John   124, 128, 131
Dilke, Sir Charles   102
Disraeli, Benjamin   17, 46, 59, 63, 66, 67, 69, 85, 87, 89, 90, 92, 94, 96, 99, 101, 102, 105, 106, 107, 110, 115, 120, 121, 133
D'lsraeli, Isaac   91
Don Pacifico   71, 76, 78
'Dreadnought' (Warship)   145, 149
Durham, Lord   34, 40

Economic Advisory Council   153, 175
Eden, Anthony   181, 182, 187, 195, 196, 199
Education League   98, 117
Edward VII, King   143, 146
Edward VIII, King   187
Egypt   90, 96, 103, 107, 121
Eire (Irish Free State)   173, 187, 194
Eldon, Lord   17, 22, 26 29, 58
Empire, the British   73, 77, 79, 82, 89, 95, 114, 115, 120, 125, 131, 139, 142, 148, 149, 167, 177, 188, 192, 195, 196, 198, 201
Exhibition, The Great   46, 52, 59
Eyre, Governor   98, 107

Fabian Society   140, 141, 147, 206
Fashoda Crisis   121
Federation of British Industry   190
Fenians   124, 126, 128, 130, 131
   and Manchester and Clerkenwell 'outrages'   124, 131, 134
   and 'Manchester Martyrs'   134
Free Labour Associations   140, 147
Frere, Sir Bartle   107

Gaitskell, Hugh   215
'Geddes Axe'   153, 159, 169, 173, 214
General Strike   154, 159, 163, 166, 168, 170, 171, 174
George III, King   20, 23
George IV, King 17, 23   See also: Prince Regent
George V, King   146, 149, 169, 180, 188, 189, 192
George Vl, King   187, 208
Gladstone, Herbert   132, 133
Gladstone, William Ewart   25, 59, 64, 65, 86, 87, 89, 90, 93, 94, 98, 99, 101, 102, 104, 106, 107, 109, 112, 114, 116, 117, 119, 124, 125, 127, 129, 131, 132, 133, 137, 138, 141, 148
Gold Standard   20, 23, 59, 64, 67, 154, 159, 161, 167, 174, 183, 187
Gordon, General Charles   103, 107
Graham, Sir James   40, 41, 64
Great Depression (1873–96)   113, 121
Greek Revolt   17, 26, 75, 77, 81
Greenwood, Arthur   159

Grey, Lord   28, 32, 33, 35, 37, 38, 40, 41, 67, 138

Haldane (Army Reforms)   143, 145
Halifax, Lord   181, 194, 199, 201, 202
Hardie, Keir   140, 147
Hartington, Lord   118
Health, Ministry of   159, 170
Henderson, Arthur   198
Henderson, Hubert   167, 175, 180, 182, 188, 192
Hoare, Samuel   194, 196, 199
Home Government Association   131
Home Rule (Ireland)   99, 103, 124, 125, 128, 129, 131, 132, 137, 139, 142, 143, 148, 149
Home Rule League   131
Hong Kong   78
Housing and Local Government Boards   159
Hunt, 'Orator'   19, 21, 27
Huskisson, William   17, 22, 23, 24, 26
Hyde Park Riots   85

Imperial Preference   153, 160, 181, 183, 186
Independent Labour Party   138, 148, 167, 186
India   77, 86, 89, 93, 121, 177, 183, 187, 207, 211, 212, 215
Indian Mutiny   78
Industrial Revolution   17
Invergordon Naval Mutiny   174, 187, 190
Ireland   31, 37, 62, 79, 89, 101, 103, 106, 112, 116, 120, 124, 126, 127, 129, 131, 133, 135, 150, 167, 173, 177
Irish Famine   53, 62, 65, 124, 125, 127, 133
Irish Free State See: Eire
Irish National League   124, 128, 129
Irish Party   90, 99, 125, 130, 132, 133, 136, 139, 143
Irish Republican Army   173
Irish Universities   99, 105

Jameson Raid   60, 112, 115, 118, 121
Jarrow   157
   Hunger March   159

Kennington Common (Chartists, 1848)   45, 48, 52, 54
Keynes, John Maynard   153, 157, 159, 162, 167, 173, 175, 181, 192, 194, 201, 210, 213
Kilmainham Gaol   131
'King and Country' Debate (Oxford Union)   194, 198

Labour Party   140, 141, 143, 146, 148, 166, 168, 170, 174, 177, 183, 185, 186, 189, 196, 200, 206
Labour Representation Committee   138, 148
Land League   89, 124, 127, 129, 134, 135
Lansbury, George   180, 216
Latin America   17, 26, 71, 72, 77, 80, 81
   Revolts   112
LCC (London County Council)   147

Left Book Club   187, 206, 215
Liberal Party   65, 85, 98, 101, 103, 112, 116, 118, 119, 125, 130, 135, 136, 138, 143, 148, 168, 175, 178, 180, 183
Lib-Lab Pact   76, 143, 147
Lichfield House Compact   42
Liverpool, Lord   17, 21, 23, 24, 26, 29, 32, 58, 75, 79, 81, 83
Lloyd-George, David   117, 138, 142, 145, 149, 153, 158, 166, 167, 169, 173, 176, 177, 181, 190
London Transport   181
London University   31, 115
Lothian, Lord   196
Lovett, William   45, 47, 51
   and London Working Men's Association   44, 47, 51, 55
Luddism   23, 27
Lytton Report   198

Macaulay, Lord   99, 104
Macdonald, Ramsey   138, 147, 160, 162, 166, 167, 169, 171, 173, 174, 177, 180, 183, 185, 187, 188, 189, 192, 198, 210, 216
Macmillan, Harold   153, 178, 207
Manchester Guardian   138, 178
Marketing Boards (Britain)   212
Marshall Plan   212
May Committee   159, 161, 167, 174, 180, 188
Maynooth Grant   59, 62, 66, 86, 98, 104
Melbourne, Lord   31, 35, 37, 38, 40, 60, 65
Methodism   21
Mill, John Stuart   49, 99, 108
Miners' Federation   147
Mond Committee (Industry)   159
Monroe Doctrine   77
Mountbatten, Lord Louis   207
Morrison, Herbert   189, 206, 209, 215
Mosley, Sir Oswald   158, 174, 175, 181, 183, 185, 187

Napier, General   49, 81
Napoleon III, Emperor (France)   76, 79
National
   Assistance   216
   Board of Education   133
   Charter Association   45, 48, 52
   Coal Board   212
   Education League   111, 113, 117
   Employers' Federation   153
   Government (Britain)   175, 176, 177, 180, 183, 186, 187, 188, 191, 192
   Health Insurance Scheme   141
   Health Service   207, 209, 212, 213, 215, 216
   Insurance   207
Nationalisation (Britain)   209, 212, 214, 216
National Liberal Federation   98, 112, 114, 116, 118, 119

National Unemployed Workers' Movement   187
Newcastle Programme   106, 107, 118, 119
'New Departure' Policy (Ireland)   124, 128, 130, 131
'New Liberalism'   141
Newport Rising   44, 48, 52, 54
New Zealand   175
Nigeria   115
North Atlantic Treaty Organisation   207, 211
Norman, Montagu   155, 175

O'Connell, Daniel   22, 24, 31, 60, 62, 65, 67, 125, 131, 133, 135
O'Connor, Feargus   44, 45, 48, 52
Osborne Judgement   145, 147
O'Shea, Mrs Kitty (Catherine)   124, 125, 130, 131, 132
Owen, Robert   45, 47
Oxford Movement   37

Pakistan   211, 212
Palestine   207
Palmerston, Lord   40, 66, 67, 69, 71, 76, 78, 79, 81, 82, 89, 94, 98, 102, 104, 106, 109
'Pax Britannica'   73, 107
Parnell, Charles Stewart   112, 118, 124, 125, 127, 129, 131, 132, 135, 136
Peace Bailot   194, 198, 204
Peace Pledge Union   187
Peel, Sir Robert   17, 18, 21, 24, 25, 31, 37, 38, 41, 64, 65, 67, 69, 78, 85, 91, 95, 98, 103, 104, 106, 130
Penny Post   38
Pentrich Insurrection   20, 23
'People's Budget'   142, 145
People's Charter   46, 52, 54, 56
People's Convention   48
Peterloo   20, 23, 25, 27, 61
Petersburg Protocol   78, 81
Phoenix Park Murders   124, 129, 131, 132
'Phoney War'   188
Pitt, William (The Elder)   116
Pitt, William (The Younger)   17, 32, 80, 88
Place, Francis   24, 39, 47
Plimsoll Line (Merchant Shipping Act)   88, 93
'Plug Plot' Strikes   45, 48, 52, 54
Police, Metropolitan   19, 22, 24, 27, 38, 58, 59, 64
Poor Law and Local Government Board   94
Port of London Authority   145
Post Office Savings Bank   105
Prague   198, 200, 202
Prince Regent   20, 23 See also: King George IV
Property Tax (1816)   17, 23

Rearmament   184, 194, 197, 200
Reconstruction, Ministry of   158
Rhodes, Cecil   112, 115, 121
Ridley, Jasper   77

Riots:
  Ely   19, 23
  Littleport   19, 23
Robinson, 'Prosperity'   17, 22, 23, 24
Rosebery, Lord   106, 114, 138
Rothermere Lord   177
Royal Air Force   185, 194, 197
Royal Commission
  on Depression of Trade and Industry   121
  on the Poor Law   145
Royal Irish Constabulary   173
Russell, Lord John   79, 105, 107
  'Edinburgh Letter'   63, 65

Salisbury, Lord   86, 103, 105, 108, 111, 117, 118,
  119, 129, 131, 132, 177
Samuel Commission (Coal Industry)   155, 159, 176
Samuel, Sir Herbert   159, 171, 174, 180, 187, 189,
  192
Sankey, Mr Justice   158, 176, 187
Shaftesbury, Lord   36
Shelley, Percy Bysshe   20, 28
Shop Stewards' Movement   139
Sidmouth, Lord   17, 23
Simpson, Mrs Wallis   187
Sinn Fein   173
Six Points (Chartism)   49, 55
Slavery, Abolition of   30, 35, 37, 39, 89
Snowden, Philip   147, 153, 157, 167, 173, 180, 183,
  187, 190
Social Democratic Federation   147, 216
South Africa   115, 121, 148
Spa Fields (London)   19, 23, 27
Speenhamland   31, 36, 37
Suez Canal   85, 89, 92, 96, 120, 121

Taff Vale Case   140, 145, 148,
Tamworth Manifesto   31, 38, 41, 58, 60, 64, 66, 67
Tariff Reform League   112, 116, 118, 120
Ten Hours Movement   59, 67
The Times   125, 132, 136, 191
Thomas, John Henry   164, 180, 187
Tillett, Ben   147
Tolpuddle Martyrs   37
Tonypandy   146
Trades Union Congress   164, 167, 170, 171, 176,
  177, 181, 188, 190, 212, 216
Transvaal   89, 92, 103, 122
Treaties:
  Aix-la-Chapelle   74
  Anglo-German Naval   705, 198
  Anglo-Turkish Mutual Assistance Pact   199
  Berlin   105, 107
  Geneva   167, 196
  Irish (1921)   173
  Kilmainham   124, 129, 131, 135
  Locarno   167

London   78
  Molotov-Ribbentrop Pact   194, 196, 200, 203
  Munich   188
  Nanking   78
  'Pact of Steel'   199
  Pekin   79
  Russo-German Non Aggression   187, 198, 199
  San Stefano   89, 92
  Stresa Agreement   196
  Unkiar-Skelessi   78
  Versailles   173, 195, 196, 201, 202

Ulster   125, 129, 131, 139, 143, 146, 150
Unemployment (Britain)   154, 156, 160, 163, 184
  Assistance Board   186, 187
United States Civil War   79, 98
  Neutrality Acts   197

Vereeniging, Peace of (Boer War)   118
Victoria, Queen   38, 71, 78, 82, 85, 89, 90, 92, 114,
  118, 121, 139

Wars:
  Abyssinian   194, 196, 199
  Afghan   92
  Boer   112, 115, 118, 120, 122, 138, 141, 148
  Crimean   71, 76, 78, 98
  First World War   139, 154, 157, 162, 166, 173
    195, 202
  Franco-Prussian   57, 102
  Korean   211, 213, 214
  Opium (Chinese) Wars   71, 78, 82
  Russo-Turkish   78, 81, 92
  Second World War   162, 199, 207
  Zulu   92

Webb, Beatrice and Sidney   145, 147, 167
Welfare State   207, 209, 211, 213, 218
Wellington, Duke of   17, 18, 22, 24, 26, 30, 32, 33,
  58, 60, 62, 68, 71, 82
Welsh Church, Disestablishment   142, 146
Wilkinson, Ellen   216
William IV, King   38,
Wilson, Harold   207, 215
Wilson, Horace   181
Wood, Kingsley   213
Woolton, Lord   207, 215
Workers' Weekly   167, 174
WSPU   139, 143

'Young England'   59, 67, 87, 91, 93
  (See: Disraeli, B)
'Young Ireland'   124, 125

Zinoviev Letter   167, 174